LAWYERS, FAMILIES, AND BUSINESSES
The Shaping of a Bay Street Law Firm, Faskens 1863–1963

LAWYERS, FAMILIES, AND BUSINESSES

The Shaping of a
Bay Street Law Firm,
Faskens 1863–1963

C. IAN KYER

Published for The Osgoode Society for Canadian Legal History
by Irwin Law

Toronto

Printed and bound in Canada by Irwin Law Inc.

ISBN 978-1-55221-310-0

Cataloguing in Publication data available from Library and Archives Canada

The publisher acknowledges the financial support of the Government of Canada through the Book Publishing Industry Development Program (BPIDP) for its publishing activities.

We acknowledge the assistance of the OMDC Book Fund, an initiative of Ontario Media Development Corporation.

1 2 3 4 5   14 13 12

CONTENTS

FOREWORD

THE LAW FIRM CURRENTLY known as Fasken Martineau can trace its roots back a century and a half to the Beatty Chadwick partnership established in 1863. As its title suggests, this history of the Fasken firm is in part a history of the close-knit families that dominated its early decades — Beatty, Chadwick, Blackstock, and, of course, Fasken. Law practice in the later-nineteenth and early-twentieth centuries was frequently characterised by such family connections, and by connections between legal and business families, in this case by connections to the Gooderhams' and Worts' extended families. This book also takes us through crucial stages in the development of not just Fasken Martineau, but many other Canadian law firms — the alliances with various businesses; the growth of two or three man partnerships into considerably larger firms; the links between leading law firms and politics. Along the way, we see how law practice changed, how remuneration was divided up, and how strong leaders stamped their individual personalities onto the collective identity of the firm. This book is a major contribution to our understanding of the changes in Canadian law practice through the twentieth century.

The purpose of the Osgoode Society for Canadian Legal History is to encourage research and writing around the history of Canadian law. The Society, which was incorporated in 1979 and is registered as a charity, was founded at the initiative of the Honourable R. Roy McMurtry — formerly attorney general for Ontario and chief justice of the province — and officials of the Law Society of Upper Canada. The Society seeks to stimulate the study of legal history in Canada by supporting researchers, collecting oral histories, and publishing volumes that contribute to legal-historical scholarship in Canada. It has published eighty-eight books on the courts, the judiciary, and the legal profession, including such topics as the history of crime and punishment, women and law, law and the economy, the legal treatment of ethnic minorities, and famous cases and significant trials.

Current directors of the Osgoode Society for Canadian Legal History are Robert Armstrong, Kenneth Binks, Susan Binnie, David Chernos, Thomas G. Conway, J. Douglas Ewart, Violet French, Martin Friedland, John Gerretsen, Philip Girard, William Kaplan, Horace Krever, C. Ian Kyer, Virginia Mac-Lean, Patricia McMahon, R. Roy McMurtry, Dana Peebles, Paul Perell, Jim Phillips, Paul Reinhardt, Joel Richler, William Ross, Paul Schabas, Robert Sharpe, Mary Stokes, and Michael Tulloch.

The annual report and information about membership may be obtained by writing to:

The Osgoode Society for Canadian Legal History
Osgoode Hall, 130 Queen Street West
Toronto, Ontario, M5H 2N6

Telephone: 416-947-3321
E-mail: mmacfarl@lsuc.on.ca
Website: Osgoodesociety.ca

R. Roy McMurtry
PRESIDENT

Jim Phillips
EDITOR-IN-CHIEF

PREFACE

"Sit down, Ian. Anita, take a memo to Mr. Kyer." It was these words that started me on three decades of research into the history of the law firm where I have practised as a student, associate, partner, and now counsel. They were spoken to me on 10 August 1982 by Ronald Rolls, a senior litigator in the law firm then known as Fasken & Calvin.[1] I had been practising law a mere four months and three days. I knew Mr. Rolls to be a very formal man, but I was surprised to learn that he gave instructions to students and junior lawyers by calling them to his office and dictating to his secretary while they looked on in silence. Sitting and listening to his dictation, I learned that his friend Burke Doran, a bencher of the Law Society of Upper Canada, had just returned from an official visit to the Law Society of Ireland. While there Doran had been approached by the secretary of the General Council of the Irish Bar, Geoffrey Coyle, who explained that he had received a set of letters from the Baker family that discussed the founding of a Toronto law firm.[2] Coyle was curious if Doran knew of this Beatty Blackstock firm. Doran did not, but he suspected the letters were about the founding of the firm he knew as Fasken & Calvin. He had noticed that they were written on the letterhead of this mystery firm and that one of the named partners was David Fasken. So Doran brought copies back to Toronto and gave them to Ron Rolls. My task was to find out if they were indeed about the founding of Faskens.

To appreciate the enthusiasm with which I undertook this task, you need to know that I was a would-be academic with a doctorate in medieval ecclesiastical history. I had turned to law when I could not find a full-time university position. Although the founding of a law firm in nineteenth-century Ontario by two Orangemen was a long way from my study of papal envoys in thirteenth- and fourteenth-century Europe,[3] it was history. Ron Rolls had given me an official excuse to blend my lifelong interest in history with my life's work at Faskens. As he knew well, the same thing had happened at the University of Toronto Faculty of Law when Deans Martin L. Friedland, Frank Iacobucci, and Robert Sharpe had encouraged me to write the history of the legal education I was receiving.[4]

Within a month I discovered that the letters, written by Edward Marion Chadwick to a maiden aunt in Ireland in the early years of the twentieth century, did indeed describe the founding of the law firm that later became known as Faskens, albeit in a very indirect and incomplete fashion. I decided to share the result of my research. John Honsberger, then editor of the *Law Society Gazette*, was good enough to publish my article "New Light on an Old Firm."[5] But what I had uncovered was so interesting that I did not want to stop there. I knew that there was much more to discover and to share with people inside and outside the firm. I began to collect materials and anecdotes from senior members of the firm. None of them knew anything of Beatty or Chadwick, although Roger Wilson had collected letterhead dating back to 1864 that showed the firm had once borne their names. Many had oral history to share, stories passed on to them by senior members of the firm, now gone. There had been two Fasken brothers, I was told. One was a fine fellow and a great lawyer and the other, a very difficult man.

I was informed that the firm was not an establishment firm like Blakes or Osler's or McCarthy's, hiring on the basis of social position, but had, instead, sought out good lawyers from out of town. Unfortunately, its lack of standing in the Toronto establishment had precluded representing a number of the big Canadian corporations, but nevertheless it had some great, long-standing clients: a bank, the Toronto-Dominion; mining clients, led by Dome Mines; and several health clients, led by Toronto Western Hospital. It had always had excellent technical lawyers who were underappreciated in the corporate sphere, but it was recognized as one of Canada's best litigation firms. Over time I came to see that each strand of this tradition had some basis in fact, but they all described the firm after it had been transformed by the two Fasken brothers. Forgotten was that the firm of the late nineteenth century, the firm of Beatty Blackstock, had been very different. Also unknown was that the firm had been closely linked to the Toronto establishment through its ties with the Gooderham and Worts families.

The many questions and comments that my investigation engendered encouraged me to do more research. I began to write short pieces to circulate to the members of the firm. When I had the time, I did more serious writing about aspects of the firm's history. Three articles appeared in the Essays in the History of Canadian Law series,[6] and a number of short biographies were published in the *Dictionary of Canadian Biography.*[7]

The interest of lawyers in the firm was piqued in 1986, when the firm was asked to represent Allied Lyons in its contested acquisition of the Hiram Walker–Gooderham Worts distillery.[8] That facility had generated wealth for the Gooderham and Worts families and indirectly for the law firm before being sold in the 1920s, and it was now one of the assets in a hard-fought take-over battle between the British distillery giant and the Reichmann family. The history that had seemed so abstract and distant was now a subject of current interest to the partners involved.

I was, of course, also conducting a demanding law practice, so time for historical research and writing was at a premium. When I declined to do biographies of people not related to the law firm, Ramsay Cook, then the general editor of the *Dictionary*, quipped to me that I did not do Canadian history or even Ontario history; I did nothing but Faskens history. That was in a sense true — I did not have time to do anything else — but it was also quite false. What I have learned is that the history of Faskens is a microcosm of Canadian and Ontario history. It both reflects and to some extent helped to shape that history.

This book represents the first time I have brought what I have learned into a single study. It builds upon and to a significant extent refines and corrects what I have previously published. The result is at once a glimpse into the social history of Ontario, an insight into the development of Canadian business and its regulation, and a chapter in the rise of the business law firm and the ascendancy of the business lawyer.

Professor Margaret Ogilvie (who briefly served as Faskens' research director in the 1980s) once lamented in a review of the *History of McMaster Meighen* that "the sort of gossipy information which makes biographies of the famous so compelling is rarely available"[9] to law firm historians. The problem, she suggested, was that "lawyers rarely kept personal diaries; never corresponded with the distant great on the big questions of jurisprudence or even with their own children at school, never mind lovers; or wrote their memoirs."[10] That was not the case at Faskens. Many people have assisted me in finding diaries, letters, memoirs, and the like written by its lawyers.

First and foremost, I must acknowledge Dr. Hugh Laurence who, as a colleague, researcher, sounding board, and friend, has been of enormous assistance. Besides Ron Rolls, who started me on this journey, a number of other members of Faskens have assisted. Any list has to begin with Richard B. "Dick" Potter and Roger Wilson. These two mentors not only helped to shape my legal practice but because they shared my enthusiasm for history also provided much encouragement and insight. Roger even shared materials on the firm's many names, as well as on the Calvin family and Garden Island. Don Affleck had collected the old partnership agreements and the memoirs of Bryce MacKenzie and J.B. Robinson, which he happily passed on to me. Ron Robertson gave me extensive material. Robert Shirriff, David Menzel, Fraser Fell, Bob Sutherland, Bill Graham, and John Campion shared their memories. Karl Harries helped me better understand hard rock mining and the role that the Fasken brothers played in the development of Ontario's North. Mae Wiseman, who had been a secretary in the firm in the 1940s, gave me photos.

Many outside the firm have also provided me with access to documents that have permitted me to tell the story. William Beatty's grandson Geoffrey provided a copy of the letter that Beatty wrote to his second son on his coming of age. Douglas Worts provided much material about the Gooderham and Worts families, as did Stephen Otto. Don Hicks, who had been a student at the firm, helped me gain access to the archives of Confederation Life, where he was working as a lawyer. A retired corporate secretary of the Excelsior Life Insurance Company, Morgan Crockford, sent me much information about the long-standing relationship between that company, Toronto Western Hospital, and the firm.[11] Victoria Vidal-Ribas of the Ministry of the Attorney-General was kind enough to donate a set of letters from the firm dated December 1879 and January 1880 that she had bought at an auction.

Sam Bowman, a local Mennonite farmer turned township reeve turned international agricultural representative of Canada, spent a wonderful day in the summer of 2001 with me and our mutual friend Hugh Laurence, showing us the plaque to David Fasken mounted on a wall in Bethany United Church and family documents in the Wellington County Museum and Archives. He took us to the original homestead of David's grandfather, to the farm where David had been born, to the one-room schoolhouse that David had attended as a youngster (now a family home), and to the Fasken gravesite in Elora. Sam, now deceased, was a source of much knowledge and insight.

Cecily Blackstock was as well, even though she initially refused to talk to me because I identified myself as a partner at Faskens. I later learned that she firmly believed the Fasken brothers had stolen the law firm from her grandfather. With Roger Wilson's assistance, I was eventually able to talk to her about her insightful family history, entitled *All the Journey Through*.[12] She explained that she had deposited the extensive Gibbs Blackstock Family Papers on which her book was based in the Thomas Fisher Rare Book Library. I spent much time reviewing the letters to and from Thomas Gibbs Blackstock and his younger brother, George Tate.

Harold Averill at the University of Toronto Archives, housed in the same building, cheerfully shared the building plans and related materials for the Oaks, William Beatty's home on Queen's Park Crescent. In the same archive, I discovered the Lash Miller Papers, which gave me a glimpse into the close personal and professional relationship between Zebulon Lash and his brother-in-law, Nicholas Miller. Tye Farrow, the noted architect, took me on a tour of what would have been St. Alban's Cathedral, now the chapel for Royal St. George's College, and introduced me to College archivist Jonathan Lofft, who provided materials not only on the history of the cathedral but also on the career of E.M. Chadwick. In March 2004, Ann MacKenzie, a daughter of Bryce MacKenzie, gave me a copy of a chatty, well-informed, and very extensive unpublished family history by David Fasken's cousin, Marion Fasken MacKenzie.[13] Other members of the Fasken family, such as Annabelle Cameron, shared photos and memories.[14]

Norbert J. Dyckman, the manager of Fasken Oil & Ranch Properties in Midland, Texas, deserves special mention. One night over dinner at the Oilmen's Club in Midland, he informed me that he had a box of materials that might help me understand why David Fasken, the managing partner of a Toronto law firm, had acquired property in Texas. The next day he had a steamer trunk full of legal documents brought into his boardroom. These materials had been compiled for a legal action fought all the way to the US Supreme Court over the Texas property, and they told the story of Fasken's investment in incredible detail through sworn statements and cross-examinations.

I also owe a large debt to Mr. Justice David Gooderham Stinson who, as a great-great-grandson of George Gooderham and one-time partner in Faskens, has long taken an interest in my history of the firm. But the debt I owe to David relates primarily to his bringing the diaries of Edward Marion Chadwick to my attention. In early 2010 at a lunch, he leaned across the table and told me that he had wonderful news. He had been at a reception at the Royal Canadian Yacht Club where he had talked with Dianne Bell, Chadwick's great-granddaughter. She had told him that Chadwick, one of the founders of Faskens, had kept a series of diaries all his adult life — and she had them. With David's assistance and through the kindness of Dianne Bell, Hugh Laurence and I were able to spend a number of happy hours in her living room in Orillia studying and copying portions of the diaries. Although much of the firm's history was well known to me by this point, several conjectures were confirmed, others corrected, and life was breathed into Beatty, Chadwick, and other early members of the firm. Dianne Bell also arranged for Barbara Rayner, another descendant of Chadwick, to supplement the diaries with some interesting letters and other materials.

All legal historians owe a debt of gratitude to David Corbett and Walter "Wally" Palmer. David, as national managing partner, and Wally, as the then Ontario managing partner, agreed to donate some of the firm's old files to the Archives of the Law Society of Upper Canada. The Law Society archivist, Paul Leatherdale, was very helpful in making this happen.

With the assistance of Mark Sweeney, I supplemented these materials with extensive documentation in the national, provincial, and Toronto archives. Mark and I located much correspondence between members of the firm and various ministers and departments about both personal and professional matters. The Osgoode Society for Canadian Legal History provided me with a research grant to retain Mark's services.

Finally I want to thank Jeffrey Miller of Irwin Law for his support, Jim Phillips of the Osgoode Society for his guidance, and Camilla Blakeley for her expert editing.

INTRODUCTION

On its 150th anniversary Fasken Martineau DuMoulin LLP is a legal behemoth with over 700 lawyers in six offices across Canada and in London, Paris, and Johannesburg, but it had a modest beginning. In 1863 it began as a two-man firm in a single, half-furnished room in Toronto. The legal work of those founding partners was neither high profile nor particularly remunerative. They did debt collection and insolvency work for mortgage lenders. They almost never appeared in court. One of the two was not even qualified as a barrister. How, then, did the firm they founded become one of the strongest litigation practices in Canada? How did a firm expert in bankruptcy that served the legal needs of banks and insurance companies come to be ranked as the world's leading mining law firm?[1] It seems a stretch to act for both bank presidents and hard rock miners, yet that is exactly what happened. The modern legal practice of the Faskens firm can best be understood and appreciated by a study of its first 100 years, the century that truly shaped it.

Originally known as Beatty & Chadwick, the firm passed through twenty-four name changes over the next 100 years and by 1963 was known as Fasken, Calvin, MacKenzie, Williston & Swackhamer. In 1967 the firm adopted the name Fasken & Calvin, which it retained unchanged until its merger with Campbell Godfrey & Lewtas on 1 November 1989 to create Fasken Campbell Godfrey. On 1 February 2000 it took on the present name, Fasken Martineau DuMoulin LLP, following mergers with Quebec's Martineau

Walker in 1999 and Russell & DuMoulin in Vancouver in 2000.[2] To avoid confusion, I have chosen to refer to the firm by its nickname, Faskens.

This is a history of a Bay Street law firm. Bay Street, which runs north–south through downtown Toronto, has long been considered the centre of Ontario's business community because the Toronto Stock Exchange had its trading floor there and because the head offices of many Canadian financial institutions are to be found nearby. Over time it has become the centre of Canada's national business community. The law firms that serve the needs of that community are often referred to as Bay Street firms, whether or not they have an address there.[3] Securing a Bay Street address took Faskens until 2010, when Fasken Martineau DuMoulin LLP moved into its current offices in the Bay Adelaide Centre. Nevertheless, it was one of the very first Bay Street firms in that it dedicated itself to serving the special legal needs of Toronto's business community.

I have entitled this book *Lawyers, Families, and Businesses* to emphasize that although it is a study of a law firm, it is also about the individual lawyers who practised in the firm, their place in society, their families, and the businesses they served. A law firm is a collection of lawyers and staff who work for and against individuals, corporations, and governments in a series of law-related activities. Those activities can be quite diverse: purchasing property; drafting wills; administering estates; buying and selling goods, services, and entire businesses; financing those purchases or business operations; collecting debts; suing for wrongs done or contracts broken. These transactions and law suits both shaped and were shaped by the law firm in question. But law firms are made up of people who have families, other interests, and other demands on their time. Certainly in the firm of the early twenty-first century, one of the challenges a lawyer faces is finding anything resembling a reasonable balance between the demands of the profession and home life. Although they were somewhat different, such challenges existed during the first 100 years of Faskens. In telling the story of how the firm has come to take its current form, I have tried to place the lawyers within their social context, to make it possible to relate to them as people and not just as lawyers. You will learn a good deal about their families and something about their extralegal interests — Marion Chadwick's genealogy and heraldry, Tom Blackstock's buffalo hunting, his brother George's social engagements, William Renwick Riddell's legal history, Munro Grier's acting, and Walter Williston's carousing.

I focus my attention on nine individuals who have significantly influenced the firm, for better or for worse: William Henry Beatty, Edward Marion Chadwick, Thomas Gibbs Blackstock, David and Alex Fasken, Robert Spelman Robertson, John Wellington Pickup, Collamer Chipman Calvin, and Walter Williston. Others, such as Zebulon Lash, Nicholas Miller, Charles Biggar, Daniel E. Thomson, Wallace Nesbitt, William Renwick Riddell, Hugh Rose, George Sedgewick, and Mahlon Cowan, had distinguished careers and also figure prominently in the story. Many are better known than the nine highlighted here. Lash, for example, is considered Canada's first great corporate lawyer.[4] Nesbitt was appointed to the Supreme Court of Canada and became treasurer of the Law Society. Riddell was a leading light on the Ontario Court of Appeal and a noted legal historian. Rose was one of the great judges of his generation, rising to become Chief Justice of the High Court of Ontario. But for various reasons these men were not as influential in shaping the firm as the chosen nine.

The early years of the law firm demonstrate the importance of marriages and family connections. In fact in those years it is difficult to separate the story of the law firm from the story of the two founding partners, William Henry Beatty and Edward Marion Chadwick, and their families. Chapter 1 reads almost like a dual biography rather than an institutional history because the firm had not yet taken on a separate persona. The founders *were* the firm, and their extended families provided important contacts and many of their clients.

To the extent that the firm developed a persona by the 1880s, it was one dictated by Beatty. It is he, not Lash, who ought to be known as Canada's first business lawyer. He trained Lash and acted as his inspiration. At a time when law firms were almost invariably led by barristers, Beatty was proud to be a solicitor. For lawyers, the focus was on the courtroom rather than the boardroom, making Beatty's choice a notable departure. He practised for twenty years before being called to the bar and even after his call he refused to be made a Queen's Counsel. He was content to make his firm Canada's largest solicitors' practice.

Beatty married into the Gooderham and Worts families, became a member of Toronto's moneyed elite, and lived the life of a wealthy businessman. But he had a work ethic that few could (or would want to) emulate and became both a legal and a business adviser. As a result, Beatty and Chadwick became in many respects the Gooderham and Worts family firm, serving the legal needs of those wealthy and powerful families and their businesses.[5] The families invested the profits from their very lucrative distillery in financial institutions such as the Bank of Toronto, Manufacturers Life Insurance Company, and Canada Permanent Mortgage Corporation.[6] Beatty's firm acted for these family-controlled public companies and became pre-eminent among law firms serving the needs of the burgeoning financial sector.

Chadwick was Beatty's partner for almost fifty years, but they could not have been more different. Ironically it is Chadwick who is much better remembered today, but not as a lawyer. He is known as the author of some of Canada's most frequently consulted genealogical studies[7] and as someone who helped shape Canadian heraldry.[8] Among many other things, he secured the maple leaf as a Canadian national symbol, helped design Ontario's coat of arms, and designed the shield for Saskatchewan when it became a province in 1905.[9] But genealogy and heraldry were just two of Chadwick's many outside interests. In addition to being an artist and painter, he was a long-serving officer in the Queen's Own Rifles militia and a key participant in the Anglican Church, especially its significant, albeit much troubled, project — the building of the Cathedral of St. Alban the Martyr.[10]

Beatty and Chadwick practised law in a very different world from today's. The Anglican Church was very important and legal ethics were assumed rather than regulated. Conflict of interest was of little concern: relying upon and helping friends and relatives was seen as a duty to be fulfilled rather than a conflict to be avoided. It was also a world in which railroads played a central role in the development of the province and the country and in which the financial services sector was being shaped. The few corporations that existed were created specially to operate banks and railroads, and many clients were individuals carrying on business as sole proprietors or partners. For lawyers, specialization was a matter of choice, infrequently exercised. There was little statute law, no administrative tribunals or regulation, and a modest if growing body of caselaw. Beatty and Chadwick acted for both individuals and corporations.

Almost from the beginning the partners in the firm cultivated relationships with political and government leaders. Personal visits and letters were a regular occurrence. Beatty thought nothing of asking Prime Minister Sir John A. Macdonald for personal and business favours. In return, he and the other members of the Gooderham, Worts, and Beatty families helped raise funds for Macdonald and his Conservatives. They even made Sir John president of one of the family businesses, Manufacturers Life. It was no accident that Beatty was chosen to head the Macdonald memorial committee, or that it erected a monument to Macdonald across from Beatty's estate on Queen's Park Crescent.

The political party in power changed from time to time, but the need for good relations with government was a constant. As Chapter 2 points out, the firm early on realized the importance of having close personal links with both the Conservatives and the Liberals. At times this meant that the firm's strong Conservative contingent had to recruit a lawyer of a Liberal stripe, Zebulon Lash being the first example. But even the Conservative members of the firm needed to build bridges to the Liberals when they were in power. Thomas Gibbs Blackstock, a lifelong Conservative, regularly visited and corresponded with Sir Wilfrid Laurier, seeking some advantage for his clients.

Blackstock is a fascinating individual. He is probably the only Bay Street lawyer whose first job was as a buffalo hunter. He also has the distinction of having laid the foundation for Faskens' reputation as a top litigation firm, even though he spent most of his own career as a business lawyer. He laid that groundwork in part by inviting into the firm his talented and well-respected but much troubled brother George, who then helped lure Nesbitt, Riddell, and Rose. Blackstock also left his mark on the city of Toronto. As the son-in-law of George Gooderham, he oversaw the construction of the Gooderham mansion on St George Street, which now serves as the York Club, and the building and furnishing of one of Canada's first luxury hotels. Few guests who come to the King Edward Hotel today have any idea that it was built under the direction of a lawyer who had once hunted buffalo for a living, and had watched a man die in the corner of a barn-like hotel in Dodge City.

As Chapter 3 outlines, the 1880s were a trying time for the firm as Beatty learned that keeping lawyers content within the firm is a constant challenge for a managing partner. Tom Blackstock benefited most from the departure of Biggar, Miller, Lash, and Thomson in the mid-1880s. It was he who incorporated Gooderham & Worts, a watershed in the firm's law practice. Overseen by Blackstock, that incorporation helped soften the blow dealt the Gooderham and Worts business empire by the untimely death of Beatty's father-in-law, James Gooderham Worts. But it had significance beyond the solution of an estates problem. From this point forward almost all of the firm's large clients would be bodies corporate.

Nevertheless, it was some time before the firm practised corporate law as defined by Gregory Marchildon, in reference to lawyers who "specialized in serving the new entities being created in the transition from an economy of small family-owned (and largely unincorporated) firms to one dominated by publicly traded and professionally managed enterprises."[11] Such specialization was decades away, but from the 1880s incorporation and organization of bodies corporate became an increasingly important skill for the firm's lawyers.

By the 1890s the firm was known as Beatty Blackstock and was providing employment for the sons and sons-in-law of George Gooderham and other relatives. The opening up of mining in the Sudbury area of northern Ontario motivated Blackstock and the Gooderhams to look to the mining sector. They invested in British Columbia's mining discoveries that would later be consolidated into Cominco. The firm, acting for the family mining ventures in Rossland, faced one of Canada's first large-scale strikes. It was the beginning of the labour movement and of labour regulation. Under Beatty and Blackstock the firm grew extremely large for its day, with fifteen lawyers in 1902. Its members generally shared a common place in the society of late-nineteenth-century Toronto. They were principally members of the congregation of St. James Anglican Cathedral. Politically, most were Conservatives. Socially, most were from prominent Toronto families.

The extent to which Beatty Blackstock was connected to the power elite in Canada was brought home to me when I read Peter Waite's biography of Sir John Thompson.[12] I was struck by how many prominent people in Canada of the day had links to the law firm. Thompson himself became a friend and client of Thomas Gibbs Blackstock and was permitted the use of Blackstock's private yacht. In light of this it is not surprising that one of Thompson's two sons articled with Blackstock. But there were many other connections. A close relationship developed between Thompson and Sir Oliver Mowat, Ontario's premier. Mowat's son-in-law, Charles Biggar, was a partner in the law firm for six years. As minister of justice, Thompson also had dealings with Chief Justice John Edward Rose in Ontario. Rose's son, Hugh, would become a partner in the firm. Robert Sedgewick served as Thompson's deputy minister before being named to the Supreme Court of Canada and Sedgewick's nephew became a partner in the firm. Beatty Blackstock was, in short, a well-connected, establishment firm.

But the world around them was beginning to change. Shifting social patterns transposed the relative importance of the Anglican and Methodist churches and brought a swing from political conservatism to political liberalism. Beatty and Blackstock oversaw the firm and became much involved in business during the last half of the nineteenth century, when

Anglicans dominated both the legal profession and the economy through family-owned businesses and Conservatives, led by their friends Sir John A. Macdonald and Sir John Thompson, governing in Ottawa for much of the time. By 1905 David Fasken, a Methodist and a Liberal, had exploited his position as Beatty's right-hand man to gain control of the law firm. He assumed leadership when Wilfrid Laurier's Liberals were in power and as dynamic, hard-working Methodists such as Hart Massey, Timothy Eaton, Wilmot Matthews, and Joseph Flavelle were coming to the fore in Canadian business.[13] It was Fasken who led the firm into an era when many businesses were being conducted by public corporations funded from the United States.

Fasken chose his brother, Alex, for his own right-hand man. The Fasken brothers had little in common with the other members of Beatty Blackstock. They were the sons of an Elora farmer. When David came to Toronto to attend university and become an articled clerk in Beatty's law firm, he had to walk everywhere because he could not afford public transit. He learned law and business administration from Beatty and was an avid student. David became not only a better lawyer than either Beatty or Blackstock but a better businessman as well. When his business interests kept him out of the office, he relied on Alex and taught him what he had learned from Beatty. Unfortunately he was unable to pass on his own ability to deal with people. Alex's personality and his strict, inflexible approach to the law office anticipated many of the characteristics of the modern law firm, but in the first decades of the twentieth century it was a jarring break with tradition and cost the firm skilled lawyers. Many left to become judges — so many, in fact, that the courts came to owe Alex Fasken a considerable debt of gratitude, even if it went unacknowledged by either Fasken or the judges.

The Fasken brothers lacked the advantageous marriages of their predecessors. Neither married into a wealthy, influential family as Beatty and Blackstock had done. David Fasken used the law firm itself as his means to wealth and influence, moving up the social ladder from his humble beginnings as a farmboy to become one of Canada's wealthiest and most powerful businessmen. The firm brought him into contact with people who could fund his business ventures, and his drive, ambition, business acumen, and ability to recognize opportunities made many millions for him and his investors. He succeeded as an entrepreneur but entered the halls of the moneyed elite as a lawyer rather than through family connections. David Fasken followed Beatty into insurance but unlike the older man, who had been invited onto the board of Confederation Life as a representative of the Gooderham and

Worts shareholdings, he began as legal counsel. He skillfully used George Gooderham's money to achieve control of Excelsior Life. Gooderham was only too pleased to fund Fasken's endeavours because they earned him a good return on his investment. Fasken also followed Blackstock into mining, again, not as shareholder but as legal counsel. This time he used money from New York investors to get his start. He and his brother, Alex, made much of their wealth through the key role they played in development of the Canadian mining industry and the opening of Ontario's northern lands and Canada's western territories.

The Fasken brothers remained outsiders in the Toronto establishment. They could not recruit their lawyers there but sought them out in communities around the city. In Stratford they found James Mabee and Robert Spelman Robertson, who would later be called Canada's greatest lawyer, and in Windsor they found Mahlon Cowan. In the process the firm developed a reputation for being more accepting than usual of people's background but also for demanding hard work and great diligence. Again they anticipated the approach of the modern law firm. Appropriately, when David died he was buried in the Elora cemetery with his farming relatives, forcing Toronto's business and community leaders to drive miles through snowdrifts to get to the gravesite.[14] His striking headstone, towering over the simple graveyard, stands as testimony to both his business success and his rural roots. When Alex died seventeen years later he, too, was buried in Elora, his grave sharing a marker with David's.

Corporate finance, the funding of corporate business, became more and more important as time went on, and the investment dealers who arranged that financing became very wealthy and powerful. The firm came to act for a number of them. Already in the last quarter of the nineteenth century, one of the firm's partners had left to become an executive of the newly created Toronto Stock Exchange. His former partners brought many flotations to that exchange. David Fasken, lacking the ties to Toronto's moneyed elite that Beatty and Blackstock had enjoyed, would develop strong ties to the sources of corporate finance in New York and leverage those ties into a substantial fortune.

Fasken recognized that industrialization and mineral exploitation required large amounts of accessible power. Once again he learned from Beatty, who had assisted the Canadian Niagara Power Company in providing power to parts of southern Ontario and New York State. Fasken applied those lessons to northern Ontario, where he established the Northern Ontario Light and Power Company to provide hydroelectric power to the mines of Cobalt and Porcupine.

When David Fasken retired from active practice in 1919, the firm continued to be managed by Alex. The younger Fasken ruled the firm, but R.S. Robertson became its leading lawyer. Following in David's footsteps, Alex was more businessman than lawyer. These were difficult years for the Canadian economy and Alex chose to focus the firm's business lawyers on serving its long-standing corporate clients. For legal advice he turned to Robertson, who was one of a small group of superb litigation counsel to whom the profession turned for skilled advocacy, especially on appeals. Not surprisingly, Robertson became a bencher of the Law Society of Upper Canada, its leader as treasurer, and eventually Chief Justice of Ontario.

In the 1920s the firm assisted David Fasken, who had amassed enormous wealth, with some of Canada's earliest estate planning. The goal was in part to lessen the tax burden imposed by such new measures as the 1892 Ontario succession duty and income tax, which was introduced following the First World War. The 1920s and 1930s also saw the introduction of administrative law. The firm provided some of the early leadership to administrative tribunals. Again Alex Fasken's management style drove partners out of the firm. One ended up heading the Railway Commission and another, the Tariff Board. The firm played a more traditional role in the development of securities regulation. Following the collapse of the Home Bank in the 1920s and the stock market crash of 1929, Robertson defended many of the business people charged with inappropriate conduct. Then, in the 1940s, when the power of the Ontario Securities Commission to discipline stockbrokers was challenged, Robertson's protégé J.W. Pickup successfully defended its powers.

From 1944, when Alex Fasken died, until 1952, when Pickup succeeded Robertson as Chief Justice of Ontario, no single individual clearly dominated the firm. Certainly, Pickup and C.C. Calvin were strong personalities and good lawyers, but they did not manage every aspect of the firm as their predecessors had done. In reaction to the iron grip of Alex Fasken, the firm no longer had a managing partner but a management committee. Management was vested in Jimmy Aitchison, the most senior and affable lawyer in the firm, and in Pickup and Calvin, who were respectively its leading litigator and its leading corporate lawyer.

After Pickup's departure in 1952 the management committee became Aitchison, Calvin, and Bryce MacKenzie. In this managing triumvirate, Calvin led the way. He continued the tradition of Beatty, Blackstock, and the Fasken brothers by combining a corporate/commercial practice with an active involvement in the business affairs of large corporate clients. Beatty had used family and political connections to build a large clientele, and the Faskens' entrepreneurial drive had created new clients for the firm. Calvin consolidated and built upon their foundation. Like Beatty, he assumed a leadership position in Toronto's financial sector. It was Calvin who prepared the firm for the modern era, recruiting many bright young lawyers and training them well. When I joined the firm as a student in 1980, all of the senior partners had been recruited and trained by Calvin in the 1950s or early 1960s.

Walter Williston fits less comfortably in the group of nine principal lawyers, partly because he was never a managing partner and partly because he marched to his own drum. After Pickup's elevation to the bench, much of the weight of the firm's litigation practice fell on young Williston. The son of an Anglican missionary father and a Jewish mother, he was born in China in 1919, but he did not follow in his father's footsteps in either his personal or his professional life. Walter is remembered by many inside and outside the law firm as a person who lived life to the fullest, enjoying long, boozy dinners and the company of many women, several of whom he married. But Walter was at his best in the law library and the courtroom. Although he spoke with a slight slur, he became a great advocate. He was an iconoclast and his penchant for taking on unpopular causes frequently brought him to the public's attention.[15] He was regularly before the Ontario Court of Appeal and the Supreme Court of Canada. It is said that he made one of the last appearances by Canadian counsel before the Privy Council in London,[16] but I have found no support for this. He did, however, make an appearance before the International Court of Justice in The Hague in the Barcelona Traction case, representing the government of Spain.

Despite his self-destructive lifestyle, Williston helped shape litigation practice for the next generation. For many years he lectured on civil procedure in the bar admission course and co-authored with Ron Rolls the leading text on court forms. He also encouraged reform of our court processes and mentored a group of bright young lawyers, including Rolls, Julian Porter, John Sopinka, John Laskin, Donald Jack, Allan Rock, and John Campion, who became the leading barristers of the next generation.

Williston is the only one of the nine whom I met personally, and only briefly. I was anxious to talk to him about his role in the fight between Caesar Wright and the Law Society over legal education for use in a book I was then writing, but I never got the interview he promised me. Regrettably, Walter died shortly after I joined the firm as a student in August 1980. One of the first formal events I attended as a member of the firm was his funeral at St. James Cathedral.[17] At the time I had no idea that I was following in the footsteps of the firm's two founders, who had started their legal careers at the funeral of Sir John Beverley Robinson in that same cathedral. Even after his death, Walter was everywhere in the firm. Hardly a day would go by without a Walter Williston story. I learned much about him from his colleague Ron Rolls and from his former juniors Bill Graham, Allan Rock, and John Campion. It was obvious that he had been a giant in the litigation department and had engendered deep, warm, enduring feelings in those with whom he had worked and played.

This study ends in 1963, but it is important to appreciate that although the modern firm was shaped by its first 100 years, it has nevertheless been transformed in many ways. An epilogue outlines its development over the next fifty years. I look briefly at the end of family connections, the increasing democratization and professionalization of firm administration, the increasing religious and ethnic diversity of lawyers, the slow growth in the number of women lawyers within the firm (as the first chapter shows, they have long had an influence from outside), the creation of specialization and practice groups, and the development of the national and international firm.

Much of the firm's growth in numbers and geographic reach has been effected through mergers with other long-standing firms. The first of these large-scale mergers was in 1989 with Campbell Godfrey & Lewtas. The two firms had been founded more than 100 years before by next-door neighbours on little William Street and had frequently interacted over the years. A son-in-law of Beatty practised for a time with a forerunner of Campbell Godfrey, and the two firms worked together on the development of Toronto's Annex neighbourhood. In 1892, when a member of the Faskens firm first appeared as lead counsel in the Supreme Court of Canada, it was against Frank Arnoldi, one of the founders of what became Campbell Godfrey. A brief history of Campbell Godfrey & Lewtas is provided in Appendix 1. Faskens did not have the same frequent interactions with its other major merger partners, Martineau Walker and Russell & DuMoulin, with whom it merged in 1999 and 2000, respectively. Those firms too, however, had developed along parallel lines, as is briefly outlined in the appendix.

This study, however, focuses on the first 100 years of the oldest branch of the Fasken legal tree. Along the way we meet some fascinating individuals, not all of them likeable — or even good lawyers — but all with stories both interesting and enlightening. There is much that they can teach us about how law was practised at various times; how wealth was accumulated, retained, and, at times, lost; of the interplay between lawyers, business people, and government; and how society and government were affected by and, in turn, influenced the law and business regulation.

᠅ Chapter 1 ᠅

TWO MARRIAGES THAT MADE A LAW FIRM: 1862–75

Anyone seeking an appreciation of the early years of Faskens should begin with a visit to Toronto's St. James Cathedral. The Anglican Church, and this church in particular, played a central role in the lives of the early partners and their families. Religion was an important part of their social fabric. St. James is replete with evidence of the strong connection between the church and the firm — a box pew long held by the family of one of the founders, a chapel donated by that family, stained glass windows, and numerous plaques all stand today as memorials to members of the firm or their families and to the roots of the firm in the Anglican community of mid-nineteenth-century Toronto, and specifically in that portion with Orange Irish roots.

Two of the memorials in St. James are of special interest. In the eastern aisle of the nave is a beautiful white marble plaque commemorating the death in 1865 of a young woman, Ellen Byrne Chadwick. Along the western aisle is a set of three tall stained-glass windows with a Latin inscription that translates as "Blessed is he that readeth."[1] These windows, which depict the role played by the Church in the revival of English learning after the Viking raids, are dedicated to the memory of Charlotte Louisa Beatty, who died at the age of eighty-one in 1928. There is no obvious link between the two women so memorialized and the Faskens firm, yet such a link exists: they were born in Toronto within three years of each other, and each married a founding partner. To understand how the firm came into existence and why it prospered, one needs to look at the women remembered by these memorials.

Even though the firm did not admit its first woman lawyer, Georgia Bentley, until almost 100 years had passed and did not have a woman partner until Eleanore Cronk in 1983, it is not an exaggeration to say that Ellen Chadwick and Charlotte Beatty were crucial to its founding and success. Ellen's courtship and later marriage to Edward Marion Chadwick gave birth to the association between the men; it is clear that but for her, Chadwick would never have gone into partnership with her brother. Once established, however, the firm grew and prospered because of Charlotte Worts and her marriage to William Henry Beatty. Charlotte provided the enormously important link to the Gooderham and Worts families and their numerous and profitable businesses, the connection that nurtured the firm's early success. In fact, Charlotte's marriage to Beatty may have been the single most important event in the first fifty years of the firm.

Much of what we know of Ellen comes from the writings of her husband, who was both a regular diarist and a published genealogist.[2] In his diary, Chadwick tells us that he met Ellen Beatty in 1862, when she was an attractive eighteen-year-old. She was born on 9 November 1843 in Toronto,[3] the fifth of eight children of James and Anne Beatty.[4] One brother, James Jr., died in infancy. When Ellen met Chadwick, her father was seventy and had long been in poor health. She had one older brother, William Henry, and three older sisters, Elizabeth, Jane Louisa, and Annie. She also had a younger brother, Joseph Walker, and a younger sister, Diana Mary. In 1862 the Beatty children, all unmarried, were living with their parents in a two-storey brick house at 29 William Street, one block west of College Avenue (modern-day University Avenue) and just north of Queen Street. This short, tree-lined street had but a few houses on large lots. The Beatty house was a stone's throw from Osgoode Hall, where Ellen's older brother, William, was attending lectures as he studied to be a solicitor.

The Beattys were in good company on William Street, living just south of the substantial property owned by the Honourable William Pearce Howland, a prosperous grain merchant and member of the Legislative Assembly.[5] Farther up the street was the home of Justice John Hawkins Hagarty, who had been a puisne judge of the Court of Common Pleas for six years and that year had become a judge of the Court of Queen's Bench.[6]

Ellen's father had come to Canada from Belfast, Ireland, at age thirty-eight, thirteen years before she was born. James Beatty had intended to make a short stopover in York, as Toronto was then known, but instead settled in the town of about 4,000.[7] In 1831 he set up a business on the south side of King Street, just a few shops east of Yonge. James soon became a prominent merchant, calling his business the British Woollen and Cotton Warehouse. He sold plain and fancy muslin of his manufacture and British woollen goods that he imported. The year after he established his business, he married Anne Byrne McKowen, who had been orphaned in transit from Dublin when most of her family died in Montreal.[8] On 10 December 1835 Anne had given her husband a son, William Henry. James closed his business in 1836, most likely for health reasons, and became a "gentleman," never working again.[9] Whatever his disability, it did not prevent him from serving in the militia, rising to the rank of major in 1846 and later to colonel.[10]

Ellen's father never worked in her lifetime. His health problems meant that William had been forced to mature early, assuming an adult's responsibility and sharing the role of head of the family with his mother. By 1862 William was twenty-six years old and belatedly studying to be a solicitor.[11] He had attended Upper Canada College, but we do not know what he did to support his family on leaving school and before he started his legal education.

It was 21 May 1862 when Ellen met Chadwick. She and her sisters were attending a party given to celebrate the accomplishment of a number of young men who had been certified as attorneys and solicitors the day before.[12] At that time, legal education was primarily a matter of apprenticeship to an established practitioner. At the end of their period under articles, candidates were examined, and if they passed they received a certificate of fitness as an attorney and solicitor. A further year of private study, followed by written and oral examinations, was necessary to be called as a barrister. As the introduction to the 1862 *Upper Canada Law List* stated, "the professions of Barrister and Attorney may be and usually are followed together."[13] One of the newly certified attorneys was Edward Marion Chadwick. Ellen's brother William was nine months away from being so certified. There was much that would have appealed to Ellen about Marion, as he was known: he was a tall, handsome, gregarious, witty twenty-one-year-old. We do not know a great deal about Ellen, but we do know that Chadwick was taken with her and her four sisters — the "sheminines," as he would later label them in the diary.[14] Chadwick makes no mention of William Beatty.[15]

It would soon have been obvious to Chadwick and the Beatty girls that they had plenty in common. Both families had come from Ireland, both fathers had served as officers in their local militia, and both had been active in the Anglican Church. Chadwick's father had come to Canada from County Tipperary in about 1837.[16] John Chadwick, unlike James Beatty, had not settled in Toronto but had taken up land farther west, originally building a white clapboard house in the rolling hills near Ancaster, in Wentworth County. Marion, his third son, was born there on 22 September 1840.[17] By 1847 John had become a lieutenant in the militia. When Marion was nine, his family moved to Guelph, where his father became a justice of the peace and served as the regional representative on the Diocesan Synod of Toronto and the Corporation of Trinity College.

Marion probably explained to Ellen and her sisters that the Osgoode Hall lectures had brought him to Toronto. In 1858 the Law Society had appointed two permanent lecturers, S.H. Strong for equity and J.T. Anderson for law, to supplement what students learned through their articles of clerkship. Marion had started his articles in Guelph with the firm of Lemon & Peterson.[18] Then on Friday, 2 August 1861, he had "started for Toronto to prosecute [his] studies there."[19] On arrival in Toronto the next morning, he moved in with the Morgan family at 24 Walton Street. This arrangement had undoubtedly been worked out before his arrival, as had his clerkship with the firm of Patterson, Harrison & Hodgins.[20] He stayed with the Morgan family for the seven months needed to complete his initial period of articles and may well have recalled for Ellen and her sisters the joy he experienced on 20 February 1862, when he noted with glee in his diary that his "articles expired and [he] was released from bondage!!!!"

It must have soon been apparent to Ellen that she and her sisters had made a favourable impression on young Chadwick. Following the party Marion began frequenting the Beatty home on William Street. He would later quip that their house was "most conveniently near Osgoode Hall."[21] A week after their first meeting Chadwick tells us that he called on the Beattys in the afternoon. On Saturday, 7 June, he "slammed about with two of the Beattys — Anna and Ellen to wit." Slamming, which he sketched in his diary for 1860, was a term he used often to refer to walking with a young woman. On 11 June he was "calling on the Beattys . . . found the whole of the sheminines on hand save Mrs. Beatty and Miss Jane." On 4 July he went to the Horticultural Grand Bazaar in the evening "and met divers Beattys there, so I repeated the performance of yesterday evening slamming with them to a reasonable hour and then seeing them home, and upon bringing them home sat awhile talking to them and Mrs. Beatty." The next day he went to

William Henry Beatty
Photo courtesy of Douglas Worts

the Royal Canadian Yacht Club (then on the mainland) and met "divers Beattys, Hancocks, Robertsons and a lot of boys collected within a short space of time." In the diary he inserted an impressive coloured sketch of the group on a sailboat known as the *Dart*. Ellen is shown on board with him. On 9 July he "went up to the Beattys for the purpose of giving Ellen Beatty a sketch of the Dart as she (the Dart) appeared last Saturday, which resulted in my staying the whole evening."

Finally, on 2 August, Chadwick first mentions William Henry Beatty in his diary, more than two months after meeting Ellen. That day Chadwick took Ellen and Miss Marsh, her cousin, out for a row in the bay. William accompanied them, probably as a chaperone. This lack of reference to William or his father reinforces the impression that neither was important to Chadwick at this time. William was too busy playing the role of *pater familias* and too much older to socialize with young Chadwick, and James was incapacitated.

In the late summer and fall of 1862, Chadwick notes that he acquired a rowboat he called the *Pollywog*, in which he would row about on the bay and up the Don River. Ellen and her younger brother, Joseph, accompanied him most often. Joseph Walker Beatty was two and a half years younger than Ellen, born on 29 March 1846. Chadwick had more in common with Joe than with William, who was not only older and more mature but seemed to lack Chadwick's wit, playfulness, and artistic bent.

By 26 September 1862 Chadwick was spending so much time with Ellen at the Beatty home that he says in his diary, "spent the evening at William Street of course." By 1 October their engagement was finalized. Chadwick tells us that he, William Beatty and "Hawkins"[22] received his father, mother, and older brother Fred at the station and then went up to William Street, where "the leading members of the Beatty family received the leading members of the Chadwick family in due form." It is interesting to note that James Beatty was not among the "leading members." Afterward Mr. and Mrs. Chadwick boarded a steamer for England, and William and Ellen Beatty went with Marion Chadwick on board to spend more time with his parents.

What would the families have thought of one another? They shared a common heritage, but the Chadwicks were better placed in Guelph than the Beattys were in Toronto. The Chadwick family had settled in Guelph in 1849 and lived along the Waterloo Road, owning Park Lot 51 of the Canada Company's survey of the town. Marion's father, John Craven Chadwick Sr., was an important figure in the community. Marion's two older brothers were also prominent locally: John Jr. was a lieutenant in the Wellington Militia, while Frederick Jasper was a provincial land surveyor, real estate agent, publisher, and city councillor. Fred would later serve a term as mayor of Guelph.[23] Marion, with Fred's encouragement, had even developed the coat of arms for the city.[24] The Beattys were not nearly as prominent. Although they had a home in a good neighbourhood and were pew holders at St. James, the achievements of the father, James, were in the distant past and William and young Joe had yet to make their mark. None of Ellen's older sisters were married, and the family seemed to lack the social and political contacts that were so important in this period.

FOLLOWING THE ENGAGEMENT, William Beatty took Chadwick for a walk. Chadwick writes of it in his diary in a surprised tone: "slammed up and down King Street with William Beatty in the afternoon!"[25] Beatty and Chadwick had spent little, if any, time alone with each other. One can imagine Beatty, as the de facto head of the family, discussing the fact that Chadwick would need to be established with a steady income before he could marry Ellen.

Such an income could come from a successful law practice, but the legal market seemed tight and Chadwick had not yet secured a position in an existing firm. He could, of course, start his own practice, but would it not be better for the two of them to go into a law partnership together? By February 1863 Beatty would be certified as a solicitor and Chadwick would be called to the bar. Why should each seek out a place with others when they could practise together?

Shortly thereafter, on Sunday, 9 November, Chadwick sat for the first time with the Beatty family in their large box pew near the front of the nave along the west aisle of St. James.[26] Chadwick had been attending services there since his arrival in Toronto, but he had no designated pew. Now that he was to be a member of the family, he could join the Beattys in their private pew at the morning and evening Sunday services.

Before William Beatty and his soon to be brother-in-law could go into partnership, they had to complete their legal studies. Specialization was largely unknown. Lawyers were required to "be conversant with the knowledge of the profession in all its branches, the practice as well as the principles, with Equity as well as Common Law, the Rules of pleading and those of evidence — in short, place themselves in a position to be able, without extrinsic aid, to advise a client on any matter in which he may require advice and to carry through a suit in all its stages."[27] They were expected to prepare themselves during a period of years under articles of clerkship. This on-the-job training was supplemented by independent reading as well as, to some extent, lectures given in Toronto at Osgoode Hall, the seat of the Law Society of Upper Canada. Students could enter legal studies at age sixteen. Chadwick could not have been much older than this minimum when he began his articles in Guelph with Lemon & Peterson. Beatty, much older, was articling in Toronto with John Leys, a barrister and solicitor who had been called in 1860 and who had his office at 39 Church Street in the City Building, just south of King Street and within a very short walk of St. James Cathedral and the court house, then located on Adelaide Street.[28] The hours that Beatty and Chadwick spent in their respective law offices probably involved assisting in drafting or engrossing legal documents (i.e., writing them out in longhand), serving and filing materials, doing legal research, and searching land titles.[29]

The idea of two young lawyers going into partnership together was not surprising. Partnerships of two or three practitioners were a common form of organizing a legal practice; in fact, partnership was then the principal method of carrying on any type of business. English partnership law, as Dick Risk has noted, had been "adopted in Ontario without significant modification . . . . Business records and the volume of litigation suggest that thousands [of partnerships] were created, for a wide range of commercial purposes."[30] In law, a partnership was and is defined as two or more persons carrying on a business in common with a view to profit. Unlike a corporation, it was not a separate legal entity; the partners were the business and the debts of the partnership were their debts. Unless otherwise agreed in writing, all partners were equal and each could bind the partnership. At the time of William Beatty's proposal to Chadwick, there was no partnership legislation, although from at least 1870 there was a requirement to file a notice of the formation and dissolution of a partnership.

It is surprising, however, that Chadwick would think of going into partnership with William Beatty. He had had little to do with Beatty and much to do with fellow law student Calvin Browne. The Tuesday after his articles expired, Chadwick had moved into the Newbigging boarding house with Browne, with whom he would live, work, and play for the year needed to qualify for his call to the bar. "Browne and I occupy together two rooms — a bedroom opening into a sitting room in which we sit and work."[31] Chadwick and Browne put in long hours and prepared an impressive 400-page book to assist other students in preparing for their law examinations.[32] The authors were quick to point out in the preface that the book was not "intended to enable students to 'cram' for their examinations" but rather was to be used by the student "as an aid to the study of the books upon which he will be examined, but never to be read in lieu of them." By 19 April they had completed a draft of the text and by 30 April had finished the index. On 3 May Chadwick went up to Osgoode Hall and filed his articles and four days later, his book went on sale with "very promising result."

Despite their friendship and their work on the book, Chadwick does not seem to have considered going into law partnership with Browne. Perhaps it was because neither had the money or connections to ensure a good start or perhaps Browne, who opened a practice in St. Catharines,[33] had never intended to stay in Toronto. In any event, Chadwick states in his diary for 29 May that he spent the day offering himself "for sale to divers legal practitioners." When he was unable to find a permanent position by 12 June, he returned to the firm with which he had articled, where he was permitted "to stay for 12 months if all goes right." Harrison in his diary for 30 May indicated that his practice as a barrister was much lighter than usual: "Never saw so little general business."[34] Chadwick, however, having not yet been called to the bar, was likely to have worked more with Patterson, who acted as a solicitor, or Hodgins, who had a Chancery practice.

Beatty and Chadwick, the two would-be law partners, completed their legal studies in early 1863. On 29 January Chadwick sat for his written examination as a barrister.[35] The next Monday, 2 February, he was to have had an oral exam, but it was cancelled due to the death of Sir John Beverley Robinson, the former Chief Justice of the Queen's Bench and then presiding judge of the Court of Error and Appeal.[36] One of the first things that Beatty and Chadwick did together in the legal world was attend Robinson's elaborate "state funeral" at St. James Cathedral.[37] The next day, 5 February, Chadwick was called to the bar. Meanwhile Beatty had been certified as an attorney and solicitor.[38]

On 12 February 1863 the Legislative Assembly of United Canada opened a new session in Quebec City.[39] Tension between the largely French-speaking Catholics of Canada East and the largely English-speaking Protestants of Canada West was a continuing problem in the union. There can be little doubt where Ellen's brother and her fiancé, as Orangemen, stood on these issues. As fervent Anglicans of Irish descent, they viewed all Catholics and all Frenchmen with suspicion. The political tensions between French and English, between Catholics and Protestants, would soon lead to a deadlock that gave impetus to Confederation and the formation of the Dominion of Canada. South of the border, the US Civil War raged on. General Grant of the Union forces was poised to capture Vicksburg and Robert E. Lee of the Confederate army was preparing for his incursion into the North, which would lead four months later to the bloody three-day battle at Gettysburg, Pennsylvania.

Beatty and Chadwick, however, had other, more mundane things on their minds: they needed to find office space for their partnership. On 9 February Chadwick wrote that he "went with Beatty to see a room in the new Bank of Toronto which is proposed to be our office." Three days later they were still looking. This time they "went to the Exchange looking for an office, the Bank of Toronto being rather exorbitant as to rent." Finally, on 23 February, the soon to be brothers-in-law announced their new partnership in the *Globe*. That day Chadwick proudly noted in his diary, "The firm of Beatty & Chadwick opened office at no. 12 Exchange." The following notice appeared in the papers announcing the new partnership:

Beatty & Chadwick
Barristers and Attorneys,
Conveyancers, Notaries Public etc
No. 12 Toronto Exchange
Wellington Street
W H Beatty E M Chadwick[40]

This notice implied that Beatty was a barrister. Certainly they were both solicitors and attorneys, but only Chadwick was a barrister. Perhaps they thought it only a formality until Beatty was called to the bar in another year. As it happened, however, he became busy with the new firm and was not called to the bar for almost twenty years.

Although less expensive to rent than the Bank of Toronto, the Toronto Exchange building on Wellington Street East was a handsome edifice.[41] It had been erected in 1855 by a group of millers and grain merchants to house a grain exchange.[42] The building boasted a pillared façade on both Wellington Street and Leader Lane. The entrance hall on Leader Lane was fifteen metres wide and twelve metres high, with two grand staircases and an ornamental glass-domed roof.[43] The space rented by the new law partners was reached by climbing the stairs to the first floor and proceeding down the hall on the right. Their office, number 12, was reached just before numbers 10 and 11, occupied by the milling and distillery partnership of Gooderham & Worts.[44] Although neither Gooderham nor Worts is listed as an incorporator of the Exchange, both were directors by 1856 and had their offices in the building.[45] Other tenants included Dun, Wiman & Company, a "mercantile agency."[46] Beatty & Chadwick's office was about eight by nine metres, into which they fitted their desk and working space for their clerk and perhaps a few client chairs. Chadwick would later say, "We commenced to practise in one room about half furnished."[47]

Although they were equal partners in law, Beatty was the de facto leader and more focused on business. Chadwick was bright and capable, but his diary suggests that his interests were elsewhere. He studied heraldry and genealogy, painted, and put time into Church affairs.

The young law partners reflected the community they wished to serve. Of Toronto's 45,000 inhabitants, 93.1 percent were of British descent, 43 percent had been born in Canada, 32 percent were Anglican, 48 percent were between the ages of fifteen and forty.[48] Nevertheless, Beatty and Chadwick faced a difficult market. As the 1862 *Upper Canada Law List* noted, "There was a time in Canada, not very long since, when all that was required to secure a competent livelihood was honesty and attention to business."[49] But this was no longer the case. They faced "competition and [the] crowded state of the profession," especially in Toronto.

The Toronto Exchange building may well have influenced the law that the partners practised. The Exchange had been incorporated by special act of the legislature at the request of the Association of Merchants, Millers and Businessmen in 1854 to provide office space and a forum for buying and selling grain and other produce.[50] A building housing these businesses would have represented an excellent source of work for commercial lawyers, who could draft sales agreements and assist in collection matters for the other tenants. It seems likely that the young lawyers intended to fulfill this need. William Pearce Howland, the Beattys' neighbour, had an office there and he may have influenced their choice. He was listed as a "commission merchant," presumably acting as a middleman in facilitating grain sales. It is unclear whether Beatty knew the two prominent businessmen whose offices were next door. William Gooderham was then seventy-three and his nephew, James Gooderham Worts, was forty-five.

If the two partners were hoping for good crops and a vibrant grain trade, they were disappointed. The president of the Bank of Toronto, Angus Cameron, reported to his shareholders in July 1863 that Canada West was suffering a "considerable depression."[51] The next year, James G. Worts, the Bank's vice-president, repeated the dire assessment, talking of "a probable deficiency in the crops . . . at the approaching harvest and the depression in business consequent thereon."[52] It is not surprising that Beatty and Chadwick did much repossession and receivership work. In the fall of 1863 they acted as solicitors for the mortgagees of a farm property within four miles of Barrie being sold at public auction under a power of sale.[53] In December they were again solicitors for mortgagees, this time of the schooner *Newcastle*, said to be in good order and have a capacity of 3,500 bushels of grain. Potential purchasers were asked to apply to Beatty & Chadwick for terms.[54] The city also hired them to collect tax debts.[55] The court proceedings columns of the *Globe* contain no notices of them at this time, but Chadwick does note in his diary that on 24 February he made his first appearance in Chancery court before Vice-Chancellor Spragge in the case of *Macdonald v Smith*. It was a "hearing on further directions. Stayner (Crooks' office) for plaintiff and myself for defendants." The leading grain merchants in the Exchange building — Howland, Gooderham, and Worts — were all in the business

James Gooderham Worts, 1864
Notman Collection, McCord Museum

of lending money on mortgages, but we have no evidence that Beatty and Chadwick were then providing services to them.[56] The one 1867 case involving the three merchants as mortgagees was handled by Mr. Hector, QC, and C.S. Patterson.[57]

ONCE THEIR LAW PRACTICE was generating income, Marion Chadwick could finally marry Ellen. On 28 June 1864 they were wed at St. James Cathedral after an engagement of approximately a year and a half. Although Ellen was the fourth daughter, she was the first to marry. Her oldest sister, Elizabeth, then about thirty, would not marry for another twelve years, when she became the third wife of Marion Chadwick's elderly father. Ellen's other older sisters, Jane and Annie, never married.

Ellen's bridesmaids were her sisters Elizabeth and Annie and her cousins Elizabeth and Harriet Marsh. The Reverend H.J. Grasset presided at the service, assisted by J. Walker Marsh, an uncle to the bride and father to Elizabeth and Harriet. Lunch at the Beatty home on William Street followed.

Afterward the newlyweds boarded the *Champion* to sail to Kingston, where they toured the Thousand Islands. The description that Chadwick provides of their honeymoon permits us a glimpse of transportation between Toronto, Montreal, and Ottawa. After sailing to Kingston the Chadwicks continued on to Montreal, arriving on the 29th at 8:00 pm. The newlyweds took a room at the Ottawa Hotel and visited Notre Dame, climbing to the top of the bell tower. The next day they went for a drive on the mountain and then visited Christ Church Cathedral, where they strolled the cemetery in which Ellen's grandfather, grandmother, aunt Mary, and other relatives were buried. On Saturday, 2 July, they left Montreal by train to Lachine to board the *Prince of Wales* mail steamer, which made its way up the Ottawa River to Carillon, where they disembarked and boarded the nineteen-kilometre-long Carillon and Grenville Railway for Grenville.[58] There they boarded the *Queen Victoria* steamer to Ottawa, arriving at the Russell House at 8:00 pm. On 5 July they left on the Prescott and Ottawa Railroad for Prescott, where they took the Royal Canadian mail steamer *Banshee*. Finally, they arrived back in Toronto the next day and went to their new residence at 32 Gloucester Street, where the Beatty family visited for tea. The next month or two of their marriage was spent in reciprocal visits with family and friends.

Perhaps the most significant comment Chadwick records in his diary about the wedding was that William Beatty was accompanied by young Charlotte Louisa Worts, then eighteen. Lotty, as she was known, would have an even greater impact on the early years of the firm than did Ellen. The reason lies in who her father was and in both the position and nature of the Gooderham and Worts extended family.

Three years younger than Ellen, Charlotte was born on 29 October 1846,[59] the third child of Sarah Bright and James Gooderham Worts but the first to reach maturity. Her parents' firstborn, Elizabeth Anne, had come into the world in July 1841 and their second, James Gordon, in December 1843. Neither had survived childhood — James dying in 1846 at age two and Elizabeth in 1849 at age eight.[60] Charlotte had two younger brothers and four younger sisters. Her family lived in a substantial two-storey house known as Lindenwold, recently built on a large estate on Mill Street at the corner of Trinity. Immediately south was the Gooderham & Worts distillery and immediately north was the equally large and impressive Gooderham house, built at the same time. We do not have a description of the Worts house but we do have one of the Gooderham home. Elizabeth "Lizzie" Blackstock, a great-granddaughter of William Gooderham, recalled that it had "a great spreading veranda, large garden, and a many-mirrored ballroom, pale green and gold . . . so convenient, hot and cold soft water to be had anytime day or night by just turning a tap . . . a fireplace in every room in the house."[61]

Charlotte's family was closely linked to the Gooderhams by marriage, business, and religion. In fact, William Gooderham was Charlotte's de facto grandfather, having effectively, if not legally, adopted her father (his nephew) in 1834. Charlotte's father, then thirteen, had left England in 1831 with his father, James Worts, who was married to William Gooderham's sister Elizabeth. They were to establish a milling business in York and to make the way easier for other members of the Worts family and the elder James' in-laws, the Gooderhams, who were to come the following year. The father and son began to construct a windmill at the mouth of the Don River, to the southeast of the town. The next year William Gooderham arrived with fifty-four people, including members of both families as well as servants and eleven children whose parents had died on the journey. William also brought £3,000, the combined family fortune, to invest in the business. The two brothers-in-law went into partnership as Worts and Gooderham, carrying on a flour-milling business. Their partnership dissolved in 1834, when, following his wife's death in childbirth, James Worts committed suicide by throwing himself down the family well.

At this point William Gooderham in essence adopted his nephew, James Gooderham Worts, and assumed sole control of the milling operation. Holding his nephew's share in an informal trust, William carried on business as a sole proprietor under the name William Gooderham Company. In 1837 he took the step that would make the family fortune by expanding the business to include a distillery to use surplus grain. Four years later he started a cattle operation to use by-products of the distillery.

In 1845 Charlotte's father, now twenty-seven, went into formal partnership with his uncle and adoptive father under the name Gooderham & Worts. In 1846 the partnership, faced with the need to bring grain from the United States for its distillery and to ship finished product to other parts of United Canada and the United States, expanded its operations into shipping and built their own Great Lakes schooners. As we shall see, the two business partners sought to control all factors contributing to the success of their operations. For this reason, Charlotte's father had taken an active role at the first meeting of the Canadian Ship Owners' Association, held in June 1857, and begun his lengthy tenure as one of the five commissioners of the

Toronto Harbour Trust, the forerunner of the Toronto Harbour Commission.[62] He would become its chairman in 1865, a post he kept until 1882.

Charlotte had a strict religious upbringing. Both her family and the Gooderhams were ardent members of the Anglican congregation of Little Trinity Church, located immediately to the north of the two houses. Charlotte's father and his uncle William served as wardens of that church for over thirty years. In his history of Little Trinity, Alan Hayes states that in this period, "the parish functioned rather like a proprietary chapel, with Gooderham, his nephew and partner James Gooderham Worts, and some other captains of industry and commerce of St Lawrence ward as the benevolent proprietors."[63] In 1850, when Charlotte was six years old, the Gooderham and Worts families had a gallery of the church constructed and reserved for their use. Cecily Blackstock, whose mother was a Gooderham, remarks in her family history, "For all their wealth, they were modest and shunned publicity; they were also exceedingly conventional."[64] They had "many laudable virtues: integrity, generosity, and a strong social conscience." William Gooderham "epitomized conservatism." An adherent of an evangelical Anglican sect, "he practised its precepts in daily living, held family prayers twice daily, and observed a strict Sabbath."[65]

It is likely that Charlotte was home schooled since the Toronto Model School, which her younger siblings would attend, opened only in August 1858.[66] In fact, before Charlotte met William Beatty, her world had to a large extent been circumscribed by her extended family. The Gooderham and Worts families largely kept to themselves. This does not mean that she would have been without significant social contact because the two were large, extended families, with many brothers, sisters, uncles, aunts, nephews, and nieces. Cecily Blackstock notes, "None in the subcontinent of Asia could have been more extended than ours."[67] William Gooderham had eight sons, five daughters, and more than forty grandchildren. James Gooderham Worts, as noted, had seven children who survived childhood. Cecily Blackstock gives the impression of a broad but closely knit family that seldom went outside the large clan, pointing out that "the Gooderham network, so closely bound by blood and trade, was a Family Compact in itself. Old William's advice to his sons is said to have been: Stick together, boys."

The families certainly followed this advice. To the extent that they needed legal, medical, or other services they patronized members of the extended families. Blackstock informs us that in 1872, Thomas N. Gibbs, a member of Parliament who was soliciting funds to finance the Pacific

Railway, approached James Gooderham Worts. He reported to Sir John A. Macdonald, "If assured half a million as the result he would not enter into it. His ideas are and his partner's the same, that wealth is only of service so long as it can be made to minister to the comfort and ease of its possessor. Any other obligation than those of self & family are ignored. They seem to have a natural aversion to have anything to do with matters not under their own immediate control."[68]

These three themes — conservatism, keeping things in the family, and controlling the businesses in which they invested — run throughout the Gooderham and Worts business history and help to explain why they eventually came to rely upon Beatty and his law firm for the legal assistance needed by the many family businesses. Both Charlotte's father and her uncle became quite knowledgeable about and active in a series of corporations in which the families invested the extensive profits generated by the distillery, including the Bank of Toronto and the Canada Permanent Building and Savings Society, both of which were incorporated in 1855 by special act of the legislature. Their partnership, with other members of the Association of Merchants Millers and Businessmen, was among the original incorporators of the Bank of Toronto and they made a substantial investment in it. From 1858 James Gooderham Worts had served on its board. By 1863 he was the second largest stockholder of the Bank and its vice-president. In 1864 when Angus Cameron, the original cashier and second president of the Bank, died, William Gooderham became president.[69] Charlotte's father was also on the board of Canada Permanent.

As for Charlotte herself, the only evidence we have of her attitudes comes from an obituary written many years later. In 1928 she was said to have been "noted for her strong, outspoken Tory views. It is not making a hackneyed use of the term to say that she was an ardent Imperialist. She was a staunch believer in the principles of the Orange Order, and always on the 12th of July stood on the verandah of her home watching the parade form up in Queen's Park."[70] What we do not know is the extent to which these later views reflected her upbringing and attitudes as a young woman and to what extent they were shaped over the years by her husband and her experiences.

While the future looked bright for Beatty and his wife-to-be, the same did not hold true for Ellen and Marion Chadwick. Their shared joy at their life together and Ellen's pregnancy was cut short when she died suddenly in February 1865. The register of St. James Cemetery lists her cause of death as "premature confinement," suggesting that she died of complications arising from a premature delivery of their first child, who also seems to have died. Ellen was only twenty-one. She was buried in the Alexander Dixon vault in St. James Cemetery, most likely because Chadwick did not then have the funds to give her a proper burial in her own plot. The Dixons were well known to both the Beatty and Chadwick families. Alex Dixon had come to Toronto from Ireland about the same time as James Beatty, and for a time their shops were side by side on King Street. Beatty had his woollen importing business and Dixon operated the British Saddlery Warehouse. They both were active members of the Anglican Church. Initially, each family had lived above its shop.[71] Alex Dixon's eldest son, also named Alexander, became the rector of the Anglican Church in Guelph, which the Chadwick family attended. Undoubtedly, the elder Chadwick knew Alex Dixon, the father, since both were very active in Church affairs.

There is no more telling testimony to the impact of Ellen's death on Chadwick than the fact that the diary he had kept diligently for ten years went silent. There is no discussion of Ellen's death or of the days immediately following, other than a brief news clipping that he pasted in: "Chadwick at 32 Gloucester Street on Friday 10th after a few hours' illness, Ellen Byrne, beloved wife of Edward Marion Chadwick Esquire, barrister at law. The funeral will take place on Monday at 3 o'clock pm."[72] Chadwick's next entry was eleven days later. On Wednesday, 22 February, he wrote, "returned from Guelph where I have been staying for a week and took up my abode at 29 William Street." He had gone to his parents' home to mourn for his young wife and child. On returning to Toronto he did not want to be alone and moved in with the Beattys instead of going to his own empty house. The next day he was "at work again as usual."

Chadwick's brief marriage to Ellen gave impetus to the creation of the partnership, but the success of the firm was intimately connected with Beatty's marriage. Interestingly both marriages were memorialized on the same day. On 26 April 1865, at a time when the newspapers were full of the news of President Abraham Lincoln's recent assassination in Washington, Beatty married Charlotte Worts at Little Trinity Church.[73] That same day, Chadwick and the Beatty family erected the beautiful white plaque to Ellen's memory that still hangs on the eastern wall of St. James Cathedral.[74]

While Chadwick continued to live with his mother- and sisters-in-law on William Street (James Beatty having died shortly after his son's wedding), William Beatty and Lotty made their home at 290 King Street East, not far from the Worts family home on Mill Street. The location of their new home illustrates that Beatty was joining the Gooderham and Worts extended family. In fact the entire Beatty family and his law partner would also be drawn into that "Family Compact." Chadwick's diary began to include entries like "spent the evening at the Worts."[75] On such visits he was often accompanied by Joe Beatty,[76] who would eventually join Gooderham & Worts as a clerk and later become its accountant.[77]

Visits to the Worts home may have provided the widowed Chadwick with a distraction. Certainly it seems that he was doing what he could to take his mind off of the loss of Ellen. To make matters worse, business was still slow. William Gooderham told the shareholders of the Bank of Toronto in July that "the year has been one of the most trying that the country has ever experienced."[78] Chadwick, however, had other interests. In his diary for 21 September 1865 he pasted a clipping from that day's *Globe* reporting that he had entered an illuminated title page and vignette of a book at the Provincial Exhibition. His entry was said to have been "very well done," showing "artistic taste."[79] This was the likely genesis of *Ontarian Families*, his study of Ontario heraldry and genealogy, published many years later. Certainly heraldic art and genealogy would be lifelong interests. Chadwick also became a member of the Toronto Lacrosse Club[80] and joined the Queen's Own Rifles militia.

— ◈ —

HIS MILITIA SERVICE PROVED timely because the next summer Fenians invaded Upper Canada.[81] Their incursion near Fort Erie was the second raid into Canada of the Fenian Brotherhood, an Irish independence group based in the United States.[82] The first had been in April against Campobello Island, New Brunswick. The Fenians planned a series of raids on British army forts, customs posts, and other targets in Canada with the hope that this would put pressure on Britain to withdraw from Ireland. Approximately 1,500 Fenians, many veterans of the US Civil War, were ferried across from Buffalo and dug themselves in at Ridgeway, near Fort Erie. The Queen's Own Rifles were one of several militia groups called up to drive out the invaders. Chadwick was not in the first call-up. The telegraph and newspaper offices opened their doors to let people see the news as it came in,[83] and he "watched news" of the Fenian raids.[84]

Chadwick soon received word that his company was to join the fight. He and his men gathered at the Toronto harbour and boarded a ship to sail to St. Catharines, joining other militia units that were to reinforce the initial troops then in battle with the Fenians. On 3 June, he and his troop took a special train to Port Colborne. There they learned that the Canadian militia under Colonel Brooker, including a number of the Queen's Own Rifles, had stumbled upon the Fenians at Ridgeway the day before. Their intelligence had indicated that the invaders were elsewhere and Brooker's Canadians had been on their way to rendezvous with British soldiers at Stevensville.

The fighting had gone badly for the inexperienced Canadians. They were no match for the much more battle-hardened Fenians, who had chosen their battleground well to give them advantage. Nineteen Canadians were killed or so seriously wounded that they would soon die. Chadwick was with the reinforcing units gathered at Port Colbourne with the expectation that they would have to drive the Fenians from Ridgeway. They were taken by train to the previous day's battleground, only to find that the Fenians had withdrawn to Fort Erie, where they had driven out a small force left to protect the town and used its ferry service to retreat to the United States. The Ridgeway site had been stripped clean of anything that could be a souvenir of the bitterly fought contest. One of those collecting souvenirs was Thomas Gibbs Blackstock, age fourteen, a Toronto boy who had hidden himself among the baggage taken to Ridgeway. In the midst of the battle, he had been noticed by a neighbour and sent back.

Throughout his life Blackstock would keep the "Fenian cartridges . . . found in a field back of the town of Fort Erie by me on the . . . day after the battle of Ridgeway which was fought between the Queen's Own Rifles and the Fenians under O'Neil."[85] Although they did not meet at the battle site, Chadwick later came to know the lad as the winner of many sharpshooter contests in the Queen's Own Rifles. A decade later Blackstock would become one of Chadwick's law partners.

Chadwick was disappointed that he and his men had arrived after the successful Fenians had retreated. The immediate threat was over, but the fear of further attacks was widely shared and would soon give impetus to the Confederation talks under way. Pride in the "successful" expulsion of the raiders was also widely shared. Lotty Beatty later recalled that her family had supported the troops sent to Ridgeway. She was fond of telling her children and grandchildren how the family yacht, the *Oriole*, had been used to take supplies over to the troops defending Canada.[86]

Lotty and her husband had reasons to remember 1866. Almost exactly a year after their marriage, on 29 April 1866, Harry Worts Beatty was born, the first of their five children.[87] Although Beatty undoubtedly had high hopes for his newborn son, Harry would prove a disappointment to his business-oriented lawyer father.

—➤◆←—

CHADWICK LATER RECALLED THAT "when we got along so well so that we were able to have a student we considered we were doing very well, and when we got on so as to be able to take another room and a few more chairs we thought our success was assured."[88] The need for the extra room is actually evidence, however, that Charlotte Worts and the Gooderham & Worts connection had not yet brought significant work to the law firm. The two partners took over room 11 in 1866, one of the two offices previously used by Gooderham & Worts, because on 2 October they had taken in a new partner. Chadwick pasted into his diary a news clipping saying, "Law Partnership. The undersigned have entered into co-partnership in the practice of the law under the firm of Robinson, Beatty & Chadwick, offices 11 and 12 Toronto Exchange Wellington Street. The Honourable John Beverley Robinson, W.H. Beatty and E.M. Chadwick." It seems that the use of an extra office in the Exchange Building was a stopgap because Chadwick reports in his diary that just a few weeks later, 29 October 1866, was their "first day in our new offices on Church Street — moved on Saturday."

The Honourable John Beverley Robinson was the second son of Sir John Beverley Robinson, the former Chief Justice whose death had led to the cancellation of Chadwick's oral examination in 1863. Robinson was forty-five years old with twenty-two years of practice behind him when he went into partnership with Beatty and Chadwick. His value was not as a lawyer, however, but as someone who could generate business through his political and social connections. Had the two partners needed assistance in legal work they could have looked to Chadwick's brother, Austin Cooper, who had graduated in 1864 and gone into partnership in Toronto with a Mr. Hodgins.[89] Robinson, however, was a very well connected former politician: mayor of Toronto in 1857; first elected to the Legislative Assembly in 1858; and a cabinet minister in John A. Macdonald's Conservative government in 1862, acting as president of the Executive Council.[90] The *Globe* reported that he became the local "dispenser of Government favours." His tenure in the cabinet had been very short, less than two months, because Macdonald's government had fallen. Significantly, in 1864 he had obtained the lucrative post of city solicitor for Toronto, which he would hold until 1880. He had also started the Western Canada Building and Loan Association and invested in the building of one of Toronto's foremost hotels, the Rossin House.[91] He had legal work that needed to be done and Beatty and Chadwick had the ability and the capacity to do it. It seemed like a perfect fit, but the prospects for the new partnership were not all good. Robinson had a combative personality and his companies would prove to be very demanding clients.

⟶✥⟵

ONE WONDERS HOW CHADWICK was able to balance his law practice and his personal life in 1867. He was promoted in the militia, he moved into a new home, and he began a new courtship. On 16 February 1867 he was commissioned with a second-class certificate as an ensign in the 2nd Queen's Own Rifles.[92] Then, on 30 May, he "obtained possession of my new house 31 Mercer St, I slept in it for the first time tonight."[93] A month later, 1 July 1867, of course marked the end of the United Canadas. Chadwick notes in his diary that "we wound up the evening [of 30 June] with some sacred music and then went to bed to sleep out the remainder of the existence of the province of Canada and to wake up in the morning in that of Ontario." The next day, Chadwick and his new love interest, Marian Martha "Mattie" Fisher, joined in the Confederation celebrations in Toronto. He took Mattie and her sisters for ice creams and to the horticultural gardens. In the harbour, HMS *Hercules*, a side-paddle steamer serving as a gun boat to protect against the Fenian raids, fired a salute.[94]

Chadwick had met Mattie through the Beatty girls. She was the daughter of Alexander Fisher, the manager of the Toronto branch of the Ontario Bank, which had an attractive office building at the corner of Wellington and Scott Streets, just three buildings west of the Exchange Building.[95] The Fishers lived above the Bank offices. The Ontario Bank had been founded in 1857 in Bowmanville, with a capital of $1,000,000. It had clearly prospered and set up a number of offices, of which the major one was in Toronto.

By 28 September there were clear signs that Chadwick and Mattie Fisher were thinking of marriage. He mentions in his diary that his mother and father came to stay with him and spent the evening at the Fishers. In November Mattie went to Guelph to spend a week with his family.[96] On Monday, 2 December, he and Mattie returned together to Toronto. Then, on 19 February 1868, Chadwick notes in his diary that "Papa, Momma and Fred came down at 12 o'clock and put up at my house." The next day he married Mattie Fisher in St. Peter's Anglican Church, located near his new house. The Reverend Samuel J. Boddy presided over the simple ceremony. Other than the immediate family, there were no guests. It had not been intended to be so. The wedding was to have taken place on 15 January and "to have been quite swell," but it had had to be rescheduled because of the death of Chadwick's eldest brother's wife, Elinor, in Guelph.[97] After the wedding, the newlyweds had a quiet breakfast at the Fishers and then left at 10:35 a.m. for St. Catharines.

Like the wedding plans, the honeymoon was an ill-fated affair. The couple were to have gone to Niagara Falls and Buffalo "but various difficulties — especially irregular trains — spoiled the intended trip." Significantly, legal business also interfered. On 24 February, "In consequence of the urgency of business matters, we were compelled to be so unfashionable as to return home — which we did. I was at the office for a while." As was typical, for the next month the newlyweds called on numerous people. The Beattys of William Street were first, followed by the Worts family, then William and Lotty Beatty, Mrs William Gooderham, and many others.

—————•⊗•—————

By 30 April 1868 Beatty and Chadwick realized that their partnership with Robinson had been a mistake. It had brought them some work, but at a price they were no longer willing to pay. Chadwick wrote in his diary that day, "The partnership of Robinson, Beatty & Chadwick came to an end, being dissolved by mutual consent on the principal ground of the meanness, stinginess, unfair dealing, disagreeableness etc etc etc of the Western Canadian Building Society, clients of Robinson's with which Beatty and I are not disposed to put up any longer."

The split with Robinson caused the partners to move again, this time to 56 King Street East, next to Rice Lewis and Son Hardware.[98] For the first and only time in the firm's history, the partners had a storefront location. The address seems to have been tied to Beatty's friendship with Rice Lewis and the ties between the Lewis family and Gooderham & Worts.[99] Rice Lewis had served as a witness at Beatty's wedding and his daughter, Margaret, married Robert Turner Gooderham that same year.[100] Although the move had been caused by the break with Robinson, King Street was then quite a prestigious address. The *Toronto City Directory* of 1856 describes it as "the main street of the city . . . one of the finest in America," noting that the "shops on this street, which display extensive stocks of goods, are finished and decorated in the English style and in appearance some of them bear comparison with Regent Street London."

Now the firm name began to be listed in the court proceedings column of the *Globe*, initially in connection with three cases — two in common law and one in Chancery. On 1 March 1869 Beatty & Chadwick moved for security for costs in *Mullarkey v Robinson*. Two days later the firm appeared in Chancery Chambers in *Rogers v Taylor* to obtain an order appointing a guardian to infant defendants. On 23 March it was in Common Law Chambers in *Mullarkey v Robinson* seeking an order for better particulars. On 26 May it appeared in Chancery Chambers in *Rogers v Taylor* to obtain an order to serve a defendant by publication. On 3 July in *Moss v Bruce* it objected to a petition for a new venue.[101] The impression is that the two partners were trying to replace the business that Robinson had brought in by expanding their barrister practice. It was a short-lived effort, probably because they had limited success with their motions. They were soon focusing once again almost exclusively on solicitors' work.

At about the time of their split with Robinson, Zebulon Lash advertised that he was opening a Toronto office as a sole practitioner. Shortly thereafter there is evidence that Lash was assisting Beatty and Chadwick. Chadwick wrote in his diary on 10 December 1868 that he had spent the "evening at work at William Beatty's and by way of variety (Lash, Joe [Beatty] and I) went on our way home to see Carty's Factory burnt down." Within two years Lash would formally join their practice as a partner, an expansion made necessary because Beatty's marriage to Lotty was about to pay its first dividend.

Gooderham & Worts was in need of legal assistance in connection with the incorporation and financing of the Toronto Grey and Bruce Railway. It was one of two narrow-gauge railways that the families supported, the other being the Toronto and Nipissing Railway.[102] Each railway was promoted by George Laidlaw, a former Gooderham & Worts employee, working with his "senior partners" William Gooderham and James Gooderham Worts. The two partners considered railway companies a natural extension of their milling and distillery operations. They needed to bring grain for their milling operation and wood for the barrels used in the distillery to Toronto from the surrounding area.

It was not their first railway venture. In the 1850s Worts had made a short-lived and costly investment in the Ontario, Simcoe and Huron Railroad Company, later renamed the Northern Railway of Canada. The Trout brothers in their 1871 *Railways of Canada* wrote that "the Northern got into so low water as to be seized by the Government for delinquencies with respect to the public lien. It became apparent that the figures paid for construction were extravagant; that the money that should have served for an ample equipment was lavishly disbursed on the permanent way, leaving the leading lines in anything else than a prosperous condition."[103]

Worts' unsuccessful experience with this railway may have influenced the decision of the partners to become much more personally involved in the financing and operation of the two narrow-gauge lines. The petition for the incorporation of each railway was made in 1868, the year of Chadwick's second marriage and the birth of his first child, William Craven Vaux.[104] The creation of the new railroad was of real importance to Chadwick. He tells us in his diary that on 20 January 1869, a few weeks after the birth of his son, he "went to the house to hear a debate on the Toronto Grey and Bruce Railway bill." *The Railways of Canada* reported the debate:

> The idea of a railway with so narrow a gauge as 3 ft. 6 in. was an entirely new idea with nearly everyone in this country, and like most other changes which conflict with interest and prejudice, excited a good deal of hostile criticism and not a little ridicule. Notwithstanding the fact that the application to the Ontario legislature for a charter at the first session of that body in 1867–68, was supported by the names and influence of many of the leading merchants of Toronto, it was only carried through by a narrow majority and after a severe contest, first in the Railway Committee, and afterwards on the floor of the House.[105]

But the charter was granted and on 5 October 1869 Chadwick joined "a monster crowd of swells, snobs, gentles and respectables interested in the welfare of the Toronto Grey & Bruce Railway Co (whereof the firm of Beatty & Chadwick are solicitors and in which I am a shareholder) — and otherwise — went out by two special trains to Weston to see Prince Arthur dig up the first handful of mud of the railway which was duly done and wetted with Champagne in the proper manner."

Three weeks later the celebratory mood was lost when the main building of the Gooderham & Worts distillery went up in flames. It began at 6:00 p.m. on 26 October when a small cask of benzene in the fermenting rooms burst and caught fire. The building sustained considerable damage, valued at between $100,000 and $120,000. There was no insurance claim to be processed by Beatty or Chadwick since business insurance was not yet available.[106] Although the fire was a setback, the distillery was quickly rebuilt and work on the railways continued unabated.

Gooderham & Worts Distillery, 1896

THE LEGAL WORK THAT the two partners began to do for the proposed new railway was very different from the debtor–creditor work they had previously done. Here for the first time they were involved with corporate law: the laws that governed the creation, organization, and operation of corporations. They dealt with bylaws and meetings of directors and shareholders, with investments and corporate loans. Corporate law was something of a novelty. The principal method of carrying on business was still by partnership.[107] Between 1841 and 1867, however, approximately 200 corporations were created by special acts of the legislature.

Corporations were seen as special-purpose vehicles to deal with such capital intensive operations as gaslight and water services, harbours, canals, bridges, roads, and railways. Incorporation facilitated the raising of funds. In the 1850s financial institutions such as banks and insurance and loan corporations were also incorporated by special act. After 1855 a few manufacturing and mining corporations were created as well. As we have seen, Gooderham and Worts had invested in and controlled a number of these special act corporations, including several financial institutions, but the Toronto Grey and Bruce would be the first corporation for which Beatty and Chadwick acted as principal counsel. Incorporation for businesses generally was still in the future, although the provisions of the general incorporation statute for manufacturing and mining corporations[108] would be extended in 1861 to permit its use for most types of business, other than railways.[109]

This new corporate work meant that Beatty and Chadwick needed assistance. On 9 May 1870 Zebulon Aiton Lash came to the office as a junior partner,[110] the firm being renamed Beatty, Chadwick & Lash.[111] Lash had been called to the bar two years before and taken room 1 in the Toronto Exchange Building,[112] where Beatty and Chadwick had themselves started out. Although he assisted Beatty and Chadwick in commercial and other solicitor's work, he also appeared in court. In 1871, for example, he appeared on behalf of Gooderham & Worts in a contract dispute over the price of "high-wines," or spirits.[113]

Even with the addition of Lash, Chadwick felt pressed for time. On 3 June 1870 he noted in his diary that he had been offered a promotion to captain in the militia. Given his earlier enthusiasm for the militia, one would have expected him to be pleased. Instead he initially refused the promotion "principally on account of the responsibilities and unremunerated and thankless trouble and expense which it would entail" and only accepted when assured that he would not be required to do anything unless in active service.

Lash was a very bright young lawyer. He was born in Newfoundland in 1846 but moved to Dundas, Ontario, at age eighteen when his father, a Presbyterian, became manager of a branch of the Bank of British North America there. He started as a law student in 1862, articling in Dundas with a son of Judge William Miller, the first judge to be appointed in Waterloo County.[114] W. Nicholas Miller, the judge's twenty-four-year-old son, was not much more experienced than Lash, having been called to the bar the year before.[115] It is not surprising, then, that this was more a case of two friends assisting each other than a typical lawyer–student relationship. In an era when it was customary to refer to someone as mister, Miller called his student Zeb. It is clear that Miller recognized Lash's intelligence and appreciated his assistance with his varied practice in Dundas and Galt, where his principal client was the Gore District Mutual Fire Insurance Company.[116] In one letter remarking on some work, Miller candidly told Zeb, "I have made a mess of this matter."[117]

Miller and Lash were more than friends; they were related by marriage. On 22 September 1864 Lash's sister, Frederica Louisa, married Nicholas at the Presbyterian church in Dundas.[118] In 1866 the couple gave Lash a nephew, William Lash Miller. Even after Lash moved to Toronto to take lectures at Osgoode Hall, Nicholas Miller wrote to Zeb asking him to do various tasks. Lash did very well as a student, finishing in the top three in his year on his exams both as a barrister and as a solicitor.[119] Robert Brown, the author of the Blake firm history, later described him thus: "Blessed with an exceptionally acute and orderly mind, he developed early in his career the ability to

Zebulon Lash
Law Society of Upper Canada Archives, Ontario Court of Appeal collection
"Photograph of Zebulon A. Lash," 994006-08P

get things down on paper clearly, concisely and in language which a client would understand. Those who worked with or for him marvelled at the way he could sort out a complicated problem and how quickly he could draft a document whether it be a letter of intent, contract or trust deed." After Lash's call to the bar, Miller used him on numerous matters. Now rather than a simple, "My Dear Zeb," Miller's letters began, "Z.A. Lash Esq., Barrister Toronto" but this was followed by "Dear Zeb."[120]

The Act that created the Toronto Grey and Bruce Railway specified that it was to extend from Weston to Mount Forest or Durham via Orangeville. At this westerly point it was to split into a northerly branch to Southampton and a southerly one to Kincardine. There was to be yet another branch commencing at either Mount Forest or Durham that went north to Owen Sound. From Toronto to Weston the railway was to travel along the Grand Trunk Railway, using a third rail between the wider five-foot six-inch gauge tracks of that line.

George Laidlaw and his partners sought to finance the construction of their two narrow-gauge railways through "bonuses" approved by a vote of taxpayers from each township and county on the route of the line. This meant that Laidlaw, his partners, and other directors had to visit each township and speak at taxpayer meetings in support of each requested bonus. Both Beatty and Chadwick joined their clients on these trips. Chadwick's diary gives us a firsthand account of one such trip.

On 24 September 1871 he "left at 8:45 with John Gordon, president of the Toronto Grey & Bruce Railway Company via that line to Orangeville, where the regular trains stop at present, thence by the engine Kincardine to Arthur, where we dined: after which ceremony we got a carriage and drove to Harriston, 22 miles, 93 miles from Toronto, where we arrived at 6 p.m." They "spent the evening arguing, consulting and negotiating and drinking bad whisky with the Native chiefs, trying to arrange a bonus" for the proposed new railway. The next day, in a steady drizzle, they went on to meet and try to win over several other township councils. They returned to Orangeville, "making in all 60 miles travelled, and accomplished a thing not before done on that line of travel, viz, dined on the borders of Turnberry and slept in Orangeville." Gordon returned to Toronto the next day on the 7:00 a.m. train, but Chadwick stayed on "to sleep off the two previous days and nights work."

A little over a month later, on 3 November 1871, Chadwick and his wife, Mattie, travelled to Orangeville by the "Ladies Tram" at 4:00 p.m. for a grand celebration of the formal opening of the railway — "the same having been running for the last three months — consisting of a monster lunch in the daytime and a ball in the evening." He mentions that about 400 came by trains for the event.

The grand opening did not mean the end of the work that Beatty and Chadwick did for the railway, although the nature of that work changed. Railways invariably created legal problems. Sparks from the engines could set a crop on fire or the engine could strike and kill a farm animal grazing on or near the tracks. These matters were often arbitrated. Chadwick tells us that on 16 January 1872, "Ridout and I went to Orangeville by pm train in order to attend arbitrations of the TG&BR." The next day he tried an arbitration in Shelburne "in which we were entirely successful." Just two days later another arbitration, in Farmington, was also successful.

There was still the occasional trip to cajole yet another town council into granting a subsidy. Chadwick wrote in his diary for 3 March 1872, "Beatty having sent up for me, went down to see him, he being too ill to go to Wingham with Gordon tomorrow morning." The next day Chadwick "started with Gordon by TG&BR at 7:10 a.m. arriving at Arthur in time for dinner with Anderson at Greens, after which we set out driving against a fearful wind and drift, bitterly cold. Drove by Harriston and Worcester to Wingham, 45 miles, without getting frozen (thanks to a shawl which I borrowed from Anderson, as far as I am concerned) — and arrived in time to attend a meeting which McMaster and Baxter were carrying on." The trip proved unsuccessful, however. The next day the bylaw that would have granted the railway the bonus they had been seeking was defeated in a vote, and the day after that the bylaw they were seeking in Turnberry was also defeated. Their frustration was made even worse when they ended up stuck in Stratford for a day because their train was six hours late.

The railroad continued to require considerable time from Beatty and Chadwick. On 13 March Chadwick spent "all day going to, staying at and returning from Charleston where I attended a Division Court respecting the death of a certain cow, cruelly slain by the engine Kincardine." It also required them to work evenings. Chadwick records that on 3 April he "spent the evening at board meeting of TG&BR offices."

The railway work was set aside in the summer of 1872 when Chadwick and Mattie took a much-deserved vacation in the British Isles. They left by ship on 18 June and arrived in Liverpool on 2 July. They then took a train to London. Chadwick and his younger brother Austin Cooper had spent time in England in 1851, when they lived with their grandfather on Hornton Street and attended a boarding school in Clapham, Surrey. Chadwick and his wife returned to Hornton Street, staying at number 7. They visited relatives, shopped, and did sightseeing in London and then visited Lewes and Brighton. Chadwick's diary suggests that he was disappointed with England, especially with its trains.

He was enthusiastic, however, about Ireland, which they visited next, spending time in Tipperary and Dublin. On 19 August, during a visit to Dublin Castle, Chadwick discussed his family coat of arms with Sir Bernard Burke, the Ulster King of Arms. (The next year, in December, Burke issued a confirmation of the Chadwick arms to Edward Marion Chadwick and his descendants.[121]) The Chadwicks arrived back in Canada on 1 September, stopping in Quebec. By 5 September they were back at home in Toronto and on 9 September Chadwick tells us that he was "at work again at the office."

Both the Toronto and Nipissing Railway and the Toronto Grey and Bruce Railway proved to be business challenges for William Gooderham and Beatty's father-in-law, James Gooderham Worts. In 1870 the partners had to make substantial loans to both railways to help give their bonds market value. Gradually their control over the operations of these railways increased. They were especially influential in the operation of the Toronto and Nipissing, whose Toronto terminus was located next to their distillery. Gooderham & Worts was, in fact, the main customer of the Toronto and Nipissing.

In 1873 Gooderham's oldest son, William Gooderham Jr., became president of the railway, a post he would hold until 1882. As Dianne Newell has noted, "Although family control of a railway built with much public funding did not escape criticism, defenders of the line pointed to the need for Gooderham's capital to launch the enterprise and to finance its chief activity, which involved buying cordwood in the north and storing it to season before transporting it for sale in the city."[122]

IN 1871 THE GOODERHAM AND WORTS family connection was to provide Beatty with another business opportunity. He became one of the twenty-one "promoters" of a new enterprise to be known as the Confederation Life Association.[123] As evidence of how important the railway work was to the law firm, Beatty signed the petition to the federal government asking that the life insurance company be chartered as "Solicitor to the Toronto Grey & Bruce Railway." His former neighbour William Pearce Howland was also a promoter, but it seems to have again been the Gooderham and Worts family connection that got Beatty involved.

One of the other promoters was William Gooderham Jr. Unfortunately, William Jr. lacked the business acumen of his father. Beatty was to assist young William in representing the family interest in Confederation Life, but he also invested some of his own money in the enterprise, becoming a holder of fifty shares and the seventh person to be insured by the company. Both Beatty and William Jr. were elected to its board.

Although William Jr. dropped off the Confederation Life board the next year, Beatty continued until shortly before his death. In 1873 he became an important member of the board's insurance committee, which reviewed all requests for insurance to assess the risk that the company ran in granting a policy. This was no sinecure. The Confederation Life letter books have letters to Beatty enclosing twenty or more applications. This work brought him into regular contact with John Kay MacDonald, the managing director of the company.

Beatty eventually became company vice-president in 1893 and president in 1902. In assessing his role it is important to remember that at this time the president and vice-president were closer to today's board chair and vice-chair. These officers oversaw operations and advised on business strategy, but they did not deal with day-to-day matters. The one thing we know for sure is that Beatty and his firm did not provide legal work to Confederation Life. This was done by James Beaty, QC, who was not related.[124]

＊—＞◊＜—＊

As IF HE DID not have enough on his plate, Beatty also undertook some property investment in 1871. Wanting to take advantage of the purchase by the new Dominion of Canada of Rupert's Land from the Hudson's Bay Company and the creation of the North-West Territories, Beatty joined John Leys, a Toronto merchant married to one of William Gooderham's daughters,[125] in purchasing two parcels of land in the Algoma District, north of Lake Superior and just inland from Black Bay, near Thunder Bay.[126] The acquired property was within Ontario but close to the boundary of the new territories. While he undoubtedly purchased them in the hope of profiting from the opening of the West,[127] not only did he fail to earn any return but he later lost title to the land parcels in a series of legal actions, culminating in an adverse judgment of the Judicial Committee of the Privy Council in London, until 1950 the final court of appeal in Canadian matters.[128]

Although the legal battle would occur decades later, the documents filed in this legal action give a rare and very revealing glimpse into Beatty's investments in land and, more important, into the financial arrangements between him, Lotty, and her family. They suggest that with her family's help, Lotty maintained control over her own money and that the financial relations between husband and wife were more formal and businesslike than one might have expected. For example, when Joe Beatty gave his brother a promissory note for $7,560, William Beatty endorsed it to his wife, with a letter dated Toronto, 25 November 1903, in which he explained that he needed her to guarantee a $50,000 loan from George Gooderham. In addition to the endorsed note he offered her a mortgage on properties he owned in Quebec and the assignment of monies owing to him from her nephew James.[129] This is just one indication that Charlotte Worts and her family did not simply permit Beatty to assume control of her substantial wealth.

Lotty Beatty and her husband had lived at 290 King Street East since their marriage. This location had the advantage of being close to the Gooderham and Worts homes on Mill Street at the corner of Trinity but had few other advantages. That part of the city had become largely industrial. The Gooderham & Worts complex itself had expanded, the Consumer Gas works had been built, and other factories and warehouses had located in the area. It was time to move: a new house needed to be built in a more fashionable neighbourhood. The house transaction provides more evidence that Lotty and her family, not her husband, maintained control of certain assets.

Some years before, the University of Toronto had been granted a large tract of land covering the area between present-day College Street on the south, Bloor Street on the north, Bay Street on the east and St. George Street on the west. It was known as University Park. The university had laid out private roads running east–west and north–south that would eventually become College Street and University Avenue. These private, tree-lined boulevards had been "laid out for the grandest possible effect." They were "120 feet wide, arranged with a central carriageway with boulevards and walkways on either side, and shaded by double rows of pink flowering chestnuts."[130] The area had originally been closed to the public, with toll booths and gates blocking their entrances, and many fine homes had been built on these roads. In 1859 the university had turned the roads over to the city and laid out fifty-one large building lots (100 by 150 feet, or about 30 by 45 metres) along the east side of St. George, the north side of College, and on a new roadway to circle Queen's Park, to be known as Queen's Park Crescent. These lots were made available for lease, provided that the lessee agreed to build a large, attractive home acceptable to the university on the site. Perhaps because the land could not be purchased outright or because it was well away from the downtown business district, few people moved into the area.

By 1875 there were still many vacant lots, including lots 12 and 13 on the southwest side of Queen's Park Crescent, almost immediately south of where the legislative buildings would be built about fifteen years later. In May 1875 Joseph Gearing, a prominent Toronto builder, took out a forty-two-year lease on lot 13 to build and sell a large brick-and-stone house designed by the noted Toronto architectural firm Smith & Gemmell, which was then designing Knox College at Spadina Circle.[131] Beatty decided to buy, but he wanted to build the house on two lots. He took an assignment of the lease on lot 13 and obtained a new lease from the university for both lots 12 and 13. He agreed with the university that the house would cost at least $14,000, a fortune at that time. The rent was $250 a year, a not insignificant amount of money in 1875.

This lease gave Beatty an immense corner property with an effective frontage of 400 feet (120 metres). The house and stable at the rear of the property were dwarfed by a large expanse of lawn and a sizable pond. Although Beatty had been practising for twelve years, he could not afford this home on his own. It seems that he and his wife asked her father, James Gooderham

Worts, and her cousin, George Gooderham, who was coming to assume an increased role in family affairs, to help finance the house. They agreed to do so but not in Beatty's name. In December, Beatty assigned the property lease to them as trustees for his wife. By the next year the house was finished and the family had moved in.[132] Lotty's obituary in the *Toronto Telegram* many years later on 21 May 1928 would state that the house was "presented to her with its horses and carriages" by her family. The same obituary has a picture of Beatty, Lotty, and their children standing in front of their new, very attractive house in 1876.

William and Lotty called the property the Oaks, and as the name suggests it was well treed.[133] None of the homes in the area had a better location, sitting as it did near the garden and fountain that then occupied the southern portion of the current legislative building site, where a statue of Sir John A. Macdonald now stands.[134] Eric Arthur, in his history of the Ontario Parliament buildings, would later say, "The estate, because that is what it was, is still fondly remembered by older members of the family."[135]

At about 8:00 am each day Beatty came out of his house and climbed into a carriage pulled by two horses. George Flute, his driver, and another man would be in the driver's box. He was then taken through the tollgate that guarded the entrance to the neighbourhood and down University Avenue to his law office.[136] All who saw him knew that he was a man of wealth and influence.

Family Connections: Gooderham, Worts & Beatty

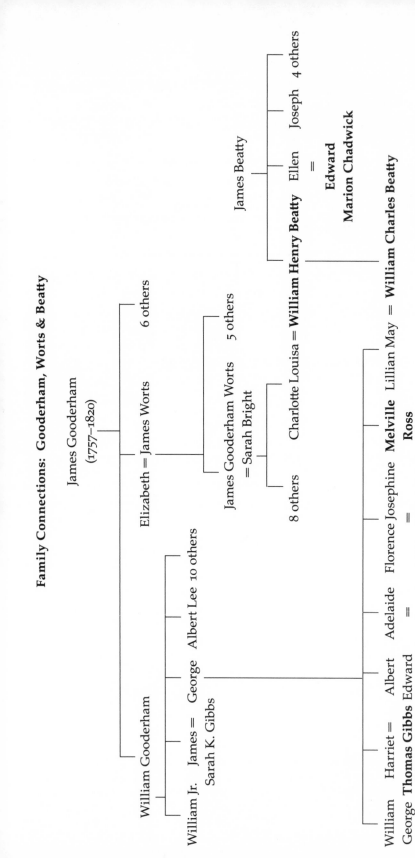

Chapter 2

POLITICS AND FAMILY TIES, 1876–80

POLITICS PLAYED A KEY role in restructuring the firm in the mid-1870s. When the firm was founded more than a dozen years before, Conservatives had been prominent in the politics of Upper Canada, even if not in power. Premier John Sandfield Macdonald may have been a Reformer, but he was more at home with the Conservative John A. Macdonald than with George Brown and the western Grits. After Confederation the two entered into an alliance of sorts: John A. Macdonald's leadership of the new national government was paired with John Sandfield Macdonald's leadership in Ontario.[1] This was good news for Beatty and Chadwick and for their clients William Gooderham and James Gooderham Worts. All were lifelong Conservative supporters.[2] They formed, as Beatty's brother Joe would later write to Sir John A., the "Gooderham/Worts/Beatty Tory faction."[3]

Beatty did not take any active role in politics. He never ran for political office or campaigned for those who did. Nevertheless, he was a "true blue Conservative."[4] At times he carried his Conservative politics to a laughable extent. When interviewed by the press years later, Lotty Beatty remarked,

> On one occasion . . . Mr. Beatty was in London, England, and went into a shop to purchase a travelling bag. When the salesman came back with the change from the purchase money he remarked that Mr. Beatty had selected a very handsome "Gladstone" bag, as the style was called. When Mr. Beatty

heard the name Gladstone used, he said: "It would burn my hand to carry the damn thing," and demanded his money back.[5]

Unlike Beatty, his father-in-law tried his hand at politics under the Conservative banner. In 1867, not long after Beatty had married into the family, Worts had been convinced by a delegation of about 200 businessmen to stand for election as the Conservative candidate in the federal riding of Toronto East. Worts agreed but soon learned that he had little support outside the business community. Resentment of his wealth and prominence proved strong, and he was attacked by the opposing candidates and shouted down by hecklers at his nomination meeting. In response, Worts withdrew. George Brown's *Globe* newspaper happily concluded that his lack of tact meant he would "never reach even a middling position as a politician."[6] But if neither Beatty nor Worts ever became a politician, they and the others did provide important financial support to the Conservatives.

By 1874 the political climate had changed and Beatty and Chadwick's Conservative leanings had become a liability. The Liberal Party of Brown and his allies had come to power both provincially and federally. Sandfield Macdonald's Ontario coalition government was the first to fall.[7] In 1871 Edward Blake became premier but a short while later, he, Alexander Mackenzie, and several others who held seats both federally and provincially were forced to choose one.[8] When Blake chose the federal position, a new premier had to be chosen. Blake joined Brown and Mackenzie in convincing Oliver Mowat to resign his judgeship and assume the premiership. Shortly thereafter, on 5 November 1873, Sir John A. Macdonald's Conservative government resigned following revelations that large payments had been made to his government by the backers of the Canadian Pacific Railway.[9] When Mackenzie's federal Liberals were asked to form a government, they promptly called an election; riding the wave of the Pacific Scandal, they won on 22 January 1874.

The firm was now without a strong link to the party in power and its government that not only passed laws but also set policy and granted favours. Lash, the Liberal junior partner, seemed the obvious way out of this dilemma. He was coming to be well known through his teaching at the Law Society and through his skilled legal practice. On 1 May 1874, shortly after the Liberals won federally, Lash was made an equal partner in the firm.[10] Lash promptly exploited his new status to invite his brother-in-law, Nicholas Miller, to join the firm.[11] The two had remained very close and were now tied together by another marriage. In 1871 Lash had married Nicholas' sister,

Elizabeth Ann.[12] They were now twice brothers-in-law. Lash had even named his first son, born in 1873, after Nicholas' father, calling him William Miller Lash. One wonders if he and his wife gave any thought to the fact that the name they had chosen was confusingly similar to the first born of Nicholas Miller, who had been called William Lash Miller.[13] The firm's new partner moved his family to Toronto, finding temporary accommodation with Lash's brother John, who married yet another member of Judge Miller's family, Cornelia Francis, on 30 October 1874.[14]

On Miller joining the firm, Beatty created two partnerships. He and Lash were members of both, but Miller and Beatty's long-time partner, Chadwick, were not. One partnership had Beatty, Chadwick, and Lash as partners; the other had Beatty, Miller, and Lash. Parallel but separate partnerships were used intermittently from 1876 to 1906. In one they described themselves as "Barristers, Attorneys at Law & Solicitors in Insolvency" and in the other as "Barristers, Solicitors in Chancery & Notaries Public," suggesting that one was a legal practice and the other an equity one. It is puzzling that this practice continued even after the *Judicature Act* merged the courts of law and equity.[15] Even more puzzling is that the dual partnership does not seem to be reflected in the firm's financial records.

Lash's contacts with the new Liberal government in Ottawa proved even stronger than Beatty or Chadwick had expected. In Ottawa, Alexander Mackenzie and his Liberal ministers were seeking out able people of like mind who could join their administration. Edward Blake was approached by the new prime minister, who was particularly interested in returning this prominent Toronto politician and lawyer to Parliament and his cabinet after Blake had resigned his seat following a falling-out between the two. In 1875 Blake agreed and in June he was elected in a by-election and made the minister of justice. Blake then asked Lash to join him in Ottawa as his deputy. On 16 May 1876 Lash was named chief clerk in the Department of Justice and in September he officially became the deputy minister.[16]

All indications are that Lash regarded his new position in Ottawa as temporary, with the expectation that he would return to the firm at some point. There is perhaps no better evidence of this than that his brother-in-law Miller remained with the firm. But even if Lash's absence was to be temporary, it left gaps that needed to be filled. Lash had been lecturing at the Law School on criminal and commercial law since 1872 so the benchers of the Law Society held a special meeting before the Trinity term to elect a lecturer to succeed him.[17] But what of the firm? The day before Lash's appointment,

Daniel E. Thomson, who had clerked at the firm and had just passed his final examinations, became a lawyer there. Might he not take up Lash's workload? It seems that the partners did not think so because on the same day they added Charles Robert Webster Biggar to the partnership.[18]

———————————

THE LIBERAL POLITICS THAT had played a large part in Lash's departure played an equally significant role in Biggar's joining the firm. Biggar had very strong ties to the Liberals. He would, in fact, later chronicle the events leading to the downfall of the political alliance between Sandfield Macdonald and John A. and the rise of Oliver Mowat, serving as our "eye- and ear-witness."[19] This was a story he was happy to tell because as far as he was concerned, Sandfield Macdonald, in taking John A.'s advice, had acted "contrary to the strongly expressed opinion of the Liberal Party," and "many of the methods by which the Ontario Premier carried on his Government were in direct opposition to the principles of the Liberal party."[20]

Biggar knew those principles well. He was the eldest son of James Lyons Biggar, a Liberal member of the Legislative Assembly from 1861 to 1867 and of the federal Parliament thereafter. Even more important, his father-in-law was none other than Oliver Mowat. In the summer of 1874, Charles enjoyed one of the favours that a government can bestow on those it wishes to reward. He was chosen as one of three barristers charged by Mowat's government with the revision and consolidation of the statutes of Ontario.[21] As a commissioner with Messrs Thomas Langton and R.E. Kingsford, he began "the minute examination of more than two thousand Statutes and the consideration . . . of questions of jurisdiction" arising from the division of powers on Confederation. The commission initially reported on 12 December 1874 and as Biggar joined Beatty and Chadwick, it was preparing further reports to be made on 11 and 30 December 1876. Biggar was thus well connected and highly regarded.

Given Blake's involvement in recruiting both Mowat and Lash, it hardly seems a coincidence that Lash's acceptance of the position in Ottawa opened a place in the Beatty firm for Mowat's son-in-law. Mowat may well have been looking for a proper place for Biggar, who for the last four years had been assisting Beatty and Chadwick's demanding former partner, John Beverley Robinson, with city of Toronto work. One can imagine Blake and Mowat working out this arrangement. Mowat found a suitable place for his son-in-law, Blake got the deputy that he wanted, and the firm got a talented and well-connected new partner.

It is intriguing to note that much of this manoeuvring took place on William Street, now renamed Simcoe.[22] The year before joining the law firm, Biggar had married Jane Helen, Mowat's eldest daughter, in a service at her family home on this small, seemingly insignificant street, just two doors south of the house where Beatty grew up and Chadwick wooed Ellen.[23] And it was on this street, as Mowat himself explained in an address to the Ontario legislature, that Blake, George Brown, and Alexander Mackenzie paid a visit to convince him to accept the premiership. As Biggar could personally attest, Mowat had needed some convincing. When first asked, he explained that he needed time to reflect. It was a momentous decision and Mowat spent the next two days in anxious thought, consulting his family and friends.[24]

It would be wrong to think that Biggar had been taken into the partnership solely because of his family and political connections. He was bright and well educated, having attended the University of Toronto, obtaining a BA in 1869 and an MA in 1873. At twenty-nine, he was also a mature, experienced counsel. Although raised a Methodist, Biggar had become a well-connected Anglican, actively involved in Church affairs as Beatty and Chadwick were.[25] He would serve for a time as registrar of the Diocese of Toronto and a member of the Diocesan Synod. All in all he seemed an excellent addition to the firm.

The firm's other addition, Daniel Edmund Thomson, lacked Biggar's political and family connections. It seems clear that business was thriving and that Thomson had impressed the partners. Then twenty-five, he had been a student in the firm since 1874. He was the son of a pioneer farmer in Wellington County and might have known the Chadwick family. Like Marion Chadwick he began his articles in Guelph, in his case in January 1872 with the firm of Oliver and Macdonald. Again like Chadwick he had come to Toronto for the lectures at Osgoode Hall. Beatty was impressed with Thomson's work ethic. He was a raw lad off the farm but one to whom you could never give too much work.[26] And he was very bright. Like Lash, Thomson had been a top student, winning a scholarship each year of his legal studies.[27] He, too, was a Liberal in politics but in many other ways was quite different from Biggar and the other members of the firm. He was the first articled clerk asked to join the firm, the first Baptist, and the first lawyer to join as a non-partner. He became what today would be called an associate but what was then referred to as a junior, or nominal, partner.[28]

——◆——

LOTTY BEATTY WAS BECOMING known as the chatelaine of the Oaks and invitations to her Friday evening parties were much sought after. But in summer of 1876 Chadwick was dining at Beatty's home to permit them to work all evening.[29] These sessions were necessitated because Beatty was spending less and less time in the office during office hours. The career paths of the two founders had started to diverge. Inside the firm, Beatty had become more of an administrator and business getter than an active lawyer. Outside the firm, he was increasingly becoming involved in the management of financial services businesses.

Chadwick, on the other hand, had become a strong technical lawyer with a relatively narrow legal practice. Like Beatty he focused much of his work on the Gooderham and Worts families, but while Beatty assisted them with their businesses, Chadwick served their personal needs, helping them buy and sell property, prepare their wills, and after their death administer their estates. He also designed most of the forms used in the firm: deeds, powers of attorney, mortgages, and the like. Known for avoiding excess verbiage and for using little or no punctuation in a document, he claimed that if the words did not speak for themselves, the document was not properly drawn.[30]

The time that Chadwick spent in Beatty's home on Queen's Park Crescent got him thinking that he and his family should also move north, away from the downtown. Chadwick and Mattie spent the fall of 1876 looking at lots on which they could build a new house. Finally on 6 November, Chadwick found a property on Saint George Street, which the next day he contracted to purchase.[31] It was slightly north of College Street and about 200 metres south of the house into which Sir John A. Macdonald and his wife had moved in May of that year.[32] The lot was just outside the University Park area into which Beatty had moved,[33] which went as far as the east side of St. George. Chadwick decided to call the new house Lanmar since his wife's name, Martha, was Lanna in Gaelic. It was his way of saying that this was Martha's house. On 29 November he opened tenders for its construction, a project that would take almost a year and often keep him from his work. He made frequent visits to check on the progress on Lanmar. On 19 September 1877 they commenced moving and three days later, on Chadwick's thirty-seventh birthday, the family was settled in their new home.[34]

Bank of Toronto, corner of Wellington and Church Streets

THE FIRM BECAME EVEN busier in 1877, when Beatty's father-in-law, James Gooderham Worts, began directing the work of the Bank of Toronto to it. The Bank had grown substantially from its beginnings in 1854 as an institution dedicated to serving flour millers and grain merchants who needed access to loans to fund their transactions. It had taken in investments from many millers and grain traders but none more important than Worts and his uncle, William Gooderham. These two had assisted in the Bank's capitalization and had for some time been providing conservative business leadership. Worts had been the vice-president since 1863.[35] By 1877, when Beatty was appointed the Bank's solicitor,[36] it had $2 million in deposits, almost $6 million in total assets, and profits of $100,000.[37]

As solicitors to the Bank, Beatty and his partners assumed responsibility for the corporate aspects of its operations. Banks were creatures of statute and thus in need of good legal counsel. Their powers were generally drawn from their incorporating statutes but, starting in 1871, banks also had to comply with a new federal *Bank Act*, one that was to be updated every ten years. That statute was the new Dominion's first attempt to apply a uniform set of rules to all the banks operating in its provinces. It imposed a number of restrictions on the business that could be conducted by a bank and the security that it could take. It also set out capital and reserve requirements and rules with respect to internal affairs such as minimum shareholdings and other eligibility requirements for directors. Finally, it required annual audits and the annual filing of various forms with the government.

The firm assisted the Bank of Toronto in interpreting these rules and regulations and dealt with changes in its charter and bylaws, called and organized meetings of the board and of shareholders, acted as scrutineers for votes taken, and so on. In addition the firm provided advice on the business of banking: lending restrictions, loan realizations and disputes, loan document preparation, and the protesting of promissory notes. The firm's opinion files contain many letters to various branches of the Bank giving opinions on a host of banking law or business matters, and its ledgers have page after page of notations about small matters done for the Bank, showing accounts rendered ranging from one or two to hundreds of dollars. From this point forward the Bank would always be one of the largest corporate clients of the firm.

The timing of the firm's retainer by the Bank is interesting. These were tough times for business. The previous year had been characterized by William Gooderham as "one of great depression in nearly every branch of business in Canada."[38] The business of the Bank had been seriously affected. In 1877 Worts, delivering the president's report on behalf of an ailing Gooderham, reported that things had not improved. The harvest that the grain merchants counted upon "proved to be an exceptionally deficient one." The depression had deepened and had "seriously affected the business and earnings of the Bank."[39] But this poor economic outlook was good news for Beatty and his firm. They had begun their practice in the hard times of the 1860s as debt collectors, and their extensive experience in insolvency and debt collection was undoubtedly one of the factors in Worts' decision to send them the Bank's work.

The next year Sir John A. Macdonald's Conservatives won the federal election and returned to power. If Beatty and his firm expected Lash to rejoin them on the fall of the Liberal government, they were disappointed. He decided to stay on in Ottawa, where he was heavily involved in matters affecting the division of powers between the federal and provincial governments. He most likely wanted to see those matters through, and no doubt Macdonald did not wish to lose his skills and expertise. It is difficult to know how Beatty and his firm reacted. They were happy to have their party back in power, but were they displeased that Lash was to stay in Ottawa? We do not know. Our only hint is found in a letter that Beatty wrote to Sir John, referring to his long-time partner as "your Mr. Lash," a reference that seems rather cold.

Beatty wrote that particular letter on behalf of the Bank of Toronto in an effort to collect a debt. He wanted the prime minister to intercede and assist the Bank in seizing money owed by the federal government to one of the Bank's debtors in connection with the building of the Lachine Canal.[40] By 1879 the business from the Bank was such that Beatty moved his firm into the Bank of Toronto building at the northwest corner of Church and Welling-ton Streets,[41] across from the site on which the Gooderham building would be built a decade later. In February 1863 Beatty and Chadwick had found this building too expensive for their first office, but circumstances had changed dramatically in the sixteen years since. Now the firm was successful and profitable and moving into the head office building of its principal client. This would be the firm's home for the next thirty-six years and until 1915 its letterhead proudly indicated, "Offices: Bank of Toronto Corner Wellington & Church Sts." The building was impressive, "rivalled by few of the other banks that crowded Toronto."[42] It rose three storeys, with broad façades on both Wellington Street and Church Street. Designed in the Italian Renais-sance style, it was faced with Ohio sandstone.

THAT SAME YEAR, 1879, BEATTY MADE a seemingly insignificant move that would shape the firm in the last quarter of the nineteenth century. As a favour to the Gooderhams, he took twenty-eight-year-old Thomas Gibbs Blackstock into the firm. The move both reflected the importance of the Gooderhams to the firm and strengthened that connection. Blackstock was well known to Beatty and his partners, but not as a lawyer. He had neither trained at the firm, as Thomson had done, nor come to the attention of the partners for the quality of his legal work, as had Lash. Beatty knew him as a young member of an extended family that spent Sundays with the Gooderhams. Chadwick knew him as an expert rifleman with the Queen's Own Rifles militia.[43] Big-gar knew him as the son of an influential Methodist minister.[44] They would soon come to know him as a dedicated, hard-working, talented young lawyer.

The request to take him into the firm came from Tom Blackstock's aunt and uncle, James and Sarah Ketland Gooderham.[45] Tom's mother, Mary, was Sarah Gooderham's younger sister. They were two of the seven children of

Thomas Gibbs and his wife, Caroline Tate, and thus from one of the most prosperous and influential families in Oshawa.[46] The two sisters had chosen very different husbands. Sarah had married into the even more prosperous and influential Gooderham family. Mary, on the other hand, had married an itinerant Methodist preacher. She and her family led a migratory existence, barely scraping by; her husband often had to accept food and other items because many of the communities to which he ministered could not afford to pay him any other way. Although living divergent lives, the sisters kept in regular contact and were both convinced that Tom Blackstock was pursuing his fledging legal career in partnership with the wrong person. They had heard that Tom smoked and drank, sometimes to excess, and they blamed Alexander McNabb, his law partner, who was known to be much enamoured of both habits.[47]

Beatty's new lawyer was the eldest son of the pairing of the influential but poor Methodist minister and the daughter of the prominent Gibbs family.[48] He and his younger brother George would both play important, if quite different, roles in the firm in the decades to come. Their contributions reflected the dissimilarities in their upbringing. Tom had left his parents' home at age fifteen because they were unable to support him, and his mother's family had taken him in.[49] Young George had remained with his parents. Ironically, however, it was George, not Tom, who came to rely on the wealth and influence of the Gibbs family. Tom was never comfortable depending on them but constantly strived to become self-supporting. Both boys ended up at Upper Canada College, Tom by winning a scholarship and George through the support of the Gibbs family. Tom worked hard and did well at school; George did not apply himself and barely managed to get by.[50] While the Gibbs family paid for George to live in residence at UCC, Tom paid for his own room and board in a rooming house. To fund his schooling, Tom took summer jobs and work part time in law offices during the school term. He went on to University College, but George was not up to university and became an articled clerk in a law office right out of UCC. Even while excelling at university, Tom felt guilty that he was not earning a living, at several points considering abandoning his studies and becoming a school teacher or an articled clerk in a law office.[51] Tom analyzed the many problems he faced and dealt with them as best he could. George faced far fewer difficulties but worried excessively over each one. In short, Tom was a hard-working, solid, dependable individual and George was a spoiled youngest son.

Tom demonstrated both his independence and his desire to make his own way when in 1872 at age twenty-one he packed a bag and headed west.[52] His uncle James Gooderham and James' brother William Jr., then the president of the Toronto and Nipissing Railway, arranged a rail pass for Tom. At this time rail travel west meant travel through the United States. Tom went first to Topeka, Kansas. "The most eastern like of western cities, the most church going," he wrote to his parents.[53] Topeka had no work, however, so he moved on to the end of the rail line, Dodge City. When he reached the plains he saw numerous herds of buffalo from the train window: "The train before us had been thrown off the track, a noble bull indignant at the invasion of his domain by a monster more terrible than himself, charged the engine between the driving wheels and soon he lay in one ditch, the engine in the other. This we are informed happens frequently."[54]

Dodge City then had fifty houses and was a far cry from the Toronto to which Tom was accustomed: "Hardly a night passes without someone being seriously hurt; pistol practice is the prevailing epidemic here." The hotel offered little or no protection. "As you enter upon the right is the bar with its tumultuous uproar, on the left the office in which you are requested to deposit your valuables. In one corner with a blanket over him lies a man in a semi-conscious state; a night or two before he received a ball in the head and there he will lie until he dies or recovers as there is not a bed to be had in the entire town."[55] But there at least Tom found that he had saleable skills. His father, who had lived in the saddle, had taught him how to ride and he was also a prize-winning marksman. Tom put these skills to use hunting buffalo. But it was soon winter and buffalo hunters, he explained to his parents, "slept on the Plain most of the time . . . . Many got lost . . . and were frozen to death or lost a limb or two."[56]

At the insistence of his father, Tom returned in early 1873, laden with buffalo skins but with little money to show for his adventure. The experience had a profound influence on him.[57] He was to prove an avid outdoorsman and hunter for the rest of his life and sustained an enduring interest in the West and in the fate of the buffalo.[58] He resumed his studies, graduating in 1874. He briefly articled with William Mulock, one of Toronto's most distinguished barristers, but he found the hard work did not permit him time to study for his examinations.[59] He joined Ferguson, Bain & Meyers, but much to his chagrin they did not offer him a position on his call to the bar. He briefly practised on his own but then in September 1877 went into the partnership that would so trouble his mother and her sister.[60]

By this point the Reverend William Schenck Blackstock was more concerned about Tom's younger brother George.[61] In August 1878 Tom's father suggested that his two sons practise together: "I am anxious to see your brother and you in the same firm. I have always thought that you were admirably adapted to do business together."[62] Tom, however, did not share his father's vision of a partnership with his brother. When George passed his examinations as a barrister he joined Rose, Macdonald & Merritt, a firm we know today as Weir Foulds. He was well suited to the drama of the courtroom. Tall, clean-shaven, and handsome, with short, wavy hair, George was much sought after as a dinner guest.[63] He was "lionized by hostesses for his handsome looks, quick wit, and skill as a speaker."[64] Although older, more experienced, more stable, and quite competent, Tom would live the rest of his life in the shadow of his attractive, appealing, but mercurial and troubled brother.

Tom formally joined Beatty at the law firm on 14 April 1879 as a junior partner.[65] He was not entirely happy with the terms, but he accepted them, expecting that he would do better in the future.[66] His agreement was for three years: $800 for the first year, $1,000 for the second, and $1,200 for the third. In explaining his new status to his father, he characterized the firm in a very telling way: "Beatty Chadwick & Biggar do the largest business as solicitors of any firm in the country." He noted that the work would be "of a more routine character than that to which I have heretofore been engaged in," but he expected "to work out of it after awhile into something better."[67]

Blackstock's junior partnership proved helpful to Thomson, who was given a promotion. On 1 May, the firm was renamed Beatty, Chadwick, Biggar & Thomson in recognition of Thomson's partnership.[68]

Tom's parents were pleased not only with his new firm but also with the fact that James Gooderham assisted the Reverend Blackstock in finding a ministry in Toronto, where he could reunite his family. Reverend Blackstock became minister at the Berkeley Street Methodist Church. The family's joy at Tom's new position and his father's Toronto ministry must have been short-lived, however, because less than two weeks later their patron died in a railway accident on the Credit Valley Railway.[69] On 14 May, at a time when they had hoped to be celebrating their good fortune, they instead attended the funeral service at the Metropolitan Methodist Church, following which James Gooderham was buried in the Gooderham vault in St. James Cemetery.[70]

It seems that Tom Blackstock was right about the routine character of the work before him. We are fortunate to have a series of letters from December 1879 and January 1880 detailing the work he did in his first year.[71] The firm had been retained to advise the inspectors appointed in the insolvency of W.G. Thomson. Thomson had given $155 to the firm of Dennistown Bros & Hall in Peterborough after he had become insolvent. Blackstock wrote on behalf of the inspectors asking that the money be repaid. As it happened, Dennistown Bros & Hall had an unpaid account with the insolvent party for $12.30. On 7 January Blackstock wrote, explaining,

> We have just had a meeting of the Inspectors herein, and on our recommen-
> dation they consented to allow your costs be paid out of the Estate if you are
> willing to accept $10.00 in full . . . . If this is satisfactory kindly send a cheque
> for the monies in your hands after deducting this amount. And let us know
> at the same time whether you are open to act with us with reference to a dis-
> pute with George A Cox Landlord of the Insolvent's premises in case we fail
> to reach a settlement with him.

Perhaps the most interesting aspect of these letters is that they are headed "Beatty, Chadwick, Biggar & Thomson; Beatty, Miller, Biggar & Blackstock." Tom now had his name on the letterhead.

TOM'S NEW PLACE IN the law firm meant that he was in a position to be taken seriously as a son-in-law. He had long admired one of George Gooderham's twelve children, Harriet Victoria, known as Hattie. Tom's aunt Sarah played matchmaker, writing to her sister that she had pointed out to Tom he was a professional now and might as well get "one of the nice girls with money." Hattie was certainly one such girl. Tom's mother was thrilled with the match: "I suppose that she must have some faults for all have them but no one seems to know what hers are."[72]

Tom married Hattie in January 1880, a year after joining the firm. The marriage took place at the bride's home on Trinity Street, with some of the festive mood muted by the recent death in childbirth of one of her sisters.[73] The couple honeymooned at Niagara Falls and then returned to Toronto to take up residence in a home provided by her family at the corner of Gerrard and Berkeley Streets, not far from Tom's father's church.

The law firm in which Tom Blackstock practised in 1880 consisted of six lawyers, and was now one of the largest in Toronto and quite prosperous. But as Tom had noted, what set it apart was that it was a solicitors' firm. To a large extent its practice was shaped by Beatty, the managing partner. Unlike other leaders of the profession such as William Mulock, Britton Bath Osler, D'Alton McCarthy Jr., or the Blake brothers, Beatty was not a barrister but a solicitor and business lawyer. The firm, following his lead, was more often in the office and the boardroom than the courtroom. Lash is often referred to as Canada's first business lawyer, but Beatty was doing the same earlier and helped train Lash and inspire his practice.

The firm's financial records indicate that the partners met in February and July of each year to review the financial affairs of the partnership. They looked at expenses, petty cash disbursed, partner drawings, and collections. Partners were permitted to withdraw amounts from the firm over the course of the year based on their share of the anticipated profits. Periodically these drawings would be reconciled against each partner's actual entitlements and adjustments made. As long overdue amounts were gradually collected, reconciliations were made for past years. Chadwick was principally charged with collecting old accounts.[74]

Those financial records show that at this time each partner was guaranteed a base amount, referred to as their "basis." The basis indicates the perceived importance of the lawyer to the firm. In calculating the pool of money available for the partners' compensation, expenses were deducted from the total amount billed (less a reserve for doubtful accounts). From this pool, each partner was first allocated his basis. Any surplus was then divided among the partners in accordance with their shares in the partnership and the annual calculation adjusted when the accounts were finally collected. In assessing how the firm's profits were allocated from 1 July 1879 to 18 March 1882 (Table 1),[75] bear in mind that the average skilled tradesman earned $452 a year.[76]

Partner	Basis	Surplus	Entitled to	Drawn	Owing to	Overdrawn
Beatty 4 shares	$18,958 (approx. $7,000 per year)	$2,330.12	$21,288.12	$21,433.56		$145.48
Chad- wick 3 shares	8,125 (approx. $3,000 per year)	1,747.59	9,872.59	9,403.97	468.62	
Miller 3 shares	7,312 (approx. $2,750 per year)	1,747.59	9,059.59	8,547.81	511.78	
Biggar 3 shares	7,312	1,747.59	9,059.59	9,173.90		114.31
Thom- son 3 shares	5,687 (approx. $2,140 per year)	1,747.59	7,434.59	7,603.85		169.36
Black- stock 0 shares	2,650		2,650	2,650		
Totals	**50,044**	**9,320.48**	**59,364.48**	**58,813.19**	**980.40**	**429.15**

The record shows that Beatty saw himself as the dominant partner, who drove the business of the firm. He received 35.8 percent of the profits. Chadwick, his long-time partner, received less than half as much, with 16.6 percent. Miller and Biggar received 15.25 percent each, Thomson took 12.5 percent, and Blackstock was left with 4.5 percent. Blackstock was right that his initial terms were not particularly favourable. But he was also correct in his assessment of his prospects. In fact, the firm was about to change dramatically in reaction to a series of events in 1881–82. Tom Blackstock would be one of the principal beneficiaries.

ॐ Chapter 3 ॐ

CHALLENGES OVERCOME, 1881–89

In 1882 the *Ontario Law List* proclaimed that the judicial system had been "completely revolutionized" by the *Judicature Act*, which merged the courts of Common Law and Chancery into "one Court of universal jurisdiction in civil cases."[1] Law courts could now hear cases that had traditionally been reserved for the courts of equity, apply both legal and equitable principles to achieve a fair result in a single hearing, and grant equitable remedies. Major changes were also being made in the law firm, but they had nothing to do with this judicial revolution. They were rooted in several deaths.

It all began on 20 August 1881, when William Gooderham died at age ninety-one. In and of itself his death was of little more than symbolic importance, as his power and influence were by then more apparent than real. He had remained the nominal head of the Gooderham and Worts businesses but de facto control had passed to others several years before, when his health began to fail. The burden of leading the extended family had fallen largely upon Beatty's father-in-law, James Gooderham Worts, and upon William's third son, George, twelve years younger than Worts. George had been selected for this role by his father twenty-five years earlier, in August 1856, after it had become obvious to William that neither his eldest son, William Jr., nor his second son, James, had the business acumen or desire to run the distillery and its related businesses.[2] James first and then William Jr. had become Methodists, joining their campaign against the consumption of alcohol; they did not wish to be partners in a business so heavily involved in

63

liquor.[3] George had been made a full partner in the core business operated as the Gooderham & Worts partnership.[4] He soon confirmed his father's judgment, bringing energy and a clarity of vision that contributed to a major expansion of the business. Beatty would later say that he "held the highest opinion of George . . . . His judgment on questions of business and finance was exceedingly sound. Although a quiet and undemonstrative man, he was a master of detail and a man of constant industry."[5]

Thus when William Sr. died, there were no problems with succession. As a matter of law, the partnership between William, his nephew, and his son was dissolved but this presented no practical difficulty.[6] William's interest in the partnership passed to George in accordance with his will and on 11 February 1882 Worts and George Gooderham formed a new partnership, continuing to operate with little or no disruption. As for the related incorporated businesses, such as the Bank of Toronto, Worts assumed the office of president previously held by William Gooderham, while George Gooderham assumed the vice-presidencies that Worts had held.[7] Again there was little or no effect on their operations.

William Gooderham's death nevertheless signalled the end of an era and was marked with much formality.[8] The funeral was held in the afternoon of 24 August 1881. The previous day the Board of Trade published a notice in the *Globe* requesting that members of the Board attend the funeral "in a body" to honour an "old and much respected member of this Corporation."[9]

A memorial service was also held at Little Trinity Church on Sunday, 28 August. The Reverend Alexander Sanson presided and delivered a glowing tribute that was subsequently published. He commented on the many things that William had achieved in his life and noted that "for nearly half a century every day was filled up with energetic toil and diligent attention to business, occasionally performing such civic duties as were entrusted to him by his fellow-citizens, and habitually keeping in view the care and government of his large family, growing up under his paternal shadow."[10]

William had indeed cast a lengthy shadow, influencing Worts, his son George, and Beatty in many ways. But that shadow had been weakening for some time and few could have expected his death to be the harbinger of troubles that would bring dramatic changes in the family businesses and in the firm that served their legal needs.

The law firm was the first to experience troubles. On 18 March 1882 Nicholas Miller and Charles Biggar left. Each had been a partner for six years and each was in the prime of his legal career. Miller had just the year before been the first lawyer in the firm to appear before the recently created Supreme Court of Canada, successfully assisting Christopher Robinson, QC, in the defence of an action by Robert Summers against the Commercial Union Assurance Company.[11] Forty-four-year-old Miller left for the Mulock firm where Blackstock had articled, which was renamed Mulock, Tilt, Miller & Crowther.[12] He remained there for many years, eventually becoming its senior partner, before moving to England.[13] Thirty-five-year-old Biggar joined his father-in-law's firm, Mowat & Maclennan.[14] Biggar would practise with the firm for six years before becoming the city solicitor on Maclennan's appointment to the bench.

The simultaneous departure of multiple partners from a law firm is usually evidence of a major rift, a fight for control with the losers departing. Is that what happened here? Chadwick's diary is of no assistance. The only hint is its silence. Chadwick recorded no entry from 10 February to 18 April, suggesting that Miller and Biggar gave their partners a month's notice. One can imagine quite a stir. There would have been files to be transferred, work assumed by others, accounts to be rendered and collected. Chadwick's silence may signal both that he was upset and that he was very busy dealing with the work they left undone.

There was most likely a dispute over what constituted fair compensation for Beatty in his roles as business developer and administrator. As we have seen, he was taking a very large proportion of the profits for himself at a time when others were actually doing the work. A general sense of unfairness was supplemented by Miller's immediate need for more money. In February he had started to correspond with Zebulon Lash and others about Dominion lands that he was acquiring out west, probably in the hope that they contained valuable minerals. The California and Caribou gold rushes had raised people's hopes that fortunes could be had in buying wilderness land. In one telegram Miller expressed concern: "I feel we cannot trust giving the figures in plain English in connection with the word California or any other word. Telegraph operators might think there were millions in it." He then set out a code to be used. At one point he explained to Lash that he was worried he would miss the opportunity to buy some lands adjoining a previous purchase, telegraphing, "Can you arrange to take? If not will try here. Must not miss chance. Answer quickly." Miller's need for money to complete his real estate deals seems to have motivated him to press Beatty for a greater share of the firm's profits. Rather than do so alone, he probably recruited the younger, well-connected Biggar. Together they could put

Thomas Gibbs Blackstock

pressure on Beatty to increase their compensation, or so they thought. The fact that they left together suggests that whatever their strategy, it failed and they sought opportunities elsewhere.

The day following their departure William Albert Reeve joined the firm as a partner. In any other circumstances he would have seemed an odd addition to a firm of establishment solicitors. Reeve, from a non-conformist, reform family, had been practising in Napanee as a barrister since his call to the bar in 1865. Lately he had also served as Crown attorney for Lennox and Addington counties and as a justice of the peace.[15] Were it not for some letters that Tom Blackstock wrote to his family, we would wonder how such a person came to the attention of Beatty and his partners and why they thought him a suitable partner.[16] While articling with Mulock, Blackstock had met and worked with Reeve. He came to respect Reeve's judgment, as evidenced by his choice of Reeve to consult in September 1877 when he was thinking about going into partnership with McNabb.[17] When the firm was faced with the impending departures of Miller and Biggar, Blackstock saw an opportunity to help Reeve get to Toronto. While Reeve's experience and practice seem a poor fit with Beatty's emphasis on business law, Blackstock could have pointed out that he himself had left a barrister's practice to become a solicitor in the firm. And in any event, Reeve's experience as a barrister could also supplement and enhance the firm's practice.

The loss of Miller and Biggar was made even worse by the fact that short-ly after they left, Lash returned to private practice in Toronto — but not to the Beatty firm. With Miller gone, Lash's link to his former firm was greatly weakened and he chose to join the practice of his former minister of justice, Edward Blake. Lash's action must have rankled Beatty and Chadwick, espe-cially when they came to realize that he intended to apply the lessons they had taught him and turn Blakes, which had built its reputation on litigation, into a true rival in their areas of specialization. In fact, with the addition of Lash it had nine lawyers, making it Toronto's largest firm and a formidable rival. Following the trail that Beatty had blazed, Lash would soon be acting for a bank, the Commerce, advising railroads, and serving on the board of numerous corporations.[18]

Even if Lash had not made Blakes such a significant rival, there can be no doubt that in a firm of six solicitors the departure of two was bound to be damaging and the addition of a little-known barrister, disruptive. When partners leave a law firm they always take some business with them. The Gooderham and Worts family businesses would have stayed, but who was to undertake the portion done by Miller and Biggar? Chadwick's silent diary suggests that he was busy with at least some of it, but he had his own per-sonal problems as well. In 1882 Mattie's father, Alexander Fisher, manager of the Toronto branch of the Ontario Bank, committed suicide. He had been having fits, unable to cope with defaults totalling $33,000 on bank money he had advanced to friends on poor security.[19] This personal tragedy must have affected Chadwick's work and left even more to be done by the other partners. It is likely that Tom Blackstock assumed a larger role, but Thomson seems to have carried the bulk of the burden.

Reeve was of little help. Beatty wrote to Sir John A., asking for a QC for Reeve. He noted that he was "fully entitled through his professional attain-ments to receive that honour. Unfortunately for himself, he is too retiring a disposition."[20] Not surprisingly we see him appearing on appeals in the Queen's Bench Division for the firm's clients, but even here he was assisted by Thomson. These were debtor–creditor disputes, fighting over the priority of the claims of rival debtors.[21] There is little evidence that he brought any work to the firm and no suggestion that he assumed any of the solicitors' work previously done by Miller and Biggar.

BEATTY MUST HAVE HOPED for a quiet period without further troubles so that the law practice could be put again on a solid footing, but such was not to be. Less than a month after these events, in April 1882, James Gooderham Worts became ill with malaria.[22] The *Globe* reported that he was "continually becoming weaker . . . with occasional brief periods of improvement, followed by relapses, leaving his condition more hopeless than before."[23] He suffered for nine weeks, the last while in a coma, before he finally succumbed to the disease on 20 June 1882. He was only sixty-four. If William Gooderham's death had been long expected and well prepared for, the same was not true of Worts' demise. His unexpected death had significant implications for the family businesses and for the law firm.

Worts had selected his son-in-law, William Henry Beatty, to succeed him in the family businesses. Just as William Gooderham had chosen his third son over two older brothers, so Worts had favoured his son-in-law over his sons, James Gooderham Worts Jr. and Thomas Frederick Worts. There is no better evidence of Beatty's business judgment and acumen than this. In a very unusual provision in his will, Worts directed that Beatty be elected to succeed him on the Bank of Toronto's board of directors.[24] This would not, of course, have been binding on the shareholders of the Bank, but it did happen, indicating the influence that Worts had and his sense of proprietorship over the Bank. George Gooderham became president of the Bank and Beatty became its vice-president. Beatty also became one of the executors of his father-in-law's estate and as such for many years directed its numerous investments and business interests.[25] His position at Confederation Life had already been taking some of Beatty's time. His new role in the family would take even more.

Worts' death also created serious problems for Gooderham & Worts. This family business had long been carried on in partnership. Conservatism, a desire to keep things in the family, and a strong wish to control the enterprises in which the families invested are themes that run throughout the Gooderham and Worts business history and help to explain why they favoured the more traditional and flexible unregulated vehicle of partnership over the more novel and somewhat regulated corporate form. But the law governing partnerships now presented a difficulty, as the death of a partner dissolved the partnership. In the case of Gooderham's death, this had proved little more than a formality. Old Gooderham had put the continuation of the business ahead of other considerations and passed his interest in the partnership to a single person, his son George. Worts, however, out of a sense of fairness wanted to treat all his children as equals.

Under the will that Beatty and Chadwick had helped Worts prepare, he left the bulk of his estate to his two sons and to Beatty and his four other sons-in-law, in trust for his daughters.[26] In the will he authorized the executors "to continue any business in which I may be engaged at the time of my decease for one year after my decease if they see fit." After ten years the trustees were to pay each of his sons a seventh of his estate and to pay quarterly thereafter the interest on a seventh to each of his daughters. He authorized the trustees to invest the money in his estate in such securities as they thought proper and gave them the power to retain any investment existing at the time of his death for as long as they thought fit.[27]

The provision, which seemed to require the sale of Worts' interest within a year, must have created great concern for George Gooderham. He faced having to raise a very substantial amount of money to acquire Worts' share of the business or having a third party acquire the interest or, even worse, having to wind up the business and sell off the assets. None of these prospects would have been very appealing. There were undoubtedly lengthy discussions with Beatty and other members of his law firm. In the end they found a way to preserve the status quo and yet comply with the terms of the will and trust — they would incorporate.

Incorporation was becoming more common.[28] On 17 February 1882 the firm had incorporated another family business, the Toronto Silver Plate Company Limited, under the *Ontario Joint Stock Companies' Letters Patent Act, 1874*.[29] The original directors included Beatty and George Gooderham's brother Albert Lee Gooderham, with Beatty acting as president and Albert Lee's son Edward George Gooderham as secretary-treasurer.[30]

On 1 August 1882, just a few months after Worts' death, Tom Blackstock prepared an agreement between his father-in-law and the trustees and the beneficiaries of the trust to incorporate a company to be known as "Gooderham & Worts" (Limited).[31] The name of the corporation, with Gooderham and Worts in quotation marks and limited in parentheses, suggests that the intent was to emphasize the family connections and the link with the past partnership. The idea was that the assets of the partnership were to be valued and transferred into the new corporation. Then shares in the capital stock of this new corporation having a value equal to the partnership interest of Worts would be issued to the trustees. In effect, the funds that the Worts' estate would have received on the sale of his interest were invested in the securities of the new business. The remaining shares were to be held by George Gooderham and the two of his sons who had reached maturity, William George Gooderham[32] and Albert Edward Gooderham.[33]

The agreement dealt with a number of management and ownership matters. To ensure adequate cash for any contingencies it stipulated that up to one-third of the profits were to be retained by the company in a reserve fund and not paid to the shareholders as dividends.[34] To facilitate the provision in the will calling for a ten-year investment period, it also provided for the eventual purchase by George Gooderham of the trust's interest in the new corporation.

It is worthy of note that not only the trustees but also the beneficiaries signed the agreement. Tom Blackstock and his firm were anything but disinterested independent legal counsel, but of course that was the way the families wanted it. Family business was done by and within the family. Nevertheless, it was prudent to ensure that all of the stakeholders accepted the terms prepared by the family's lawyers.

The incorporation permitted the Worts family to maintain its interest in the business and saved George Gooderham the expense and uncertainty of the other options. But did it comply with the trust? Seven years later an action seeking interpretation of the will would be brought by the executors and trustees of one of the Worts sons. Beatty himself would give evidence under oath that what had been done was consistent with Worts' intent. The argument put forward by the legal counsel representing Beatty and the other trustees hinged on the fact that the will provided "very unlimited powers of investment." The legal counsel would note that "no new moneys were invested in this business." Referring to the power of the trustees to retain existing investments as well as their power to invest the money from the then current business, he stated that the trustees had retained the investment but had not continued the business; they had formed a joint stock company to which they turned over the whole business: "In one sense they retained the money in the business; in another they invested the money in the business. We say both the retention and the investment were authorized. We say there is here no breach of trust."[35]

In essence, the argument went, Worts had stipulated that the trustees of his estate were to continue his current businesses for only one year. The Gooderham and Worts business was a partnership. That partnership had not been continued beyond the stipulated one year. The will had provided that on discontinuance of the business, the money was to be invested in "securities." The incorporation of "Gooderham & Worts" (Limited) had created securities: namely shares of the incorporated business. It was result-oriented legal analysis at its best.

The Ontario Court, however, would not be impressed.[36] Chancellor Boyd found that "technically there was a breach of trust." He held it to be an "improper investment," noting that although the will had authorized the trustees to invest in securities it was not intended to permit them to continue the business beyond a year. Nor did it justify "any change of form such as made here, whereby a partnership was superseded by a company of limited liability." Nevertheless the value of the business had increased substantially and so there were no damages.

That decision, however, was years in the future. In 1882 the question was where to incorporate. The Toronto Silver Plate Company had been incorporated under the 1874 Act in Ontario but it was also possible to incorporate federally under the 1869 *Companies Act*.[37] The issue of whether to incorporate federally or provincially was then much on lawyers' minds. The case of *Citizens Insurance Co. of Canada v Parsons* had recently been decided by the Supreme Court and affirmed by the Privy Council.[38] It found that there was a valid federal power to incorporate companies under the constitution.[39] The choice between jurisdictions hinged on the words "companies with provincial objects" in the *British North America Act* and the words "objects to which the legislative authority of the Parliament of Canada extends" in section 3 of the federal *Companies Act*.

Beatty and his firm chose to incorporate "Gooderham & Worts" (Limited) federally, probably because of the territorial scope of the company's operations. It was then commonly thought that an Ontario corporation could not carry on business outside the province.[40] The objects of the new corporation specifically stated that its business could be carried on in and extended to "any or all of the Provinces of the Dominion of Canada."

Whether federal or provincial, the incorporation was to have at least five shareholders in the company petition to the government. The petition had to be advertised in the appropriate gazette one month before it was made. Like the petition itself, the advertisement had to set out the full names, addresses, and occupations of the petitioners, as well as the name of the proposed company, its objects, place of business, amount of capital stock, share structure, names of the three or more shareholders who would be directors, the stock to be taken by the petitioners, and how it had been paid for (cash, services, transfer of property, et cetera). The petition was to be signed by all petitioners and their signatures confirmed by statutory declaration of witnesses. The name of the company could not be the name of any existing company. Statutory declarations were required to prove compliance with these regulations.

One of the challenges that Blackstock faced in preparing the incorporation documents arose from the diverse nature of the Gooderham & Worts operations. At the time corporations were permitted to carry on only the businesses specifically listed in their objects. In drafting those objects he first made a general statement that the new corporation was "to carry on the business at one time carried on by the late James Gooderham Worts and George Gooderham as distillers, maltsters, etc., at the City of Toronto." But of course they wanted to grow the business so he added "to extend the same to any or all of the Provinces of the Dominion of Canada." Then, just in case the wording was not sufficiently specific, he added that the business could carry on "manufacturing, distilling, rectifying, aging, buying and selling and dealing in all kinds of spirituous or alcoholic liquor and malting and any business which may be appropriately or conveniently carried on in connection with such business." But even that might be too narrow so he added "to carry on the business of warehousing, elevating and forwarding" and, to catch their cattle operation, "to carry on any business which may be necessary or expedient for the consumption or economic use of the refuse of any such manufacturers."

The letters patent for the new corporation were issued on 24 November 1882.[41] They provided that George Gooderham and the trustees of the estate of the late James Gooderham Worts, together with William Henry Beatty, Worts' two sons, Thomas and James Jr., and George Gooderham's two oldest sons, William George and Albert Edward, were "created, a Body Corporate and Politic." The capital of the company consisted of 20,000 shares with a value of $100 each. Of this $2 million share value, $1.6 million was paid in and deposited in the Bank of Toronto. Table 2 shows the shareholder allocation in the incorporation.

George Gooderham	12,202	61.01%
Trustees	7,748	38.74%
W.H. Beatty	10	00.05
W.G. Gooderham	10	00.05
J.G. Worts	10	00.05
E.A. Gooderham	10	00.05
T.F. Worts	10	00.05

The small holdings for Beatty and the Gooderham and Worts children (totalling 0.25 percent) suggest that these were what would later be called qualifying shares. They gave the corporation more than the minimum number of shareholders it required under the Act and qualified these individuals to be directors. It also suggests that it was thought the shares held by several of these individuals as trustees did not qualify them as shareholders and directors.

The letters patent ensured control remained with the families by stating that none of George Gooderham's shares could "be transferred to a stranger so long as any Shareholder [was] willing to purchase the same at the prescribed price," essentially equal to the amount paid up on the shares. There was an exception for transfers by his executors or administrators to any of his sons or daughters or sons-in-law or grandchildren. These restrictions did not apply to the trust shares or the qualifying shares, most likely because it was feared that such restrictions might prohibit the trustees from fulfilling their duty to maximize the value of the trust assets.

It is interesting to contrast this family incorporation with ones being done by the firm for other clients. In 1883 the firm incorporated and organized the Fergus Brewing & Malting Company under the *Ontario Joint Stock Companies' Letters Patent Act, 1874*.[42] As in the case of Gooderham & Worts, there was an existing business, Holland & Company, a small brewing and malting operation that had commenced twelve years before. Here, however, a number of individuals were seeking to acquire and finance the business, and it is likely that their potential investors would want the protection that a limited liability company provided. The number of shareholders and provisional board members was similar to that of Gooderham & Worts, although the amount they paid for their shares was not. In this case, seven people — five from Fergus, one from Orangeville, and one from Guelph — agreed to pay $100 for each share in the company to be incorporated and to act as provisional directors. Three of the petitioners were to receive 100 shares each, representing an investment of $10,000. The others received between five and twenty shares.

Unlike "Gooderham & Worts" (Limited) this new corporation needed to raise additional capital — $50,000. Beatty's firm put together a prospectus to assist in these efforts. A modern prospectus is essentially a disclosure statement setting out all material facts, but this one was a sales pitch. After setting out the seven provisional directors, the bankers of the company, and their "secretary pro tem," it stated that the company was being formed to acquire and carry on, on an enlarged scale, the brewing and malting business of Holland & Company. It noted that the business had expanded "upon the excellent reputation which its products have always enjoyed, to about 5,000 barrels per year." Potential investors were assured that "this output can readily be increased with the aid of additional capital for the necessary building and plant . . . . A business of 10,000 barrels per annum can be reckoned on, which would result in a very handsome profit upon the investment being contemplated." The prospectus went on to talk of the "remarkably fine water" in Fergus and of "barley of the best quality" being grown in the vicinity. It touted the fact that "taxes are light, wages low and fuel cheap," and insisted that the "profits of brewing are large." Given all the conditions, "it is reasonable to expect the maximum return from this enterprise."

Although the incorporation procedure was similar to that of Gooderham & Worts, the motivation could not have been more different. In each case an existing business was incorporated, but one did so to overcome problems of succession and the other to raise capital from outside investors. One adapted its structure to fit within the corporate requirements without changing the family nature of the business, using qualifying shares held by family members, restrictions on share ownership, and a shareholders agreement, while the other took advantage of the corporate statute to structure its operations and assure potential investors that it represented a good investment.

The incorporation of Gooderham & Worts was a watershed in the firm's history. Beatty's firm had always focused on business law in its many forms. Now it had effectively become a corporate law firm — its largest clients were corporations.

* —❦— *

If BEATTY AND CHADWICK thought that their troubles were over by late 1883, they were mistaken. As the year was coming to an end, Thomson told his partners that he, too, was leaving, in his case to form his own firm. Thomson had risen in the firm but not far enough or fast enough to satisfy him, and he was tired of being the workhorse, doing the bulk of the work but not being compensated proportionately. He may have also been concerned about Tom Blackstock's growing influence. It could not have been lost on him that Blackstock was the son-in-law of George Gooderham, who, as we have seen, was an increasingly important man in the Gooderham and Worts extended family. Blackstock had done the work to incorporate Gooderham & Worts. Might Thomson have questioned his future in a firm that was increasingly linked to the businesses of a family of which he was a not member?

Thomson formed the firm of Thomson, Henderson & Bell,[43] which became important in its own right, coming to be known as Tilley, Carson &
Findlay.[44] Like Lash, Thomson learned to practise with the Beatty firm but
rose to distinction after leaving. While with the firm he developed expertise
in insolvency law and would later be regarded as one of Canada's leading
authorities in that area, with one of the country's largest insolvency practices.[45] He practised as both a barrister and a solicitor, being involved in several celebrated commercial cases and advising on general mercantile and
partnership business.[46] In addition he would become the president of the
Baptist Convention of Ontario and Quebec in 1889, a Queen's Counsel in
1890, and a governor of McMaster University that same year. He was also
one of the owners of the British American Business College.[47]

Thomson's departure was one more blow to the firm. In the late 1870s
and early 1880s, six lawyers had been actively working in the firm, making it one of Toronto's largest. The departure of Biggar and Miller and the
added responsibilities of Beatty outside the firm had changed that, reducing
it to three full-time lawyers: Chadwick, Thomson, and Blackstock. Reeve
had not yet proven able to fill even part of the gap. When Thomson left it
must have seemed as if the long-term future of the firm was at risk: it had
effectively shrunk to just two full-time, experienced lawyers. Meanwhile
its competitors were growing stronger and following its lead in establishing corporate commercial practices. In addition to Blakes, there was now
another important competitor. On 1 September 1882 the firm of McCarthy,
Osler, Hoskin & Creelman had been created when D'Alton McCarthy and
Britton Bath Osler, two of Ontario's leading litigation counsel, merged their
law practices to pursue a corporate law opportunity. On the same day the
Canada North-West Land Company retained the new firm. This company
had recently been incorporated in England by Freshfields on behalf of the
Canadian Pacific Railway to manage the sale of the 25 million acres of land
out west that it had received for building the railway to British Columbia.
Osler's brother Edmund, one of the directors, ensured that the Canadian
legal work went to his brother's new firm. The McCarthy Osler firm of six
lawyers joined the Blakes firm as serious competitors to Beatty's for corporate commercial work.[48]

The profit allocation for the twenty-three months from 19 March 1882 to
31 December 1883 (set out in Table 3) tells many tales. First, it makes quite
clear that the departures of Biggar and Miller had had a financial impact on
the firm. In the earlier period the average annual profit had been $22,317 but
it was now $19,200. But it also shows that Beatty tried to address his partners'

issues. He reduced his compensation from about $7,000 to $4,800 per year so that each of the others could increase the amount they received. Chadwick, for example, went from approximately $3,000 to $3,840 per year. Thomson was put on par with the much older and more experienced Chadwick. Blackstock, too, received a substantial increase in compensation. It is worthy of note that Reeve, who was much more senior, received the same share in the partnership as Blackstock. It was an early indication that Beatty and his partners were doubtful of the value that Reeve brought to the firm.

Partner	Shares	Entitled to	Drawn	Owing to	Overdrawn
Beatty	5	$8,400 ($4,800/ year)	$8,504		$104
Chadwick	4	6,720	6,667	53	
Thomson	4	6,720	6,583	137	
Blackstock	3.5	5,880	5,390	490	
Reeve	3.5	5,880	6,545		665

Beatty's adjustments to compensation seem like a case of too little, too late. In late 1883, when the law directory asked the firm to update its listing for the next year, only four names were provided: Beatty, Chadwick, Blackstock, and Reeve.[49] Things looked bleak. In 1884 the firm's letterhead listed its major clients for the first and last time. It proudly stated, "Solicitors for The Bank of Toronto, London and Ontario Investment Co., Credit Foncier Franco Canadien, Gooderham & Worts, Limited, Commercial Union Assurance Co. etc etc etc," as if to prove to itself and the world that the firm was still as strong as ever. The reality, however, was that it had been significantly weakened by the events of the last two years.

——◆◇◆——

AMID ALL THIS PROFESSIONAL disruption and personal tragedy, a recent graduate from the University of Toronto began serving as an articled clerk. David Fasken could not have chosen a better time to start work. The firm needed all the assistance it could get and his hard work, attention to detail, and good judgment were soon noticed.[50] He reminded Beatty of Thomson and, as he had done with Thomson, Beatty started to rely heavily upon him.[51] Like Thomson, Fasken was a young lad from a farming family in Wellington County. He was born into a world where a day's hard work on the farm was followed by fishing in the Grand River, except on Sundays, of course, when Fasken and his family worshipped in the small, unadorned Bethany Methodist Church in Pilkington Township, near Elora.[52]

With Beatty as the driving force, the first twenty years of the firm's existence had seen it grow from a struggling partnership of two brothers-in-law doing debt collections into Canada's largest solicitors' practice. It had done so by focusing on serving the day-to-day needs of businesses rather than on high-profile litigation. Of course, it had been helped enormously by Beatty's position as the son-in-law of one of the two partners of Gooderham & Worts. But by 1883 Beatty had become both a blessing and a curse. He was no longer primarily a lawyer but was a significant businessman in his own right. Beatty was president of the Toronto Silver Plate Company; vice-president of Gooderham & Worts, the Bank of Toronto, and Confederation Life; and on the board of Canada Permanent Mortgage Corporation and the newly incorporated Toronto General Trusts.[53] As the chosen successor to James Gooderham Worts and executor of the Worts estate, he wielded significant power in the Gooderham and Worts extended family and in the Toronto business community generally. But now the firm needed Beatty to focus his attention on his role as its managing partner and its rebuilding. Despite the calls on his time by these other businesses, he did just that:

> Beatty remained the guiding and controlling spirit of the firm, keeping a strong grip on the reins and looking after every detail of business. A shrewd judge of character, he displayed excellent judgment in his choice of associates. He was essentially a business lawyer and seldom appeared in court, devoting the major portion of his time to questions of organization and management, leaving the execution of his plans to the staff of counsel, consulting lawyers and expert office men with whom, like the good legal general he was, he surrounded himself. An able and tireless worker, he was chiefly responsible for building up what finally became the largest legal business in Canada.[54]

Beatty was able to rebuild the firm and still work on the affairs of the many businesses with which he was involved because with him it was always work. As he wrote in August 1892 on the twenty-first birthday of his son Charles,

> Life is very stern and business is a very jealous jade. She does not brook any other lover. She demands her votaries' entire attention . . . . If you wish to

succeed, it is not simply doing what is given to you. That, of course, should be attended to first. No matter how insignificant it may appear, do it as if your whole life depended upon it and ask for more to do. Be not one moment idle. One will rust out a great deal faster than wear out . . . . But with all of your work the first thing is to do your duty and be truthful . . . . There will be plenty of fun for you. But it must be work, first, first and first and then play afterwards.[55]

By January 1884 the firm had added two young lawyers: Thomas Percival "Percy" Galt and Rufus Shory Neville. Galt was the twenty-seven-year-old third son of Thomas Galt, a justice of the Court of Common Pleas who in 1887 would become Chief Justice of Ontario.[56] Percy was also the nephew of Alexander Tilloch Galt, a former minister of finance and one of the Fathers of Confederation. Galt would remain with the firm for almost thirty years. Neville, who had practised for two years in Lindsay before joining the firm, had none of Galt's lineage, connections or, as it turned out, skill.[57] He stayed a mere thirty-four months, leaving to form his own firm in partnership with W.J. McWhinney.[58]

Galt's addition helped enormously and behind the scenes the young student, David Fasken, did everything that could be asked of him and more. Tom Blackstock also stepped up, assuming an ever more important role in the firm. Chadwick helped by putting considerable effort into collecting unpaid accounts. With the challenges that the firm faced and the need to better compensate its partners, collections had become a priority.[59]

One person who did not rise to the occasion was Reeve, who continued to be of little assistance. It soon became clear to Beatty that while Reeve had good judgment, he was not the lawyer he had hoped for. As a result Reeve ceased to be a partner on 31 December 1883. He remained with the firm but his compensation, to the extent that it was in excess of what his work had brought in, was taken from the share of the two partners who were principally responsible for his having joined the firm — Tom Blackstock, who had put his name forward, and Beatty, who had agreed to admit him.[60] In 1884, for example, Reeve had drawings of $1,900 but brought in only $230. Beatty and Blackstock each had to contribute $835 to meet the firm's obligation to him.

Needless to say this arrangement did not last long, and by 1885 Reeve would be gone. Both Beatty and George Tate Blackstock, Tom's brother, soon began to write to Sir John A. Macdonald suggesting that Reeve was a bright, talented person who was misplaced in the practice of law but would make

Beatty addressing the Toronto Board of Trade, 1888
LAC

an excellent judge.[61] No judicial appointment was forthcoming but in 1889 Reeve did find a role for which he was quite suited, becoming the first principal of Osgoode Hall Law School.[62] Regrettably it was a role that he would not play for long. He died suddenly at age fifty-two in 1894.[63]

AT LEAST ONE ASPECT of Beatty's position as the heir to the business position of his father-in-law was good for the firm — it brought a significant new client. Worts had been active in the Toronto Board of Trade for some time, serving as its vice-president for several years and then from 1865 to 1869 as president. He had in fact used his presidency to encourage the Board to support the building of the Toronto Grey and Bruce Railway and the Toronto and Nipissing Railway, both because the railways were seen as engines of growth for the city's economy and also because of their lower construction costs.[64] In 1885 Beatty began to be listed as solicitor to the Board of Trade, a position he was to hold until at least 1896. He cleverly reminded the members of his link to Worts by donating a portrait of his father-in-law (with a suitable name plate acknowledging his donation) to be hung on a wall of the Board offices.

Beatty also had his own portrait done. In 1886 E.J. Lennox, the thirty-one-year-old architect who would soon be chosen to built the new city hall, completed the Beatty Building at 3 King Street West. Beatty's sculpted head looked out on Toronto's business community from the fourth-floor façade.[65] The building was not very wide but "nearly every surface of the façade was embellished . . . a conspicuous testimonial to the wealth of its owner."[66]

He celebrated his new prominence by joining a Board of Trade delegation to London, England, to attend a Canadian exhibition. On his return Sir John A. Macdonald wrote to say that he hoped that Beatty had "appreciated its value to Canada." Macdonald added that he was to be in Toronto shortly and would "be glad to see the manufacturers showing their appreciation of the venture in some tangible measure," which no doubt they did.[67]

Beatty was soon a prominent member of the Board of Trade.[68] In a photograph of the Board's council taken in 1888, Beatty is front and centre. As the members sit about a large table, Beatty is shown standing and addressing the group. Spread in front of him are various papers.[69] Some of them might well have been accounts from his firm because the Board's annual report for 1888 notes that the fees paid to Beatty, Chadwick, Blackstock & Galt from 1885 to 1887, inclusive, totalled $547.75. They also show that Beatty had fees connected to the *Board of Trade Bill* of $202.26 and to a proposed amendment to the Board charter of $124.20.[70] By 1892 the Board paid fees to the firm totalling $3,282.80.

In 1887 the Gooderham & Worts connection paid two further dividends, one in the form of a new lawyer for the firm and the other in the form of a significant new client. The new lawyer was William Henry Brouse Jr., who had married Florence Josephine Gooderham, another of the eight daughters of George Gooderham.[71] The twenty-eight-year-old Brouse was the son of the Honourable William Henry Brouse, MD, a senator from Prescott who had been one of the incorporators of the Royal Canadian Insurance Company in 1868.[72] In 1887 the firm assisted Gooderham & Worts in the incorporation and organization of its own life insurance company, Manufacturers Life. By this point the family distillery was the largest in Canada and would soon be producing more than 2 million gallons of whisky a year (more than 7.5 million litres).[73] It was a very lucrative operation and the family was always looking for other businesses in which to invest its profits. The family used its influence with the then prime minister, Sir John A. Macdonald, to get him to assume the presidency of Manufacturers Life Insurance Company. George Gooderham became the vice-president and dominant personality behind the company. Given that Beatty was then vice-president and very active in the rival Confederation Life, it seems safe to assume that Blackstock did the legal work for this new client. It proved an excellent and lucrative one. By 1892 the firm had done over $61,000 worth of work for Manufacturers Life.

Interestingly, at the same time the Gooderhams were involved with the incorporation of the Dominion of Canada Guarantee and Accident Insurance Company. For whatever reason, the Beatty firm did not do the legal work for this company, but by 1901 Tom Blackstock was nonetheless its vice-president.[74]

CHADWICK'S OUTSIDE INTERESTS ALSO created a business opportunity for Beatty and some additional work for the firm. Chadwick was heavily involved in the affairs of the Anglican Church in Toronto, favouring the High Church rather than the evangelical Low Church of the Gooderham and Worts families.[75] In his own words, he "engag[ed] in Church work during all of the time he [could] spare from his business."[76] That seems a bit of an exaggeration, in that Chadwick was also a noted genealogist, heraldist, and artist. To assist in his estates practice but also to feed his love of genealogy, he had begun to keep a series of notebooks in which he recorded information on the many Ontario families with which he came into professional and social contact. He studied family coats of arms, many of which he expertly sketched or painted.[77] In addition he remained active in the militia. The Official Army List for April 1882 shows Chadwick as Quarter-Master of Infantry, 2nd Battalion, Queen's Own Rifles.[78] Nevertheless, the Church was extremely important to him.

In 1884 Chadwick's Church work and Beatty's business acumen merged in a significant real estate project just north of the then city boundaries. The part of Toronto that came to be known as the Annex on its annexation to the city was just beginning to be developed. The portion bounded by Bloor on the south, Dupont on the north, Spadina on the east, and Bathurst on the west was owned by William Pearce Howland, Beatty's former next-door neighbour on William Street. It was thought that this area could be developed for middle-class families, whereas the area around St. George Street was destined for the upper class. Howland sold his land to a syndicate headed by Beatty and Howland's son, Oliver, then managing partners of different law firms.[79] Chadwick became intimately involved in the project because the centrepiece of the development was to be St. Alban the Martyr, a magnificent new Anglican Cathedral to be built on the site.[80]

Archdeacon Arthur Sweatman had been elected Bishop of Toronto in 1879, and he favoured the building of a cathedral church in the city. St. James, although referred to as such, was not a true cathedral. As Chadwick himself would later write, "The Cathedral, duly constituted, is not the Church of a parish, but of the whole Diocese, every inhabitant of which, even non-Anglicans (except the Romanists, who are under the jurisdiction of a separate Bishop) has full right to attend and to claim a seat, or indeed one might say, to claim a share in the ownership of it."[81] St. James had sold its seats to a series of pew holders (including Beatty) and was thus disqualified to serve as a cathedral. The pew holders refused to give up their pews.[82]

In 1881 the Diocesan Synod passed a resolution approving Bishop Sweatman's plan, and in 1883 a bill was passed in the provincial legislature incorporating the Cathedral Chapter.[83] The Bishop considered whether it might be possible to convert one of the parish churches but none seemed both willing and suitable. To the Bishop, the key was having sufficient land to support not only an expansion of the church but also the building of a See House to accommodate the Bishop and a school. Chadwick tells us that "after considering such sites as were proposed, and after consulting with a number of churchmen who seemed disposed to assist, the Bishop and Chapter decided upon the site between Howland and Albany Avenue offered by a syndicate of owners who had purchased the block of land afterwards known as St. Alban's Park, and who offered the site on very favourable terms."[84]

What Chadwick does not tell us is that he and Beatty had played a key role in moving the proposed cathedral to the land being developed by the Beatty–Howland syndicate. Chadwick, who was undoubtedly aware of the Bishop's search for a site, seems to have approached Beatty and Howland about the possible sale of the land the Church needed at a low price, suggesting to them that such a sale would heighten the value of the land they were seeking to develop and make lot sales easier and more profitable. Chadwick was on the building committee for the new cathedral, but he also acted for the syndicate in doing the real estate and conveyancing work. The deed conveying the property from Beatty and Howland to the Bishop and Chapter was drawn by Chadwick (without any punctuation). It was dated 31 December 1884 and signed by the parties in the presence of Chadwick, who acted as witness. Under it the Chapter agreed to pay $10,288, all but $1,000 of which was a downpayment. The conveyance was in trust, pending the passing of the necessary legislation. A supplementary agreement of the same date was also prepared by Chadwick, under which the Chapter agreed to built a cathedral within the next ten years on the southerly part of the land acquired.

In 1912 the *Canadian Churchman*[85] stated, "It is nearly thirty years since the acquisition of the site of St. Alban's was effected. We gladly preface an account of the present service by acknowledging again the debt which the Church in the diocese owes to Mr. E.M. Chadwick for the foresight with which he acquired the site, and the constant interest that he has shown in the undertaking."[86] As Blackstock and the firm had done two years before for the incorporation of Gooderham & Worts, Chadwick and his partners wore many hats in the transaction. Chadwick was a representative of the Cathedral Chapter but also the lawyer for the syndicate and the partner of one of the key members of the syndicate. His involvement became even more complex in 1886, when under a power of attorney, he became Beatty's agent "in respect of all matters connected with lands and mortgages of lands in St. Alban's Park."[87] But it is likely that neither he nor Beatty saw any real conflict. Chadwick's many roles were known to and accepted by all. Beatty, Howland, and their syndicate were more than pleased with the business opportunity that he gave to them. The Cathedral Chapter was also pleased with both the site and its price.

Chadwick himself moved into the district to live opposite the cathedral on Howland Street, named after William Howland.[88] Completing the project became a task that would absorb much of Chadwick's time and energy for the next thirty-five years. For numerous reasons, including the death of the original architect, a fight over who would replace him, mounting costs, and flagging enthusiasm, the bankruptcy of chief fundraiser Sir Henry Pellatt, and the building of a rival "cathedral," St. Paul's, for Canon Henry John Cody[89] by his Low Church supporters (including the Gooderhams and the Blackstocks), St. Alban's was never finished. The foundation for the entire building was completed, as was the chancel and the bishop's house, but by the early 1920s the project had been abandoned. The one-third of the cathedral that was finished still stands today as a monument to Chadwick's fruitless efforts.

Because of his seemingly conflicting roles on the building committee of the cathedral and as the lawyer for the syndicate, the failure of the project brought Chadwick much criticism. A review of the materials suggests that it was largely unwarranted. The cathedral was separately represented by Moss Falconbridge & Barwick, and Chadwick does not seem to have participated in the final negotiations.[90] Certainly, he was hurt by the disapproval. Shortly before his death, at a time when the cathedral had been all but officially abandoned, he published a pamphlet to affirm that "the effort to establish a worthy Cathedral in this great city and important diocese, was an act of faith, begun in faith and carried forward year by year from the smallest beginnings in the face of discouragement and unanticipated opposition."[91]

THE FIRM'S ROLE IN ST. ALBAN'S PARK is notable for another, very different reason. It was the first project for which documents were typewritten. In the previous year documents for the incorporation of Fergus Brewing had been either printed or written by hand. The expense ledger shows that the firm acquired its first typewriter on 24 April 1884 for the substantial sum of $120.20, representing almost 25 percent of expenses for the month. Although the typewriter had been invented in the United States and patented in 1868 by Christopher Latham Sholes, the Beatty firm was an early adopter. It had taken Sholes years to find funding and support for a machine that even he doubted was useful. In 1872 he wrote that "for a while there may be an active demand for them, but . . . like any novelty, it will have its brief day and be thrown aside." He could see no business use for it and thought that its market would be clergymen and men of letters. Fortunately for him, in 1874 Remington was a Civil War munitions manufacturer seeking a new set of products and agreed to manufacture some. But they sat on the shelves unsold. The $125 price tag made it "an expensive gamble on an unproved technology."[92] Gradually sales grew, but by the beginning of the 1880s fewer than 5,000 were in use and it took until the late 1880s for the machines to be widely accepted in business.

On 30 April, a week after it had acquired its typewriter, the firm rented its first telephone, for $25. The telephone had been invented by Alexander Graham Bell in 1876 and the Bell Telephone Company of Canada had been incorporated in 1880. Again the firm was among the first to use the new invention. Access to the device was carefully controlled, however, and it was kept in the firm's vault.

THANKFULLY FOR THE HISTORIAN, the telephone did not replace letters as the principal means of communication. In the 1880s both Beatty and Blackstock were in regular correspondence with prominent Conservative politicians in Ottawa. In Beatty's case the letters were usually to Prime Minister Macdonald. Tom Blackstock, on the other hand, usually wrote to the minister of justice, initially Alexander Campbell and later Sir John Thompson.[93]

One of the subjects Beatty wrote regularly about was his refusal to be considered for a QC. He saw himself as a business lawyer and neither expected nor wanted an honour intended for barristers. On 21 July 1887, for example, Beatty wrote to Sir John on firm letterhead to make it clear that if his name was put on the list of those to be made a QC, "I will take steps that the public shall know I have declined."[94]

When he thought it necessary, Beatty used his political connections and his personal friendship with Sir John A. Macdonald and Sir Charles Tupper to assist his family and his clients. In January 1888 he wrote to Sir John, calling on the prime minister to assist his eldest son, Harry, in securing a promotion in the North West Mounted Police: "In April last year you were kind enough to ease the way for my son on his entering the N W M Police force. He now writes to me about a promotion and is very anxious to be made a corporal . . . . I hope that you will see he gets his step."[95] Macdonald wrote on the back of the letter, "What about this youngster? Find out. Beatty is an important man."

Then in April, Beatty again called upon the prime minister, this time to assist the Gooderham & Worts Distillery in preventing the Canadian Pacific Railway from using the former estate of his father-in-law, located just north of the distillery, for a shunting yard.[96] In that letter Beatty stated that he and Mr Gooderham considered themselves to "have a claim not only as citizens upon you and have a right to ask you to protect the public and also protect us from what may be an irreparable damage and an incalculable loss."

The same attempt to expropriate the Worts property caused Tom Blackstock to complain to Minister of Justice Sir John Thompson,

> The Canadian Pacific . . . now say in effect that if we will give them lands upon their own terms for the Branch Line (not for the yard) and will abandon any claims for damages they will not put their yard there but put it somewhere else. If the Railway Act contained adequate provisions for the payment of compensation for the exercise of these powers by the Canadian Pacific they would not be in a position to coerce my clients into accepting their terms under the threat of surrounding the property with a Railway Yard.[97]

Neither Beatty nor Blackstock was able to win the day against the CPR. They would not give the railway what it demanded and so the shunting yard went in just north of the distillery.

BLACKSTOCK'S POSITION IN THE firm was noticeably improving in the late 1880s, but not all was good news. In the same year as the struggle with the CPR, Tom wrote a heartrending letter to his father: "It has just struck 2 am which reminds me I should date this 23rd February. Dear Hattie lies on the Library Lounge beside me while upstairs our Darling Tommy is in a death struggle with the dreaded Diphtheria and not expected to last till morning."[98]

They called in Dr. James Ross, who was married to Hattie's sister, Adelaide.[99] But Ross could not save Tommy. Hattie, especially, was devastated. She shut up the Sherbourne Street house and took the rest of the family to England, where she remained for two years.

Tom Blackstock did as he usually did when things became difficult. He worked harder. By 1889 he was determined that his hard work be properly rewarded, even if it brought him into conflict with Beatty. Their struggle is recorded in the firm's financial records in the dry, matter-of-fact fashion of an accountant, but it must have been a very trying time for both men.[100] It began with Tom Blackstock preparing a page dated "1889, 1st Jan." that set out what he proposed for each partner's compensation for the previous five-year period, based on a profit of about $100,000 (Table 4).

Partner	Entitled	Drawn	Due
W.H. Beatty	$20,000	19,363.53	636.47
E.M. Chadwick	25,755.59	25,586.63	168.96
T.G. Blackstock	30,755.59	20,372.63	10,382.96
T. Galt	15,022.26	12,179.25	2,843.01
R.S.N. [Neville]	5,201	5,201	-
W.H. Brouse	3,400	3,400	
Totals	**100,134.44**	**86,103.04**	**14,031.40**

Beatty undoubtedly recognized that Blackstock was doing the bulk of the work, but it must nevertheless have come as a shock that the younger lawyer expected to receive substantially more than the two founders. Beatty scratched out the original $20,000 that had been set out for himself and wrote in $25,000. He then reduced Blackstock's amount from $30,755.59 to $25,755.59. Beatty's counterproposal would have effectively made Beatty, Chadwick, and Blackstock equals. But an entry on the page dedicated to the drawings by Beatty has a note recording that Blackstock won the day: "My arrangement with T.G. Blackstock is that after I receive $20,000 from the firm of BCB&G for the past 5 years to 31st Dec. 1888, all in excess of that amount is to be credited to him." The note, dated 18 March 1889, is signed by Beatty. It had taken Blackstock two and a half months but he had prevailed over his managing partner.

This new financial order was also followed in 1889. The amount that each partner was permitted to withdraw in that year for the new, reconstituted firm of Beatty, Chadwick, Blackstock & Galt (in which, for the first time, David Fasken is shown as a partner) has Tom Blackstock at $5,360, Chadwick at $4,250, Galt at $2,975, and Beatty at $2,450 plus an additional $545 in his capacity as executor for the Worts estate. A note following states, "amount earned but not drawn estimated at $12,000." For the year, assuming that the additional $12,000 was collected, Blackstock would have earned $8,825.52, or just over 28 percent. Tom Blackstock was now the most highly compensated partner in the firm, well ahead of both Beatty and Chadwick.

Beatty had, in fact, fallen to fourth place in partner compensation in the firm that he had earlier dominated. A new era was dawning.

Chapter 4

BEATTY BLACKSTOCK,
1890–1906

ALTHOUGH BEATTY REMAINED THE managing partner, by 1890 Tom Blackstock had become the principal lawyer. With Beatty otherwise occupied, it was Blackstock who acted as solicitor for the Bank of Toronto, Manufacturers Life, Gooderham & Worts, and other businesses in which the Gooderhams invested their funds. It was also Blackstock to whom Judge Stevenson Burke, a noted corporate lawyer from Cleveland, turned when he and his associates were fighting for control of the Central Ontario Railway, or COR.[1]

This railway had begun in 1873 with a line in Prince Edward County linking Picton with Trenton. The discovery of gold in the hills to the north at a spot soon named Eldorado spurred a line north. Then the discovery of iron ore near Bancroft led to the line being extended to that area.[2] The prime mover behind the COR was a financier and mining entrepreneur from Akron, Ohio: Samuel J. Ritchie invested in the iron ore discoveries and also helped develop the Copper Company of Canada in Sudbury.[3] After a time, with the railway in financial difficulties, other investors led by Judge Burke lost faith in Ritchie and seized control of the company. Ritchie, Burke, and various bondholders spent more than a decade in court fighting over the railway. Blackstock not only oversaw the litigation undertaken by the firm's lawyers, including his brother George and Percy Galt,[4] but he also joined the board of COR and acted as an agent for the Burke group, buying up bonds and shares on its behalf. Blackstock's litigators were generally successful in their many skirmishes, but they would ultimately prove pyrrhic victories because the COR went bankrupt.

Beatty, meanwhile, had other things on his mind. On a business level, he was busy overseeing the planning and construction of the massive new head office building for Confederation Life, which still towers over the northeast corner of Yonge and Richmond.[5] The company had announced its decision to build a head office in 1889 because Beatty and the other board members wanted the company housed in a building that reflected its importance and potential.[6] It would be completed in 1892 and on 9 May 1893 Beatty, as vice-president, presided over the first annual meeting held in the new building.

On a personal level, he was engaged in a bitter family dispute with his sister-in-law Mary Worts, the widow of James Gooderham Worts Jr., his father-in-law's youngest son. When J.G. Worts Jr. died in 1884 at age thirty-one, Beatty and Mary Worts had become his executors. Mary was left with two young children, a boy and a girl. In 1887 Beatty, who considered her an alcoholic and an unfit parent, convinced her to relinquish her executorship as well as her home and the custody and control of her children. In 1890 she sued him, alleging that he had procured her agreement by fraud and mis-representation and that he had used threats and duress against her. Herbert MacRae, her brother-in-law and a lawyer with Watson, Thorne, Smoke & Masten, brought the action on her behalf. Beatty retained Samuel Blake to defend what he had done. It was regarded by the *Montreal Herald* as "the most sensational case on the docket."[7] Blake and Watson, the senior partner in MacRae's firm, met extensively in December to settle the action and rob the *Herald* of "the latest cause célèbre" to which it was so looking forward.

⸻

BLACKSTOCK'S NEW STATUS WAS reflected in a new firm name in 1892. For virtually all of the first twenty-nine years the first two names on the firm's letterhead had been those of its founders, Beatty and Chadwick. For the next twenty-three years the firm would be known as Beatty Blackstock.

Chadwick, although more senior, had clearly been eclipsed by Blackstock. He was slowly losing his hearing, and his interests in heraldry, genealogy, and the building of St. Alban's Cathedral were consuming more and more of his time. He had celebrated the Ontario centenary of 1891 by issuing a book on the genealogy of his family.[8] The positive public reaction to this study and frequent requests for genealogies of other families soon led him to plan a more ambitious genealogical study, entitled *Ontarian Families*, the first volume of which would be published in 1894.

Blackstock had not only become prominent inside the firm but was coming to be well known and respected outside of it as well, as a noted business lawyer and as George Gooderham's right-hand man. Tom and his father-in-law had become close and clearly George trusted Tom's judgment and enjoyed his company. They not only worked together but they played and travelled together. Both were prominent members of the Royal Canadian Yacht Club, or RCYC. While George favoured a sailing yacht, calling his craft the *Oriole*, Tom chose a motor yacht, which he dubbed the *Cleopatra*. Tom might well have chosen the name because in 1889 George had taken him and their respective families on an extended vacation to Egypt, where they had ridden camels out to the pyramids.[9]

The high regard in which Tom was held is reflected in the fact that George entrusted him with supervising the building of Gooderham's new palatial house on St. George Street just north of Bloor, as well as homes for his children on adjoining Prince Arthur Street. Hattie and Tom, his favourites, were to have a mansion modelled on his and built immediately north of it, at the corner of St. George and Prince Arthur. Each of these impressive new homes was designed by David Roberts Jr., the Gooderham family architect. Once Gooderham had approved the designs, he left for Europe and put Tom in charge of the construction of both houses.[10] Tom took the job very seriously, personally selecting the building materials. He even went to Italy to recruit skilled tradesmen to come to Toronto to mould the ceilings.

Although there can be no doubt that Hattie had much to say about the furnishing of their new home, Tom's interests were clearly reflected. He found places for his hunting trophies, especially his beloved buffalo. The library walls featured moose and buffalo heads, and a massive buffalo head was a principal feature of the entrance hall. The large head in the entrance was a gift from the federal government in recognition of his donation in 1898 of a small buffalo herd to Canada's new national park in Banff, Alberta.[11] Given in the hope of saving the species from extinction, the donation had a profound impact on the philosophy of Canada's national parks.[12]

As IMPORTANT AS BEATTY and Blackstock had become in the Toronto business community, they had little impact within the Law Society of Upper Canada, the self-governing body overseeing the legal profession in the province. The legislative arm of that body was referred to, in the tradition of the English Inns of Court, as Convocation, its members as benchers, and its leader as treasurer. The benchers were almost to a man barristers; Beatty and Blackstock, as solicitors, were not elected as benchers and did not stand for that office. This meant that they had no say in a battle then being fought at Convocation over the admission of women to the legal profession.[13]

In May 1891 Clara Brett Martin, a recent graduate of the University of Toronto, applied for acceptance as a student at law. The benchers rejected her application on the basis that when the *Law Society Act* referred to persons seeking to enter the profession, it had not meant women. Martin put together a political coalition and obtained the support of Premier Mowat. To ensure that there could be no doubt, a bill was passed in the Ontario legislature permitting the Law Society to consider the admission of women as solicitors. Nevertheless, in September 1892 the benchers declined to exercise their new power. Mowat was not pleased. As a former attorney-general he was an ex officio bencher. He personally attended Convocation in December and made a motion that women be permitted to join the legal profession. It passed twelve votes to eleven and Martin was admitted as a student at law. By 1896 she had convinced the Ontario legislature to permit women to be called to the bar as barristers as well. The next year she became the first woman called to the bar in the British empire. She and others after her would not, however, find a place in the Beatty Blackstock firm or any other large Toronto firm.[14] Beatty Blackstock would not hire a woman as a lawyer for another sixty years, long after Beatty and Blackstock were gone.[15]

— ❖ —

BLACKSTOCK'S RISE TO PROMINENCE ushered in a period of stability and growth. By 1894 the firm had grown to eleven lawyers, making it the second largest in the city. Blake, Lash & Cassels was slightly larger with thirteen lawyers, six of whom were members of the Blake family. McCarthy Osler was third, at nine. By 1901 Beatty Blackstock had surpassed Blakes and with fifteen lawyers became Canada's largest law firm, only slightly smaller than the largest in the United States, Sullivan & Cromwell. After a period during which lawyers came and went, it is notable that for over a decade only one, William Brouse, would leave the firm.[16] He joined the young, increasingly important Toronto Stock Exchange, eventually becoming its president.

Two recent additions, Robert J. McKay and Harper M. Armstrong,[17] had clerked with the firm, Armstrong starting in 1887 and McKay as a student in 1889.[18] Even though Armstrong was called to the bar in 1890 and McKay in 1892, both officially joined the partnership as junior partners in 1893, with McKay listed first on the letterhead. This suggests that Harper Armstrong had articled right out of high school whereas McKay had a university degree.

⋆⟶⟞⟝⟵⋆

PERHAPS NO EVENT BETTER illustrates that Tom Blackstock was a force in the firm than the addition of his brother George Tate Blackstock in 1892. Finally the Reverend Blackstock's vision of his two sons in partnership was realized. On the surface, George seemed an excellent addition, filling the need for a strong barrister. On joining Beatty's solicitors' practice in 1879, Tom Blackstock had hoped for "something better and more suited to my tastes." He had never given up that desire to establish a barrister's practice in the firm and finally, in 1892, he was in a position to do something about it.

Tom undoubtedly assured his partners that George had developed an active litigation practice in both civil and criminal actions throughout the province and as both a defence counsel and a Crown prosecutor. With his addition, the firm would not need to look outside for expert counsel. Tom could point to 1890, when his father-in-law, George Gooderham, the firm's foremost client, had launched a legal action against the city of Toronto and the law firm had had to go outside for a lead counsel. Gooderham had been seeking to prevent the city from extending Saulter, Strange, and McGee Streets through a 22.5 acre (9 hectare) property south of Eastern Avenue that he had acquired for the family's cattle business.[19] Although Percy Galt had assisted in the action, the first chair had been Charles Moss, QC, of Moss, Hoyles & Aylesworth, one of Ontario's leading barristers.[20]

Although George had recently triumphed in the Supreme Court of Canada,[21] his addition had much in common with Blackstock's addition of Reeve a decade before. Each was an act of kindness rather than an exercise of good business judgment. Like Reeve, George would be a problematic addition despite his excellent reputation as a litigator. He had proven himself a poor fit in several firms already. He had stayed with Rose, Macdonald & Merritt for just over two years.[22] In 1882 he had joined Wells, Gordon & Sampson, but this affiliation was also short lived. Soon George was practising as a barrister on his own. He had acted for the Bank of Toronto on occasion, most likely work referred to him by Tom. He had also for a time been counsel to the Canadian Pacific Railway[23] and in the 1880s had been involved in arbitration between Canadian Pacific and the federal government over the character of the road handed over by the federal government.[24] Then in 1890 he had earned much admiration for his skillful, although unsuccessful, defence of Reginald Birchall in a famous Woodstock murder trial.[25] By 1892, however, Blackstock was experiencing serious personal problems and it seems clear that he was offered a position in the firm to assist him through a difficult time.

The previous year George had gone down to defeat in the federal election in West Durham, despite his ability as a gifted speaker. He was bitterly disappointed. He so wanted to be a successful politician, but his efforts to win a seat had consistently failed. He had run unsuccessfully for office provincially in 1884 in Lennox and federally in 1887. His third loss seems to have destroyed his self-confidence and self-esteem. This was made worse by the fact that his American wife was rumoured to be having an affair and wanted a divorce. Thus, when his brother Tom offered him a position in the firm, it was in the hope that George might benefit. He was finding it more difficult to give his law practice the attention it required.

George's friend Wyly Grier, a noted portrait painter, later wrote in his memoirs that "domestic worries . . . at times when he was the leading barrister on one or other side of cases of great moment, which called for his undivided absorption in the issues at stake — made him distraught and preoccupied."[26] His wife would divorce him in 1896, but it is unclear whether his family problems were the source of or the result of his personal difficulties. Wyly Grier wrote,

> A sinister cloud had arisen on the apparently brilliant horizon of this gifted lawyer, nor am I able to say he was entirely blameless when it enveloped him. Battles in court and minor conflicts at home gradually undermined the nervous system which had evoked my father's admiration and bereft Osgoode Hall of one of its most brilliant figures. I remember that a symptom of the approaching breakdown of our friend was confided to me (or more correctly, to my brother, Alex Munro). Blackstock had stated that when waiting for his turn to address the court the perspiration would drop off his finger-ends.[27]

George's personal problems meant that he did not deliver on whatever representations Tom had given his partners, ultimately proving to be more a burden than a benefit. George spent considerable time out of the office seeking cures for his various perceived ailments. Dr. Daniel Clark, who would later give his name to Toronto's mental health centre, later remarked, "He has travelled hither and thither as his fancy dictated in the vain hope that he could get away from himself."[28] A year after joining the firm, George was in a hospital in Quebec City. Tom wrote to him pleadingly on 29 January 1893, "Nesbitt has looked worried for some time, I fairly feel he could not hold things together in your absence." But George, unmoved by the concerns of his brother or the needs of his junior, remained in Quebec.

━━◆◆◆◆━━

THAT JUNIOR WAS THIRTY-THREE-YEAR-OLD Wallace Nesbitt. He had joined the firm shortly after George, whom he knew through their work for the Conservative Party and through Canadian Pacific Railway matters. In 1891 George had strongly recommended Wallace's brother, John W. Nesbitt, QC, of Hamilton, for the senior judgeship of the Wentworth County Court.[29] Wallace was born in Woodstock, Ontario, the youngest of eleven children of John and Mary Nesbitt. His father, a Scot, had immigrated to Canada in 1837 with his Irish-born wife. They settled on a farm in Oxford County and it was there that Wallace was born. After high school, Nesbitt served as an articled clerk and studied law at Osgoode Hall, where he excelled, winning scholarships and serving as president of the Osgoode Literary and Debating Society.

On his call to the bar in 1881 he joined his older brother in a law practice in Hamilton. There he met and impressed Britton Bath Osler, who in 1883 asked Nesbitt to join him and D'Alton McCarthy in their new firm in Toronto. Wallace Nesbitt practised with Osler and McCarthy for almost ten years, assisting these two leading litigators in several notable cases, including the suit between Conmee & McLennan and the Canadian Pacific Railway over excessive fees charged by the former to build the portion of the railroad that ran north of Lake Superior.[30] The CPR was an important client of McCarthy Osler and brought Wallace Nesbitt into contact with George Blackstock. When Wallace joined the Beatty firm it was renamed Beatty, Blackstock, Nesbitt & Chadwick.

━━◆◆◆◆━━

ONE OF THE THINGS troubling George Blackstock in the early 1890s was the death of his long-time mentor, Sir John A. Macdonald, on 6 June 1891. One wonders if it bothered George that it was Beatty, and not him, who was chosen by the local Conservatives to chair the Macdonald Memorial Committee of Toronto and that the statue of Macdonald erected by that committee was installed at Queen's Park about 100 metres from Beatty's home.[31] Macdonald's death deprived George of an important political ally and ushered in a period of great instability in the ruling Conservative Party.

As Stephen Leacock would later write, "With Macdonald's death the Fates began to cut the threads of the Conservative destiny."[32] He was succeeded by Sir John Abbott, but Abbott was seventy years old and soon developed health problems that led to his resignation in the fall of 1892. Abbott was succeeded by forty-seven-year-old Sir John Thompson.

For a time this must have seemed like good news to both Blackstock brothers. Thompson was younger, a skilled orator and lawyer, and a proven, if somewhat reluctant, politician. Although Thompson was a convert to Catholicism, Tom had developed a friendship with him when he was the minister of justice and deputy prime minister, and the two had corresponded regularly on personal and political matters as well as business.[33] In 1894, when Thompson was prime minister, Tom Blackstock offered him the use of his yacht *Cleopatra* for a few weeks, and the two spent time together in the Niagara region, along with Thompson's two oldest sons, John and Joseph. Joseph, then twenty, had just started as a student at Beatty Blackstock. His older brother, John, was articling at McCarthy Osler. Lady Aberdeen, the wife of the governor general, noted that "Sir John thought that they would learn more practically in a law office than by going to the University."[34] Tom used the occasion to host a reception for Thompson on board the yacht, at which Thompson met Tom's brother-in-law, Dr. James Ross, by then the head of gynaecology at Toronto General Hospital and a professor of medicine at the University of Toronto.[35] Ross was the Gooderham family doctor just as Tom was the family lawyer.

Soon Ross became Thompson's personal physician and a month later diagnosed him with heart disease.[36] Thompson was on his way to London to be sworn in as a member of Her Majesty's Privy Council and Dr. Ross gave him a referral to a leading London doctor. Regrettably, Thompson never returned from London, dying there in December. His death must have been a terrible blow to both of the Blackstock brothers, but especially to Tom.

Thompson's unexpected death also caused Lady Aberdeen to express concern in her diary about Thompson's two boys. She noted that both McCarthy Osler and Beatty Blackstock "have been very kind. Although no salary is generally given to students, one gets $10 a month & the other $12 a month because they are so much help."[37] The firms' kindness, however, did not extend past articling. Neither son joined the Toronto firm for which he had worked as a student. John ended up practising in Ottawa, Joseph in Toronto.

IN THE SPRING OF 1893, Wallace Nesbitt became the first person in the firm to argue a case as lead counsel before the Supreme Court of Canada. Assisted by Percy Galt, he argued before Chief Justice Sir Henry Strong and Justices Fournier, Taschereau, Gwynne, and Sedgewick.[38] They were acting for George Burfoot, the plaintiff in the original action and the respondent on the appeal to the Supreme Court. It was a dispute over a restrictive covenant in an agreement for purchase of land. The firm's client had won at trial, but this had been appealed to the Divisional Court, which had reversed the judgment. An appeal to the Ontario Court of Appeal had been successful in restoring the trial judgment but that decision had in turn been appealed to the Supreme Court. Justice Sedgewick gave the judgment, once again restoring the trial judgment. Beatty Blackstock had its first win at the Supreme Court thanks to Wallace Nesbitt's able advocacy.[39]

Nesbitt would often be in the Ontario Court of Appeal and at the Supreme Court of Canada.[40] Not long after Nesbitt and Galt appeared before the Supreme Court of Canada, Nesbitt appeared with another lawyer from the firm, Alexander Munro Grier. They successfully defended a finding of non-suit in a negligence action brought by Henry Headford, a factory worker, against his employer, the McClary Manufacturing Company.[41]

Like Nesbitt, Grier had joined the firm when George did. He had assisted Blackstock in the 1880s arbitration between the Canadian Pacific Railway and the federal government and other, similar work.[42] Munro Grier was born in England, where his family had travelled from Australia. He had spent some time in Toronto in 1876, when he and his brother first met George Tate Blackstock, and then returned with his family to England, where he studied law. Grier had an abiding love of the theatre, however, which would later lead him into amateur acting. He used his time in London to attend plays as well as to study law. Much to his later renown, he attended one of the first performances of Gilbert & Sullivan's *Patience*.[43] But he managed to suppress his interest in the theatre long enough to be called as a barrister in 1882. He then returned to Toronto, where he was called to the Ontario bar in 1884. Munro Grier was one of the founders of the York County Law Association in 1885, and like his brother Wyly, he was artistically inclined and a noted speaker. He was praised for "concise, well modulated diction" and his "logical thinking, couched in clear, decorative, sometimes rhetorical language."[44] Like Nesbitt and the Blackstocks, he was a Conservative.

IN 1895, WITH GEORGE BLACKSTOCK ILL, the firm decided to add another outstanding litigator: thirty-nine-year-old William Renwick Riddell. Riddell was exceptionally well educated. He had three university degrees (a BA, a BSc, and an LLB) and had taught school for a few years before completing his legal studies. He had been thirty-one on his call to the bar in 1883 and the gold medallist. Riddell began his practice in Cobourg and by 1890 had taken on two associates, A.J. Armstrong and H.W. Nesbitt, both of whom had articled with him and been called to the bar that year.[45] By 1891 he had opened additional offices in Brighton and Northumberland County. In the same year he was elected a bencher of the Law Society. Then, in 1893, he opened yet another office, this time in Toronto in partnership with established lawyers Charles Millar and R.C. LeVesconte. Although he maintained his practice in Cobourg, in 1894 he moved into a large house at 109 St. George Street in Toronto, just up the street from Tom Blackstock's home at number 79.

As a bencher (the firm's first) and a noted litigator, Riddell was clearly a worthy addition, although one cannot help but wonder whether the offer was at least partly motivated by his strong Liberal ties. The Conservative Party was in disarray, as a quick succession of prime ministers culminated in 1895 with the disastrous choice of seventy-year-old Mackenzie Bowells, creating a rift in the party that soon led to his resignation. It seemed very likely an election would soon be called that would bring Wilfrid Laurier and the Liberals to power. As in 1876, when the firm had added Biggar, Riddell gave the firm a strong voice in the Liberal Party that it otherwise lacked. Beatty, Chadwick, Blackstock, and Nesbitt were all too closely tied to the Conservative Party. David Fasken was a Liberal but had no profile and lacked strong credentials in that party. Riddell, on the other hand, was a fervent Liberal supporter with extensive party connections.

Almost immediately, Riddell's Liberal connections paid a dividend. In February 1895 the student body at the University of Toronto had gone on strike to protest the firing of a popular professor. There was much tension between university president James Loudon and the students, led in part by a hard-working, intelligent, and somewhat radical William Lyon Mackenzie King. King saw himself following in his grandfather's footsteps in leading a rebellion against an oppressive regime, asserting, "His mantle has fallen on me."[46] The affair drew much attention and led the provincial government to establish a five-person commission of inquiry headed by Chief Justice Thomas Taylor of Manitoba to look into the matter.[47] Young King's father, John, was a close personal friend of William Mulock, the noted litigator turned Liberal politician who acted as vice-chancellor of the university. John King turned to Mulock for advice and Mulock recruited his fellow Liberal, Riddell, to act for his son and the other student leaders before the commission.[48] It would turn out to be a good brief for Riddell and the firm. After graduate work in Chicago, young Mackenzie King later became a deputy minister in Laurier's government and as such a highly influential Liberal and very useful contact in Ottawa.

With Riddell's addition it became even clearer that Beatty Blackstock would be a different firm from Beatty & Chadwick. Symbolic of the changes that Tom Blackstock had introduced, Nesbitt was named a Queen's Counsel in 1896 and Riddell in 1899, the first lawyers to receive that honour while members of the firm. George Blackstock had been made a QC in 1889 prior to joining the firm. Beatty, as a solicitor, had refused the honour and Chadwick, under Beatty's influence, had not sought it. But this was no longer the firm of solicitors specializing in business law and insolvency that Beatty had created. Beatty Blackstock had become a force in litigation. George Blackstock had the reputation; Riddell and Nesbitt had the skills and aptitude; Munro Grier could ably assist. But none of them did litigation exclusively. When necessary each could also do some solicitors' work.[49]

Nesbitt and Riddell were soon mentoring another significant addition to the firm. Hugh Rose was the son of John Edward Rose, a judge of the Ontario High Court of Justice. Born in 1869, Hugh earned a BA in 1891 at the University of Toronto and an LLB in 1892. He began his articles with Maclaren, Macdonald, Merritt & Shepley but transferred to the Beatty firm. On his call to the bar in 1894 he joined the firm.[50] Rose was to become known for his care and thoroughness, as well as for his politeness and courtesy. Although he could be austere and aloof, he was generally well liked.[51]

———— ••◦•• ————

THERE CAN BE LITTLE doubt that Tom Blackstock had become a powerful member of the firm, but Beatty was determined to retain his position as managing partner. He remembered well his tussle with Blackstock over compensation. If he was to maintain his place in the firm, he needed a trustworthy assistant to deal with matters that arose in his absence. He turned to the hard-working farm lad from Elora, David Fasken. David's new role is reflected in some correspondence Beatty had with George Bennett, the local agent of Ocean Accident & Guarantee Corporation of London, England, in 1896.[52] Bennett wrote about putting the firm on a retainer. Beatty belatedly responded, apologizing that both he and "our Mr. Fasken to whom all matters of this sort are usually referred" had been away from the city. This is a very telling remark. Retainers with a substantial company would have been very important to the firm. The fact that they were usually referred to Fasken and not to Tom Blackstock is of significance.

The correspondence with Ocean gives us an insight into law firm economics. What were businesses willing to pay their lawyers in such retainers, and what services did they expect to receive? George Bennett said in his letter of 31 July 1896 that the firm had "been mentioned to [them] in the highest possible terms." As a result, he had been instructed by his general manager to ask if Beatty Blackstock would act as its Toronto solicitors for an annual retainer of $150. For this, Ocean Accident & Guarantee would expect the firm to handle all consultations, opinions, document drafting, collection of outstanding accounts when necessary, and assistance in settling claims as between lawyers.

Beatty replied that he was happy to "note a general retainer" for Ocean but that it would cover only consultations and opinions. If a claim arose that necessitated entering into negotiations with the parties or their solicitors, an additional fee should be paid. Such negotiations could extend for weeks, and Beatty suggested that if such a situation arose, the firm would indicate that it did not consider the work to be "fairly covered by the retainer" and the parties would discuss it and settle on "what charge if any should be made." He also suggested that either party should be at liberty to end the retainer if it considered that the work was either insufficient to justify the amount or copious enough to warrant more.

Bennett replied that the general manager believed the amount of consultation and opinion work alone would not justify a fee of $150 a year and that the initial proposal was the best he could offer. Beatty accepted but added that if the work turned out to merit a greater fee, they would discuss the matter and arrive at an arrangement.

This is a revealing glimpse into the now uncommon retainer arrangement. The obvious advantage for the firm was that it was paid in advance, and the obvious disadvantage was that it might end up doing unpaid work. Beatty's gentle insistence that the parties be at liberty to make suitable arrangements if there was more work than originally contemplated was thus a clever response.

While Blackstock was building litigation expertise within the firm, Beatty added yet another position to those that kept him occupied outside of it.

In 1894 he and William George Gooderham, the eldest of George's sons, engineered a reorganization of the board of Upper Canada College.[53] Both were graduates. Beatty, who was very proud of his years at UCC, was the president of the Old Boys Association, as the alumni group was called. The college administration had been facing serious financial problems for years. The thought was that the college would better prosper if it involved its distinguished alumni in school affairs, thus encouraging them to give generously to the school.

In 1894 a new Act changed the college board, which now was to have five appointees from the lieutenant-governor and four from the Old Boys. Beatty and Gooderham were appointed by the Old Boys along with W.T. Boyd and W.J. McMaster. Four holdovers from the previous board resigned. Beatty and the other members of the newly constituted board did indeed get involved. The next year the entire teaching staff was replaced and many new policies adopted.[54] Standards were raised and a new emphasis was placed on better aligning the college curriculum with that of the university. Modern languages were stressed, as were the sciences.

—◦◆◦—

BEATTY KEPT ADDING OUTSIDE involvements, such as UCC, but one client he did keep was the Board of Trade. In the last few years of the nineteenth century the Board provided Beatty with his only publication. It had established a Chamber of Arbitration, which had been conducting arbitrations between its members for some time. Beatty, as counsel to the Board, wanted to attract arbitrations from non-members under the new *Boards of Trade General Arbitrations Act* of 1894. The preamble to the new Act stated that the Board's previous experience in arbitration justified "its extension to persons and corporations other than members of the Board" and that this system of arbitration and its advantages should be extended "to other cities where Boards of Trade have been established, in case such boards desire to avail themselves of this Act." Beatty and Nesbitt wrote a guide and forms book to familiarize people with the Act and to facilitate their use of it.[55] While Nesbitt, as an experienced counsel, undoubtedly wrote much of the book, it is clear that Beatty had shaped the tenor of the remarks, writing an introduction that reads like the work of a businessman and corporate lawyer (and an unrealistic one at that):

The majority of cases . . . may be finally disposed of in a couple of hours. There will be no lingering about courts day after day waiting for a hearing. . . . Forensic displays will not be encouraged, nor will the practice of cross-examination be permitted to be abused, the conduct of the Chamber being under the control of men of business "anxious to get at facts, and arrive at a common sense conclusion as speedily as may be, with due regard to efficiency." . . . [T]here will necessarily be a vast reduction in expense. . . . The entire proceedings of the Chamber will be considered strictly private and confidential . . . .

Beatty and the Board did their best to have another piece of legislation passed in 1894, a federal bankruptcy act.[56] Provincial debtor–creditor and winding-up legislation existed, but Beatty knew only too well that it was not the comprehensive legislation necessary to deal with insolvent debtors, especially in situations where the insolvent party did business in more than one province. After representations from the Board, Mackenzie Bowell introduced the sought-after bankruptcy act in the Senate, but it was never passed. It was not until 1920 that the Canadian parliament enacted the law that Beatty had tried hard to get.

BEATTY AND RIDDELL WERE chosen to attend the third annual Congress of the Chambers of Commerce of the Empire in London in 1896 as Toronto Board of Trade delegates, but a region closer to Toronto was proving more important to the Board and the firm. In 1884 the boundary between Ontario and Quebec had been settled and Ontario was given a large tract of land stretching from North Bay to James Bay. The Toronto Board of Trade was approached by delegations from the new communities of Haileybury and New Liskeard to assist in encouraging settlement in their "Little England," located in the Clay Belt west of Lake Temiskaming.[57] The Toronto business community recognized the importance of claiming this region as part of its hinterland. French-speaking Quebeckers, following the new Canadian Pacific Railway line out of Montreal, had already started to move into the area.

The Ontario government supported this goal and wanted to open the region to farming and the timber industry. It decided to build the Temiskaming and Northern Ontario Railway (T&NOR as it was then referred to, or the Ontario Northland Railway, as it has come to be known) to facilitate settlement and build a strong link between the region and Toronto. In 1897 the president of the Board, J.F. Ellis, said of the T&NOR, "I believe that it will prove of inestimable value in developing and settling the fertile wheat lands of New Ontario and the West — lands that are now practically valueless because of the want of railway facilities. Ontario and particularly Toronto will be the great gainers."[58]

To further settlement, the land around Lake Temiskaming was surveyed and townships delineated. Many of the new townships were named after members of the Board of Trade. To record the contribution of the law firm, three of the new townships were named after its members: Beatty (near Cochrane), Blackstock (on the shore of Night Hawk Lake in the Cochrane district), and Fasken (on the northern boundary of the Timiskaming District, southeast of Timmins and just west of Kirkland Lake). In 1890 the Royal Commission on Northern Resources was established and a delegation from the Board of Trade visited the mines in the Sudbury area, the first of many such delegations to go north over the next few years. The development of the mineral resources of northern Ontario was soon to reshape the firm.

For a time the Gooderhams considered buying one or more of the companies that had started to mine copper and nickel in the Sudbury basin but ultimately decided against it. Although Wallace Nesbitt personally invested in the Copper Company of Canada, which would eventually merge into Inco, the Gooderhams looked west. Tom had maintained his interest in the region and now focused it on several mines in the BC interior along the border with the United States. In the early 1890s gold, silver, and copper had been found in the Kootenays. Later lead mining would also develop. The Canadian Pacific Railway had linked British Columbia with central Canada and Tom became a frequent traveller on the CPR, visiting the small mining town of Rossland, near Red Mountain, and nearby Trail, along the Columbia River.

In January 1897 Tom Blackstock and George Gooderham's eldest son, William George Gooderham, put together a syndicate that included Beatty and Senator George Albertus Cox.[59] They paid $850,000 to buy the War Eagle gold mine and its associated mines, known as the Poorman, the Iron Mask, and the Virginia. Tom was given the task of overseeing these investments. He feared that War Eagle would be forced to pay exorbitant rates for shipping ore and for its refining, later explaining that "mining is in the nature of a manufacturing business which requires the utmost economy in every detail to enable it to be carried out successfully upon a large scale."[60] Frederick Augustus Heinze of Butte, Montana, had built a smelter at the mouth of Trail Creek, about ten kilometres from the Red Mountain mines, and a narrow gauge railroad to connect the mines to his plant. From the tone of Tom's letters, it seems that he found Heinze aggressive and demanding. In late November 1897, when Tom learned that the CPR was planning to buy out Heinze, he had a new concern. He wrote to Sir Richard Cartwright, the federal minister in Ottawa, that he feared "we shall have to pay the piper in some way."[61] Tom was concerned that the price the CPR would have to pay to buy out Heinze would drive up freight and smelter charges and that if the CPR had a monopoly, those costs would be passed along to War Eagle.

Tom expected the federal government to "bonus" the CPR for building a line from Robson to Penticton and wanted it to insist on reasonable freight and smelter rates for commercial customers using the line. He assured Cartwright that "the Camp will . . . certainly amply repay your looking after its interest." The next month he renewed his request that any bonus be conditional upon the CPR setting a rate of $7.00 per ton for freight and treatment for Rossland ores.[62] A few days later Tom wrote to Thomas Shaughnessy, vice-president of the CPR, assuring him that he and his group favoured the CPR buyout of Heinze but again seeking assurance of a $7.00 per ton rate.[63] The same day he wrote to federal minister of railways A.G. Blair to point out that the ownership group he headed had more "hard cash" invested in that country than did Heinze[64] — over a million dollars. And they were prepared to invest even more money "if we receive any reasonable encouragement."

In January 1898, frustrated at the lack of response from the government, Tom wrote to Sir Wilfrid Laurier personally. Unlike the typewritten letters to the others, this was a handwritten note on War Eagle stationery. He enclosed the other correspondence and ended with the following:

> The American Smelter built at Northport to treat Rossland ores is offering better rates than either Heintze [sic] or the CPR. What does it profit the B.C. miner that the Govt spend millions on Branch lines in B.C. when American Roads and Smelters without State and Federal aid will offer us better terms than our own state-aided enterprises? It is obvious that the money has not been spent for the miner.[65]

Laurier's response makes it clear that Tom Blackstock was an important, influential man whose concerns were to be taken seriously. The prime minister assured Tom that he personally would be "very glad to see you any day that may be at your convenience."[66]

The negotiations must have gone well because in April 1898 the Gooder-ham–Blackstock syndicate bought another Rossland area mine, the Centre Star, and its associated mine, the Idaho, for $2 million. They incorporated the Centre Star Mining Company, Limited, with George Gooderham as titular president and Tom as vice-president to hold their interest. Shortly thereafter, in October 1898, they incorporated a sister company, the War Eagle Con-solidated Mining and Development Company, to hold their other mining interests in the area. George Gooderham was listed as a director and Tom as president.

Mining was a labour-intensive endeavour and the hours were long and hard. Strikes pushing for an eight-hour work day were launched in other areas of the province in 1899 and 1900, part of a wider wave of labour unrest that was affecting railroads and mines in British Columbia and manufactur-ing in Ontario. In reaction the federal government adopted the *Conciliation Act* in 1900, trying to encourage conciliated settlements.

Then, in 1901, labour problems arose at Rossland. Tom telegraphed Lau-rier on 12 July saying, "Miners have struck at Rossland. Managers say quite useless attempt rebuild working force until fully protected. Will government guarantee protection before any overt act violence committed? If not, mines will have to close completely."[67]

Blackstock was asking Laurier to bring in the militia to protect any re-placement workers. But he did not rely solely on government intervention. On behalf of the Gooderham–Blackstock syndicate he took legal action. The *Trade Union Act, 1872* had granted workers immunity from being prosecuted for criminal conspiracy in combining in a union to improve working condi-tions. Nevertheless, employers were still able to bring a civil action alleging that workers were engaged in an unlawful conspiracy in restraint of trade or that the union was inducing workers to breach their contracts of em-ployment. By October, Blackstock's BC counsel had obtained an injunction against the union and had started a legal action in the name of each of their companies against the Western Federation of Miners (WFM) for damages suffered in the strike.[68]

Laurier, recognizing the political sensitivity of the issue, referred the matter to his new Department of Labour and its recently appointed and quite young deputy minister, William Lyon Mackenzie King. King, as a for-mer strike leader at the University of Toronto, was something of a social reform expert. He had done graduate work in industrial relations at Chicago, Harvard, and the London School of Economics and had authored several papers.[69] He believed in conciliation, in listening to the two sides and, once fully informed, guiding them to a settlement. In doing so he relied upon the *Conciliation Act*. His goal was to get the workers back on the job; he encouraged management to address worker concerns and workers to return to work while he mediated a settlement. He came at his new role with sympathy for the working man and a desire to effect social change.

Nevertheless, when he personally travelled to Rossland, what he recorded in his diaries sounded much like what Tom Blackstock had been preaching: "All of Canada can learn from BC; the province speaks a note of warning in strongest terms against the dangers of labour democracy. Industry will be fettered and the source of wages and wealth left undeveloped, if change does not come. Where men without a stake rule those who have everything to lose, or at least at risk, the alarm is great."[70]

On his return to Ottawa, King came out against the strikers, or at least against those who defied the injunction to return to work. Again he confided his thoughts to his diary: "I have at least been fearless and honest in this exposé of Rossland proceedings . . . . It is the first time I have had to come out against the workingman and it pained me to do it, but if the cause is to prosper honesty must characterize it."[71]

One wonders if King was being completely honest with himself. Did it occur to him that he might have been prejudiced to some extent by his personal relationship with the lawyers of Beatty Blackstock? Did their defence of him at the 1895 Commission of Inquiry influence him to support Tom Blackstock?

The Rossland strike was an early sign that the world of business was changing and that from this point forward labour relations would be an important aspect of business and of business law. Tom Blackstock learned that lesson. Even after the strike was settled at the end of January 1902, War Eagle and Centre Star continued their legal actions for damages. He wanted a clear legal precedent — strikers were to be held liable for the damages they caused to their employers. The Centre Star case took two years but this Gooderham–Blackstock company won $12,500 in damages. The War Eagle then settled for $1,000 in the spring of 1905. By then the local chapter of WFM had gone bankrupt.[72]

While these labour troubles were being dealt with, Tom petitioned the federal government to encourage the development of lead mining and smelting in British Columbia. He made "an urgent plea for a bounty on lead refining."[73] Although he was willing to accept limits on the amount, its duration, and the tonnage to which it would apply, he was confident that much benefit would accrue to other mining interests from such a policy. Laurier agreed.

As if Tom Blackstock did not have enough to worry about, his younger brother George was going from bad to worse. Following his divorce in 1898, he became quite unstable. Specialists in Toronto and in New York, including Dr. Daniel Clark of the Provincial Lunatic Asylum, suggested that he be committed. Eventually Tom went along with these recommendations, saying that his brother was to be lodged in a mental institution "out of which he cannot come for a period of years unless cured and until then I do not wish to hear more about him for I am wearied beyond expression by the whole business."[74]

THERE WERE TWO POSITIVE notes for Beatty and the firm in 1898. Three years after being called to the bar Beatty's second son, Charles William, joined the firm. Significantly, Charley Beatty was also George Gooderham's son-in-law, having married Lillian May Gooderham two years earlier.[75] Second, Nesbitt, whose first wife, Louise, had died in 1894, married Amy Gertrude, Beatty's third child and oldest daughter, thus becoming Beatty's son-in-law.[76] So Beatty ended the century with both his son and his son-in-law practising with him in the firm.

By 1901 Tom Blackstock had become "one of the best known members of the Ontario Bar."[77] But, as often happens, becoming well known outside the firm meant that he was spending less time within it. The correspondence we have from him in those years suggests that he had, in fact, moved his office across the street from the Bank of Toronto building into the Gooderham ("Flatiron") Building. That structure had been built in 1892 and it was where George Gooderham had his personal office as well as the offices of the various companies that he controlled.[78] Tom had stationery printed showing an address of the "Gooderham Buildings, Cable Blackstock Toronto."[79] Moving between the two buildings would have been easy. The Bank of Toronto head office and the Gooderham Building were connected by an underground tunnel that he and Gooderham must have used many times.[80]

These days, however, Tom was in neither Toronto office. He had already been taking trips to British Columbia to deal with the mining companies and to Ottawa to lobby the government. Now he was off to Italy and other parts of Europe to personally choose marble and other materials for his newest project. About the time that Tom was overseeing the construction of the family homes, business people in Toronto had begun to talk of the advantages of having a premier hotel at the corner of King and Victoria. Montreal had the Windsor Hotel and Quebec the Chateau Frontenac, but Toronto lacked a "palace hotel." George Gooderham provided the funding, and Beatty was an incorporator and a first director. But it was Tom who became the president of the King Edward Hotel Company and who personally oversaw the work of the firm's client and noted architect, E.J. Lennox, along with the construction itself.[81]

Beatty, too, was often out of the office. In 1901 he added the presidency of the Canadian Niagara Power Company to his many outside business interests and in 1902 he became the president of Confederation Life. The power company was in the process of building the world's most advanced hydroelectric power plant, in Queen Victoria Niagara Falls Park on the Niagara River. Beatty's son-in-law, Wallace Nesbitt, had represented the company in an 1898 lawsuit to uphold the monopoly contract that it had signed in 1892 to generate power on the Canadian side of the river.[82] Now Beatty was taking a role in the company. As with his other presidencies, he was not tasked with running the company. As its vice-president the American lawyer William B. Rankine had more responsibility for day-to-day operations. But it is unlikely that Beatty's position was a sinecure. It was not in his nature to leave management of an enterprise entirely to others. Perhaps as some evidence of his importance in the company, on 2 January 1905 when the powerhouse was officially opened it was Beatty who turned the switch for the first of the 10,000-horsepower generators.[83]

Here, too, Beatty wanted to have his own man in the company. He arranged for Munro Grier to leave the firm to become the secretary and in-house solicitor to the power company.[84] There was an irony in his position. Twenty-five years before, Grier had attended performances of Gilbert and Sullivan at the Savoy in London, the first theatre to be lit by electricity. He later remarked that if someone had told him at the time that he would become personally involved in the development of power "made simply by means of tumbling water" — and that the electricity produced would be enough to illuminate myriad theatres — he would never have believed it.[85]

———◦◦◦◦———

THESE BUSINESS SUCCESSES OUTSIDE the firm meant that within the firm the era of Beatty and Blackstock was coming to an end. Although in theory Beatty was the managing partner, he was leaving matters to others. His wife, Lotty,

David Fasken as President of Excelsior Life
Photo courtesy of Aetna Canada

later remarked that "after a trip out of town, [my husband] had to be taken around and introduced to his new partners."[86] So who was running the firm? It was not Tom Blackstock. Like Beatty before him, Tom had ceased to be a lawyer in any meaningful sense and was now a businessman. The person running the firm was Beatty's trusted Methodist farmboy, David Fasken. By this point, however, David certainly knew his way around the law office and the boardroom. He had administrative abilities, drive, and ambition beyond those of his colleagues at the firm. As one biographer later said, "His out-standing traits were a capacity for sustained and concentrated effort, close attention to detail, and absolutely unprejudiced weighing of facts."[87]

Fasken's role in the development of Excelsior Life Insurance Company is very revealing of his business judgment and opportunism. In the late 1880s a number of members of the Orange Lodge had incorporated a provincial company that they called the Protestant Life Insurance Company. Shortly thereafter they approached David Fasken about becoming its legal counsel. He agreed and bought ten shares in the new, as yet unorganized company, becoming a member of its board.[88] One of the first pieces of advice he gave to his new client was to change its name. Drawing their inspiration from

Longfellow's poem "Excelsior," they settled on the Excelsior Life Insurance Company.[89]

The company got off to a slow start, but Fasken saw potential. When it needed funds in 1893, Fasken was one of five directors who arranged and guaranteed a $5,500 loan from the Bank of Toronto. In 1895 he bought an additional five shares and encouraged George Gooderham to buy sixty. Then, in 1898, a takeover was rumoured. Rather than have a third party acquire control, Fasken approached disgruntled shareholders and bought up many of the shares of the struggling company on his own behalf and on behalf of Gooderham. Fasken personally ended up with 1,896 of the 5,000 shares, at a cost of about $30,000, and Gooderham acquired an additional 813. Their shares together gave Fasken control. On 13 February 1900 he was elected president, a position he was to hold until his death. He worked in the law office during the day and helped direct the company's operations in the evenings.

By 1901 David Fasken was already well established. That year he was having a stately home constructed on Queen Street East in the Beaches under the watchful eye of E.J. Lennox, who had become the architect of choice for all firm-related projects. His new house was to feature a Greek temple–like façade facing Queen Street with a series of paired giant columns supporting a large, impressive pediment.[90] Nor was this his only home. Six years earlier he had bought a 300-acre (120-hectare) farm in Clarkson that included a large stone house built in 1820 by Colonel Adamson, a veteran of Wellington's Peninsular War. David had extensively renovated the house for his use.[91]

Fasken may have had a new house, but he seems to have had little desire to spend much time in it. Unlike Beatty and Chadwick, whose marriages had been so influential in their professional advancement, he had married badly. After graduating from Elora High School, he and his cousin George had been able to convince their parents that they should be the first in the family to go to university. They enrolled at the University of Toronto and moved to the city. The family provided a small allowance for Fasken but there was nothing left for sports or concerts, or even transportation. Fasken walked everywhere.[92] During those early years in Toronto, he boarded with two sisters who were older than he was.[93] Although engaged to Nellie Bye in Elora, David had an affair with Alice Winstanley, one of his landladies. When she became pregnant, duty and honour dictated that he marry her, which he did in 1891. The baby, Mary Isabel, was born 24 February 1892 but died just over three months later. David found himself in a loveless marriage, mourning the death of his first child. He and his wife did have another child in 1893, a son, Robert Alexander. As soon as the child was born David enrolled him in the Toronto Model School, but Robert did not do well in school and David soon realized his son was not likely to follow in his footsteps.[94] In fact, Robert was to be a regular source of trouble and concern for his father. So David turned away from his family and focused his considerable energy and attention on the law firm and his business ventures.

Like Tom Blackstock before him, David Fasken evidenced his new power in the firm by arranging in 1901 for his younger brother, Alex, to join him. At first glance this addition might have seemed in keeping with the nature and history of the firm. There were already many family connections. But those families had been prominent, Conservative, Anglican, Toronto families. The Fasken family was quite different and Alex Fasken, the youngest of nine children, would prove especially disruptive. He had been born on the family farm ten and a half years after David, on 27 June 1871. Like David, he entered the University of Toronto, graduating in 1891 with a BA.[95] Alex then went to Osgoode Hall Law School, where he studied under the firm's failed partner, W.A. Reeve, who proved to be a better academic and pedagogue than lawyer.[96] Alex did not article with his brother's firm but with Cassels and Standish, and on his call to the bar in 1894 he opened a sole practice in Fergus, Ontario.[97] The letterhead for "Alex. Fasken, B.A. Barrister, Solicitor, Notary Public and Conveyancer" stated, "Money to loan at lowest rates." Alex had neither the legal reputation of Nesbitt or Riddell nor the political connections of Biggar, nor the social standing of Galt or Rose. His sole qualification for joining Beatty Blackstock was that he was the younger brother of David Fasken, but in 1901 that was enough.

David needed his brother to play the role in the firm that he himself had played for Beatty. Like Beatty and Blackstock before him, the older Fasken brother was finding himself out of the office regularly. His younger brother may not have been the best lawyer, but he was a trustworthy, careful, diligent person who could look to day-to-day operations in David's absence. But if Alex, a junior member of the firm, was to play that role he needed to know what the more senior people were doing, and in the early years of the twentieth century that meant having access to the mail. So, in 1903, the Fasken brothers added a note to the firm's letterhead requesting that all letters be addressed to the firm and that all cheques be made payable to the firm. The note went on to explain that members of the firm were frequently absent, and thus letters addressed to them might be delayed.

To justify what many partners would have seen as an intrusion into their practice and their personal lives, the brothers undoubtedly pointed out that many of the firm's fourteen lawyers were seldom in the office or even in Toronto. Certainly Beatty and Blackstock were busy elsewhere and Chadwick was increasingly disabled and distracted. George Blackstock was out of the mental institution but now living at the Waldorf Astoria (at Tom's expense) and "working" in New York, as counsel to the Beatty Blackstock firm.[98] When not in New York, George was in Quebec City or London, where he was wined and dined by the cream of society. In the United Kingdom, the conservative Unionist Party regularly called on him to campaign on their behalf and several times pressed him to run for Parliament. What George and the others did not do much of was spend time in Toronto working at the firm.

— ◆ —

WHILE DAVID WAS TRYING to secure his place in the firm through his brother, Riddell was trying to help his much-loved Liberal Party weather a threatening political storm. In late 1902 there was a particularly close provincial election. Sir George William Ross's Liberal government was barely returned to power. Almost immediately the Conservative MP for Manitoulin, Robert Roswell Gamey, made a surprising announcement — he would support the Liberals. Then, when the legislature convened in March 1903, Gamey rescinded his statement. In fact he went further, asserting that his earlier pronouncement of support had been purchased by the Liberal Party secretary, J.R. Stratton.

This raised a hue and cry both inside and outside the legislature. By April, Premier Ross felt compelled to establish a royal commission into the allegations of bribery. Chancellor Boyd of the old Chancery Court and Chief Justice Falconbridge were appointed as commissioners for what became known as the Gamey Commission. Riddell was one of three counsel retained by the Liberal Party to defend Stratton.[99] The Commission sat for 27 days, hearing evidence from 119 witnesses who gave 3,512 pages of testimony. In the end, Riddell and his co-counsel could claim victory. The commissioners found that the evidence was contradictory and irreconcilable and would not support a finding of guilt against Stratton or the Liberal Party.[100]

Riddell's joy in his victory was tempered by his unhappiness with what was happening in the firm. Much of what David wanted was a harbinger of changes that were coming to the profession, a move to a more business-like approach. Change is always difficult but this was aggravated by the character of the person whom David chose to implement his changes. David called his brother "Dutch" and knew him as a fishing companion and a skilful administrative assistant. Others, like Riddell, saw Alex very differently. These were proud, accomplished "gentlemen." They found Alex gruff, presumptuous, and demanding, and he did not give them the respect they expected. A long-time acquaintance described him as "a short, wiry man with a low boiling point."[101] A cousin who would write the Fasken family history tells us that Alex "being the youngest . . . soon became the baby tyrant of the family, . . . and he carried this tyrannical characteristic with him throughout the rest of his life, demanding to his very last day immediate and complete obedience to his every whim from associates, family and all business firms with which he had dealings."[102]

One of the people who could not abide Alex was Nesbitt. Beatty's son-in-law could see that the days of his father-in-law as the dominant managing partner were at an end, and he had no desire to stay around to be managed by the Fasken brothers. But what was he to do? He did not want to hurt his father-in-law by joining a rival firm. The death of Justice David Mills of the Supreme Court of Canada on 8 May 1903 offered Nesbitt a way out.[103] Just over a week later, on 16 May 1903, Laurier appointed Nesbitt to the Supreme Court of Canada at the very young age of forty-five.[104] The *Canada Law Journal* noted the "remarkable and commendable promptitude" with which the vacancy had been filled and applauded the appointment of a Conservative by a Liberal administration and especially one "in the prime of life." Knowing nothing of Nesbitt's real motivation, they praised his decision because "no counsel who enjoys a large and lucrative practice . . . can be persuaded to leave and go to the Bench, at least before he reaches an age when his faculties are declining and his strength waning."[105]

Shortly after Nesbitt's appointment, Riddell wrote to Laurier to indicate that he too would accept a judgeship. He sought the position of Chief Justice of the newly created Exchequer Division of the High Court. He informed Laurier that the minister of justice would be putting his name forward, adding "I shall feel hurt if it is not approved as tho' I were either not a good enough lawyer or a good enough Reformer."[106] Laurier was not swayed and Riddell was passed over.

Nesbitt proved to be an energetic and able judge. He produced a number of well-written and well-analyzed judgments, often winning the support of

Wallace Nesbitt in his Supreme Court of Canada robes, 1903
LAC

his fellow judges for his views. He did not always reciprocate their high opinion. Some of his dissenting judgments were extremely critical of the majority. One such "dissent" was given in a case presented to the Supreme Court by Nesbitt's former partners, George Blackstock and Riddell. The firm's client had received what it perceived as a promise from a supplier that it would always get the lowest wholesale price. When the client learned that others were getting a lower price, it retained the firm to sue the supplier. The trial judge had held that there was no contract, only an unenforceable intent. The Court of Appeal had agreed. At the Supreme Court, Justice Nesbitt gave what has to qualify as one of the oddest concurring judgments of that Court:

> Had it not been that no useful purpose is attained by dissenting, I should
> have held that, in my view, the contract was based upon the agreement that
> an export stock should be established and maintained in Montreal and after-
> wards in Toronto. I do not think it was intention; I think it was bargain and
> I view the case as just one more instance of a party suffering for the gen-
> eral good by the enforcement of the salutary rule that business men should
> be careful to have their understandings in writing . . . . [N]o matter how
> strongly one represents he intends to do so or so and induces another to act

to his prejudice, he can, in breach of all principles governing men of common honesty, abandon his intentions. Such is the law, apparently, but I would unhesitatingly say, here, it was not intention but bargain. However, as the majority are for affirming I concur, as I assume I must be in error in my view.[107]

In late 1904 the Fasken brothers set out to fill the hole created by the departure of Nesbitt. They knew that there were other good lawyers like themselves who were practising in smaller communities outside Toronto. One such was James Pitt Mabee, a litigation counsel with extensive political experience.[108] Mabee was born in Port Rowan, Ontario, in 1859. A graduate of the University of Toronto, he was called to the bar in 1882 at the age of twenty-three. After practising for five years in Listowel, he moved to Stratford, where he entered into partnership with F.W. Gearing.[109] He was made a QC in 1899. A prominent Liberal, he served as president of the Stratford Liberal Club and ran unsuccessfully in the federal election of November 1904. He did, however, win election as a bencher of the Law Society. When the Faskens approached him, he agreed to move his practice to Toronto and join the partnership.

Mabee promptly proved to his new partners that he was well connected when, on 7 January 1905, Prime Minister Laurier named him first chairman of the International Waterways Commission, created to deal with boundary water disputes. His career at the firm was off to a good start but it was to be short lived. Whether he, too, could not get along with Alex Fasken or it was just a case of a better offer coming along, in November 1905, after only ten months with the firm, he was appointed by Laurier to the Ontario High Court. In 1908 he would become chairman of the Railway Commission, considered to be "next to the position of a Cabinet Minister."[110]

In retrospect Mabee was not the most important addition in 1904. That distinction must be reserved for a young student — Lionel Davis.[111] What makes Davis's addition both significant and intriguing is that he was a member of one of the oldest Jewish families in Toronto.[112] Russian-born Isaac Davis, Lionel's grandfather, had been a dry goods merchant in Toronto in the 1850s.[113] Lionel's father, Henry, carried on the family business as the Henry Davis Company. Although Lionel would ultimately take over the business, he trained to be a lawyer. He began the five-year program required of those without a university degree, attending Osgoode Hall and clerking with the firm.

Lionel Davis
Law Society of Upper Canada Archives, Osgoode Hall Law School fonds
"Law School Osgoode Hall, final year 1909," P443

How did a young Jewish man come to join the firm? It was probably at the suggestion of one of its clients, Sigmund Samuel, a leader of the Toronto Jewish community. Samuel would become a lifelong friend of David Fasken and serve as a pallbearer at his funeral. Following in his father's footsteps, Samuel promoted civil rights for members of the Jewish community. Might he have reminded Fasken that he himself, as a Methodist farmboy, had been an outsider who benefited from joining the Beatty firm? Could he not do the same for young Davis? We know that Samuel and Fasken did many things together. Samuel later recruited Fasken for the new museum board and Fasken would, in turn, recruit Samuel for the board of Toronto Western Hospital. Davis seemed to be one more means by which Fasken was seeking to change the old ways.

⸻✦⸻

By the time that Mabee and Davis joined the firm in 1904, Tom Blackstock was seriously ill. His frequent travels and many responsibilities had taken their toll. As early as July 1903 he wrote to his mother from Rossland, trying to reassure her: "I had a pleasant journey out and am comfortably settled in my own room here . . . . I am taking particularly good care of myself in diet, exercise and rest. The various interests at present dependent upon me are such as to make it impossible for me to take even the slightest liberties with myself."[114] Nevertheless, he contracted typhoid, which led to nephritis, which in turn led to blindness. He was confined to bed, unable to do anything inside the firm or out.

This presented a serious problem for the family businesses because George Gooderham died on 1 May 1905.[115] Tom, who had been his right-hand man and was to have assumed his father-in-law's responsibilities, was unable to do so. As had happened years before when Worts had been unable to direct the businesses after William Gooderham's death, much of the weight of responsibility fell on the already burdened Beatty. Now he became the president of both the Bank of Toronto and the Canada Permanent. Although his name continued to appear first on the firm's letterhead until his death seven years later, he ceased to have any active involvement in the firm after Gooderham's death.

One of the first things Beatty did was to sell the BC mining interests. In June 1905 the *Monetary Times* reported that the sale had been necessitated by the death of George Gooderham and "the enforced temporary retirement from business of Mr. Blackstock." Blackstock and the Gooderham estate sold their controlling interest in the War Eagle, St. Eugene and Centre Star mines to a syndicate of Toronto, Montreal, and New York capitalists representing the Canadian Pacific Railway for $825,000, a fraction of what the Gooderham–Blackstock syndicate had put into these properties. The next year Beatty as president of the Bank of Toronto closed the bank's branch in Rossland.[116]

Beatty knew that he could not long play this expanded role in the family businesses. He began to prepare for the future by tutoring William George Gooderham and Albert Edward Gooderham, the two oldest sons of George Gooderham, in business with the thought that they would assume their father's role on his own retirement. On George Gooderham's death, each had become a substantial shareholder in Gooderham & Worts. William George became its president and Albert Edward its managing director. William George left the running of the distillery business largely to his brother, putting his time and energy into other family businesses, namely the Bank of Toronto, Canada Permanent Mortgage Corporation, and Manufacturers Life Insurance Company. He had been a director of the Bank of Toronto from 1881 and a director of Canada Permanent from 1889. From 1905 to 1910 he served under Beatty at both Canada Permanent and the Bank of Toronto.

Once Beatty ceased to be active in the law firm, his son-in-law Nesbitt resigned from the Supreme Court on 4 October 1905, for "reasons purely private."[117] Significantly he did not return to the firm but instead approached McCarthy Osler, which was happy to work out an arrangement with him. Its two leading litigators, D'Alton McCarthy and Britton Bath Osler, had both died, McCarthy in a carriage accident in 1898 and Osler of a heart attack in 1901.[118] Nesbitt offered litigation expertise and profile that they had been lacking, but as a retired judge there was some question about whether he could join a law firm.[119] In any event, Nesbitt wanted a level of independence. He did not want to take orders from his new firm any more than he had wanted to be dictated to by the Fasken brothers. His agreement with McCarthy Osler made him counsel to the firm. They provided him with office space and secretarial support and first right of refusal on all work to be referred to an outside counsel. In return, he would give McCarthy Osler all of his solicitors' work. He drew no revenue from the firm nor did he share any with them.[120] He continued his distinguished career, becoming treasurer of the Law Society in 1927.[121]

Tom Blackstock's "enforced . . . retirement from business" was not temporary, as the *Monetary Times* had hoped. He died in June 1906.

⟶ ⟶◈⟵ ⟵

DEATH HAD ALSO TOUCHED the Chadwick family. Chadwick's diary for 10 January 1905 and the days following are filled with the illness, death, funeral, burial, and memorials for his much-loved daughter Marion, known as Fanny, whom he called "the light and life of our family." A century later she is still remembered in the arts community as one of the first actors, playwrights, and producers of stage plays in Toronto.[122] Chadwick was devastated. He continued to come into the office to administer several estates, but his days as a full-time, active member of the firm were drawing to an end.[123]

His diaries for 1905–6 stand as evidence of his many outside activities. There is a clipping of a news item regarding his donation of an illuminated buffalo robe to the provincial museum. There is also reference to his heading a delegation of United Empire Loyalists to the Ontario government to lobby for monuments to Colonel John Macdonell, killed at Queenston Heights, and to Tecumseh.[124] On 13 April 1906 Chadwick tells us, "I had to go to present the Bishop with a pastoral staff which, after several years of gathering gems and material, has been in the course of manufacture, from my design and under my supervision for the past three months." The staff had been manufactured by Beatty's Toronto Silver Plate Company.

Health was also on the mind of David Fasken in 1906, but not his own or his family's. His concern was more general and philanthropic. In that year he was approached by his friend and colleague Dr. John Ferguson to assist in erecting a new building for the Toronto Western Hospital. Ferguson had been one of the founders and was the chief medical officer of the Excelsior Life Insurance Company, of which David was legal counsel, a large shareholder, and president. In 1899 Fasken's partner Riddell had been one of the original sponsors of the hospital when it was incorporated as a public hospital. Now Ferguson hoped that Fasken could help to raise funds for its new building. Fasken himself provided the funding for the 1906 addition to the modest original building. It was but the first of many ways in which he would help the hospital, forging a triangular link that would exist for a century between Excelsior Life, Toronto Western, and the Faskens firm.[125]

————

WHILE THE SKIRMISH BETWEEN Nesbitt and the Fasken brothers was going on, Beatty was fighting a legal battle over the land north of Lake Superior that he and John Leys had acquired decades before. In the fall of 1903 Beatty was approached by a Mr. Gregory.[126] Gregory indicated that he was acting on behalf of Mr. McConnell, who wished to buy the property that Beatty and Leys had purchased in 1871. Gregory noticed, however, that the title to the property was clouded. In the 1880s Beatty, or perhaps more likely John Leys, had let the taxes fall into arrears. The result was that the property had been sold by the province for back taxes to Thomas Bull in 1887 along with a large number of other properties. Bull did not obtain a clear title, however, but instead received a series of tax certificates that entitled him to have the title registered in his name if Beatty and Leys did not redeem the property by paying the back taxes. In 1889, when this came to Beatty's attention, he asked Leys to deal with the problem. Leys purchased the tax certificates from Bull and delivered them to Beatty, who placed them in his file with the title deeds and, thinking that he had resolved the problem, forgot about the matter. Gregory seems to have tried to convince Beatty that he should accept a lower price because Bull was still shown in the Ontario Treasurer's records as the purchaser of the property. But Beatty had already granted a Mr. Longworthy an option on the property exercisable for $7,500.

When Gregory was unable to purchase from Beatty, he went to Bull, who had no recollection of either his original purchase or his sale of the tax certificates. At Gregory's suggestion Bull petitioned the Ontario Treasurer to execute a deed of sale for this property and certain others to perfect Bull's title acquired at the tax sale. Why the Treasurer did so without requiring Bull to deliver the tax certificates is unclear but nevertheless he did so. Bull then sold the property to McConnell.

Meanwhile, Beatty took legal advice. He learned that once he had purchased the tax certificates, he ought to have surrendered them to the Provincial Treasurer and obtained clear title. He also learned that because Bull had not had a deed registered in his name within eighteen months of the tax sale, his claim to the property could be defeated by "a purchaser in good faith who has registered his deed prior to the registration of the deed from the . . . treasurer."[127] Like any good lawyer, Beatty turned his mind to how he could fit himself within the statutory exception. He needed a good faith purchaser. He decided to sell the property to his brother, Joe. He could not share his purpose with his brother, as to do so would have rendered the sale pointless. It was crucial that his brother be considered to be acting in good faith and not colluding with Beatty to defeat the rival claim.

How was Beatty to structure the purchase? He decided to offer the property to his brother for $7,500, the value of the option granted earlier to Longworthy. The purchase price would be satisfied by a promissory note. In this way Joe Beatty did not have to pay anything at the time but if Longworthy exercised the option Beatty could call upon the note and receive the option price. On 6 November 1903 Beatty registered the deed to his brother. The deed recording Bull's title was not registered until 14 December. Beatty had come up with a highly technical argument that would not withstand much judicial scrutiny,[128] but it might give someone otherwise inclined to side with Beatty a basis upon which to do so.

If Beatty thought he had won the day, he was wrong. Notwithstanding the registration in favour of J.W. Beatty, the sale from Bull to McConnell proceeded. Beatty decided to take legal action. George Tate Blackstock, out of the mental institution and back in Toronto, Wallace Nesbitt (now an independent counsel working from the offices of McCarthy Osler), and Percy Galt were charged with asserting Beatty's claim, or more properly his brother's claim, to the property. They brought an action in Joe Beatty's name to set aside the tax sale deed and subsequent conveyance and to recover possession of the lands. The defendants were McConnell, Bull, and Gregory. They also sought permission of the court to add the Attorney General of Ontario as a co-plaintiff. At trial the Deputy Attorney General appeared and consented to this motion.

In addition to the technical argument concerning the good faith purchaser, Beatty's legal team alleged fraud and misrepresentation. But the evidence available to support these allegations was slim. Beatty himself appeared as the key witness for the plaintiffs. Unfortunately John Leys had died and could not give evidence. Beatty's counsel convinced the judge to admit, over objections from defence counsel, certain letters from Leys to Beatty written in 1889–90 in connection with the purchase of the tax certificates from Bull. Bull and his agent, a Mr. Ledyard, were called as witnesses but did not recall anything of the transaction with Leys. The only evidence of the transaction besides the Leys correspondence was unearthed during the trial itself when the Ontario Treasurer's office found a letter in its files from Bull dated 26 January 1889 in which he asked the office to return the certificates that he had submitted to obtain the deed because he had agreed to assign them. The letter did not say to whom. When Street J. rendered his judgment, he found the evidence insufficient to demonstrate fraud and flimsy in establishing Beatty's purchase of the tax certificates from Bull: "There is nothing in writing between them, and there is no evidence even, which I am at liberty to consider, that Beatty ever paid Bull any money."

In his first judgment Street J. omitted to deal with the technical argument that the registration of the sale to Joe Beatty had defeated Bull's claim. He was called upon to consider this matter and rendered a supplementary judgment in which he found that Beatty's brother had never been a true purchaser. Beatty himself admitted in cross-examination that he had had no intention of ever calling upon the promissory note unless the Longworthy option was exercised, and Joe Beatty admitted that he had had no interest in the property. He had just left the matter to his brother.[129]

Beatty appealed to the Ontario Court of Appeal. As evidence of the importance of the matter, the Chief Justice of Ontario and four other appeal judges heard the appeal. George Blackstock, who had returned to London, did not participate in the appeal, and Nesbitt and Galt argued it alone. The appeal court decided in Beatty's favour and overturned the trial judgment. Justice Osler stressed that Bull had agreed to be redeemed. The Chief Justice in a separate set of reasons found that the Ontario Treasurer could not have lawfully issued the deed of conveyance to Bull since Bull was not then the holder of the tax certificates.

The defendants again demonstrated the value of the property at stake by appealing to the Judicial Committee of the Privy Council in London. George Blackstock, then in England, took the appeal with an English barrister, W.B. Broderick. Sir Arthur Wilson (one of three members of the Canadian Supreme Court who sat with Lords Robertson and Collins on the bench) found for the appellants, setting aside the decision of the Ontario Court of

Appeal and restoring the trial judgment. Beatty had lost despite his significant efforts and those of his best litigators.

———※———

MEANWHILE, DAVID FASKEN WAS seizing the reins of the firm. He was intent on making changes that would ensure the firm of Beatty Blackstock was all but buried with Tom Blackstock. The Fasken era was about to start. For the first time in the firm's history, the dominant partner would not draw his influence and power from his relationship to the Gooderham and Worts families.

A NEW DIRECTION,
1906–18

IN 1906 BEATTY, AS president of Canada Permanent Mortgage Corporation, issued a warning to his shareholders that was very much in the fiscally conservative tradition of William Gooderham and James Gooderham Worts. Although it was an "unrivalled period of expansion," Beatty noted that "speculation, high prices, extravagant living and extended credits" were prevalent. He advised that it was not a "time for the mariner at the helm of a business ship to throw out a reef in his mainsail, but rather to double-reef it against storms that may be gathering."[1]

David Fasken did not share his mentor's caution. Having mastered business management, he intended to grasp the helm of the law firm and sail it in a new direction as quickly as possible by applying the same principles and rigour. But this was a partnership and he needed his partners' consent. So he began by asking them to commit the terms of their partnership to paper. David wanted the new agreement to give formal recognition to the enormous changes that had occurred in the firm since 1901 — to make it clear that although Beatty and Blackstock remained the first names on the letterhead, he was in charge. Not only would a written agreement have been seen as unnecessary just a few short years earlier, given the ties that knit the partners together, but the precise terms of this 1906 document would never have been acceptable to those partners.

At first it seemed that David would prevail. On 1 September 1906 he convinced Beatty, Chadwick, Riddell, Harper Armstrong, Alex Fasken, and

Hugh Rose to join him in signing a partnership agreement that made them "co-partners" for five years in the practice and profession of barristers, solicitors, and notaries public under the firm name of Beatty, Blackstock, Fasken & Riddell. Unfortunately for David, to be binding the agreement required the signatures of all the partners and two of them, Percy Galt and Ross Gooderham, refused to sign.[2] They saw that David's proposal would give him a level of control that even Beatty had never enjoyed. The elder Fasken was described in the agreement as the "manager of the business of the firm." As such he could decide what line of work was to be undertaken by each partner, severely curtailing their independence. They also saw that they were to dedicate themselves to the practice of law — there were to be no more social butterflies or part-time practitioners who ran other businesses on the side. Partners were no longer to be free to come and go as they pleased. Each would be entitled to one month's holiday during the year. If absent beyond that, the delinquent partner was to pay to the firm such amount for each day as the majority in interest of the partners thought appropriate. Riddell was permitted to take two months without deduction on condition that "if he shall argue any case in England [before the Privy Council] during the said months he shall not claim any extra vacation on that account."

Several of the provisions seem to have been intended to ensure that there would not be another George Blackstock. The agreement stated that no partner was to be a candidate for or contest any municipal, parliamentary, or any other public election and that the practice was to be carried on in the City of Toronto and each partner was required to reside there. Someone like Blackstock who had political aspirations and who spent little time in Toronto was no longer welcome. Ironically it was probably Fasken's insistence on these measures that brought Blackstock back to Toronto and his law practice. In 1906 and 1907 we again see his name as counsel for the firm in several cases that made their way to the Supreme Court of Canada.[3] But his renewed dedication to his Toronto law practice was relatively short lived, and by 1908 he had dropped from sight once again.

Even David Fasken himself was not to be entirely immune from the requirements outlined in the agreement. He was permitted to maintain his arrangement with the Excelsior Life Insurance Company and to receive "the emoluments therefrom," provided that if he looked after the business of that company during the day he had to arrange for a proper retainer to be paid to the law firm to compensate it for his time.

Beatty was shown as a partner but his value was in goodwill: his name and contacts. He would not be required to perform any "actual solicitor work" but was to use "his best endeavours to procure business for the firm" and to "give all of the influence he [could] towards the promotion of the interests of the firm." He was not, however, to interfere with David's operation of the firm. He could retain any fees from acting as a director or trustee and any amounts that he received from any other business outside of the firm with which he might be connected — hardly surprising when one notes that he did not receive any income from the firm. His "emoluments" and "the use of a room at the north east end of the building without charge" were all that he got.[4]

In an attempt to placate Ross Gooderham, the agreement also made special provisions for him. On George Gooderham's death, Ross had been appointed executor of the estate. He was to be permitted to retain any commissions to which he was entitled as executor as well as any director's fees payable to him for serving on any company's board in connection with the estate. He was, however, not to participate in any fees received by the firm from his father's estate.

The net profits of the practice were to be divided among the partners as follows:

1 Of the first $30,000.00 each year, David Fasken and William Renwick Riddell were to receive $8,500.00 each, Alex Fasken $2,500.00, and all others either $2,000.00 or $2,250.00.

2 Profits over $30,000.00 were to be divided in varying percentages depending on the level of profit achieved. For example, if the profits fell between $30,000.00 and $45,000.00, David Fasken and Riddell would each get 35 5/6 percent, but if the profits were over $60,000.00 they received only 22 1/2 percent. In this way Fasken and Riddell would be compensated for the base business that they brought to the firm, but there was some incentive to the younger partners to work hard and bring in new business.

The 1906 draft agreement created a ripple of discontent throughout the firm. Many began to actively seek out other opportunities. With his father no longer active in the firm and David Fasken in charge, Beatty's son, Charles William, left.[5] Young Robert McKay also left. These departures paled in comparison with the loss that occurred on 10 October 1906, however, when Riddell accepted an appointment to the bench.[6] With Nesbitt gone and George

William Renwick Riddell
Law Society of Upper Canada Archives, Archives Department collection
"Photograph of William Renwick Riddell," P785

Blackstock off on his various ventures, Riddell had become the lead litigator, as his proposed compensation made clear. His departure meant that the firm's only litigators were Percy Galt, one of the dissenters, and Hugh Rose. Neither had the reputation or the skills of Nesbitt or Riddell — or George Tate Blackstock at his best.

Justice Riddell, as he became, gave an address the next year to the newly created Ontario Bar Association.[7] Although he cloaked his comments in generic terms, there can be no doubt that they were pointed at David Fasken's assumption of power from Beatty and Blackstock. He told his audience,

> The old family lawyer, the repository of the family secrets for years, the guide, the philosopher and friend of old and young, has become largely, a thing of the past. His place has been taken by the business man, the acute pulse feeler of the money market, who is ever on the look-out for investments for his clients, whether real estate, bank stock, or shares in a mining company.[8]

He noted, "No lawyer can make rich out of the practice of law," but added that some "have . . . in other ways and by other means outside of the practice of their profession acquired considerable wealth." Can there be any doubt that Riddell had David Fasken in mind?

Justice Riddell's address was one of many in which he looked back long-ingly at the way things had been. Between 1912 and 1932 he became an au-thority on Canada's legal past, authoring innumerable articles and giving many addresses on the history of the legal profession in the province.[9] He also spent much time thinking about the ethics of the profession, and one suspects that at least some of David Fasken's dealings with his clients en-couraged him to do so. He lectured on the subject and encouraged lawyers to think about ethics and adhere to high ethical standards, but interestingly enough he never joined the movement promoting a mandatory code of legal ethics. At the 1919 Canadian Bar Association meeting he even spoke out against such a code, saying that it was simplistic and an Americanism that went against the traditions of the English bar.[10]

THE FIRM HAD BEEN reduced to Beatty and Chadwick, who were members in name only, the two Fasken brothers, Harper Armstrong, Hugh Rose, Percy Galt, and Ross Gooderham, the latter two of whom were in open rebellion against Fasken and his draft partnership agreement. David Fasken's attempt to impose his will had failed, and no partnership agreement was signed fol-lowing Riddell's departure. Instead, the partners carried on without one and the profits were divided according to a statement made by the bookkeeper of the firm, Mr. Struthers.[11] David Fasken would not seek to impose a written agreement on his partners for another four years.

In 1906, faced with rebuilding the firm, David added George Herbert Sedgewick, then twenty-eight years old. He was born in 1878 to a prominent Nova Scotia family. His grandfather, Robert, had come to Halifax County in the mid-nineteenth century to serve as pastor of the Presbyterian Church in Musquodoboit, a position he held for many years. At the time of George's birth, one uncle, Thomas, was a prominent Presbyterian minister in Nova Scotia and another, Robert, was a prominent lawyer and local politician. In 1888, when George was ten years old, his uncle Robert had become Deputy Attorney General for Canada under Tom Blackstock's friend, John Thomp-son. He helped to prepare Canada's *Criminal Code* in 1892 and became a judge of the Supreme Court of Canada, serving from 1893 until his death in 1906. Like his uncle Robert, George attended Dalhousie College (graduating with a BA in 1902) and Osgoode Hall. While attending lectures at the law school, he read law with Riddell.

Ross Gooderham's refusal to go along with him must have caused David Fasken much concern. Almost from the beginning, the firm had looked to the Gooderham and Worts families for its business. Even David's position in the Excelsior Life Insurance Company had initially been secured with the help of Ross's father, George Gooderham. David was in the process of building the insurance company into a very successful and profitable business. That success and his interactions with George Gooderham led to David being called to testify before the Royal Commission on Life Insurance in 1906, which was looking into the inner workings of an industry that people alleged was investing its huge store of cash with related companies to the detriment of its policy holders.[12] The stimulus for the inquiry had been the actions of Senator George Cox in directing Canada Life to buy securities from his own company, Dominion Securities, for the benefit of other companies that he controlled.[13] Fasken, as president of Excelsior Life, was questioned about his involvement with the Gooderhams, who were not only shareholders in Excelsior but also controlled Manufacturers Life and a host of other businesses.[14] The shares that George Gooderham's estate had in Excelsior, when combined with Fasken's, represented control of that entity.

In light of the close connection between George Gooderham and the firm and the fact that George's son and executor, Ross Gooderham, was one of Fasken's partners, the Commission assumed that these parties acted together. Fasken's testimony is very revealing:

Q I suppose it is fair to say that the Gooderham Estate shares would vote along with your shares?

A I don't think it is fair. If it suited them they would vote just the opposite. They would do just what was in their interest.

Q You have many interests in common with them do you not?

A No.

Q You think not?

A No.

Q You think that it is not a fair statement to make?

A No. I act as their solicitor in a good many matters.

Q With emphasis upon the good many. But outside of your professional work as a solicitor you say that there are not many financial matters that you are interested in together?

A No.

Q You are referring now to the present time?

A Yes.

Q Since when?

A Well, since Mr. Gooderham's death.[15]

While the Commission counsel may have doubted the veracity of Fasken's replies, his comments seem to have accurately reflected his changed relationship with at least Ross Gooderham. At this time Ross had no desire to help Fasken with Excelsior Life. He was interested in Manufacturers Life instead and was using some of the money he had inherited from his father to re-establish control of that entity. To assist in this endeavour, he recruited a former supporter of Excelsior Life, his brother-in-law and the family physician Dr. James Ross, who to this point had represented the family as a director of David's company. Ross Gooderham succeeded in enlisting the doctor's allegiance and assumed for himself the role of second vice-president at Manufacturers Life (a position previously held by his father). Law ceased to be his principal interest and gradually he drifted into insurance.[16]

Fasken's changed relationship with Ross Gooderham meant that he could no longer look to George Gooderham's wealth to fund his ventures. This led him to develop other contacts with money in New York. He had met a number of US investors in the Sudbury and Copper Cliff mines and would soon get to know them very well. These new American contacts would in part change the nature of the law practised by the firm. Under Beatty the firm's key clients had been financial institutions such as the Bank of Toronto, Credit Foncier, Canada Permanent, and Manufacturers Life. Tom Blackstock and Wallace Nesbitt had advised some mining clients but that had been incidental to the firm's financial work.[17] Fasken was about to focus the firm on mining law and corporate finance. As a heavily regulated business with high demand for capital and frequent labour problems, the mining industry would prove to be a very rewarding source of work for Fasken's firm.

- ❈ -

AT THE END OF the nineteenth century the Ontario government had seen the possibility of encouraging settlement in the Clay Belt west of Lake Temiskaming. This desire to open the region to farming and the timber industry spurred the development of the mineral resources of northern Ontario. The government began to build the Temiskaming and Northern Ontario

Railway. By 1903 it had reached the north end of Long Lake, where evidence of cobalt, nickel, and some silver was discovered.[18] The initial discovery was made by J.J. McKinley and Ernest Darragh, contractors for the railway. On 30 August 1903 they registered their claim but waited three years to find investors. Meanwhile, Fred LaRose, a blacksmith employed by brothers John and Duncan McMartin, other contractors to the railway, made an even bigger find. LaRose shared his discovery with his employers and together they filed a claim on 3 September. Then, on a trip to Montreal, LaRose showed some samples of his find to the Timmins brothers, who operated a store in Mattawa. The brothers and their lawyer, David Dunlap, decided to invest in the LaRose property, buying half of LaRose's share for $3,500.

There was yet another discovery that year. Tom Hebert, a timber cruiser, staked a large area on the east side of Long Lake. He sought financing from Arthur Ferland, a hotel owner in Haileybury. Ferland happened to be the brother-in-law of the Timmins boys. He recruited two other investors and together they staked further claims, amassing 846 acres (342 hectares). They planned to retain a small portion for themselves and to operate what became the Chambers-Ferland mine. But their immediate goal was to sell the bulk of the property and make a quick profit. Ferland boarded the train and headed to New York with his ore samples to seek out Ellis P. Earle, a wealthy New York–based investor who had made his money in Standard Oil and was then considered "one of the most widely known metallurgists in the US."[19] The person Earle in turn sought to assist in his purchase of the claims was David Fasken.

As a later observer said, "David and Alex Fasken, in the late 1890's, were among the first to see the possibilities of mining development in Northern Ontario."[20] Their interest had resulted in work for some of the investors in the Sudbury and Copper Cliff mines, one of whom was Earle. When Earle asked them to assist with the discovery at Long Lake (soon renamed Cobalt), David acted quickly to form a company to finance its development. Nipissing Mining Company Limited was incorporated with Earle as president and David as a director. By 1904 they had secured Ferland's claims. In 1910 the Cobalt Daily Nugget would characterize Nipissing's operation as "the very centre of the Cobalt Camp."[21]

The initial agreement drafted by David Fasken on behalf of the newly created Nipissing Mining Company stated that the owners of the original claims were to be paid sixty-five cents for each pound of cobalt mined to date. There was also mention in the agreement of nickel and arsenic. There was no mention of silver, which seems to have been thought of as incidental to the other minerals. But by the summer of 1904 high-grade silver ore was being shipped out by the carload. As news of this spread, prospectors and miners converged on Cobalt. By 1908 the Provincial Geologist reported that Cobalt was "not only the world's largest producer of silver, but it absolutely controls the market for cobalt."[22]

At the time many bemoaned the fact that Americans and not Canadians had come to control the Cobalt mines. The *Monetary Times* noted, however, that although Canadians had originally held almost all of the claims, they had chosen to sell their interest before its full value was known. It pointed out, "The president of the Nipissing Mines Company is understood to have paid $250,000 for the properties which were chiefly of prospective value. The sellers thought that they had outwitted a Yankee. Now, probably, they are assuring themselves that they were foolish to part with so great a property at so small a price."[23]

The truth is that Earle and the other American investors were willing to invest the large amounts of money that commercial development of the finds required. David and Alex Fasken proved important in securing both the capital and the sources of power and other utilities necessary to mine in what was then a remote and rugged locale. From the beginning Earle had relied upon Fasken's guidance. In the early days many had doubted the commercial viability of the venture because the Cobalt ore was complex, but David Fasken never lost faith.[24]

In reporting the discoveries in 1905, the *Monetary Times* suggested caution in light of a limited market and a low price for cobalt, and the adulteration of the cobalt with silver, warning that "no process yet discovered suffices to meet the peculiarities of this Canadian silver cobalt ore."[25] The newly elected Conservative premier of Ontario, James Whitney, spoke in guarded language of the ore's "very complex and refractory character."[26] In 1906 the province's leading geologist, Professor W.A. Parks, spoke to the Empire Club, noting that "in Cobalt . . . mines are in advance of the facilities for treatment of the ore. In most mining regions capitalized companies are formed and expensive machinery is put in before they have ore to treat. In Cobalt, they have ore already mined before they have machinery to treat it."[27] As these men expressed their concerns, original test work on cyaniding the cobalt ores was being carried out at the School of Mining at Kingston, and by 1907 silver and arsenic would be produced at Deloro, Ontario, from the ores of the Cobalt district.[28]

David Fasken's belief in the viability of Cobalt is illustrated by his development of hydroelectric power for the camp. After the surface finds had been exhausted in the early years and subsurface mining began, the operations required sources of power and other utilities, including air. Initially steam plants were fuelled by burning trees, but the wood was soon used up and coal had to be imported at great cost. The answer seemed to be hydroelectric plants, as had recently been developed in Niagara. In 1909 the newly created Cobalt Power Company built a hydroelectric plant at Hound Chute on the Montreal River, about eleven kilometres from Cobalt. Then Mines Power Limited built another plant on the Matabitchewan River, just under thirty kilometres away. Finally the Cobalt Hydraulic Power Company built a compressed air plant at Ragged Chutes on the Montreal River, about fifteen kilometres from Cobalt. In 1911 Fasken acquired all three companies and merged them to form the Northern Ontario Light and Power Company Limited, of which he was president.[29] These plants furthered the commercial exploitation of Cobalt's finds by making power less expensive and more reliable. The cost of mining fell from over $3.00 per ton to $1.31.[30]

David became heavily involved in many of the region's mines. He served for a substantial time as Nipissing's president and one of its directors. He was also a director and substantial shareholder of both La Rose Consolidated Mines Limited (which owned Violet Mining Company, Limited) and Trethewey Silver Cobalt Mine Limited, each of which had its mines at Cobalt. His brother Alex also became involved. By 1909 Alex was on the board of two other Cobalt mining companies: the Chambers-Ferland Mining Company, Limited (Harper Armstrong was its vice-president and George Sedgewick was on the board), and the Temiskaming Mining Company, Limited, for which he also acted as secretary-treasurer.

With all this involvement, David and Alex were spending considerable time in the Temagami area; they became sympathetic to the vision that Dan O'Connor had for the area. O'Connor was convinced that investors in the Cobalt mines needed accommodation and transportation and would enjoy spending time in the area hunting and fishing. Investors going north on the *Cobalt Special* had become so common that Stephen Leacock poked fun at them in his *Sunshine Sketches of a Little Town*:

> On a winter evening . . . you will see the long row of Pullmans and diners of
> the night express going north to the mining country, the windows flashing
> with a brilliant light, and within them a vista of cut glass and snow-white

The Steamship *Belle* on Lake Temagami

linen, smiling Negroes and millionaires with napkins at their chins whirling past in the driving snowstorm.[31]

O'Connor wanted to build a series of hotels linked to the railway and each other by steamboats. The Faskens decided to support his proposed Temagami Hotel and Steamboat Company, but they needed additional funding.

They turned to William George Gooderham, who was by this time vice-president of the Bank of Toronto. With some encouragement from David Fasken, the Bank had followed the mining operations north to Copper Cliff, Sudbury, and Cobalt, providing loans and banking services to prospectors, mine owners, and workers.[32] Duncan Coulson, who had been head cashier (chief operating officer) at the Bank since 1878, sat with David Fasken on the boards of several mining companies.[33] Gooderham agreed to join them and when the new venture was incorporated, David served as president, Gooderham as vice-president, and O'Connor as general manager. They built and operated the Ronnoco Hotel, the Temagami Inn, the Lady Evelyn Hotel, and a general store in the new lakeside village of Temagami, as well as several steamships.[34] Alex used his influence to have the lead steamship in their new fleet named *Belle* after his wife, Isabel.[35]

Unbeknown to the Fasken brothers, one of their employees at the Temagami Inn would later find world renown. Eighteen-year-old Archie Belaney had come to the area from England. Under the mentorship of a local guide and colourful character by the name of Bill Guppy, Belaney had become a guide at the inn. He spent much time with the Algonquians, who had a settlement nearby, and adopted many of their ways. He later assumed the persona of Grey Owl and became a noted author and one of the world's first environmentalists.[36] The link to Grey Owl and a wonderful moosehead logo, however, were among the few positive things that came out of this investment.[37] After a few unsuccessful years of operation, the Faskens sold out in 1914.

⚬

THIS FAILURE WAS EXCEPTIONAL. Generally, everything that the Faskens did in the region proved successful. In 1909 the *Montreal Star* listed David Fasken among the seventeen Canadians and eighteen Americans whom Cobalt had turned into millionaires.[38] David and Alex Fasken became key players in what would prove to be one of the most important mining operations in Canadian history. Morris Zaslow has called Cobalt "the opening victory in the long campaign waged by Canadians to wrest mineral wealth from the Precambrian Shield."[39] Another mining historian, Douglas Owen Baldwin, has stated, "For the next half century, nearly every major discovery in Canada — from Noranda to Eldorado to Elliott Lake — owed its life to the skills and financial resources acquired at Cobalt."[40]

The success of the Cobalt discovery spurred exploration throughout the region. In the summer of 1909 the Dome gold discovery was made near Night Hawk Lake, not far from Timmins. The first person to rush to the Porcupine district, as it was called, was W.S. Edwards, a Chicago businessman who had made his money in plumbing. He barely survived the trip. After the train dropped him in Kelso he needed to take a twenty-kilometre stagecoach ride over a corduroy road, a steam launch across a lake, a sixteen-kilometre hike, and two canoe trips. But he and his enthusiasm both survived and he staked his claim. His problem was that he did not have sufficient funds to develop the property. He returned to Toronto and sat in a room at Tom Blackstock's King Edward Hotel for several weeks interviewing prospective investors. When none proved satisfactory, he sought out money in New York. Through Joseph de la Mar, one of the organizers of International Nickel Company of Canada in Sudbury, he was introduced to Ambrose Monell, one of the principals in that firm. After three days of intense negotiations, Monell called Alex Fasken in Toronto and asked him to draft a twenty-page option agreement.

John Francis Hope McCarthy incorporated Dome Mines Limited on 23 March 1910 but it was Alex Fasken, on behalf of Monell's New York syndicate, who put the deal together that made the mining development possible. The New York businessmen packed their bags and went to see the site for themselves. After an inspection, Monell decide to exercise the option and exploit the claims. Alex was named as a director (as was Sedgewick) and as corporate secretary at the shareholders meeting of 22 March 1911. The younger Fasken was to take an active role in the management of the new company, and later became a vice-president. When the story of Dome Mines was written, Alex Fasken and Jules S. Bache, who became president in 1918, were said to have been the "dominant personalities in the company structure."[41]

Alex Fasken was also involved in another shrewd business move in 1911. In March, on behalf of a syndicate that controlled the Cobalt Power Company, he acquired the financially troubled Nipissing Central Railway, an electric trolley service that ran between Cobalt and Haileybury. The rolling stock, line, and land holdings had been valued at $500,000 but Alex Fasken's syndicate picked them up for half that figure. They then sold just the rolling stock and line for $250,000 to the Temiskaming and Northern Ontario Railway, leaving them with the valuable land holdings at no cost.[42]

Following their successes at Cobalt and Porcupine, the Fasken brothers became active supporters of numerous mining exploration initiatives, and their law firm incorporated and did the legal work for many of them and for the Ontario Mining Association that they helped organize. By 1912 David Fasken had become a player in a powerful and very well-connected group of wealthy Canadian and American businessmen who formed the Canadian Mining Exploration Company, a venture that had 400 properties under consideration.[43] He served on the board with Ambrose Monell of International Nickel and Dome Mines, Sir Edmund Walker of the Bank of Commerce, Sir Edward Clouston of the Bank of Montreal, W.E. Cory of US Steel, P.A. Rockefeller of Standard Oil, J.A. Stillman of City Bank of New York, and his old nemesis, Wallace Nesbitt.

One of the properties that the Faskens were considering was in far off Flin Flon, Manitoba. In 1915 they visited this remote site on the border of Manitoba and Saskatchewan, more than 600 miles (966 kilometres) north of the Canadian border. It was best reached by water from Hudson Bay but they approached it from the south. This meant travelling at times by oxen as well as by canoe. Following the visit they formed part of the Toronto-based

Fasken riding an ox at Cumberland House, one of the oldest trading posts
of the Hudson's Bay Company, in Northern Saskatchewan, 1915
Courtesy of Wellington County Museum and Archives

investors' syndicate that optioned these claims. While the others sold their
interest before the Flin Flon mine was developed, David Fasken hung on.
W.F. Currie, one of the original grubstakers, noted in 1927, "We got out and
were quite satisfied to do so. Only David Fasken was left and I hear he's
made a very good thing out of sticking to the end."[44]

⁘

WITH ALL OF THIS going on David still found time to do his family a favour
that only a few had it in their power to do. His brother William's daughter,
Ellen Maria "Nellie" Fasken, had secretly married Harry Parr, who worked
on her father's farm. Both William (known as Bud) and his wife, Mabel Bye
(the sister of young Nellie Bye of Elora, who was to have married David)
were quite upset. Nellie and Harry were under age and he was an Anglican. Knowing that her parents would not agree, the young couple had asked
the rector of the Anglican church to marry them secretly, which he did on
19 April 1906. Within a week William and Mabel discovered the marriage.
Surely, they thought, it could not be a lawful.

They turned to David for advice, and he agreed that the marriage ought
to be invalid.[45] Not only was the couple under age but they had not con-
summated the marriage. But there was no procedure to seek a declaration

from the court of its invalidity. To David this seemed inappropriate. His work with the mining interests in Cobalt had brought him into contact with Premier Whitney's Conservative government at Queen's Park. Fasken approached his government contacts and asked them to pass a law creating such a procedure. An amendment to the *Ontario Marriage Act* was included in the 1907 *Statute Amendment Act* — strong evidence of David's importance and influence.[46] The amendment permitted an application for a declaration that an unconsummated marriage between two underage people was not valid under federal law. David then prepared an application on behalf of his brother William to have his daughter's marriage declared of no force and effect. The *Toronto Daily Star* correctly noted that the legislation seemed to have been passed especially to permit this very application.[47]

On the morning of 9 August 1907, David's former partner James Mabee, now a judge, heard the application and granted the declaration. The marriage was said by the *Toronto Daily Star* to have been annulled, but it is more proper to say that the court declared no valid marriage had ever been effected. Marriage, of course, is a federal matter, as the federal government reminded Ontario Attorney General James Joseph Foy on noting the press coverage. Whitney's government dutifully revoked the legislation but David had already obtained what he had been seeking.

———

MEANWHILE, BEATTY'S CANADIAN NIAGARA POWER COMPANY was in a fight with Adam Beck and the new Hydro-Electric Power Commission of Ontario, which Beck headed. The Canadian Niagara Power Company, like the other private-sector developers of Niagara Falls power, wanted no part of Beck's proposed publicly owned power lines and publicly set power rates. Beatty and Munro Grier looked to their law firm for assistance. On 14 September 1909 Percy Galt applied to the Attorney General of Ontario under the provisions of Ontario's *Power Commission Act of 1909* for a fiat for leave to proceed with an action seeking an injunction restraining the construction of transmission lines from Niagara Falls to Berlin and other municipalities in western Ontario, along with the expenditure of public moneys and pledging the credit of the ratepayers of the province on such lines. The claim was that the Niagara River, being an international boundary and also a navigable river, was under the exclusive jurisdiction of the federal government, and that the province of Ontario in assuming to grant franchises to the power companies at Niagara Falls, had exceeded its constitutional powers.

Hugh Rose
Law Society of Upper Canada Archives, Wallace Rankine Nesbitt collection
"Photograph of Hugh Rose," P141

On 17 September Hugh Rose wrote to Charles Murphy, the secretary of state and acting minister of justice, in Ottawa, with a copy to Sir Wilfrid Laurier: "Judgment has not yet been delivered on the application, . . . [but] the indications were that the fiat would be refused. Under the circumstances we feel it our duty to bring the facts to your notice that you may be made aware immediately of the attitude of the Ontario Government towards the question at issue."[48]

This was but one battle in a long, hard-fought war between the private and the public sector over control of hydroelectric power in the province. The large monument to Sir Adam Beck on University Avenue makes it clear who ultimately won. What makes this particular battle worthy of note is that it was to be one of the few fought by the firm; in November 1910 the firm's principal link to the Canadian Niagara Power Company was broken. Because of poor health, W.H. Beatty resigned his various positions, including this one.[49] Nesbitt, no friend of Fasken and his firm, assumed a leadership role at the power company. From this point forward McCarthy's would do its legal work.[50]

———※———

BEATTY'S DECISION TO RESIGN his positions triggered a number of tributes. The Bank of Toronto board noted, "His wide experience in commercial affairs and his far-sighted and well balanced judgement made his counsels of the highest value and his deep sense of responsibilities . . . made him most scrupulous in the discharge of [his] duties."[51] It also moved closer the loss of the Gooderham estate work and the work for Manufacturers Life because Ross Gooderham began to think about leaving as well. William Gooderham Blackstock, a son of Thomas Gibbs Blackstock whom Ross had hired to assist him, left the firm shortly thereafter in 1911.

Gooderham's departure would be a while in coming and would not be a surprise. David Fasken seems to have been anticipating it. Earlier in 1910 the young Lionel Davis had joined the firm as a lawyer, one of three new members that year. Another junior, G.E. McCann, and one established litigation counsel, Mahlon K. Cowan, also joined. None would last very long. Chadwick noted the arrival of the latter in his diary, pasting in an article from the *Mail and Empire* of 23 April 1910: "Toronto Law Firm Secures Mr. Cowan; Noted Counsel Joins Beatty Blackstock firm; Resigns as GTR Solicitor; Will remove to Toronto on May 1st to enter upon his new duties." The article, failing to notice the changes that had been taking place, referred to the firm as "this old-establishment firm of Toronto lawyers." It added, "Mr. Cowan is aggressive in the highest sense of the term, and at times waxes caustic, but this is mellowed by a saving sense of humour and a broad spirit of generosity."

Again, the Faskens had looked beyond Toronto. Cowan was an experienced lawyer with strong political ties, enticed to Toronto and the firm by an offer of higher compensation. He was from a farming family in Essex County and had been called to the bar in 1890. Given little chance of defeating the sitting Conservative incumbent of twenty-three years, he had nonetheless been elected as a Liberal MP in 1896. Laurier had appointed him chairman of the Private Bills Committee. Although he had been successful and highly regarded in the House of Commons, he resigned in 1904 to pursue his legal career and served as counsel to the Grand Trunk Railway from 1904 to 1910.

Cowan was described as "a brilliant convincing jury lawyer" with "a powerful and vibrant voice which he used to good effect. At times he was witty. His tact, courtesy and attractive manner combined to make his presence an exemplar. To his great natural powers, he added from his earliest days, remarkable powers of application."[52] He used those powers and abilities shortly after joining the firm in acting as counsel to the governments of Saskatchewan and Alberta against the railway companies in rate hearings.

Cowan was impressed with young McCann, who was the president of the Osgoode Legal & Literary Society. Cowan wrote to Laurier to point out that

McCann was "quite as zealous a Liberal as I am; in fact he is a Grit through and through."[53] The next year the firm would add yet another young lawyer, Austin G. Ross, who had been a medallist at Osgoode Hall Law School in 1907. Like Fasken, Cowan, and McCann, he was a "staunch Liberal."[54]

In the fall of 1911 the Fasken brothers brought their nephew James "Jimmy" Aitchison into the firm on his call to the bar. Although he was a new lawyer he was a well-known face in the firm, where he had already been a student for five years, "running errands, delivering mail, travelling on foot with it . . . and being at the call of each and every Member at all times."[55] Like his uncles, he was born on a farm on the Grand River, in Pilkington township near Elora. His birth came at midnight on Christmas Day in 1887. He was the fifth of ten children of William Aitchison and Ann Fasken, an older sister of David and Alex. At the age of fourteen he had gone to Hamilton to stay with his grandmother Isabel Milne Fasken and her two daughters, Sarah and Belle, while he attended Central Collegiate. He was a quiet fellow, "a perfectly groomed young gentleman with his jet-black glossy hair, combed and brushed until every hair was in its proper place in its proper position."[56] He would quietly practise with the firm for the next sixty years.

* ⟶•⟩◆⟨•⟵ *

ONE OF THE LAST decisions that Beatty had presided over at the Bank of Toronto was to choose an architectural firm to build a new head office building on the southwest corner of King and Bay Streets. The decision to move the head office to this location had been made in 1901 but it had taken several years to assemble the land. Then in early 1910 an American firm, Carrière and Hastings of New York, had been selected.[57] When the choice of a foreign firm was made known by the *Toronto Daily Star*, the outcry from the Canadian architectural community led Beatty and the Bank executives to institute a competition. Several Canadian firms were invited to submit proposals, but in the end the original decision stood and by 1912 the building was under construction. The striking building opened in 1913, featuring fluted Corinthian columns and arched entranceways on the exterior and marble, bronze grillwork, and brass fixtures on the interior.[58] The Faskens firm did not move with the Bank of Toronto but remained in the former head office at Church and Wellington, which became a branch with rented offices on the upper floors.[59]

Beatty never got to see the Bank in its new head office. He died at his home on 20 November 1912. Chadwick pasted Beatty's death notice in his diary: "Deaths: Beatty On Wednesday the 20th inst. William Henry Beatty, at his residence, 6 Queen's Park. Funeral private. Please omit flowers." The funeral may have been private but it was no simple affair. The Anglican Bishop of Toronto personally presided at the service. Chadwick wrote, "William Beatty and I commenced practice in February 1863: if he had lived three months longer it would have completed the fifty years. There are no two other lawyers in the province who have been so long in partnership." Then on Saturday, 23 November 1912, Chadwick wrote, "The funeral took place in the forenoon. Our office was closed all day" — a reminder that the law firm was open for business six days a week.

⋅ ⋅⋆⋅ ⋅

IN SEPTEMBER 1912, SHORTLY before Beatty's death, David Fasken found himself in court, not as legal counsel but as plaintiff.[60] The lawsuit says a great deal about the blurring of Fasken's roles as lawyer and businessman.[61] In February 1908, at a lunch at the King Edward Hotel, David had been introduced to John McMartin by a mutual friend, W.A. Fraser. McMartin had explained that the owners of the La Rose Consolidated Mines — John and Duncan McMartin, Louis and Noah Timmins, and David A. Dunlap — were looking to sell their shares in La Rose and related mining properties in Cobalt for $6 million. David thought that he could arrange a public offering through his contacts in New York, E.P. Earle and William Boyce Thompson, a mining engineer turned mining financier.[62] David alleged that McMartin and the other owners then retained him as their agent to effect the public offering at the customary commission of 10 percent. He went to New York with the La Rose owners and introduced them to Earle and Thompson. Flotation agreements were prepared under which the shares would be offered to the public at $9 million.

On reflection the New Yorkers decided to reduce the offering price to $7.5 million, and then in another meeting in New York Thompson suggested that $7 million was more appropriate. With commissions and other expenses they would have netted less than the desired $6 million. At this further reduction David expressed concern to Thompson, explaining that he was in an awkward position, acting for both sides and taking a commission, but Thompson apparently had little sympathy, saying that perhaps David ought "to bear some of the load." McMartin and the ownership group then looked elsewhere and found an English engineer who offered better terms. McMartin asked David to see if Thompson would let them out of the flotation agreements. Again David went to New York with the owners to meet Thompson, where he was successful in obtaining the sought-after release.

After the meeting McMartin asked David if he would accept $50,000 for his services if the English deal went ahead. David was non-committal. That deal did go forward and the owners received $4.4 million in cash and property with a value of $2.25 million. David decided that their offer of $50,000 was inadequate and sought his full 10 percent commission. He asked for $640,000, but the owners replied that the retainer had been as legal counsel only and the fee had been set at $50,000. David sued.

While this was going on, the *New York Times* noted in October 1909 that there were "rumours of dissension in the management." The article reported that following the annual meeting of the La Rose Consolidated, John McMartin was replaced as president and David Fasken became vice-president.[63] David had supplanted his client in management. The results were positive; in April 1911 the *New York Times* reported that 1910 had been the most profitable period in the mining company's history.[64]

The owners paid into court $50,000 plus $1,184.24 in interest. The trial took a week, with David on the stand for several days.[65] Legal counsel for the defendants was none other than Wallace Nesbitt, Beatty's son-in-law who had quit the firm when David Fasken took over. One can imagine how much delight Nesbitt must have taken in cross-examining his former partner. The presiding judge commented that there was "more personal feeling apparent than in any other case he had handled for years. It was very painful for the court."[66] In the end the matter settled, regrettably without leaving any evidence of the extent of the payment that David received.

———❧———

On 13 March 1913 Chadwick, now seventy-three years old, wrote to a relative in Ireland about a "remarkable entertainment" that had been held at his house in late February to celebrate the fiftieth anniversary of the founding of the firm.[67] The event was held on 20 February. Riddell was the only former partner to attend. Lash and Nesbitt both politely declined. Riddell, on behalf of the firm, presented Chadwick with a portrait of himself that Wyly Grier,[68] Munro's brother, had painted.

It could not have been lost on some of the attendees that the celebration was also a wake, marking the passing of one of the great law firms of its time. They knew that the firm Chadwick had helped to found fifty years before was no more. It had been completely transformed by David and Alex

Edward Marion Chadwick, KC
Courtesy of Mrs. Reginald Walsh, his granddaughter

Fasken. They also knew that the Fasken transformation had not been without its casualties and tensions.

———◦◦◦———

A FEW MONTHS LATER, on the afternoon of Monday, 14 April 1913, David Fasken attended a business meeting at the Queen's Hotel in Toronto that was to dramatically change his life and that of his family. He had received a telephone call the previous day from Chicago asking if he could meet to discuss a possible investment. David was no stranger to deals and investments, but the size and nature of this one would challenge even his business acumen.

David met with two men that afternoon. One, William Harvey, was well known to him.[69] The other, O.W. Kerr, a businessman from Minneapolis, was a stranger.[70] Harvey had articled at the Beatty Blackstock firm in 1886, when David was in his first year of legal practice. Although Harvey had left the firm he stayed in contact with David. In 1900 he joined Excelsior Life, serving as the western manager in Winnipeg and helping the company get up to 10 percent return on its investments in Manitoba and what would come to be known as Saskatchewan and Alberta.[71] And in 1904 he had become vice-president and managing director of the Standard Trusts Company, in which capacity he helped David invest money in western Canadian properties.

Harvey and Kerr had been working together for three years on "colonization" projects in Alberta.[72] Colonization consisted of purchasing large tracts of raw land and subdividing it into farm lots, which could then be sold to people in Europe who wished to come to the Canadian West. The Standard Trusts Company had arranged funding for the purchase of the lands. The O.W. Kerr Company had acted as sales agent, selling the farm lands for a commission.[73]

Harvey and Kerr had just arrived in Canada from Chicago, where they had tried unsuccessfully through several weeks of negotiations to purchase a very large tract of land in Texas from the Morris family on behalf of a syndicate of English and Scottish buyers.[74] The property under discussion was enormous — 104,000 hectares. Known as the C, or Chicago, Ranch, it was located just north of Midland, Texas. When they were not able to reach agreement with the Morris family on the terms required by the British syndicate, Harvey told the family that he had a valued client in Toronto who might agree to buy the property. That client was David Fasken.

Harvey explained to Fasken that in February of that year he had gone to Texas to see some properties in the Pecos Valley that Kerr thought could be acquired cheaply for colonization. Harvey had not liked them, however, so one of the party visiting these properties, T.O. Kimber, suggested that Harvey stop in Midland on the way back to see another property, the C Ranch, then being offered for sale. Harvey liked the ranch, which was a single, very large tract of land, conveniently located near Midland and the Texas and Pacific Railroad.[75] He told Fasken that he "had faith in the Ranch, and its possibilities as a money maker." It had been owned and operated by Nelson Morris, a Chicago meatpacker who had purchased the land from the state of Texas. He operated it as a cattle ranch for Black Angus and gained notoriety as the first rancher to use barbed wire to fence his property.[76]

Kerr explained that his methods of buying and selling land had proved very profitable in Alberta and offered to do the same for the Texas property if Fasken were to buy it. Fasken would not have to develop the property. Kerr would enter into a sales agreement and take care of sinking wells, erecting buildings, breaking land, and settling retail prices.[77]

Fasken was told that the property could be acquired for $6.50 an acre or better: Harvey showed him a letter from O.W. Frances, the confidential clerk of the Morris estate, offering the property at that price.[78] That would mean a purchase price of $1,456,000, but Fasken was assured he would not have to come up with that much money. The $400,000 he then had invested with the

Standard Trusts Company would more than cover what he would have to pay, and after the downpayment the sale of the farm lots would more than meet the future payments.[79]

Harvey, Kerr, and Fasken discussed the possible formation of a land company in the name of which the property could be put. This company could then collect the sales revenue. They also agreed that they would need to satisfy themselves that there was sufficient water for irrigation.[80] David, relying in part on his experience with Harvey and on Harvey's "unbounded faith" in the O.W. Kerr Company,[81] authorized him to go to Chicago and make an offer to the Morris estate to buy the ranch. It was a fateful decision; David's investment in west Texas would take much of his money, energy, and time over the next dozen years.

Shortly after David agreed to buy the ranch, he learned that non-residents could not hold or have an interest in real property in Texas.[82] He retained the best Texas lawyers he could find, Baker, Botts, Parker & Garwood of Houston, to help him structure the land deal in a way that permitted the purchase but complied with the law.[83] He was advised that a farm company should be incorporated because such companies could acquire and hold land for resale. This suited his purpose well. He had already discussed with Harvey and Kerr the use of a company to hold the land for sale as farms, and Midland Farms Company was formed. Fasken was also advised to act through a trustee, so he assigned the agreement of purchase and sale for the C Ranch to the Midland Farms Company in exchange for 2,997 of the company's 3,000 shares. The remaining shares were for directors' qualifying shares. He then authorized the trustee to lend the company the money needed for the downpayment.

Almost immediately things began to go wrong. David discovered that the deal with Kerr contained undisclosed terms whereby Kerr had been made exclusive sales agent with a first charge on the property for his fees. Even worse, the land was almost useless for traditional farming because it lacked sufficient water.[84] On 30 October 1913 Fasken wrote to Kerr expressing "anxiety that even at this late date I have no report that we have a good well on the property."[85] He added that the reports "were very discouraging and I feared that we merely had a ranching proposition on our hands."[86]

His two agents had not done enough due diligence. They had noted abundant water during their visit but had not realized that 1912 was a year of abnormally high rainfall.[87] Normal annual rainfall was a mere 330 to 355 millimetres. There were no rivers or other permanent surface water in the immediate area. Most of the 178 ranches and farms in Midland County did cattle and sheep ranching — there were 29,000 cattle in the area — which relied upon wells.[88] The C Ranch had seventy-nine wind-powered wells, but well water was insufficient for irrigation farming. Crop farming in the county had started but was limited: 2,438 acres (986 hectares) of sorghum, 1,755 acres (710 hectares) of cotton, and 421 acres (170 hectares) of corn.[89] In neighbouring Andrews County the story was largely the same.

One wonders why the agents thought that farming was a viable alternative. Certainly David would later suggest that either they were negligent or they had intentionally misled him. He threatened litigation against Standard Trusts, Harvey, and Kerr. The lack of water made sales more difficult, and David found himself being called upon to pay the remainder of the purchase price as well as to fund improvements to the property. He wrote to Harvey that he was already financing his purchase of the Cobalt area power plants and now he had to come up with additional funds: "I hate having everything on earth I have tied up." [90]

Having invested well over $1.5 million in it, he could not and did not give up on the property. He visited it in the fall of 1913 and again in 1916. On his second visit he met the manager, E.H. Morgan. He was not impressed. In January 1917 he moved his nephew Andrew Fasken down to Texas to manage the property.[91] They tried dry farming with crops like cotton on a model farm. To support would-be purchasers of farms, Fasken founded a small town that he called Fasken, with a school, stock pens, and a hotel, and he built a 100-kilometre railroad, the Midland and Northwestern, running from the mainline of the Texas and Pacific Railway to the ranch.[92] As the Midland Farms Company improved the land and built the railroad, Fasken lent the company more money through the trustee, bringing the value of his investment to $2,374,461.99. Some lots were sold but few people moved in and Fasken, Texas, died in the 1920s.[93] The only good news was that his nephew Andrew proved an excellent manager and was able to turn the property back into a prosperous cattle ranch. David, who had bought a property expecting to profit from its development and resale, found himself a reluctant rancher with a huge property in distant Texas.

Plaque on the C Ranch commemorating the building of
the Midland & Northwestern Railroad by David Fasken
Photo taken by the author

MEANWHILE, FASKEN HAD A law firm to run. The partner compensation for
him and his brother for the fiscal year 1912–13 makes it very clear that David
saw himself as the dominant partner and his brother as a key player in the
firm (see Table 5).[94]

David Fasken	$25,884.34
E.M. Chadwick	$5,420
Harper Armstrong	$6,570
Alexander Fasken	$10,866
M.K. Cowan	$10,990
Hugh E. Rose	$8,090
M.R. Gooderham	$8,090
Thomas P. Galt	$3,900
George H. Sedgewick	$2,485

At the end of this fiscal year, David brought the ongoing conflict with
Gooderham and Galt to a head. Out of a sense of loyalty to Beatty and Chadwick, Fasken had waited until Beatty died and Chadwick had celebrated the
fiftieth anniversary. It was now time to make it clear that this was his firm.
He insisted that all partners accept his leadership on his terms. The dissenters responded by packing their things and marching out the door. In May
1913 George Blackstock, who had just returned from a stay in England, Percy

Excelsior Life Building on Toronto Street 1915 and the doorway to the building
Photo on the right taken by the author

Galt, Ross Gooderham, and young G.E. McCann moved across Wellington Street from the Bank of Toronto building to the Gooderham Building and formed Blackstock, Galt & Gooderham.[95] Lionel Davis also left but he did not join the dissenters, going into practice instead with Samuel M. Mehr.[96]

The two firms practised opposite each other on Wellington Street for only a short time. In 1914 the firm's architect of choice, E.J. Lennox, working closely with David, designed a new building for Excelsior Life at 36 Toronto Street, on the southwest corner of Toronto and Adelaide.[97] The *Toronto Directory* had an advertisement for the Excelsior Life Building, "the most modern and up-to-date office building in Toronto — excellent light, reasonable rates."[98] Rising eleven storeys, the building was one of the tallest in the city. The top two floors formed a "highly original two-storey attic. Florid Corinthian engaged columns and coupled pilasters at the corners provided the building with a rich appearance."[99] David put his law firm at the top of his new building. One of the lessons he learned from the Gooderhams and his mentor Beatty is that you should always keep your business in the family — but that family was no longer related to the Gooderhams or the Worts.

Chadwick described the new offices as "quite high toned . . . a handsome suite of rooms with stylish new furniture." Located on the southeast corner of the tenth floor, they offered a grand view, and he could sit and watch the aviators learning to fly at the island airport and the comings and goings of

Young J.W. Pickup
Law Society of Upper Canada Archives, Osgoode Hall Law School fonds
"Law School Osgoode Hall final year 1913," P447

the Niagara steamers.[100] The floor was divided into a series of small offices by wooden and glass partitions. In the centre on the east side was one large room for the secretaries. Just inside the front door was a semi-circular desk surrounded by glass, with an opening like a bank teller's old-fashioned station. Along the walls the law books were shelved from floor to ceiling.[101] Clients and other visitors sat on long benches. At the end of each bench was a large brass cuspidor to permit the cigar-smoking mining men from the north country to expectorate freely.[102]

Harper Armstrong did not move with the firm into the new premises. He was having health issues and withdrew from the partnership on 30 April 1915.[103] The man who had assisted Alex Fasken with the incorporation and organization of many mining companies over the previous decade developed tuberculosis and died at his home in Muskoka in 1919.[104]

Two YOUNGER MEN DID move with the firm into that new, well-lit building: John Wellington Pickup and Collamer Chipman Calvin. The first was a recently called lawyer. The second was an articling student, reading law with Alex Fasken.

J.W. Pickup was born in Millbrook, Ontario, on 6 August 1892, the youngest of seven children.[105] His father, William Scott Pickup, had moved his family in the 1880s to Millbrook, where he set up a tinsmithing business.[106] Later he purchased the long-established Cosgrove hardware store. William Pickup was very active in community affairs, serving as reeve for a time.[107]

C.C. Calvin
Law Society of Upper Canada Archives, Osgoode Hall Law School fonds
"Osgoode Hall, law school, final year 1920," P1323

Wellington, as J.W. was then known, did very well in school, as had his four brothers and two sisters before him. His two oldest brothers became Presbyterian ministers, another brother became a doctor, and the fourth, a pharmacist. J.W. had other ideas. He and his lifelong friend George Walsh wanted to become lawyers.[108] They articled locally, Pickup with Robert Ruddy in Peterborough.[109] Each then went to Toronto in 1910 to attend the lectures at Osgoode Hall. In Toronto, Pickup continued his articles with Matthew Crooks Cameron of Marten, Starr, Spence & Cameron, where he stayed for two years.[110] Then in 1913, having won the Osgoode gold medal, Pickup switched firms, completing his final months under articles with Mahlon Cowan at Beatty Blackstock.[111] Finishing first at Osgoode Hall was no small feat for Pickup.[112] In addition to Walsh, his graduating class included J.C. McRuer, Nathan Phillips, Percy Wilson, Lewis Duncan, and a number of others who would go on to very successful careers. Just after being called to the bar, J.W. married his childhood sweetheart and next-door neighbour in Millbrook, Kathleen Fitzgerald.[113]

Like Pickup, C.C. Calvin was not from Toronto. In most other respects he was more reflective of the firm's establishment past than of Fasken's reconstituted firm. He himself seems to have thought so — in the later years of his life he would say that he had articled with Beatty, Blackstock, Fasken, Cowan & Chadwick, even though that was the name of the firm for only a few months of his student tenure with the firm.[114] Like the members of the old Beatty firm, he was from a Conservative family that had had dealings with Gooderham & Worts. Both his grandfather, Deleno Dexter Calvin, and his father, Hiram Augustus Calvin, had been elected as Conservative members of Parliament for Frontenac County.[115] His grandfather had supported Sir John A. Macdonald. At the time of C.C. Calvin's birth in 1894, his father was sitting as a Conservative in Parliament during the years when a series of Conservative prime ministers tried unsuccessfully to succeed Macdonald. His father had been re-elected in 1900, serving until 1904 in Borden's Conservative opposition. Borden had, of course, become prime minister by the time that C.C. Calvin joined the firm.

Like his father, C.C. Calvin was born on twenty-six-hectare Garden Island, about three kilometres south of Kingston. Garden Island was a self-contained community of about 700 people with its own school, post office, custom office, farm, bakery, library, and general store. His grandfather, originally a timber merchant from New York State, had relocated there in 1844, where he had been renting land since 1836. He chose the island because it had an excellent harbour on its southeast side, where he was able to take pine and oak logs from the Great Lakes and form them into rafts up to a kilometre long, which were floated down the St. Lawrence to Quebec City for shipment to England.

In the summers C.C.'s grandfather and father dealt with timber and in the winter their firm built ships, which they used both to bring squared timber to the island from as far away as Michigan and Minnesota and also to tow their huge timber rafts to Quebec City. Initially they built lake schooners, called "timber droghers." In 1877 Hiram launched a large barque, the *Garden Island*, which was used for ocean voyages, but generally the Calvin ships were used in their timber trade. In 1880 on the retirement of D.D. Calvin's brother-in-law, Ira Breck, Hiram Augustus, the oldest surviving son, went into partnership with his father under the name Calvin & Son. Starting in 1883 the Calvins began to build steam tugs and barges. The next year D.D. Calvin died at age eighty-six and Hiram assumed leadership of the family business and the island, now entirely owned by the family. He incorporated the business as the Calvin Company, Limited. All told the Calvins built more than sixty ships. They were distinctive-looking vessels, built specially for the timber trade. Considered "sturdy and conservative," they were painted a bright green with white trim and a black funnel. In some cases, the boiler and machine shops of Garden Island even built boilers for the ships and made related hardware and sails.

Much of this was in the past when C.C. Calvin won a scholarship to Queen's University. One summer during his university days he worked in northern Manitoba on a government surveying party. He later explained to the *Globe and Mail* that when he came out of the muskeg and mosquito clouds he had one simple, yet firm conviction. "It was one hell of a life and I didn't want any more of it."[116] Ironically, when he graduated with a BA in 1914, he joined a firm that had built up a large clientele in the muskeg and mosquito clouds.[117] He chose law in part because the early years of the twentieth century had seen the decline of the family businesses. The last Calvin ship launch occurred in 1906. The last timber raft had floated down to Quebec City in 1911. By 1914 the market for exported timber had largely disappeared and Calvin's company sold its fleet of timber vessels to the Montreal Transportation Company Limited, which later became part of Canada Steamship Lines. Ironically and wisely C.C. Calvin's grandfather had hated lawsuits: "As for law, I think it the height of folly for either you or us to waste money on it."[118]

❦

FASKEN USED THE OCCASION of the move to change the firm's name. The 1 May 1915 partnership agreement between Chadwick, David Fasken, Mahlon Cowan, Alex Fasken, and Hugh Rose provided that the firm name was to be Fasken, Cowan, Chadwick & Rose.[119] There was to be no trace of the Beatty Blackstock name under which the firm had become a force in the Toronto legal community. The agreement went further, providing that on the dissolution of the partnership, none of the partners would use the name "Beatty and Blackstock, or either of them as a firm name or part of a firm name" without the consent of a majority of the partners, thus effectively ensuring that the former name would never again be used. So as not to lose all the goodwill in the old name, however, the next year in the *Canada Law List* the firm appeared both as Beatty, Blackstock, Fasken, Cowan & Chadwick and as Fasken, Cowan, Chadwick & Rose.[120]

David Fasken continued to manage the business of the firm and to "determine what line of work shall be done by the various partners," but increasingly he was delegating these duties to his brother Alex. The agreement noted that every partner other than David was "entitled to one calendar month's holiday during the year." David Fasken, by contrast, was "entitled to such holidays from time to time as he shall desire to take."

David, and through him Alex, had tremendous power in the partnership. The agreement, provided, for example,

In case of the death or retirement of any member of the firm or of the dissolution of the said partnership the value of the assets of the firm shall be left to
the arbitrament of David Fasken, K.C., and the Accountant of the firm and in
the event of the death or inability of either of them to act the same shall be
fixed by the other and their or his decision shall be final and binding upon all
parties and from which there shall be no appeal . . . . [121]

Despite David's dominant role, his compensation from the firm was limited,
reflecting that it was no longer his principal source of income. Net profits
up to $18,500 per annum were to be divided so that Cowan and Alex Fasken
received $4,700, Chadwick $3,600, David Fasken $3,000, and Rose $2,500. The
profits in excess of this were to be divided with 36 percent each to Cowan
and Alex Fasken, 15 percent to Rose, and only 13 percent to David Fasken.
Old Chadwick got nothing of the excess.

Notwithstanding David's smaller financial rewards, the agreement gave
him, and to a lesser extent Alex, very special treatment. All other partners
were required to devote all their time to the partnership, accounting to it for
all commissions and revenues that they received in any way connected with
the law practice. David Fasken, however, was entitled to have connections
with corporations or other businesses in which he was financially interested
and to receive commissions and other fees from them, so long as all moneys
that he received by way of retainer or other legal services rendered were the
property of the firm. Alex Fasken was entitled to retain all commissions and
other fees from his directorship in the Excelsior Life Insurance Company so
long as the meetings of directors were held in the evening.

In November 1916 David, who had just returned from his ranch in Texas,
made the front page of the *Toronto Star*, but he was anything but pleased.
Allegations had been made that his client, International Nickel, the US-
owned company that had indirectly helped him make his fortune, was shipping Canadian nickel to the United States, where it was being put aboard
German submarines for use in the German war effort. Needless to say the
story caused quite a stir. Premier William Howard Hearst himself denied the
allegations. David Fasken, who was referred to in the press as "the local legal
counsel of the International Nickel Company," did not deny that such shipments had been made in the past. Rather he stressed that the practice had
ended. He noted that Inco had not made such sales "since the agreement was
reached with the British Government."[122] To further combat the rumours,
International Nickel began refining its nickel in Canada at Port Colbourne.[123]

As David was trying to convince the press that his client was innocent of war profiteering, Mahlon Cowan was forced to leave the firm because of illness. He would die at his home in Toronto on 28 October 1917 at the age of fifty-four. His departure left a large hole in the firm's litigation practice. That hole was made even bigger when Hugh Rose, who had worked extensively with Cowan, took Cowan's departure hard and decided to rethink his future.[124] One is reminded of Wallace Nesbitt a dozen years before. Cowan's "jovial, hospitable and generous" personality and "personal magnetism"[125] had helped Rose to tolerate Alex Fasken. With Cowan gone, Rose followed Nesbitt's example. Although only forty-seven years old and a KC with bright prospects in private practice, Rose accepted appointment to the Supreme Court of Ontario on 4 December 1916. Rose, however, would not shortly return to practice as Nesbitt had done. He served on the court for twenty-nine years, the last fifteen as Chief Justice of the High Court.[126]

The aging Chadwick noted Rose's departure in his diary on 1 January 1917. His entry makes it clear that although that Chadwick knew generally of the changes in the firm, he was no longer fully informed:

> Hugh Rose the junior partner of our firm having been appointed to a High Court Judgeship (fourth judge taken out of our firm within the last few years) and Cowan having gone out, the firm was reconstituted by taking in — — — Robertson late of — — — in Cowan's place and the advancement of Sedgewick, one of the nominal partners, to Rose's position.[127]

In May 1915 Sedgewick had been given a share of the profits to supplement his $250 per month salary. Now, in 1917, he became a named partner in the firm, to be known as Fasken, Robertson, Chadwick & Sedgewick. The Robertson referred to was Robert Spelman Robertson and his addition to the firm was a real coup for the Fasken brothers. To get him to come, Alex Fasken had to guarantee him a minimum of $10,000 a year.[128]

ONCE AGAIN THE FASKENS had sought out an experienced out-of-towner. R.S. Robertson was born in Goderich, Ontario, on 11 December 1870. His father, William Roderick, had come to Upper Canada from Churchville in Pictou County, Nova Scotia, in 1858.[129] He stayed just a year before joining the Gold Rush to California, then returned to Upper Canada in 1861, settling initially in Caledonia. There he married a local girl, Fanny Augusta Smith. They moved to Brampton, where four children were born, and then in 1870 to

R.S. Robertson
Law Society of Upper Canada Archives, Fasken Martineau DuMoulin LLP fonds
"Robert Spelman Robertson — Who's Who in Canada," 2009006-43P

Goderich, where an additional three children were born. Initially William operated a dry goods shop but for most of his time in Goderich he ran an insurance brokerage and real estate business. He was a staunch Liberal and an active member of the North Street Methodist Church.

R.S. Robertson's three brothers were an accomplished group. John Charles, the eldest, was a gold medallist at the University of Toronto and did graduate work at Johns Hopkins. He became a noted classical scholar and by 1917 was serving as dean of the Faculty of Arts of the University of Toronto.[130] Alexander Morton was also a university graduate and a teacher of modern languages and mathematics. In 1917 William, the youngest, was the editor of the *Goderich Signal*.

R.S. was clearly very bright like his brothers but not academically inclined. He attended elementary and high school in Goderich but then chose to forgo university in favour of reading law with J.T. Garrow, who would be appointed to the bench and whose son would later join Robertson at Faskens. Robertson was sworn in as a solicitor in 1892 and called to the bar in 1894. He began his practice in Stratford, Ontario, in partnership with John Idington, thirty years his senior and a very well-established and highly regarded graduate of the University of Toronto.[131] Idington had earlier served as Crown attorney and clerk of the peace for Perth County and by 1894 had become president of the Western Bar Association. They practised together for ten years. In 1904 Idington was appointed a judge of the Ontario High Court, and the next year he went to the Supreme Court of Canada.

Robertson was tall, "slight of build and genial in manner" and "a family man."[132] Bryce MacKenzie would remember him as "a very fine and somewhat severe gentleman" with "crisp white starched linen, his cuffs practically shone they were so glistening white." In politics he was a Liberal. In religion he was a Methodist and an advocate for temperance. In fact in 1914, in his only venture into the political arena, he unsuccessfully ran in a provincial election as a candidate under the "banish-the-bar" banner. This was part of a nationwide evangelical prohibitionist movement that, although unsuccessful in the election, motivated the Ontario government to create the Ontario Liquor Licensing Board under the chairmanship of Joseph Flavelle.[133] Robertson was unaccustomed to defeat. Certainly, it came seldom to him in the courtroom. That same year he demonstrated his skills by successfully defending an appeal of an insolvency case brought before the Supreme Court of Canada in the matter of the Stratford Fuel, Ice, Cartage and Construction Company.[134]

Robertson had been too old to fight in the First World War but his cousin John Gordon Robertson, born in Churchville, Nova Scotia, in 1890, had been severely wounded while serving as a lieutenant in the army at Vimy Ridge.[135] After spending two years convalescing in England, Robertson's cousin returned to Saskatchewan, where he had moved before the war, and resumed his duties as provincial livestock commissioner. Just before going off to war, John Gordon had married Lydia A. Paulson of Minnesota. They had two sons who would go on to very successful careers that brought them into contact with their Toronto lawyer relative. The older son, Robert Gordon, became a very important civil servant in Ottawa, serving for a time as personal assistant to Robertson's friend and client, Prime Minister Mackenzie King. The younger son, Ronald, eventually become a lawyer in the Faskens firm and one of the best insolvency lawyers in Canada.

While R.S. Robertson assumed leadership of the firm's litigation practice, young Pickup and Calvin were also at war. In 1916 each had taken a leave of absence from the firm. Pickup served as a lieutenant in the army. Calvin joined the Queen's University Battery as a gunner but then transferred to the activated Royal Navy Volunteer Reserve, having been given the rank of sub-lieutenant. In Greenwich, England, Calvin studied for service in the British Naval Motor Boat Patrol and was assigned to the Dover Patrol. In April 1918 he proved his mettle under fire as the second-in-command of a newly commissioned motor launch and was mentioned in dispatches, in what the *Globe and Mail* described as "the daring, dangerous but completely success-

ful attack on the German submarine base at Zeebrugge in 1918."[136] He told
the story, in a typically self-effacing way, in an article he wrote for the *Naval
Officers Association of Canada Journal* in February 1958.[137] The ability to remain
calm and keep his wits about him as things went wrong would prove to be a
valuable asset to Calvin in his career, both inside and outside the firm.

WHILE CALVIN WAS IN Europe fighting for his country, David Fasken was
facing conflict of a different sort. In the summer of 1917 James Swinson,
vice-president of the Trades and Labour Congress, announced that 1,100
of Cobalt's 1,200 workers had voted to strike. The *Toronto Star* noted that
"President Earle and Mr. David Fasken of the Nipissing board are in Cobalt watching developments."[138] The operators of the mines agreed that they
would not recognize the union; they held firm and the strike was averted.
Two years later, however, over 2,200 Cobalt miners went on strike for eight
weeks. In Kirkland Lake another 525 workers struck for twenty-one weeks.
The mine operators again held firm and would not recognize the union.
Again the operators won out, forcing the workers back to work.[139]

Although the Fasken brothers were no less concerned about unionization
than others in the mining industry, they believed the best way to ensure that
a union did not interfere with mining operations was to convince workers
that they did not need one. Granting some concessions to workers might al-
leviate any pressure on them to form a union. With Alex Fasken's assistance,
Dome Mines had adopted this approach and successfully avoided a union
for sixty years. To achieve this Dome paid workers five or ten cents an hour
more than neighbouring mines and offered them a pension plan that was
unique in the industry.[140] When the Western Federation of Miners organized
1,000 workers at the other South Porcupine mines — Hollinger, McIntyre,
Vipond, Jupitur, and Plenaurum — and went into a bitterly contested strike
in November 1912 that lasted seven months, Dome Mines was able to continue production.[141]

DAVID FASKEN ALSO HAD another union on his mind in 1917 — Borden's Union
government, which included both Conservatives and several Liberals. On
15 December 1917 David was one of sixty-four Liberals who placed an advertisement in the *Toronto Star* calling on voters at the coming election to
cast a ballot for Borden's government.[142] The electorate was convinced and

Wilfrid Laurier's weakened Liberals went down to defeat.[143] That put in motion a process to find a new Liberal leader to replace the defeated and aging Laurier. In 1919 Canada's first leadership convention would choose the firm's former client, William Lyon Mackenzie King, to lead the Liberal Party.[144] In 1921 he went on to win the first of many elections and become the tenth prime minister of Canada. Once again the firm had a friend in Ottawa.

MINDERS, GRINDERS, AND ROBERTSON, 1919–38

NOVEMBER 1918 FINALLY BROUGHT an end to the war in Europe. For the firm it meant the return of Pickup and Calvin from military service. For many businessmen it meant that they were again able to dedicate themselves to their businesses. In a 12 February 1919 report to the shareholders of St. Mary's Cement Limited, George Horace Gooderham, George's third son, set out the challenges business faced following the war: "labour shortage, high wages, exorbitant prices for supplies, and increased freight charges to say nothing of the epidemic of influenza during the months of October, November and December" and a workforce made up of returned soldiers who had to be paid full wages but could not be expected to be as productive as before the war.[1]

St. Mary's Cement had faced management issues from its very inception. On 18 April 1914, not quite four months before Britain declared war and brought Canada into the conflict, the firm had incorporated the company, which was being financed by the Gooderham family. It was done using members of the firm as the first incorporators and directors. Thus the letters patent listed the incorporators and provisional directors as four of the lawyers in the firm — Alex Fasken, George Sedgewick, Jimmy Aitchison, and J.W. Pickup — as well as the firm's accountants, Archibald Struthers and Thomas Ormsby Cox, and a student-at-law, Peter Randolph Ritchie. The expectation was that shortly after incorporation these interim shareholders and directors would resign and transfer their shares to George H. Gooderham and other members of the Gooderham family. The declaration of war meant that this did not happen until late 1918. Throughout the war, members of the law firm acted as directors and assisted Alex Fasken in the management of the cement company to permit their clients to focus on the war effort. As lawyers came and went in the firm, the directors changed but the firm's commitment continued.

At about the same time as the returning men were starting work, David Fasken formally retired from active practice. He turned his focus completely away from law, so much so that when David and Arnold Hoffman, two Boston mining engineers, met David in the 1920s in connection with work they were doing in Flin Flon, they did not realize that he was a lawyer. To them he was "a wealthy Haileyburian . . . lumberman and waterpower magnate."[2] Alex they knew as a lawyer in Toronto, "flinty, shrewd, over cautious,"[3] but David was associated with northern Ontario and his extra-legal businesses. They may have been confused about David's profession but they were in no doubt about his personality and that of his "wily lawyer" brother: "Dave . . . was bluff and generous as his brother Alec was curt and frugal."[4]

David had begun to experience health problems arising from high blood pressure that would plague the last decade of his life. Much of his attention continued to be directed at the C Ranch in Texas. The purchase of the Texas property had cost him a great deal of money and had led to litigation. When Fasken discovered that he had been misled over the presence of water on the property, he contemplated legal action against his business agent, William Harvey, who had arranged the purchase.[5] Instead he found himself defending an action by W.J. Moran, who claimed to have brought the property to the attention of Harvey and to be owed a real estate commission on the purchase. To Fasken, the Moran litigation was adding insult to injury. He had never wanted to purchase and operate a ranch in Texas. This was to have been a land development deal. To be unable to resell the land because there was no water (something he had expressly told Harvey to be sure of) and then be sued for a commission on the purchase was galling to him. Nevertheless, while working with Andrew Fasken to make his investment worthwhile, he defended and won this action.

———◦∞◦———

DAVID WAS ALSO DISTRACTED by some long-simmering family troubles that ended up before the courts in Texas. In 1913 his son Robert married a Roman Catholic woman he had met at Fasken's cottage in the Temagami region. The Ferland family had a cottage nearby and while in his late teens, Robert met and fell in love with May Ferland. She was a student at the Toronto Conservatory of Music. When David's wife learned of the relationship, she promptly took her son on an extended visit to Europe. On his return, however, Robert discovered that May had gone to Boston for further musical study. He found an excuse to visit Boston and the couple were married there in a Roman Catholic service. As Robert had no job, he and May moved into his parents' home on University Avenue.

Although it was a large house, it was not big enough for mother- and daughter-in-law. When David Jr. was born on 22 April 1915 and baptised Catholic, matters became even worse. May found the stress of dealing with her mother-in-law too much and suffered a nervous breakdown. She went to a sanatorium in Barrie, leaving her baby in the care of her husband and mother-in-law. After a time she returned to the Fasken home in Toronto but nothing had changed and she again broke down. Her husband agreed to let her go to stay with her parents up north but insisted on having his mother look after the baby. When May left, Robert's mother packed up her son and grandchild and went to Texas, where they lived in a house that Fasken had bought for them in the town of Midland, near the ranch. David Fasken and his wife never again lived together.

May did not learn of the move until she received notice that her husband had filed for divorce in Texas. She successfully defended the 1917 divorce action, which Robert had unscrupulously brought on the grounds of her abandonment of him. May's lawyer successfully argued that there had been no abandonment and that Robert's residence in Texas had not been bona fide but was undertaken to qualify to bring a divorce action that would not have been permitted under Canadian law. Robert and his mother filed for divorce again in 1919, and when they were once more unsuccessful filed yet again in a different town in Texas in 1920.

The 1920 trial lasted four days. David Fasken was required to give testimony to refute an allegation made by May that he had tried to buy her off with an offer of $50,000. He did not deny making the offer but explained that he did not want to see his son's wife dependent on anyone else, no matter what the circumstances. (Robert had provided no support to his wife for the last four years.) David also stated that he had no objection to her religion: "Lots of my friends and business associates are Catholics." For him the problem lay elsewhere: "Two families ought not to live under the same roof. I am talking of two wives and husbands. Two young people and two old people should not, do not fit in the same house."[6] This time the court granted Robert his divorce. The jury found that May had voluntarily absented herself for three years with the intention of abandonment and that Robert had neither caused, procured, nor consented to the separation.[7] The judge gave Robert custody of the child for nine months of the year. May was granted custody for the summer months but only on condition that she not take the child out of Texas.

She returned to Toronto and never saw her son again. But it was not for lack of trying. She appealed the divorce decree to the Court of Civil Appeals for the Eighth District. She asserted that the evidence was insufficient to show that she had voluntarily left and that in fact the undisputed evidence disclosed that Robert and his family caused her absence. The appeal court upheld the jury finding, relying on a letter that she had written to Robert in October 1916 in which she said, "If you practice your [Roman Catholic] religion openly, also your Father knowing that you are doing so, I shall consider returning to you, otherwise I never shall." Still May tried to have the divorce set aside. Her lawyers asked for a rehearing and argued that the letter, as a confidential communication between spouses, ought not to have been admitted into evidence. This argument also failed.[8]

This whole affair put an even greater distance between Fasken and his wife and son. Mrs. Fasken and Robert moved to Ross, near San Francisco, where Robert married Inez Ratcliffe. David, in search of a cure for his health problems, travelled extensively, often stopping at famous hot springs in the United States. His niece Nellie became "his constant companion."[9] Nellie's life had been seriously affected by the secret marriage that David had helped her parents annul in 1907.[10] The next year she had wed Donald Wallace, a marriage brokered by her uncle David, who gave the young couple a fifty-acre (twenty-hectare) farm as a wedding present. Despite, or perhaps because of, Fasken's help, the marriage did not last. After a few years Donald left Nellie, and her "Uncle Dave" helped her sell the farm and obtain a divorce. More important, he offered her room, board, and a job. She moved in with Fasken and his wife in Toronto and became his personal secretary, one of only five people whom he trusted and relied upon. The others were Alex; his wife's nephew Charles Q. Parker, who managed investments for Excelsior Life; his nephew Andrew Fasken, who managed the C Ranch; and his cousin Sam Fasken, who managed David's Ontario farm properties.

Alex Fasken
Law Society of Upper Canada Archives, Fasken Martineau DuMoulin LLP fonds
"Alexander Fasken — Who's Who in Canada," 2009006-03P

WHILE DAVID WAS DISTRACTED in Texas or travelling from spa to spa, Alex was very much focused on the law office in Toronto. His assumption of the title of managing partner might seem to have been a formality, but such was not the case. Alex's management style, when freed of David's moderating influence, was to have a profound effect on the firm for the next two decades. His cousin Marion MacKenzie recalls that Jimmy Aitchison "enjoyed his work [at the firm] as long as his Uncle Dave was in active leadership," but that changed when Alex took the helm. From that time, everyone in the office was expected to run to carry out his bidding.[11] The simple fact was that David was more attuned to people than was Alex.[12] He related better to his farming relatives but, more important to the firm, he was able to relate to members of Toronto's moneyed elite in ways that Alex could not.

With Alex the emphasis was on efficiency, strict adherence to rules, and careful, detailed attention to client matters. He saw himself and R.S. Robertson as the leaders of the firm. Each had a corner office and his name on the glass. The others did not. He had no desire to give anyone else in the office "an unreal sense of permanence."[13]

He personally oversaw all aspects of the firm's operation, beginning with the daily mail. Each morning he examined all incoming mail and arranged for its distribution among the partners. If he was late, the mail was held until his arrival.[14] Alex also insisted on strictly adhering to set office hours: 9:00 a.m.

Alex Fasken with his secretary Marion McLelland
Law Society of Upper Canada Archives, Fasken Martineau DuMoulin LLP fonds
"Photograph of Alex Fasken and Marion McLelland in his law office," 2009006-07P

to 5:45 pm. Monday to Friday, with a 5:00 pm closing in July and August. On Saturday the office was open from 9:00 am to 1:00 pm. An attendance register was maintained, with each person's arrival and departure times duly noted.[15] Alex also insisted that no lawyer shut his door.[16] They were all to be available to him when and where he wanted, no matter what they were doing or whom they were with. In the manner of an aristocrat who summons the servants when required, he had an electric bell system installed in each office. In his office was a panel of buttons that he could press to ring any or all of the bells in the other offices. To summon everyone, he simply put his arm across the whole panel to ring every bell at once.[17] Even R.S. Robertson, his star counsel, was expected to drop whatever he was doing to answer a summons.[18] To those in the office, Alex's methods seemed intrusive and overly controlling. To Alex they were both necessary and efficient.

Alex assumed many of David's positions outside the law firm as well. As a result he had much on his plate, most of it business administration rather than law, as reflected his natural interests. When he needed a legal opinion, he turned to Robertson.[19] Alex thought so highly of Robertson's legal advice that he had him added to the board of Excelsior Life. Alex Fasken and R.S. Robertson — the businessman and the lawyer — were the two personalities who would dominate the firm in the period following David Fasken's retirement.

It is often said that lawyers can be classified as finders, minders, or grinders. David had been a finder, someone who found clients for the firm. Alex would prove to be a minder, someone who carefully handled the clients that his brother and others had attracted.[20] To meet client requirements, he used a number of grinders, careful lawyers who would do as they were told, preparing and implementing routine matters: conveyances, collections, protests, annual reports, and the like. Jimmy Aitchison was one such grinder. John Beverley Robinson, a great-nephew of the John Beverley Robinson who had been Beatty and Chadwick's first partner, would be another. He had joined the firm as a student in 1918. As a matriculant he spent five years articling before his call to the bar in 1923. Robinson would gradually move from collections and corporate filings into real estate conveyancing, work that Alex did not value very highly. In real estate he worked primarily with Jimmy Aitchison. Like Aitchison, Robinson was a quiet person, willing to put up with Alex Fasken's many demands. Bryce MacKenzie recalled that Robinson "did not assert himself effectively at any time . . . . [H]e was fired every other day by Mr. Fasken and immediately rehired." He was a kind, religious man, generous and forgiving.[21]

Luckily, both Pickup and Calvin were accustomed through their military experience to taking orders from demanding commanding officers and were not put off by Alex Fasken's personality. Both thrived at the firm, learning how to practise with great care and attention without adopting the quiet, unassuming manner of either Aitchison or Robinson.

Under Alex Fasken's leadership the firm provided a broad range of legal, business consulting, and administrative services to a relatively narrow group of clients — financial services firms such as the Bank of Toronto and the Excelsior Life Insurance Company, mining firms such as Nipissing Mining Company and Dome Mines, collection firms like R.G. Dun, hospitals like Toronto Western. All of these clients had been brought to the firm by Beatty or by Alex's brother David. Alex kept these clients happy by meeting their every need. What he could not do, however, was grow the corporate commercial side of the firm. Growth came on the litigation side because of the outstanding abilities of Robertson, who not only handled the litigation for the firm's clients but also acted as litigation counsel for other lawyers who lacked his expertise and experience. Ironically, the Fasken firm was moving in the opposite direction to its traditional rivals, McCarthy's, Osler's (now two separate firms),[22] and Blakes. Those had begun as litigation firms and over time come to emphasize corporate commercial work. Faskens had begun as a solicitors' firm but was becoming widely known as a litigation shop.

By way of contrast with Robertson's growing and exciting counsel practice, the firm's solicitors' practice devolved into many routine tasks.[23] There was a separate collection department to handle small claims, some as little as $5 or $10. This department, headed by Norman Caudwell, had its own books of account. From time to time fees were transferred to the main office ledgers. The bulk of this work came from R.S. Dun & Co. (later Dun & Bradstreet). The Canadian and US offices of this company would send claims to be collected from local debtors. The minimum fee was $3.34. Above this threshold it was based on a percentage of the amount collected. Various form letters demanding payment had been developed. If the dunning letters were not successful, further instructions were sought and, where approved, a legal action would be launched.

The firm assisted the Bank of Toronto in another form of collection by "protesting" bills of exchange that for some reason had not been paid or accepted upon presentation. A protest form was filled out and signed by a notary. A notice of protest was sent to all parties appearing on the bill. At 3:00 p.m. each day, when the Bank closed, the firm's receptionist called six to eight of the Bank's downtown branches to see if they had any bills for protest. A fifty-cent fee was charged for each protest (plus streetcar fare and postage) and a twenty-five-cent fee for each notice. The firm was also often called by the superintendent for Toronto Western Hospital to go out to draw a will for a patient. J.B. Robinson "didn't care much for this because you usually had to do something in long-hand and on one occasion the patient wasn't able to speak and could only make unintelligible sounds. I don't remember any of these wills ever coming into the office to be probated. There certainly was no opportunity for Estate Planning."

For Dome Mines Limited the firm prepared dividend cheques and handled the printing and mailing of the annual report. The trust company that maintained the shareholder list would send the then current list, into which Robinson would insert the computed dividends. One of the stenographers, Mrs. Cora O'Brien, typed names and addresses on the cheque forms (which were in duplicate), and teams then proofread the list and the cheques and sent any mistakes back for correction. The cheques would be compared a second time and Robinson signed them as assistant secretary. The cheques were then mailed out on the dividend payment date. This was done for a number of years "until there were over 5,000 shareholders and it was impossible to do this in the three weeks that we were allowed and the Trust Company took over." A similar process was followed for annual reports and share certificates. The volume of mailing at the Adelaide Street post office, across the road from the firm's offices, became such that the post office insisted the firm take its mailings to the larger Front Street branch.

Considerable correspondence went between the firm and the offices of its mining clients in South Porcupine and Cobalt. Often staff or students were entrusted with urgent letters to be taken directly to the postal clerk on the T&NOR train, which left Union Station every night about 6:00 p.m. Apparently, "It was not always easy to work your way through right to the train."

THIS GRINDER PRACTICE WAS a far cry from the thriving and important counsel practice of R.S. Robertson. Robertson knew the law, but he also knew that litigation is about persuasion. He stressed to those assisting him in trial preparation that he wanted them to be concise and focused and not to clutter their memos with too much law:

> You were required to know the essence of a legal problem and to give him a memorandum that was short and dealt directly with the essential point. . . . Each legal point required to be dealt with in a case was supposed to be dealt with by one citation. The insistence was on a strong authoritative case for each point rather than a large collection of cases dealing with the point. When Mr. Robertson went into court, he always wanted to have one or perhaps two books and three only if he was convinced so many books were necessary. This was in sharp contrast to the long rows of books some counsel assembled before presenting their arguments. Searching for the essential point and insisting upon a few good authorities had the result that you clarified and simplified your thinking well in advance of going into court.[24]

That clear, simple thinking was evident when, in 1919, Robertson defended David Fasken's Northern Ontario Light and Power Company against a claim of negligence. A pipe conducting compressed air had been installed by Fasken's company across a ravine on trestles and an electric wire crossed at right angles 1.2 metres above it at the centre. Barriers had been erected across the pipeline on both sides of the wire and on each barrier was posted a warning of danger. Nevertheless, a twelve-year-old boy had attempted to cross the ravine by the pipeline and having climbed around a barrier came into contact with the wire and was badly injured. Robertson had been successful at both trial and the Ontario Court of Appeal. At trial the jury had found that children were not in the habit of going on the pipeline at the place where the accident occurred and the action had been dismissed. The case was appealed to the Supreme Court of Canada, where once again Robertson won the day. One of those deciding in his favour was his former mentor and law partner from Stratford, John Idington.[25]

Justice Idington was not swayed by Robertson's arguments in another negligence action in 1920, however, the case of *Wabash Railway Company v William Follick*.[26] To Idington this was a clear case of negligence. A train had struck a railway worker because it had not stopped as required by statute on approaching a level crossing and because it had been travelling too fast, just as the jury had found at trial. It rankled Idington that Robertson had been able to convince the trial judge the case should be dismissed. In his judgment he accused Robertson of absolutely discarding the statute and making a mockery of it. In Idington's view the Court of Appeal had been entirely correct in restoring the jury findings and granting judgment against the railway. Now Idington found himself having to resort to strong language because Robertson had worked his magic on the other judges.

Both Chief Justice Davies and Justice Anglin went out of their way to say that they had been extremely impressed by Robertson. The Chief Justice stated, "I frankly confess that at the close of the argument at bar, Mr. Robertson had by his able argument and clear presentation of the case for the railway company almost, if not quite, convinced me that the appeal should be allowed and the action dismissed." Anglin remarked, "I was much impressed during the argument by Mr. Robertson's ingenious and forceful contention that the failure of the employees of the defendant company to stop its train at a reasonable distance east of the distant signal could not have been the proximate cause . . . of the injury to the plaintiff, but was at most a remoter cause." Even in this loss, Robertson showcased his considerable abilities as an advocate.

THE YEAR THAT DAVID FASKEN retired was the year C.C. Calvin was called to the bar and joined the firm as a lawyer. Both Pickup and Calvin knew that Robertson was the star of the firm, and they both assisted him in litigation matters. For Pickup litigation would be the focus of his practice throughout his career. Calvin, however, was destined to be a corporate commercial lawyer — in fact one of Canada's best — but in the early years he spent a considerable amount of his time in the courtroom or at least getting Robertson ready for the courtroom. He later claimed that while waiting to be called upon in Weekly Court, he worked on drafts of trust deeds and other commercial documents.

Bryce MacKenzie, a later addition to the firm, recalls, "In Mr. Calvin we had a very careful and conscientious commercial lawyer who in his later years did not go into court, working in the shadow of Mr. Robertson and Mr. Pickup. Mr. Calvin took the position that he was not competent as a court lawyer but in truth he was extremely competent and much better than he was willing to believe."[27] Calvin may not have thought he was particularly good at litigation but he nevertheless valued the insights that it gave him. He came to the view that one could not draft good contracts until one had had the experience of litigating bad ones.[28]

AFTER HIS RETIREMENT FROM the firm, David Fasken became one of its most important clients. In the early days of Canadian estate taxes, he turned to brother Alex and the firm to help him with some estate planning, a move that provided later generations with insights into the tools and techniques of such planning. David undertook his planning within a decade of the introduction of income tax in 1917[29] and within thirty years of Ontario enacting legislation in 1892 to collect succession duties.[30] It was quite extensive, involving *inter vivos* gifts[31] and discretionary trusts,[32] charitable donations, foreign investments, a form of estate freeze, and a skillfully prepared will. His planning reflected a desire to reduce succession duties and taxes, but even more a wish to ensure that his wealth was used to fund projects that he supported and to help family members in need. Fasken abhorred the *Succession Duty Act*: "He didn't see why the Governments should be able to gobble up most of his wealth when he died, so he decided to do something about it."[33] Tax planning was certainly a motivating factor but the steps he took also reflected his fervent wish to do his duty to his family, both nuclear and extended, while at the same time keeping control of his assets out of the hands of his wife, whom he disliked, and his son, whom he did not trust.

The period from 1920 to 1925 was when David Fasken put much of his estate planning into action. He prepared his will and established a series of trusts in 1920, the trust for the Texas loan in 1924, and a trust for Nellie Wallace and his grandson in 1925.

Fasken's plans for dealing with his substantial assets was shaped in large part by the Ontario *Succession Duty Act*. This statute had been passed to defray the "very large sums [expended] annually for asylums for the insane and idiots, and for institutions for the blind and for deaf mutes and for the support of hospitals and other charities."[34] It had been re-enacted and amended several times before Fasken's death to close perceived loopholes and broaden its scope.[35] Essentially it was a tax imposed on the beneficiaries of a will or other instrument that passed title to property on or in contemplation of death. The estate itself was not the taxpayer, although it had an obligation to pay the duty on behalf of the beneficiaries within eighteen months of the testator's death.[36] Succession duty was not a tax on the value of the estate but rather on the value of any property that beneficially passed to one or more beneficiaries.[37] The rate of duty was determined by the relationship between the testator and the beneficiary, with parents, spouses, and children enjoying a lower rate.

Being an Ontario statute, it applied only to property situated in the province.[38] Fasken had not bought the Texas property to avoid provincial succession duty, nor had he set up the elaborate ownership structure for that purpose. He did, however, transfer ownership of the shares and the benefit of the interest in his debt owed as a part of his 1920 estate plan. The net effect was that a very valuable asset, worth more than $2 million, would not form part of his estate for the purposes of income tax or succession duty.

Fasken's will was completed on 17 November 1924. In preparing both it and the *inter vivos* trusts, he had three guiding principles. First, he wished to keep his wealth intact for the benefit of future generations. He made no specific bequests of property, all of which on his death was to be held in trust for specific purposes. Second, he wished no one to receive more than what he deemed they needed to live comfortably but not lavishly. Third, he wanted all investment decisions to be made by, or at least strongly influenced by, the small circle of people in whom he reposed trust.

In his will he named four executors and trustees: his wife, Alice; his son Robert; his brother Alex; and Charles Parker. These four trustees clearly divide into two groups: his wife and son, who were to be the principal beneficiaries of the trusts established under the will, had a personal interest in its administration; his brother Alex and his investment manager and nephew, Charles Parker, had professional experience and judgment.

After payment of any debts and taxes, the estate was to be held by the four trustees on a series of trusts. His wife was permitted the use and occupation of his homes in Toronto, Clarkson, and Temagami (not, interestingly, his part of the family home in Elora). She was also to be paid quarterly for the rest of her life the net income derived from an investment of $500,000. The trustees were to retain any of Fasken's investments they chose but otherwise to convert the remainder of his assets into money in a capital fund. Essentially, it was first to be used to ensure that his son received $30,000 in income each year of his life. To the extent that Robert had income from other sources, the amount paid from the capital fund was to be reduced.

On Robert's death the capital fund was to be divided into separate capital funds for each of Robert's children or their issue then living. Each such fund was to be used at the discretion of the trustees to give such children $10,000 per year. The amount could be increased at the discretion of the trustees on marriage of the children or on their starting a business. On the death of each such child the separate capital fund would go to that child's children in equal shares, or otherwise as the deceased child had directed by will or living declaration. The capital fund was to be maintained for the maximum period allowed under the *Perpetuities Act,* namely the life of the last surviving child of Robert born before Fasken's death plus twenty-one years less a day. At that point the fund would be distributed in accordance with the appointment made by the last surviving child or on the failure of a declaration to the next of kin of David Fasken as if he had died intestate.

Clearly Fasken did not want Robert, his son, to inherit his millions. In fact, he seems to have intentionally denied Robert more than an allowance, something he had been giving him for years. Neither did he want his wife, Alice, to inherit his fortune. She was to have the use of three of the homes and the household goods from four of them, but she was then living in California and would thus draw little benefit from these. Thus the bulk of the estate was not paid out and continued to accumulate in the capital fund.

In 1920 David had set up a series of discretionary trusts for his extended family, including a fund for relatives who might need financial assistance from time to time for health or other reasons.[39] He also established trusts for the churches he had worshipped at as a youngster. Today Bethany United Church, at the intersection of Sideroad 10 and 4th Line East in Pilkington Township, is a wonderfully maintained rural church in part due to a trust that Fasken established for it and the Elora Methodist Church in the 1920s. There is a modest plaque in Bethany United, thanking David Fasken for his generous gift.[40]

Fasken did not leave any money or property to his niece Nellie in his will, although in the last decade of his life she was his secretary and constant companion. He did, however, set up a trust fund for her and his grandson.

We can assume it was substantial, not only because of who they were but also because more than sixty years later its residue would be the subject of a court action.[41] Nellie was to be eligible to receive the net income from the trust property until her remarriage or death. David Jr. was to be eligible until his death, provided that he openly and publicly professed the Protestant religion. This requirement is somewhat startling in light of David Fasken's assertions at his son's divorce hearing in Texas that he had no objection to his daughter-in-law's religion. There is no evidence that his wife influenced any of Fasken's estate planning, so we have to assume that it was his choice to include this religious condition.[42] Interestingly, this aspect of the trust attracted no judicial comment whatsoever from Justice Arbour when she was asked to rule on other aspects of the trust. She simply noted that it was not an issue between the parties because David Jr. had remained a Protestant.[43]

It is worthy of note that in 1925, when Fasken set up this particular trust, he did not make either his wife Alice or his son Robert a trustee, even though his grandson was a beneficiary. Instead he chose Nellie herself and Charles Parker. Clearly he used the same approach as with his testamentary trusts — one trustee who had a personal interest and the other who was a professional adviser. With this trust he also satisfied two of his concerns. He gave Nellie money to sustain her lifestyle, and he ensured that his grandson had a source of income independent of and inaccessible to his father. Unfortunately we do not have many details about the trust.[44]

Fasken had poured millions into the building and upkeep of the Western Hospital and its nurses' home in Toronto. "That was his real baby," according to Marion MacKenzie.[45] He first came to support the hospital in 1906 because one of its founders, Dr. John Ferguson, was also a founder of Excelsior Life.[46] Fasken had become one of the hospital's earliest and most important supporters, funding an addition in 1906 and a new building in 1911 before turning his mind to estate planning. He also made two large donations during the 1920s, when he was implementing his estate plan: in 1923 he donated money to permit another extension of the hospital; and in 1924 he made a matching grant when a citywide appeal raised $200,000.

The *Toronto Daily Star* tells us that Fasken donated "about $500,000" to the hospital.[47] His cousin Marion, however, talks of "the millions he poured into the building and up-keep of the Western Hospital and its nurses' home." We do not know what he actually donated, but one comment in a brief history of the hospital prepared in the 1950s suggests that Marion's estimate may be closer to the truth. It states that Fasken was "by nature a quiet, unassuming man, who did not desire public recognition or even knowledge of his many generous acts."[48] These words echo a remark made by his good friend the Reverend Andrew Robb in Fasken's funeral oration. Robb stated that Fasken "had amassed a great fortune but he had spent liberally . . . on others, not himself. He had given away hundreds of thousands of dollars unknown to the world at large, unknown even to all but a few of his closest friends. In all his givings he abhorred publicity."[49]

Another charitable organization that Fasken supported was the Salvation Army.[50] As was often the case his support had a link to his family. His older sister Mary and his younger sister Margaret, born about 1862, had both joined the Army.[51] Margaret became an officer and moved to Vancouver as a captain.

One of the motivations for Fasken's planning was his realization that he was unlikely to be able to sell his Texas ranch. He knew that if he retained a personal interest in it he might be faced with succession duty or run afoul of the Texas law prohibiting foreign ownership. He therefore decided to relinquish any personal connection with the property and the loans, ceasing to be a shareholder, director, or officer of Midland Farms and transferring the shares to his son Robert, who had become a US citizen.[52] This was the equivalent of what today we call an estate freeze. Robert received the shares but they were of limited value because Midland Farms acknowledged the debt then held for David Fasken by three trustees: Alex Fasken, Charles Parker, and Andrew Fasken. The trustees in turn acknowledged the terms under which they held the debt. One of these was that 8 percent interest should be paid to David Fasken. Under this arrangement Robert thus owned the Midland Farms Company but would benefit only from future growth in the value of the ranch in excess of 8 percent per year. Then, in 1924, the interest entitlement was transferred to Fasken's wife, Alice.

If David's transfer of the property was intended to insulate him and the ranch from possible seizure by the Texas government, his plan did not work. The state government brought an action to seize the land as having been illegally acquired. Fasken, of course, had bought the property in the knowledge that there was a prohibition against foreigners owning Texas land, but he had been advised by legal counsel in Texas that there would be no problem if a farm company was formed to purchase and resell the land. The flaw in this strategy was that the land was not resaleable as farms. Years later Fasken found himself as the indirect owner of a Texas ranch property, and that is why he had transferred his indirect holding to his son. The Texas seizure had proceeded anyway.

Fasken fought this action through most of the last years of his life, ultimately succeeding at the US Supreme Court in 1927 on the argument that the Texas law was contrary to public policy, being in contravention of the US treaty with Great Britain under which each country had agreed to grant reciprocal treatment to the subjects of the other.[53] Since Great Britain (of which Canada was still a colony) permitted US citizens to hold land, it was inappropriate for the American states not to do likewise. Had the case arisen less than a decade later, after the Treaty of Westminster, the result might have been different.

———— ❖ ————

HAD DAVID FASKEN DONE his estate planning twenty years before, he probably would have turned to his senior partner, Marion Chadwick, but Chadwick played no part in the Fasken estate plan. He was still coming to the office, but by this time he was quite deaf and any conversation was difficult.[54] He employed a public stenographer and worked on his heraldry and genealogy.

The last entry in Chadwick's diary was for October 1921: "Engaged a maid, Sarah M. Rooney, tall and quite aristocratic looking, but not young. She came from Brantford." Edward Marion Chadwick died two months later, on 15 December. His obituary in the *Globe* appeared on the front page. The one in the *Mail and Empire* was headed "E. M. Chadwick Dies, Was Noted Historian." It opened with the words "Edward Marion Chadwick, KC, member of the law firm of Fasken, Robertson, Chadwick & Sedgewick," but it stressed his many non-legal accomplishments.[55]

If anything these obituaries underplayed his importance. His *Ontarian Families* is still one of Canada's most frequently consulted genealogical studies.[56] Although an amateur armorist, he heavily influenced Canadian heraldry, securing the maple leaf as a Canadian national symbol. He also designed heraldic shields for the city of Guelph and the new province of Saskatchewan (1905), as well as the coat of arms of the General Synod of the Anglican Church of Canada (1908) and a new augmentation of the Ontario shield (1909).[57]

Of his family the obituary mentioned only that he was survived by his wife, Martha, five sons, and a daughter. It casts no light on Chadwick's notable children: Marion (Fanny) the amateur playwright and diarist whose career is considered the forerunner of professional live theatre in Toronto;[58]

Vaux (to rhyme with box), the noted architect;[59] Richard (Dick), the distinguished engineer;[60] and Brian, an architect who shared his father's artistic
talents.[61] *no mention of our grandfather 'Pink' aldshue banker.*

—◆—

THE YEAR THAT CHADWICK died, Robertson was made a King's Counsel. The
next year Lionel Davis sought the new KC's litigation expertise. Davis represented the Ontario Metal Products Company, which was suing the Mutual
Life Insurance Company of New York over its refusal to pay out on a policy.
The insurer alleged that the application for insurance contained inaccur-
acies. Davis sought his former firm, and specifically the advocacy of Robertson. They presented the case together, arguing that the *Ontario Insurance Act*
provided that no inaccuracy in the statements contained in an application
for insurance voided the policy unless it was material to the contract. They
pointed out that the life insurance policy itself had declared "the policy and
the application . . . constitute the entire contract between the parties" and
that the statements made by the insured should "be deemed representations
and not warranties." They won at trial but lost on appeal.[62] Robertson then
took the case to the Supreme Court, where he was successful in having the
trial judgment restored.[63]

Shortly thereafter Robertson found himself part of a 1920s defence
"dream team," to use a modern expression. William Norman Tilley,[64] Newton Wesley Rowell,[65] Isadore F. Hellmuth,[66] Gordon Shaver,[67] and R.S. Robertson were retained to defend the officers and directors of the failed Home
Bank. The early 1920s had proved a difficult time for the banking industry
in Canada.[68] Although bankers lobbying the government with respect to the
upcoming ten-year revision of the *Bank Act* in 1923 assured the government
and the public that all would be well, many banks faced severe financial
difficulties. The root cause was that Canada did not enjoy the boom of the
Roaring Twenties that the United States did, and it took longer for the economy to return to normal after the First World War. In 1920 the high inflation
of the immediate postwar years broke and prices began to tumble. The cost
of living dropped 15 percent in that year and a further 10 percent the next.
Many businesses were stuck with inventory that they had produced at high
cost but could now sell only at a low price. Business bankruptcies went way
up, from 873 in 1919 to 2,451 in 1920 and 3,695 in 1921. To this was added a
severe wheat crop failure out west.

Many banks had not anticipated these changes; they had grown too big, too fast. In 1920 there were 4,676 bank branches in Canada, an increase of 1,661 over the preceding three years. The first sign of the changed time was the rising number of bank mergers and acquisitions of smaller banks by larger ones.[69] In 1921 Bank of Montreal bought the Merchants Bank of Canada. In 1923 the Banque nationale of Quebec was acquired (with some provincial government assistance) by the Banque d'Hochelaga, which changed its name to Banque canadienne nationale. The Bank of Hamilton was acquired by the Bank of Commerce. Then the Union Bank of Winnipeg announced that most of its reserves had been lost through bad debts and improper foreign exchange transactions. The Standard Bank of Toronto announced that its reserves had been reduced and it lowered its dividends. But the worst was yet to come.

The Home Bank, also of Toronto, to outward appearances seemed to have avoided many of these problems. It announced that it had net profits of over $200,000 and was in "splendid financial condition."[70] Then, on 17 August 1923, the Home Bank collapsed. Its seventy-one branches were closed and those who had money on deposit were denied access to their funds. The biggest loser was Sir Henry Pellatt, who had to declare bankruptcy and put his home, Casa Loma, up for sale. But many others also suffered severe losses. The public outcry was such that on 3 October the Home Bank's president, vice-president, general manager, chief accountant, and chief auditor were all arrested and charged with fraud, as were five directors.

Attorney General W.F. Nickle retained D.L. "Lally" McCarthy as chief prosecutor and gave him as his assistant the young but extremely hardworking and focused Crown prosecutor James McRuer.[71] In response the executives who had been charged lined up their strong defence team. J.W. Pickup, a classmate of McRuer's from Osgoode Hall but not a friend, assisted Robertson. The evidence against the executives was strong. It seems that the Bank had been misrepresenting its poor financial position for some time. The Crown won each case at trial, but the convictions were reversed against the directors on appeal.[72] One casualty of the case was the relationship between Robertson and McRuer. Patrick Boyer, McRuer's biographer, has written that "at times [McRuer] was like a horse with blinkers on: he could only see one thing — the course ahead on which he had set himself."[73] Robertson, as a skilled defence counsel, undoubtedly thought that McRuer was unnecessarily inflexible. His dogged persistence in this and other prosecutions during this period meant that there was no love lost between the two. Later, when McRuer served under Robertson on the Ontario Court of Appeal, he discovered that what goes around comes around.

— ❦ —

As THE HOME BANK was failing, the engine that had driven the law firm's early growth was being sold. In 1923 William George Gooderham and his brother Albert Edward oversaw the sale of the family distillery business to Harry Hatch, an entrepreneur from Deseronto, Ontario. It had been years since the distillery was the main source of the family's wealth. During the First World War the family had donated the use of its distillery complex in Toronto to meet the needs of the imperial government for a facility to produce acetone for use in the manufacture of cordite. All it asked in return was that the government pay the taxes. The repurposed facility produced more than half of Great Britain's supply of acetone. Now, after the war and with prohibition gaining favour, the family decided to sell the facility entirely. Hatch was happy to buy it. He was a former hotel owner turned liquor retailer. In 1921 he had been hired by the Canadian Industrial Alcohol Company, which had bought the Corby and Wiser distilleries to develop business in the United States. He had set up a very successful rum-running operation to get alcohol to US bootleggers. Now he wanted to use the profits to get into the business of making liquor. He left Canadian Industrial Alcohol and bought Gooderham & Worts. Three years later he would buy Hiram Walker and create Hiram Walker–Gooderham Worts.

Much wealth continued to be generated in a number of the family businesses. Although the legal work for Manufacturers Life Insurance Company had departed with Ross Gooderham, two of those businesses continued to be served by the Fasken firm: the Bank of Toronto and Canada Permanent Mortgage Corporation. William George Gooderham provided management for all three. His brother Albert Edward served as a director of the Bank of Toronto, vice-president of Canada Permanent, and president of the Dominion of Canada Guarantee and Accident Insurance Company, but his real interests were elsewhere. William George, like his grandfather and father, was an excellent, if very conservative, businessman, but Albert Edward was best known as a philanthropist and patron of the arts.

Albert also became an important benefactor of medicine. In 1913–14 Dr. Robert Defries and Dr. John G. Fitzgerald of the Department of Hygiene of the University of Toronto worked to establish a university-based laboratory for antitoxin production. When the First World War started, the Canadian

Expeditionary Force needed tetanus antitoxin. The Canadian Red Cross initially tried to obtain it in the United States. Albert, then serving as chair of the Ontario division of the Canadian Red Cross and on the university board of governors, approached the fledgling laboratory about producing the antitoxin. They were able to do so at a much lower price than the Americans wanted. Gooderham was impressed. The next year he purchased a twenty-three hectare farm just north of Toronto and financed the construction and equipping of a facility on the farm to support the work of the laboratory in the preparation of the antitoxin. He donated it all to the university. In 1917 he participated in the official opening of what was called Connaught Laboratories after the Duke of Connaught, Governor General of Canada. Albert then served as chair of Connaught Laboratories for many years. Later, in the 1920s, Connaught became the first to commercialize insulin after its discovery by Frederick Banting and Charles Best, and Albert Edward chaired the Insulin Committee.

Following in Beatty's footsteps, William George was for a time the president of the Old Boys of Upper Canada College and for many years chaired the board of governors of the school. His leadership and generosity were recognized in the 1920s when the lieutenant-governor of Ontario presented a full-length portrait of him to the college to hang in its library. At the ceremony the lieutenant-governor stated that none who had guided a college had ever been held in more affection by the student body.

Meanwhile, Albert Edward had become heavily involved in the Toronto music scene. He served as director of music at St. James Cathedral. More important, he was crucial in the creation and early nurture of two musical institutions: the Toronto Conservatory of Music and the Toronto Symphony Orchestra.

NOT LONG AFTER THE sale of the Gooderham & Worts distillery, Alex alienated yet another lawyer in the firm. By 1925 George Sedgewick had had enough of his domineering managing partner.[74] Sedgewick is said to have possessed "qualities of cool judgment and kindly courtesy" and "a gentleness which conduces to peace in any assembly of which he is a member."[75] But peace with Alex Fasken was hard for anyone to achieve. Sedgewick was "a gentleman at all times" but Alex was not and as result Sedgewick "found the strain and pressure at the office very hard."[76] He felt added pressure in 1925 because the Presbyterian Church of Canada, of which he was an active member, was in the process of merging with the Methodists and the Congregational Church to form the United Church of Canada. As an elder of St. Andrew's Presbyterian Church, George was much involved, as was his brother, the Reverend W.H. Sedgewick.[77] Leaving the Fasken firm, Sedgewick joined Malone, Malone, Sedgewick & Montgomery.

His departure hurt Alex Fasken and the firm much more than it did Sedgewick, who would go on to a distinguished career and be made a KC in 1928.[78] He was a good man with a strong sense of social responsibility, serving as chairman of the board of the Canadian National Institute of the Blind, an adviser to the Salvation Army, president of the board of Central Neighbourhood House in Toronto, and chairman of the Literature Service of the League of Nations.[79] He was twice chosen as president of the University Club and became president of the Canadian Club in 1926. On 19 December 1930 Sedgewick was appointed to the High Court Division of the Supreme Court of Ontario. Ironically, he again filled a vacancy created by Hugh Rose, who had become Chief Justice of the High Court.[80]

Sedgewick's tenure as a judge was short and not very distinguished.[81] The highlight occurred in 1932 when he served on an Ontario royal commission with his former mentor Riddell, now a member of the Ontario Court of Appeal. They were asked to investigate allegations made by the young leader of the Ontario Liberals, Mitch Hepburn, that payments had been improperly made by the Hydro-Electric Power Commission of Ontario to John Aird Jr. in connection with the purchase of certain power rights. Riddell and Sedgewick acted quickly, being appointed on 19 August and, much to the chagrin of Hepburn, delivering their report clearing the Hydro-Electric Power Commission and Aird on 31 October 1932.[82]

That same year Prime Minister R.B. Bennett presided over an Imperial Economic Conference in Ottawa. After his election in 1930, Bennett had sought to deal with the Depression in part by using significantly higher tariffs to "blast his way" into foreign markets.[83] British textile interests, among others, complained. At the conference Bennett agreed to seek out someone who could preside over his newly created Tariff Board to look into the appropriateness of Canadian tariffs in light of local and foreign costs of materials, labour production, and distribution. Bennett approached Sedgewick, who seems to have negotiated for better terms because in February 1933 Parliament introduced an amendment to the *Tariff Board Act*, increasing the pension of board members and raising the annual salary of the chairman from $12,000 to $15,000.[84] In March, Sedgewick was appointed chairman and immediately undertook an investigation of the tariff on British textiles, travelling across Canada and to England. His report was warmly received in both Canada and the United Kingdom and contributed to his being named a companion of the Order of St. Michael and St. George by King George V in 1935. In March 1939, while still chairing the Tariff Board, he had a heart attack during a meeting with government officials. He died shortly thereafter at his Rockcliffe home in Ottawa at the age of sixty-one and was buried in his native Nova Scotia.

Sedgewick's departure triggered a new partnership agreement. On 1 August 1925 Fasken, Robertson, Jimmy Aitchison, Pickup, and Calvin signed an agreement making it crystal clear that in all matters that counted this was Alex Fasken's firm. Each partner other than Alex was required to devote his full time to the practice, accounting for all commissions and other "emoluments" that were in any way connected with the practice. Alex was permitted to devote only such time to the partnership business as he saw fit and to retain for himself all directors' fees and salaries that he received from any company other than the annual retainers from the Northern Ontario Light and Power Company and the Excelsior Life Insurance Company. Those were to be shared with his partners. The agreement even stated that "all office furniture, furnishings, library, typewriters and equipment are the sole property of the said Fasken but this does not refer to current supplies." Alex also took the lion's share of the profits. His base entitlement was $12,000, Robertson's was $8,400, and Aitchison, Pickup, and Calvin got $3,000 each. Alex also received 42 percent of any additional profits and Robertson 32 percent. Aitchison, Pickup, and Calvin were guaranteed at least 2 percent each, with the remaining 20% to be distributed as Alex thought fit. As the manager of the partnership business, Alex had full authority to engage and discharge employees, to fix their remuneration, and to define their duties. He could also admit new partners and let partners go "without dissolving the partnership."

IN 1927 ROBERTSON WAS again retained in a much-publicized legal action. This time he was asked to assist Percy Smiley of Johnston, Grant, Dods & Macdonald in an action by Florence Deeks against H.G. Wells. Deeks was alleging that Wells had improperly used her manuscript, "The Web," in writing his best-selling book *The Outline of History*.[85] She had submitted the manuscript to Macmillan Company of Canada in late summer 1918. They had not returned it until the following spring, when it had been rejected. A year later Macmillan published Wells's book, and Deeks noted many similarities between it and her manuscript. She began to suspect that the publisher had shared her manuscript with Wells, who then used it in preparing his own. It was not that he had copied lengthy passages but that he seemed to have used her approach, structure, and some of her conclusions. She began to study the lengthy work carefully and decided that Wells must have been given access to her unpublished manuscript.

Supported by her wealthy brother, she initially retained Norman Tilley of Daniel Thomson's firm, Tilley, Johnston, Thomson & Parmenter. But in 1927 Tilley walked away from her case. The Johnston, Grant, Dods & Macdonald firm assumed it but Smiley, to whom the Deeks action was assigned, knew that he needed a well-respected litigator to take the lead if Florence was to have any chance against the very well-known and much-respected Wells and his publisher. He turned to Robertson, who soon recognized that while Florence was quite likely right, the case presented difficulties, one of which was that Florence was not a good witness on her own behalf. She was too hesitant and defensive. There was also no conclusive evidence that Wells had even seen the manuscript, let alone improperly used it. It was a case that needed to be built on logic, inference, and textual analysis.

When Robertson presented her case at trial, he opened by saying, "I should like to say perhaps a little more than one generally does, because of the nature of the case, what we claim and how we expect to go about proving it."[86] He relied heavily on expert witnesses, some of whom unfortunately proved too prolix for the judge's liking. Despite what today looks like a strong, well-presented case against them, Wells and his publisher won the day. The judge could not bring himself to find that such a distinguished author and such a respected publisher had done as Florence alleged. Robertson took his client aside and suggested that she not appeal. He knew that his was a message she would not want to hear but he thought he owed her his best assessment. He explained that an appeal would seldom overturn a judgment where the complaint was with the findings of fact of the trial judge and not with errors of law. She later recalled he told her that "the Judges of the Appellate Division would just follow the trial judge who had the advantage of seeing and hearing the witnesses."[87] Robertson helped Smiley prepare the appeal but he himself withdrew.

In the end Florence herself argued her appeal. Another former partner of the firm, Justice William Renwick Riddell, was the key judge of the four who sat on the appeal. As a historian and writer he took great interest in the case. It was Riddell, "with an attitude of supreme self confidence," to whom the others seemed to defer. Regrettably Riddell's judgment accepted the trial judge's findings. He seemed focused on proving that his scholarship was better than that of Robertson's experts. In short, the appeal court did exactly as Robertson had predicted.

Florence still would not accept the judgment against her. She took the case herself to the Privy Council in London but met with a similar fate. Ironically, history has been better to her than either Canadian or British justice at the time. Most of those today who are familiar with her case believe that Wells did in fact do as she alleged. But, of course, in the court of public opinion the burden of proof is much lower than the one that Robertson faced.

THE DECADE ENDED WITH the death of David Fasken. He passed away on 2 December 1929, making front-page news.[88] The Toronto papers noted his many achievements as a lawyer and managing partner of an important law firm; as president of the Excelsior Life Insurance Company, the Nipissing Mining Company Limited, the Northern Ontario Light and Power Company, and the Northern Canada Power Company Limited; and as a major benefactor of the Salvation Army and the Toronto Western Hospital.

On 4 and 5 December his funeral was again front-page news, including pictures of Toronto's leading citizens who not only attended the funeral at his home on University Avenue but also drove through deep snowdrifts to his gravesite in Elora — business leaders such as Albert Edward Gooderham, Edward Rogers Wood, and Sigmund Samuel; Ontario Court of Appeal judges such as William R. Riddell and Cornelius A. Masten; prominent doctors like John Ferguson; and the leading architect Edward James Lennox. Many of them acted as honorary pallbearers.[89]

Later, on 3 January 1930 on the probating of his will, the newspapers yet again gave his affairs extensive front-page coverage. Relying on the will and the probate documents, the Toronto Daily Star reported that he had left an estate of nearly $2 million.[90] The newspaper coverage underestimated the size of his estate and missed its real significance because it failed to take into account the series of estate planning steps that he had taken over the preceding decade or so.[91] David Fasken was far wealthier, one of Canada's wealthiest men. He had accumulated many assets during his life that were not referred to in his will or listed for probate purposes but that had a much greater value, many millions of dollars more, than the $1,792,328.11 shown for Ontario probate and succession duty purposes. David's assets were in fact so valuable that they would ultimately make his grandson, David Fasken Jr. a billionaire.[92]

—————◆◆◆—————

MICHAEL BLISS IN HIS HISTORY of Canadian business describes the decade following the market crash of October 1929 as the Dark Years, a time when Canada, like the rest of the world, was faced with tough economic times: a flight from the stock exchanges, low prices, and glutted markets.[93] For the Faskens firm this was a decade of little growth and declining revenues, but it was also a time when Alex Fasken was at his best. The strategy that he had adopted in the 1920s of focusing the firm's attention on a limited number of long-standing loyal clients and on the litigation reputation and expertise of R.S. Robertson was the key to the firm's survival in the 1930s, which were not as dark as they might have otherwise been. Alex had "human frailties that did not always endear him to his subordinates,"[94] but those with whom he dealt came to recognize that "he was a man of great ability and devotion."[95]

This was also the decade when Robertson reached the summit of his litigation career. He kept himself and his juniors very busy, taking on a large number of cases, many as counsel to lawyers outside the firm. When these lawyers knew their clients needed litigation expertise and experience beyond what they themselves possessed, they turned to Robertson. Sometimes all they needed was a written opinion prior to trial.[96] At other times they asked him to take the trial or the appeal.

Robertson's position as a top litigator was evidenced in the fall of 1929, when the stock market crashed. Many people lost substantial amounts of money and there was much criticism of the practices of investment brokers. Many were arrested and released on bail. When Robertson arrived at the firm's offices the morning after the arrests, it was crowded with brokers all wanting to retain him to defend them.[97]

The economic troubles in the stock market generated a good deal of work for Robertson. Typical is the case of *Re Trust & Guarantee Co. v Brennan et al.* Robertson acted for two stockbrokers, Stobel and Forlong, caught up in the consequences of the crash. These stockbrokers carried on business in partnership. Brennan, a commissioned salesman, brought them a Mr. Miller, who bought shares through them on margin, meaning that he bought them on credit. Thereafter, unbeknown to them, Miller became seriously ill and was rendered unable to give instructions. When prices began to fall and it looked as though there would be a call on the shares, Miller's son approached Brennan and asked him to sell his father's shares. The problem was that his father was unable to authorize the sale and had not given his son a power of attorney. The son was very concerned that if nothing were done, his father would suffer a serious loss that he could not sustain. Brennan agreed to arrange for the sale of the shares but, not wanting to admit that he lacked due authorization, led Stobel and Forlong to believe that he was acting on Miller's instructions. The shares were sold, with Stobel and Forlong obtaining a net gain of $41,822 for Miller.

Had matters rested there, nobody would have been hurt. Brennan, however, saw an opportunity to earn a further commission. He convinced Miller's son that they should reinvest the money. Brennan again misled Stobel and Forlong, suggesting that he had instructions from Miller to invest the profit from the sale in other stocks. When the market did not recover and in fact fell even further, Miller lost everything. Stobel and Forlong, like many stockbrokers, had their own problems and filed for bankruptcy.

When Miller died the Trusts & Guarantee Company, as his executors, noted the share-trading history and realized that he could never have authorized either the initial sale or the reinvestment. They approached Stobel and Forlong for compensation, which the two stockbrokers refused. They had acted in good faith, they alleged, and they themselves had been wiped out. The executors retained Luxenberg & Levinter. On a review of the facts, these lawyers realized that their client had a clear case of misconduct against Brennan, the commissioned salesman but, of course, he had no money. They decided to bring action against Stobel and Forlong, as well as Brennan, for conversion, breach of contract, and fraud.

Robertson defended the stockbrokers by seeking to convince the trial judge that his clients had also been duped by Brennan. In any event, he argued, the Trusts & Guarantee could not take action against his bankrupt clients without leave of the court, which they had not obtained. Despite Robertson's arguments, the executors were successful at trial and the defendants were found to be jointly and severally liable for $41,822, the profit on the original sale that had been lost by the reinvestment. Robertson appealed and was successful at the Ontario Court of Appeal. Although the judgment was affirmed against Brennan, the case was dismissed against his clients, Stobel and Forlong. The appeal court, however, was reluctant to let the stockbrokers completely off the hook. They ruled that the dismissal was without prejudice to the executors proceeding against Stobel and Forlong in the bankruptcy proceeding.

Luxenberg & Levinter, aware that Brennan did not have the ability to satisfy the judgment and unwilling to stand in line as an unsecured creditor in a bankruptcy proceeding, retained D.L. "Lally" McCarthy as counsel and appealed to the Supreme Court of Canada. They sought a ruling that the money their client was owed properly belonged to Miller and was not subject to the bankruptcy. Although the Supreme Court restored the trial judgment with some variations, it was not a total loss for Robertson. The Court accepted that Stobel and Forlong were innocent of fraud but found that they were still trustees of the property and in reinvesting the proceeds of the sale had acted without instructions, to their client's detriment. The Court also accepted that the action against Stobel and Forlong ought to have proceeded only with leave of the court but saw this as a technical matter. It granted leave retroactively. Of significance to Robertson and his clients, however, the Court required that any recovery from Stobel and Forlong would have to be in accordance with the bankruptcy proceedings. Robertson had been able to ensure that the executors did not get the preferential treatment they had been seeking.

DURING THE 1930s ROBERTSON demonstrated again and again that he was one of Canada's top litigators. He may have played second fiddle to Alex Fasken in the firm, but beyond the walls of their Toronto Street office he was one of the leaders of the profession. He appeared many times before the Ontario Court of Appeal and the Supreme Court of Canada and at times before the Judicial Committee of the Privy Council in England. He also became a key member of the Law Society of Upper Canada. In 1930, when a vacancy occurred in the ranks of the benchers of the Law Society, Robertson was chosen by Convocation to fill it. The next year was an election year for the benchers. Robertson ran and was elected by the profession. Following his election, he was appointed to the Legal Education Committee, serving with Michael Ludwig, Norman Tilley, Shirley Denison, and several other leaders of the profession.

Dean John D. Falconbridge and his teaching staff at Osgoode Hall Law School, led by young Cecil "Caesar" Augustus Wright, were trying to convince the benchers of the direction that legal education should take in Ontario.[98] In the 1920s Wright had come to the Law School, as it was then known, from the University of Western Ontario, where he had been an award-winning young scholar. During his student years, Dr. Donald A. MacRae and Dean Falconbridge had begun to change the Law School from a trade school to an academic institution. Traditionally it had been seen as supplementary to the real education that young would-be lawyers received in law offices as articled clerks, an approach that had changed only marginally since Reeve became the first principal of the school. The lectures were most often delivered not by professional law teachers but by practising lawyers like Zebulon Lash in the early years and like Robertson now. MacRae and Falconbridge had sought to recruit young scholars to do graduate work in law in the United States and then to join their faculty. Wright was one of those recruited.

Following graduation and with the encouragement of these early law teachers, Wright had spent a year at Harvard Law School, earning an SJD degree. In 1927 he had returned to join the teaching staff at Osgoode Hall. Wright's year at Harvard taught him that a professional three-year university law degree was infinitely superior to the combined part-time law course and articling program then prevalent in Ontario. In the 1930s he took on the cause of MacRae and Falconbridge and lobbied extensively both in person and in print for professional law teachers and for a more academic instruction of law students in Ontario.

But Wright was to be disappointed. Robertson and the committee decided to undo some of Dean Falconbridge's advances rather than adopt the approach advocated by Wright. Robertson would later say that the university undergraduate degree and three-year academic law program Wright sought would put students "far beyond the stage of learning to do accurately and carefully the innumerable small things that fall to the lot of the young lawyer in his practice."[99]

Robertson ran again successfully for bencher in 1936 and subsequently served as chairman of the Law Society's Discipline Committee. Then in 1937 he became the first active member of the firm to be elected treasurer, the Law Society's highest office. Nesbitt had been elected treasurer in 1927, but that was several decades after he had demonstrated his dislike of the Faskens by leaving the firm to go to the Supreme Court.

———

WHILE ROBERTSON WAS EARNING accolades and winning cases (and frustrating Caesar Wright), Alex Fasken enjoyed the life of a man of position, influence, and wealth. In addition to being managing partner of the firm, he had been elected a director of Toronto General Trusts Corporation and of the Provincial Paper Mills Limited, and he had consolidated his position and that of his firm with the Bank of Toronto, the Excelsior Life Insurance Company, Toronto Western Hospital, and Dome Mines. He had been corporate secretary of Dome Mines from its inception and in the 1930s became its vice-president. Alex assumed David's position as president of Excelsior Life and became president and chairman of the board of Toronto Western. He was also serving as vice-president of Nipissing Mines Company, the parent holding company, and as president of the operating company, Nipissing Mining Company, Limited. By 1933, however, the Cobalt silver operation was winding down.[100]

While Alex was never named to the Bank of Toronto board, he continued to provide many legal services to that institution. The turbulent economic times meant that the Bank looked regularly to Alex and his firm for opinions on such matters as their security for troubled loans. Alex ensured that the Bank always got a prompt, helpful response. With Fasken taking a leadership role in each of these companies, there was no doubt they would continue to send their legal work to the firm. He had made the firm's ties to its principal clients more or less unbreakable.

With his many business dealings, he had also become a wealthy man. He showcased that wealth by acquiring a forty-hectare property on Mississauga Road adjacent to the Mississauga Golf and Country Club. He had a large, stately mansion built that he and his wife dubbed Ialfa. The "I" stood for Isabel, the "Al" for Alex, and the "Fa" for Fasken. There the two of them lived happily, but alone. Isabel is said to have "almost worshipped him. They had no family, except . . . 'an extravagant dog.'"[101]

Each day he drove into Toronto: "Although he kept a chauffeur, he loved to drive his own car by himself, and . . . he would drive like the wind."[102] Unfortunately for Alex, the towns of Port Credit, Long Branch, New Toronto, and Mimico through which he drove posted a speed limit and because he paid no attention, he was often charged with speeding: "One day . . . he was stopped by a policeman for breaking the speed law, but Alex just put his hand in his pocket, drew out his business card, threw it at the policeman, when he growled out 'You can get me there' and drove on as fast as he could." Alex invariably had a student in the office try to get him off. J.B. Robinson recalls that Alex would give the student the summons and tell him to take it to a magistrate with some explanation or other: "It wasn't easy

Alex Fasken's home, IALFA
Law Society of Upper Canada Archives, Fasken Martineau DuMoulin LLP fonds

to find a free magistrate and when you did the invariable answer was that if he wanted to dispute the summons he must appear in Court. Finally we just paid the fines which were then $3 or $5."[103]

Despite the economic downturn, or perhaps because of it, there was much work to be done for Dome Mines. Precious metals are always in demand during downturns in the stock market. Certainly Alex realized how fortunate the firm was to have a large gold-mining operation as a client. While other businesses were in difficulty, Dome was growing. In 1934 it expanded into Quebec at a place to be known as Val d'Or. On 21 April, at a time when Alex himself was out of the office, Jimmy Aitchison, Calvin, and Robinson incorporated a new subsidiary for Dome under the name Sigma Mines. The three of them were named directors. Aitchison was elected president in Alex's absence. On his return Alex, of course, assumed that office. Later in the decade when gold was discovered north of Lake Superior in the western reaches of Ontario at Geraldton and then near Red Lake, Dome became interested.[104] Later it would acquire the Campbell Red Lake mine. Alex, who had become vice-president of Dome, dedicated much time and energy to its success.

Alex also put much time into Excelsior Life. He had been on its board since 1901. Now as its president and with his office in the Excelsior Life Building, he could "keep in close, daily touch with its affairs,"[105] overseeing all aspects of its operations. He also began to make annual visits to each of the company's branches and agencies across Canada. Despite the Great Depression he helped to develop the company into a $100 million business.

The management of Toronto Western Hospital also made frequent calls on Alex's time.[106] He had become a member of its board of governors in 1922, at a time when David was its honorary chairman. The actual chairman by this point was Thomas Crawford, and when Crawford died in 1928 Alex became president of the hospital and chairman of its board of governors. His first vice-president was Edward Rogers Wood of Dominion Securities. This was an important time for the hospital. With David Fasken's help, it had merged with the Grace Hospital. Again Alex helped administer one of his brother's projects. David may have brought about the merger, but it was Alex who made sure that the facilities were rationalized and the staff integrated. A Grace Hospital Division continued for some time, but by 1936 operations were centralized at the Toronto Western site on Bathurst and the name Grace Hospital was passed to the Salvation Army for its hospital. Like David, Alex gave generously of his time and money to the hospital. Its administrators would later say that "his sacrifice of time and the wisdom of his counsel were invaluable . . . . Rarely was such a strong and courageous spirit blended with such sound judgment."[107]

It was Alex's sound judgment that had in large part motivated his brother David to make him a key executor of his estate, with wide discretionary powers. Alex exercised that judgment to make the most important decision in his family's history. One of the key assets of David's legacy, even if not formally part of his estate, was the C Ranch in Texas. It was not a good time to be a cattleman, given the Depression and the drought that plagued the region, but Alex knew that in 1927 oil had been discovered to the southeast of the ranch, near Odessa. He decided to ask the ranch manager, his nephew Andrew Fasken, why no one had considered drilling for oil. Alex went to Texas to inspect the ranch and consider how best to proceed.

On 18 March 1931 in El Paso, Texas, he met with David's son, Robert, and Robert's wife, Inez, who had come from Ross, California, to meet him.[108] The announced purpose of the meeting was for Alex to resign as president of Midland Farms Company and Robert to be elected in his stead. They all knew that after David's unsuccessful efforts to sell the ranch land for farming, it had been operated by Andrew Fasken as a prosperous cattle ranch. But, Alex asked, was this the best way to exploit this valuable asset?

It was decided to invite Andrew Fasken to a meeting in Toronto, where he could give an account of his operation of the ranch. At 10:00 am on 4 May 1931 in the firm's offices, Andrew provided his report. Alex wanted to know why others in the Permian Basin were drilling for oil and they were not. Andrew, who had been raised as a farmboy in Elora, had a love for the land not shared by the others in the room. He saw drilling for oil as evil, a process that would pollute the land and make his cattle sick.

That was not the answer Alex and the others wanted to hear. They looked at the ranch as a business and found it hard to look beyond the potential profits. When the two sides could not reach agreement, the meeting was adjourned until 2:00 p.m. Andrew still would not agree. A further adjournment was called until 2:00 p.m. the next day. Andrew yet again opposed drilling, so a third adjournment was given until 2:00 p.m. the following day. Finally, on 6 May, Andrew submitted his resignation as a director and vice-president of the company. The way had been cleared.

It was decided that Robert Fasken and Jimmy Aitchison, newly elected as a director to replace Andrew, would go to Texas to retain a new property manager and to consider their options. The company lacked any knowledge or expertise in drilling for oil so offers were considered to sell some of the land to a third party that could conduct the drilling operations. By the fall talks were underway to sell ninety square miles (about 230 square kilometres) for $460,800 and one-quarter of the usual one-eighth royalty in the oil, gas, and other mineral rights in the land to J.E. Mabee of Tulsa, Oklahoma. This represented less than a quarter of the ranch, brought in an immediate and substantial cash payment, and was a way to test the proposition. The deal was ratified by Alex and the other members of the board in a meeting held on 15 December 1932 in a room at the Pennsylvania Hotel in New York City.

When Mabee found substantial oil reserves on his portion of the land, it was decided that no further sales would take place. Instead oil leases would be granted. This was now too important to entrust to Robert and Jimmy Aitchison. The board of Midland Farms Company authorized Alex and Charles Q. Parker to assume control of the discussions. Finally in March 1937, leases were granted to Seaboard Oil Corporation of Delaware. The Fasken operations in Texas were about to make certain members of the family very, very rich.

In the 1930s Alex also decided that it was time to realize the value of the Northern Ontario Light and Power Company, which David had founded. He arranged for the sale of the company to the Power Corporation of Canada.

This publicly traded holding company had been formed in Montreal in 1925 by two investment bankers, Arthur J. Nesbitt and Peter A.T. Thomson, to hold investments in electrical utilities in Quebec and later in Ontario, Manitoba, and British Columbia.[109] In the 1930s they went about acquiring many such companies. Ultimately the northern Ontario power plants would be sold to Ontario Hydro.

THIS WAS ALSO THE time when J.W. Pickup and C.C. Calvin, who had honed their skills in the 1920s, began to establish themselves as strong lawyers in their own right. It was Calvin, working under the supervision of Alex, who handled all the major corporate commercial matters that came to the firm. Calvin became assistant secretary to some of the major corporations for which the firm provided services, such as the Bank of Toronto, Excelsior Life, Dome Mines, and Toronto Western Hospital. He was clearly being groomed by Alex to take his place when Fasken retired. Calvin also prepared commercial and corporate cases for the courts. In 1937 he even appeared before the Supreme Court of Canada on an appeal of a judgment of the Ontario Court of Appeal. At this time commercial cases of significant value could be appealed without seeking leave from the court. *Cameron v Excelsior Life* was such a case. Calvin was convinced that there was no reasonable ground upon which an appeal could succeed and he moved to have the Supreme Court summarily quash the appeal based on the written record. The Court agreed and granted Calvin's motion.

Meanwhile Pickup had matured into a skilled litigator and was made a KC in 1933. He was brusque but energetic.[110] On many leading cases, Robertson was lead counsel and Pickup was his increasingly able and experienced "junior." One such was the action brought by the province of Ontario against the estate of David Fasken.[111] The Ontario government had learned of the extensive land holdings Fasken had acquired in Texas and of his efforts in the 1920s to transfer the property to a trust. In November 1933 it brought an action against the estate and its trustees to collect unpaid succession duty.[112] By the government's calculation it was owed about $500,000. Initially the province brought its case before Justice Garrow in Assize Court, but Garrow died before rendering a judgment. On 17 October 1934 the case reopened before Justice McEvoy.[113] Ontario's Deputy Attorney General I.A. Humphries and J.B. O'Brien appeared for the province. Robertson and Pickup appeared for the Fasken estate.

At issue was whether the $2,374,461.99 debt that had been owed to David Fasken by the Midland Farms Company qualified as "property" under the *Succession Duty Act* and whether that property had passed on or in anticipation of David's death. If it did and it had, a succession duty ought to have been applied to it and paid in 1930. Under section 19 of the Act the original duty was collectible together with a 50 percent penalty and 8 percent interest per year, and this amount was collectible from the estate and the trustees of the debt personally.

The definition of property in the Act was very broad, extending to every form of property, real or personal, that was capable of being passed or bequeathed to another.[114] Section 8 stated that the Act applied to the transfer of all property in Ontario. The province argued that the declaration of trust of 1924, whereby the three trustees held the acknowledgment of the debt, was an Ontario document. It had been prepared and signed by two of the three trustees in the firm's offices on Toronto Street (Andrew Fasken had signed in Midland, Texas). This had the effect of making the debt Ontario property, the province argued.

On 9 January 1935 Justice McEvoy held that the property in question was a contract debt situated outside of Ontario. In any event, he noted, David Fasken had transferred it during his life and no interest had passed on his death. No succession duty was found to be owing.

The province appealed. A panel of five judges was quickly put together to hear the appeal.[115] By today's standards the make-up of the panel is surprising. It included Riddell, a long-time partner of David Fasken and an honorary pallbearer at his funeral, and Cornelius A. Masten, another friend of David Fasken who had attended his funeral. Their relationship to Fasken was well known yet the case report does not note any objection by the province or any suggestion of impropriety. Perhaps the addition of two judges to the usual panel of three was intended to offset what seems an obvious bias. The province argued that the acknowledgment had been signed under seal in Ontario, and that the trust was created in Ontario by a person resident in Ontario and had originally two — and now that Aitchison had replaced Andrew Fasken, three — Ontario trustees. Further it argued that David Fasken had retained full control over the debt, notwithstanding the purported trust and gift. Robertson and Pickup in reply stressed that David Fasken had signed nothing. He had no interest in the trust. The beneficiaries were in the United States and substantial amounts had been paid to them since the trust had been established. No one in Ontario had received anything.

Justice Middleton,[116] who merely reiterated what the trial judge had said, wrote the majority opinion. Masten wrote a longer, concurring judgment. In addition to the points made by the majority, he noted that although there was the power to tax individuals resident in Ontario, here no such residents benefited from the acknowledgment of indebtedness or the trust. He also noted that the trust was not an Ontario trust because it had been created in Texas when David Fasken gave his directions to the Midland Farms Company to acknowledge that the three trustees were holding the debt.

THE DEPRESSION SAW LITTLE or no growth in the firm. During this period the only way it hired a new lawyer was if he was related to a partner. In 1929 twenty-two-year-old Bryce MacKenzie was in Toronto taking part in a debating competition as part of the team from the University of Saskatchewan. His aunt, who was a Fasken, took him to meet Jimmy Aitchison in the hope that Jimmy could arrange for Bryce to be articled to the firm on his graduation that year.[117] Bryce Robertson Parker MacKenzie was born on 6 April 1907 in Souris, Manitoba, the first of four children for Kenneth Robertson MacKenzie of Prince Albert, Saskatchewan, and Isabelle (Parker) MacKenzie from Wiarton, Ontario. Shortly after Bryce's birth the MacKenzie family moved to Moose Jaw, Saskatchewan, to an old framed house on River Street. Soil had to be banked on the sides to help keep it warm in the cold winters, as it was heated only by a wooden stove. Kenneth operated a funeral parlour on the ground floor and the family lived upstairs.[118]

Aitchison was undoubtedly told by his aunt that MacKenzie had done well in school. Later, on his call to the bar, the Moose Jaw Times Herald would brag that it had employed MacKenzie for two summers as a reporter: "During his school life in Moose Jaw, Bryce MacKenzie was noted for his proficiency along academic lines and made a name for himself as a debater and essayist of no small merit."[119] Aitchison offered him a job and MacKenzie began as a student on 1 May 1929. He was called to the bar in June 1932.

When Bryce MacKenzie joined the firm, he shared an office and large table with J.W. Gaius Thompson, who was then running a separate collections practice. The "collections department" maintained its own filing system, books, and bank accounts. Thompson, a First World War veteran who had been called to the bar in 1923, was "ploddingly conscientious" but did not have "the disposition and the quickness of mind" that suited the senior partners. Calvin used his influence to have Thompson appointed to the office of Official Guardian in Ontario.[120]

In 1933 R.S. Robertson's son, John Farley, graduated from the University of Toronto with a BA. He, too, joined the firm as an articled clerk. He worked with his father for his three years as a student and was called to the bar in September 1936 at age twenty-six. In 1938 J.W. Pickup's son, John Douglas, started as a student, also working with his father. He was called to the bar in June 1941. Unlike MacKenzie and young Robertson, he did not immediately start with the firm as a lawyer but chose instead to enlist in the army and serve as an officer with the Queen's Own Rifles. It was a fateful decision that both he and the firm would long regret.

The limited hiring of lawyers was mitigated by large numbers of students and administrative staff. In fact one of the ways in which the firm managed to serve its clients was to provide each lawyer with a student and an assistant. So when MacKenzie joined in 1929, he was one of seven students, each paid $5 a week. The others were L.W. Mitchell; F.E. McMahon; James T. Garrow, the son of Justice Garrow, with whom Robertson had articled in Stratford years before; J.K. Laird; D. Ruddy, the son of Judge Ruddy of Whitby; and Jessie D. McCarthy.[121]

The administrative staff was headed by the firm's accountant, D.A. McCrimmon. Fern Johnston assisted McCrimmon and was paid $17 a week. The secretaries were all paid $22 a week. Miss Brookstein, who as the head stenographer in the real estate department was paid $23 a week, acted as a paralegal. MacKenzie recalled that she had a knowledge of real estate matters as good as any lawyer in the firm.[122]

Miss McLelland, Alex's secretary, was noted for her care and diligence. As soon as he came through the door he invariably called out for her and she was at his heels before he reached his office. Pickup's secretary, Miss Nicholls, was very attractive and people wondered whether he had hired her for her looks. Certainly he paid her close attention, always rising when she came into his office and tucking her chair in behind her. Miss O'Brien assisted Aitchison in real estate and also prepared minutes and dividend cheques for Dome Mines. Calvin's secretary, Mrs. Roe, was "a good natured plump lady who usually got into trouble by thinking."[123] Mrs. Follinsbee was Robertson's secretary and, like him, was tall and thin. He had high standards and "she worked very well and very carefully." Miss Bond, the file clerk, became a legend in the firm. She knew where everything was and who everyone was. She followed the careers of all the people in the firm and kept a box of news

Legal assistant staff circa 1928
Law Society of Upper Canada Archives, Fasken Martineau DuMoulin LLP fonds

clippings. Mrs. Train was the switchboard operator. She insisted on knowing the names, addresses, and relatives of everyone in the office or who visited it regularly — for her job, of course. She was assisted by Miss Ferguson, who was also the firm messenger.

ONE OF ROBERTSON'S LAST appearances before the Privy Council in London was to be of national importance and demonstrates the position he had assumed at the bar in Canada.[124] In January 1935 Prime Minister Bennett made a series of radio broadcasts in which he announced his New Deal approach to getting Canada out of the recession.[125] The measures outlined included the *Employment and Social Insurance Act* and the establishment of a number of marketing boards under legislation such as the *Natural Products Marketing Act*. Mackenzie King's Liberals did not want to be seen to be standing in the way of any remedial efforts to help the economy recover so the measures passed into law. Mackenzie King knew, however, that Bennett had to call a fall election, which his Liberals easily won. Now that he was again prime minister, Mackenzie King referred each of Bennett's pieces of legislation to the Supreme Court of Canada for a ruling on its constitutionality.[126] The issue was whether the federal government had the right under the trade and commerce power of the *British North America Act* to regulate particular industries that were otherwise under provincial jurisdiction.

Mackenzie King appointed Louis St. Laurent from Quebec and Newton Rowell from Ontario as counsel for the federal government in defending the legislation.[127] They lost at the Supreme Court of Canada and it was decided to appeal the series of cases to the Privy Council. Rowell, however, was no longer available because he had been appointed Chief Justice of Ontario, and Mackenzie King thought of Robertson to replace him. The prime minister knew Robertson well and had on several occasions tried to convince him to become a judge. In 1924 and again in 1926 Robertson refused his friend Mackenzie King's request, saying that a man with a growing family of five could not afford the honour.[128] This, however, was a mandate that he was willing to accept. Robertson joined St. Laurent in London in November and December 1936. They had no better success in London than Rowell and St. Laurent had had in Ottawa, but Robertson was acknowledged as a superb counsel and an excellent choice as Rowell's replacement.

While Robertson was in London on this appeal, he was receiving regular correspondence from Calvin in connection with *Patton v Yukon Consolidated Gold Corporation*.[129] Yukon Consolidated had resulted from the merger of Joe Boyle's Canadian Klondyke Mining Corporation with the Guggenheim-controlled Yukon Gold Corporation.[130] The company owned and operated huge dredges that had automated gold mining in the Yukon by systematically digging up Bonanza Creek and other Klondike waterways. Calvin had begun to do its legal work and had joined its board. Company actions generated several shareholder disputes that Robertson handled with Calvin.

None was more litigious or annoying than *Patton v Yukon Consolidated Gold Corporation*, which began in 1933 and would drag on for more than a decade.[131] It was precipitated by an officer of Yukon Consolidated named Treadgold, who had allegedly made a secret profit in a transaction between the company and a company that he controlled. Patton, on behalf of the shareholders of Yukon Consolidated, brought an action against Treadgold and Yukon Consolidated for an accounting and to cancel shares in the company that Treadgold had received as part of the transaction. Robertson, representing Yukon Consolidated, did not try to defend the actions of Treadgold. His task was to ensure that Treadgold and not the company was held to account. At trial Treadgold lost and the shares he had received were ordered to be cancelled. He appealed, and Robertson again appeared for the company. The Court of Appeal upheld the trial judgment.[132]

Some months went by and when there was no further appeal, Yukon Consolidated cancelled Treadgold's shares and issued new shares to other, unrelated parties. Nevertheless, Treadgold did not give up. In 1936 he had his lawyers bring an application before Justice Middleton of the Ontario Court of Appeal to allow an appeal to the Privy Council in London. In connection with this application, Treadgold paid $2,000 into court as security for costs. With Robertson heavily involved with the federal government's constitutionality case, Pickup appeared for Yukon Consolidated on this application and explained to the court that the company, in reliance on the Court of Appeal's finding, had moved on. It was inappropriate to permit a further appeal at this time, more than two years later. Middleton agreed and dismissed the application.[133]

The next year Treadgold tried again. He appealed Middleton's dismissal to the Court of Appeal. Robertson, back from London, appeared for the company. Chief Justice Rowell wrote the judgment of the court, upholding Middleton and again refusing leave to appeal.[134]

Having dealt with the Treadgold matter, Robertson travelled once again to London to represent Yukon Consolidated in a different shareholder action before the Privy Council. This was an appeal from a decision of the Ontario Court of Appeal launched by Leslie Colbatch Clark, trustee of the estate of Vernon Wright Worsdale, a bankrupt. As he argued his client's case, Robertson must have been anxious about what was going on across the English Channel. Adolf Hitler was building his war machine and massing troops near the Sudetenland, a region of Czechoslovakia that was home to three million Germans and that Hitler claimed as part of Germany. Britain's Prime Minister Neville Chamberlain was preaching conciliation, a concept well known and much liked by Canada's Prime Minister Mackenzie King, who had personally visited Hitler in Berlin in 1937.[135]

--◦◦◦◦◦--

ROBERTSON WOULD SOON HAVE his own visit from Mackenzie King. In May 1938 the seventy-one-year-old Chief Justice Rowell had a heart attack, followed by a debilitating stroke.[136] Rowell had been co-chairing the Royal Commission on Dominion–Provincial Relations (the Rowell–Sirois Commission), which had been established in the aftermath of the Privy Council's decisions on Borden's New Deal legislation. The prime minister looked to Robertson again to succeed Rowell, not as royal commissioner but as Chief Justice of Ontario. Mackenzie King was no longer inclined to accept Robertson's protestations that his large family meant he needed his partner's compensation. The prime minister knew that "his family had now been educated and were away from home, that he had had a very good practice and undoubtedly provided for himself and the time had come when he could very properly act as Chief Justice."[137] Robertson sent a telegram to Alex, who was in Florida, to inform him he had been offered the position. He then consulted his other partners, who reluctantly agreed that they would not stand in his way.[138] In December 1938 Robertson was named to the post.

Even on being appointed to Ontario's highest judicial office, Robertson remained humble and down to earth. MacKenzie recalls that when people in the firm began to call him "My Lord" or "Chief Justice," Robertson "pointed out . . . that he was only entitled to the honorary salutations when he was in court and that he was not entitled to them when he was just a man walking along the street." He also "declined the chauffeur driven car provided for him and tried to insist upon his right to come from his home in Rosedale to Osgoode Hall in a street car." When this was deemed unacceptable for a Chief Justice, "he finally compromised by having his son John drive him around."[139]

On Robertson's appointment to the bench, the *Globe and Mail* stated that he was "regarded by the profession as one of the Dominion's most brilliant lawyers, and an authority on constitutional law." Even though sixty-eight when he was appointed, he would serve as Chief Justice of Ontario for the next thirteen years.

Calvin and MacKenzie prepared a corporate case for argument at the Court of Appeal shortly after he went to the bench. Calvin was of the view that it would be inappropriate to appear before Robertson and his court so soon, so they hired an outside counsel to argue their case. That counsel had been limited to a few hours' preparation and MacKenzie, especially, was not happy with the way the case was presented, but they need not have worried. Even though he was now a judge, Robertson found it difficult to set aside his advocate's approach to getting to the heart of a matter and putting forward what he saw as the best argument. About three weeks later Robertson came to the office and met MacKenzie. He had heard that MacKenzie was not happy and wanted to assure his former associate that he had done his own analysis of the materials and noted that a key aspect of the case had not been presented to the court. "It was then my job, behind the scenes," Robertson said, "to argue the case all over again with the rest of the court." The result was a decision entirely favourable to his old firm.[140]

PICKUP AND CALVIN, 1939–52

Despite R.S. Robertson's departure, the partners continued to call their firm Fasken, Robertson, Aitchison, Pickup & Calvin. There was a Robertson in the firm, John Farley, but it was the firm's past association with the new Chief Justice that was being invoked. Going forward, however, the last two names, Pickup and Calvin, were the bright lights in an otherwise unimpressive roster. J.W. and "Coll," as they signed their letters to each other, had developed a good working relationship over the last twenty years, to go with their legal skills and growing reputation.[1]

Only four partners remained to sign the partnership agreement of 1 January 1939: Fasken, Aitchison, Pickup, and Calvin. The document reflected Alex Fasken's age and changing role.[2] He was still a force to be reckoned with, but he was now sixty-seven years old. He remained "manager of the partnership business with full authority to engage and discharge employees and to fix their salaries or remuneration and to define their duties and to fix and allow bonuses and gratuities," but "in the absence of said Fasken those powers were to be exercised by a majority of the said Aitchison, Pickup and Calvin, or such one of them as they might appoint." It was agreed that

> so long as said Fasken is able to attend to business all office furniture, furnishings, library, typewriters and equipment are the sole property of said Fasken. On his death or inability to attend to business all said assets and cash on hand and accounts and bills receivable and all other assets of the firm

shall belong to the remaining partners of the firm pro rata according to their respective interest in the partnership.

Each partner was to receive a base "salary." Fasken received $2,400, but Aitchison, Pickup, and Calvin got $3,000 each and Alex's entitlement to any excess was not to exceed 10 percent.

Freed of some of the administrative burden of the firm, Alex and Isabel took a world cruise and when they returned he spent more time on his hobbies.[3] He was an ardent golfer, playing all year. He was a member of the Mississauga Golf and Country near his country estate, Ialfa, on the Credit River and played there from spring till fall. During the winters, he went to St. Petersburg, Florida, so that he could continue to play. He was such a regular winter golfer that he hired his own permanent caddy in St. Pete's, a Black man by the name of Henry Willows.[4]

In 1942 Alex gained considerable notoriety for another of his hobbies — high-stakes poker. He was a regular member of a Friday night game at the King Edward Hotel. One night John Scully of Owen Sound played. It was a night when Alex Fasken was acting as the clearing house for poker winnings. Scully thought that he had won $1,437 in one of the games, but Alex disagreed and would not pay him. Nothing came of Scully's complaint for some time; he spent the next few years in the United States. When he returned to Canada, however, he took to stalking Alex in an effort to coerce him into paying. He knew that Alex was in the habit of eating lunch each day at the National Club on Bay Street, a short distance from the law office. Scully began to hang about the lobby of the Excelsior Life Building on Toronto Street. When Alex walked through the lobby on his way to lunch, Scully would badger him, walking beside him all the way to and from the club. Alex began to fear for his safety and had Pickup pay a visit to Inspector Vernon of Police Station No. 1, on Court Street, to ask for a police escort. The escort was not immediately granted but shortly thereafter Pickup called the inspector, saying that Scully was physically in the firm's office, refusing to leave. The inspector promptly sent over an officer to show Scully out. From that point, Alex was given his police escort. Scully was not put off. He continued walking along with Alex, badgering him. On 18 April 1941 Scully was arrested by Officer Leonard Bentley and brought to the police station.

Scully was incensed and brought a lawsuit against both the arresting officer and Alex for conspiracy, assault, false arrest, and imprisonment.[5] These were serious charges. Initially Pickup and Calvin prepared Alex's defence, with Calvin examining Scully for discovery. But Alex did not think it appropriate to look to his own firm for his defence. He retained Binkley & Harries and they in turn retained D.L. "Lally" McCarthy, a very senior litigator who had left McCarthy & McCarthy in 1929, when his cousin Leighton McCarthy had begun to emphasize corporate work at the expense of litigation. Lally was then practising on his own. Alex and his legal team aggressively defended the action. On 26 May 1942 the matter came before Justice Hope and a special jury in the Court of Assizes. McCarthy asked that the matter be dismissed against Alex on the basis that the police, in arresting and detaining Scully, had been acting on their own and not under his instructions. The judge agreed and granted Alex costs of $616.23. He then heard the case against Bentley. The jury found the police officer innocent of the charges and he, too, was awarded costs, in his case, $450.10.[6]

———❧———

ABOUT THE SAME TIME, Pickup and Calvin were called upon to deal with another persistent nuisance. Treadgold, Yukon Consolidated's disgruntled former executive, brought yet another application for leave to appeal to the Privy Council, nine years after the original trial.[7] This time both appeared for the company. Treadgold's counsel argued that there was no time limit on appeals to the Privy Council and that the Ontario Court of Appeal did not have discretion to deny an application for leave, provided that security for costs had been paid into court. The court disagreed and yet again refused leave. It noted that to do otherwise would create real hardships since "great changes in the positions of the parties and important new rights and obligations have grown on the strength of the finality of the judgment of the Court of Appeal." It ordered Treadgold to pay Yukon Consolidated's very considerable costs.

Calvin would later note that Yukon Consolidated had legal expenses of $25,000 in Treadgold's various applications.[8] Three years later, those costs had not been paid. Calvin himself appeared for Yukon Consolidated in an application to have $4,000 paid into court as security for costs paid out to the company.[9] To the further frustration of Calvin's client, the application was contested by the party that had put up the money on behalf of Treadgold. While Yukon Consolidated was awarded the bulk of the $4,000 that had been paid into court, it had to return some of the money to this third party.

———❧———

J.W. Pickup
Law Society of Upper Canada Archives, Fasken Martineau DuMoulin LLP fonds
"Photograph of J.W. Pickup," 2009006-22P

WHEN PICKUP WAS NOT dealing with such annoyances, he was being regularly retained by the federal and provincial governments. In 1943 the federal Department of Justice was concerned by evidence of misappropriation and fraud by those involved in the very extensive government procurement being undertaken for the war effort. The new deputy minister of justice, Frederick Varcoe, recruited Pickup to prosecute Rodolphe Brule, J.A.P. Hayden, Hector K. Carruthers, and J. Richard Grant, who were charged with fraud against the government in connection with wartime contracts.[10] In preparing these cases, Pickup worked with a future Chief Justice of the Federal Court, Wilbur R. Jackett.[11] Instructions and commentary were exchanged by mail. They worked well together, both being dedicated hard workers.[12] Jackett especially was known for turning out first-class work in a timely fashion. This was to be the first of many retainers that the Department of Justice in Ottawa would give to Pickup.

A few years later, it was an agency of the provincial government, the Ontario Securities Commission (OSC), that retained Pickup. The Commission looked to him to defend its power to make orders withdrawing the registration of sellers of securities.[13] The Security Frauds Prevention Board, as it was originally known, had been created under the *Securities Fraud Prevention Act* of 1928, at a time when stock manipulation had become a real concern. In 1933 a new, more comprehensive *Securities Act* renamed it the Ontario Securities Commission. Then in 1945, in response to many allegations of "boiler room" operators selling junior mining stocks over the telephone, the OSC had been given a new chairman, former judge Charles McTague, and even broader powers.[14] One key power was the ability to remove a stock dealer from the register of permitted sellers if the Commission was of the opinion that to do so was in the public interest.

Armed with these powers, McTague set out to reform the securities industry. The important first step was to review the registrations of all securities dealers and any complaints against them. The Commission could then decide where it was appropriate to cancel registrations. The OSC then proceeded to do so. Those against whom the orders were made launched an aggressive counter-attack. Their livelihood was at stake. Each of them exercised his right under the statute and asked for a hearing before the Commission.

A series of hearings was duly held, but each hearing resulted in a confirmation of the initial order. The deregistered dealers then retained John Cartwright to appeal each order to the Ontario Court of Appeal. Having classed the appeals into groups, the court then heard them.

In each instance Cartwright challenged both the Commission's power and its exercise of that power. His argument was that the OSC was acting as a judicial body and not an administrative one. It ought therefore to have followed the principles of natural justice by giving notice of the initial review and the opportunity to be heard before the initial deregistration orders had been made. Formal hearings ought to have been held at that early stage and evidence ought to have been taken under oath, subject to cross-examination and challenge. Pickup defended the Commission's jurisdiction and its actions, arguing that the legislature had intentionally and wisely chosen a different path.

The case attracted much attention because people knew that the Court of Appeal's judgment would shape future regulation of the securities industry.[15] Robertson and his court looked favourably on Pickup's arguments. They showed remarkable deference for the legislative purpose and for the regulatory regime, holding that the OSC needed to have broad discretion to protect the public. They rejected the appeals, saying that in the review phase the "Commission exercises the functions of an administrative body . . . and its procedure is left pretty much to itself." In turning to the holding of hearings by the Commission, the court stressed that the wording of the statute made it clear that "the purpose of the Legislature was to relieve the Commission of the restrictions imposed by the rules of evidence by which our Courts of Justice are governed."[16] Pickup could not have had a better result for his client. The OSC's jurisdiction had been upheld and its enabling statute interpreted in the most favourable fashion.

⁕

WHILE PICKUP WAS DEVELOPING his reputation as a leading litigator, Calvin had become a noted corporate lawyer and had begun to collect the director-ships that usually accompany that status. He was already on the board of Excelsior Life, Yukon Consolidated, Nipissing Mining, and Moneta Mines.[17] Nevertheless, it was not in Calvin's nature to boast of his achievements. His greatest source of pride was that Justice Middleton, one of Ontario's best judges, had described him as "a careful solicitor" in a published judgment in 1934.[18] Calvin was, of course, much more. Jimmy Aitchison might be termed a careful solicitor, but he had neither the presence nor the intellect to do the corporate work that Calvin was now starting to attract.

One of Calvin's strengths was the ability to remain calm and unemotional in tense situations, as he had done years before as a young naval officer. Bryce MacKenzie recalled Calvin as "a prince of a man," noting that while "little irritations, neglects and mistakes used to infuriate him and he used to make his objections known in a loud voice with appropriate gesticulations," nevertheless, "if anything serious was wrong he was quiet, self-contained and not abusive in any way . . . [dealing] with the situation in a self-con-tained unemotional manner."[19]

Calvin's growing reputation meant that after years of getting few new clients, the firm began to attract many. Otis Elevator had come to the firm in the 1930s. In the 1940s it was joined by insurance brokers Johnson & Higgins, Pilot Insurance, and Toronto General Trusts Corporation.[20]

⁕

THE PRINCIPAL LAWYERS ASSISTING Aitchison and Calvin, John Beverley Rob-inson and Bryce MacKenzie, were finally admitted as partners, effective 1 January 1943 without "dissolution of the existing partnership." Robinson had waited over twenty years for partnership and MacKenzie more than ten. MacKenzie recalls that he owed his partnership to the fact that Robin-son had received an offer to leave the firm to join National Trust.[21] The firm wanted to retain him but could not make him a partner over MacKenzie, who was even more valuable. They were each permitted to draw $3,000 per

Walter B. Williston
Law Society of Upper Canada Archives, Fasken Martineau DuMoulin LLP fonds
"Photograph of Walter Williston," 2009006-47P

annum, but Robinson was entitled to only 1.5 percent of the firm's profits whereas MacKenzie got 2 percent.

On 20 June the new partners joined Calvin and two students, Walter Bernard Williston and Edward King, as the incorporators and first directors of Garden Island Limited, an Ontario private company set up by Calvin to purchase and hold the island on which he had been born. It was an aspect of his management of the estate of his father, who had died in 1932. Four hundred shares were created so that ownership of the island could be shared and passed from generation to generation without having to subdivide the island property itself.

Both Williston and King are students of note. Williston, the son of an Anglican missionary and his Jewish-born convert wife, was born in China in 1919. He came to Canada with his parents in 1928 and they settled in northern Ontario. His youth there might explain his love of the outdoors and canoeing. He had begun his articles with Grey Hamilton, QC, in 1941–42, but it had not been a good experience and he had switched to the Fasken firm. He would be called to the bar in 1944. Ed King was the nephew of two of the earliest Jewish lawyers in Ontario, Samuel and Oscar King, who practised real estate law together.[22] He would stay for a few years but then joined his uncles at their firm.[23]

WILLISTON AND KING DID not have the opportunity to practise long, if at all, with Alex Fasken. Early in the evening of 19 September 1944 Alex was driving home along the Queen Elizabeth Way. He was very upset. Earlier in the day Jimmy Aitchison had gone to his office and demanded a raise. Alex left the office in a huff. The QEW was then four lanes wide but there was no median or barrier between the east- and west-bound lanes. "It was dusk as he sped along . . . [L]ooking neither right or left nor ahead as he mulled over his disturbed emotions, and without giving a thought to where he was going, when he caught up to a car in front of him he wheeled to the left to pass it, only to be sliced by a large truck going in the opposite direction. In the instant the left side of his car was sliced off and his neck was broken by the sudden jar."[24] He died instantly. His car was dragged for some distance.[25] An inquest was held on 12 October and the five-person jury found that Alex was at fault and the driver of the truck, Ernest J. Elliott, was blameless.[26]

On hearing the news, Jimmy Aitchison went to his uncle's office and personally tore out the much-hated buzzer system. That same day, however, he confessed to MacKenzie that he felt partly to blame.[27] Even in death Alex made things difficult for Aitchison.

It would be wrong to think that most people were pleased at finally being rid of Alex. Certainly some were, but many had seen the good that he could do. While Alex had lacked David's legal and personal skills, he had shared his entrepreneurial spirit and business judgment. The partnership had not thrived under Alex as it had under David, but Alex must be given some credit for steering it successfully through the difficult 1920s, the Depression, and the war years. Certainly those at Excelsior Life, Toronto Western Hospital, and Dome Mines knew that although he had been difficult to work with at times, he had been truly dedicated to their companies. They filled Old St. Andrew's Church in Toronto for his "simple and impressive funeral service" on 22 September.[28] Ontario's Lieutenant-Governor Albert Matthews came, as did Chief Justices Robertson and Rose. His pallbearers were Charles Q. Parker, with whom he had administered David's estate and who worked at Excelsior Life; T.O. Cox, who managed Excelsior Life; his law partners Jimmy Aitchison, J.W. Pickup, and C.C. Calvin; and the firm's accountant, D.A. McCrimmon. Like David, Alex was buried in the family plot at the Elora cemetery.

The most important person to attend the funeral was seventy-one-year-old Albert Matthews,[29] who had recently become the controlling shareholder of Excelsior Life and would soon succeed Alex as its president. He was a force in the Liberal Party, a supporter of Mackenzie King who had worked to get Mitch Hepburn elected provincially.[30] He had amassed the money to buy Excelsior through his stock brokerage, Matthews & Company Limited. Neither he nor his brokerage were then clients of the firm, but he, and more important his son, would soon be working closely with Calvin and MacKenzie — and they would be impressed.

The strong ties that Alex had nurtured between the law firm, Excelsior Life, and Toronto Western Hospital ensured that Calvin and the firm got the chance to work with Matthews, but there were no guarantees the legal work would stay with the firm. Any time a new party becomes controlling shareholder of a company, there is a chance it will result in the legal work being directed to lawyers whom such party knows and trusts. The fact that Calvin and the firm not only kept the Excelsior Life work but also received more work from the Matthews family was a testament to their skills and Calvin's personality.

It would be some time, however, before Albert Matthews' son, Bruce, got to know and work with the law firm. He had other pressing matters on his mind. Better known as Major-General Bruce Matthews, he was just about to assume command of the Second Canadian Army, which was battling its way through Belgium.[31]

Alex left an estate for succession duty purposes of more than $1,000,000, but like David's estate, that did not reflect the full extent of his wealth. The bulk of his estate was in a trust that paid his wife an annuity for her life, and after her death was to be distributed among his twelve nieces and nephews.[32]

———————

WITH ALEX GONE, JIMMY AITCHISON insisted that a different atmosphere prevail in the firm: "Jim treated each and every one like human beings, wanting all in the Office to be happy at their work, and arranged that such should be the case after . . . the death of Alex."[33] In reaction to Alex's previous dominance, the remaining partners decided that there would no longer be a managing partner. Instead, Aitchison, Pickup, and Calvin were designated as the management committee.

One of the changes that the new committee made was with respect to draws. Previously as money had been collected for work done and billed, partners had been permitted to draw out money, but there had been no steady cash flow. These sporadic permitted drawings had been tracked and the amount taken was later reconciled against the amount allocated to that partner as their share of the profits. Following Alex's death it was decided that each partner would receive a base payment of $250 a month. This would provide a regular, if modest, cash flow. Their share of the profits differed, of course. Although Jimmy Aitchison was the most senior, he was given only 18 percent, while Pickup and Calvin received 32 percent each. Robinson and MacKenzie got 4 percent, and the remaining 10 percent was available to be allotted to "such partner or partners or associates from time to time and in such proportions as the said Aitchison, Pickup and Calvin or any two of them may from time to time determine."

The new management committee retained one practice that had been initiated by Alex Fasken. All mail was to be opened and reviewed before it was distributed to the lawyers. That practice would continue until at least 1988. In her address in 2005 on being awarded an honorary degree at the call to the bar, Jane Pepino recalled her time as a receptionist at the firm:

> When I was a summer student, having just completed my first year of undergraduate work, I secured a job as a switchboard operator, relief receptionist and general dog's body at the venerable law firm of Fasken Calvin Williston Swackhamer and Rolls. My day started at 7:00 am when I assisted the person who really ran the office, the commissionaire, Charlie, to open every piece of mail and stack it into 3 piles for the respective heads of the litigation, corporate, and commercial/estates/other departments. Each department head read every piece of correspondence before forwarding it to the responsible file lawyer.[34]

At about the time that Alex met his untimely end, David G.C. Menzel joined the firm as a student. He had been born in Pennsylvania but grown up in Hamilton. Having lost an eye in childhood, he was ineligible for service when the Second World War came. While his friends went to war, he went to McMaster University. After graduating in 1943 he spent a year working for the National Trust Company but saw no future for himself there and decided to go to law school. He secured an articling position with the firm. On his call to the bar in 1947, he was asked to join the firm as a lawyer working primarily with Calvin.[35]

John Douglas Pickup returned from the war in June 1946, and despite his lack of legal experience was admitted as a partner. This could not but rankle

John Farley Robertson and Bryce MacKenzie, who had toiled as associates for more than a decade. Although Pickup had won distinction in the war as an officer in the Queen's Own Rifles, he had not practised as an associate at all, enlisting immediately after his call to the bar in 1941. The decision to make Pickup's son a partner was undoubtedly seen as favouritism, but it was justified on the basis of his military record and the fact that he came back wounded. He had been an acting major when he and his men were clearing the Rheiderland peninsula. They spotted the enemy grouping for a counter-attack. Pickup led his men against them, killing or wounding twenty-five Germans and capturing five others without a single loss.[36] He was awarded the Bronze Lion by the government of the Netherlands.[37] Unfortunately, he was badly injured later in an accident and would be in pain the rest of his life. His partners and the others in the office would soon learn that his constant pain and the medication he took for it made him irritable and difficult to work with.

Also returning from the war was Albert Matthews' son, Bruce, soon to be the firm's most important client. While his father was serving as lieutenant-governor, Bruce Matthews had been working his way to the top ranks of the Canadian Army. He proved to be an excellent officer, rising steadily from the command of a battery in 1940 to counter-battery officer at headquarters, and to brigadier in 1943 at the age of thirty-three. In July of that year, he and his troops landed in Sicily. For his leadership in the Italian campaign he was later awarded the Distinguished Service Order. In January 1944 he was transferred to the II Canadian Corps as commander of artillery. As such, Matthews developed the artillery firing plans for the invasion and subsequent battles in Normandy. In November, Matthews was promoted to major-general and appointed commanding officer of the 2nd Canadian Infantry Division, which took part in the Rhineland battles of 1945. It was his division that liberated the northern Netherlands.

On his return he was not only the conquering hero, a much-decorated and esteemed major-general, but also the son and heir of a wealthy, influential member of Toronto's moneyed elite who had served as lieutenant-governor of Ontario from 1937 to 1946 and was the major shareholder and president of Excelsior Life. Bruce Matthews, who Peter Newman would later describe as possessing "a look which . . . has that forward slant of jaw that suggests participation in great deeds," was soon elected vice-president and a director of Excelsior Life and a director of Dome Mines and Standard Broadcasting.[38] Calvin, the naval officer mentioned in dispatches, and Matthews, the decorated major-general, hit it off. To Calvin and his partners, Bruce Matthews would always be "the General." The two deepened the already close and long-lasting relationships that had developed between the law firm and the Fasken ventures Excelsior Life, Dome Mines, and Toronto Western Hospital.

Later that year, on 17 September, John Farley Robertson became a partner. Like the others he was permitted to draw $250 per month and granted 1 percent of the profits. The same financial terms were offered to John Douglas Pickup. By January 1947 the percentage of profits for each was increased to 2 percent.

A year later, on 11 September 1947, Walter Williston was admitted as a partner after only three years of practice. The early offer was motivated in part by the fact that he was exceptional — a prodigious worker, going home late every night[39] — but also because the partners knew he was being enticed by Cecil "Caesar" Augustus Wright to join the law faculty at Osgoode Hall Law School.

Despite his workload at the firm, Walter had been assisting Arthur Kelly in carrying out the oral examination programme at Osgoode. The partners thought that if they did not act, teaching might become Walter's full-time job, and indeed for a time that seemed likely. In 1948 Wright became the dean of Osgoode Hall and was given the right to hire two new lecturers. Walter Williston was the first person he approached. Walter decided to try full-time teaching, taking a leave of absence from the firm.[40]

It was to be a very eventful year at the law school. Wright was still battling with the benchers over the direction legal education should take in Ontario. Despite the discouragement of the 1930s he had continued to lobby for professional law teachers and a more academic law school. His cries for reform fell largely on deaf ears. The benchers, who were themselves products of the old system, could see no reason why legal education ought to change. The summer of 1945, however, proved a turning point in Wright's efforts. That summer his lifelong friend and ally, Sidney Smith, became the president of the University of Toronto. The first person whom the two men sought to convince was R.S. Robertson. Years before he had spoken out against the changes that Falconbridge, MacRae, and Wright had been seeking; now, as Chief Justice, he was more receptive. With his support secured, Wright and Smith put every form of pressure they could upon the benchers to reform legal education and to establish the university law school they so much wanted.

The benchers would not budge. The special committee they had established to study legal education reported in March 1949 that there was no need to create a university law school. Wright had clearly alienated the benchers. They did not even give him, the dean of the law school, a copy of their final report on legal education. He read about it in the *Globe and Mail*. He called together the small faculty at Osgoode Hall — Stanley Edwards, John Willis, Bora Laskin, and Walter Williston. The group decided to resign en masse to force the Law Society to relinquish its control of legal education in the province. When, to their surprise, the Law Society accepted their resignations and hired new faculty, Wright, Willis, and Laskin went to the University of Toronto and established a rival law school.

Williston, however, had by this point already decided to return to the firm. When asked by the *Toronto Telegram* why he had not signed the resignation letter or posed for the famous resignation picture with the others, he quipped that it would have been overly dramatic to resign a position for which he had already given notice.[41] He made it clear, however, that he supported Wright's decision. The benchers refused to be bullied into changing their views. Instead they recruited new faculty and added a number of practitioner lecturers, including Williston.[42]

⟶ ⟶◆⟵ ⟵

WHILE WALTER WAS TRYING his hand at teaching, Pickup was once again faced with defending David Fasken's estate plan. This time the attack came from the federal tax authorities. In 1944 they reassessed David Fasken's income tax returns for 1925 to 1929 under the *Income War Tax Act 1917* to collect the tax they claimed was owing for those years as a result of the transfer from Fasken to his wife, Alice, of the right to receive income from the C Ranch debt repayment.[43] On 31 December 1924 Midland Farms Company had acknowledged its debt to David Fasken, and Fasken's three trustees (Alex Fasken, Charles Q. Parker, and Andrew Fasken) had acknowledged the terms under which they held the debt. One of those terms was that the interest be paid to Alice. She had received $10,000 in 1925, $5,000 in 1926, $11,000 in 1927, $15,000 in 1928, and $20,000 in 1925.

The federal minister of national revenue relied upon section 4(4) of the Act, which said that a person who sought to reduce his or her tax by transferring property to a spouse was liable for tax on that amount. That section had been amended in 1926 to include transfers of income from property. The section was stated to apply to the years 1925 and following.[44] The trustees of

David's estate acknowledged the facts but disagreed over the applicable tax treatment. They appealed the reassessments.

The appeals were heard by Justice Thorson of the Exchequer Court in October 1948. Pickup had four arguments. He explained to the court that there had never been a transfer of property from David to his wife within the meaning of the Act; that in any event what was transferred was not property in the legal sense but only an intangible right to receive income; that the relevant section of the Act applied only to transfers made for the purpose of evading tax, which was not the case here; and finally that the law to be applied was the law in force when the tax returns were prepared, not the law in effect later when the reassessments were made.

In delivering his judgment, Thorson ruled that the right to receive the interest payable on the indebtedness was property for the purposes of the Act and that there had been a valid transfer of property from husband to wife. While the property was transferred due to an act by the trustees, this was merely an indirect way of doing so and what mattered was the result of the transfer, not whether the transfer was done directly or indirectly. In the end, however, Thorson held that no tax was payable since the tax in question applied only to transfers after 1925, and in this case the date of the transfer was 1924 (when the trustees had acknowledged the interest owed to Mrs Fasken). Pickup's last argument won the day.

⸺⸢✢⸥⸻

In June 1949 Williston was back in the firm and shown in the annual revision to the percentage of drawings under the partnership agreement. Despite his potential and the undoubted pleasure that those in the firm felt on his return, he was given only 3 percent. J.W. Pickup and C.C. Calvin were at 30 percent, Aitchison at 16 percent, Robinson and MacKenzie at 6 percent, and Robertson and J.D. Pickup at 4 percent. The only person receiving less than Williston was young David Menzel, a newly recruited lawyer, who continued to receive 1 percent but not as a partner.

After Williston returned to practice, he got a call from his former Osgoode Hall colleague Bora Laskin. Laskin headed a committee of the Canadian Jewish Congress that was assisting with an appeal to the Supreme Court of Canada of *Noble v Wolf and Alley*. This was a restrictive covenant case. A group of cottage owners had agreed that they would not sell to anyone of "the Jewish, Hebrew, Semitic, Negro or coloured race or blood" and that they would insist that any purchaser of their property also agreed to be bound by the covenant. When Noble's widow wanted to sell the family cottage to Bernard Wolf, a Jewish businessman, her lawyer and his lawyer agreed to apply to the court for an order under the *Vendor and Purchaser's Act* holding the covenant void. They intended to rely upon an earlier decision of Justice Keiller Mackay in *Re Drummond Wren* holding that such covenants were contrary to public policy. The neighbouring cottagers, however, opposed the order and hired noted lawyer Kenneth Morden, KC, to oppose the application. Wolf countered by hiring the equally noted John Cartwright.

To the surprise of the Canadian Jewish Congress, Justice Schroeder refused to follow the ruling in *Re Drummond Wren* and upheld the restrictive covenant, stressing the need for freedom of contract. Then a five-person panel of the Court of Appeal, including Chief Justice Robertson, unanimously confirmed the trial judge's decision. Laskin wanted Williston to junior for J.J. Robinette at the Supreme Court of Canada. Walter, who loved to fight for the underdog and was proud of his mother's Jewish heritage, readily agreed. Robinette and Williston appeared before the Supreme Court in June 1950. They made an interesting pair. Although both were brilliant, they were very different in many ways:

> Robinette was the embodiment of every student's idea of a barrister. He always seemed to be in total command of the situation . . . . Williston, on the other hand, often appeared dishevelled and somewhat disorganized. He spoke in a halting way . . . . Williston sometimes seemed to approach the point rather awkwardly . . . . Because the point was unpolished, judges sometimes had to struggle to grasp it themselves, but, having done so, they regarded it as their own, and could not be dislodged from it.[45]

Different or not, they were successful. The Court, however, did not take up their invitation to find the covenant contrary to public policy. Rather, it preferred the narrower, technical (but equally effective) argument that the covenant did not affect the land and therefore was not the sort of covenant that could ever bind a subsequent owner.[46]

WILLISTON'S USUAL SENIOR, J.W. PICKUP, was now at the peak of his career. At the end of the 1940s and beginning of the 1950s, he was retained on a number of matters of public importance. In late 1949 Justice Roy Kellock of the Supreme Court of Canada chose him to be lead commission counsel for a Court of Investigation into the circumstances surrounding the burning of the S.S.

Noronic in Toronto Harbour on 17 September 1949.[47] The *Noronic*, the flag-ship of Canada Steamship Lines and the largest passenger ship on the Great Lakes, had burned while docked in Toronto, with a loss of 118 lives.[48] Within days Lionel Chevrier, the federal minister of transport, rose in the House of Commons and called for an inquiry.[49] Kellock was appointed as the commissioner, with Neil B. Gebbie, Captain H.S. Kane, and Captain Robert Mitchell assisting him as assessors. The first meeting was held just eleven days after the fire.[50] Pickup was assisted by John M. Godfrey of Arnoldi, Parry & Campbell. Hearings were held in Toronto in late September, October, and early November and in the city of Ottawa on 21 November. In Toronto the hearings had to be held in the council chambers of the city hall to accommodate the press and spectators.[51]

As the investigation progressed, J.W. Pickup and his legal team "remorselessly and painstakingly developed a multidimensional picture of negligence, corner-cutting, and gross unpreparedness on the part of those responsible for the Noronic and the safety of the passengers."[52] The report was published just two months after the fire.

Following the *Noronic* inquiry, Pickup was retained by the Bell Telephone Company to represent it in several rate hearings and by the federal government as a special prosecutor when it was alleged that both military personnel and civilians workers were guilty of theft from the army base in Petawawa.

---◆◆◆◆---

DAVID MENZEL FINALLY BECAME a partner on 1 August 1950 when a new partnership agreement was signed.[53] It had been six years since the last agreement but very few changes were made. The name of Fasken, Robertson, Aitchison, Pickup & Calvin was retained, as it had been since 1925. The annual revision to the percentage of drawings shows a modest shift of income to the more junior ranks: J.W. Pickup and C.C. Calvin were reduced to 28 percent, Aitchison was reduced to 14 percent, Robinson was reduced to 5 percent, while MacKenzie rose to 7 percent, Robertson stayed at 4 percent, J.D. Pickup rose to 5 percent, and Williston to 4 percent. David Menzel, now a partner, received 3 percent. The remaining 2 percent was to be allotted as Aitchison, J.W. Pickup, and Calvin decided.

Around this time Calvin was approached by Bruce Matthews, who explained that his sister's son, Fraser Fell, was looking to become a lawyer. While pursuing an economics degree at McMaster, the Baptist college where his grandfather Albert Matthews had been chairman of the board, young Fell

Fraser Fell
Law Society of Upper Canada Archives, Osgoode Hall Law School fonds
"Graduating class, 1953, Osgoode Hall Law School," P486

had tried his hand at actuarial work, working for the summers at Excelsior Life. Law was much more appealing, he concluded. Might there be a place for his nephew at Faskens, the General wondered? Calvin, of course, agreed to accept the young man as an articling student. In fact he was very pleased to have been asked. He knew that Matthews used Gordon Peter Campbell of Arnoldi, Parry & Campbell for his personal legal work; that Campbell, like Matthews, was heavily involved in the Liberal Party; and that both the Matthews and the Fell families socialized with the Campbells. To be asked was to be given an opportunity to do a favour for a valued client and a very influential man.

Calvin was motivated in large part by loyalty and friendship but also by enlightened self-interest. One wonders in light of the many ties to Peter Campbell, however, why Calvin was given this opportunity. The reason was that Calvin, like the Matthews and the Fells, attended Yorkminster Baptist Church.[54] It was a request that arose from a shared sense of community and values.

Calvin's decision to take in young Fell is reminiscent of the decision that Beatty made seventy years earlier when asked to take in Tom Blackstock. Each proved to be very good for the firm. Blackstock had solidified the relationship with the Gooderhams and provided superior legal skills and good business judgment. Fell solidified the relationship with the Matthews family and provided superb organizational skills and business judgment. The addition of Fraser Fell brought to Faskens the sort of extensive connections to Toronto's moneyed elite that Charlotte Worts had brought when she married

Beatty. His mother, Grace, was the sister of Bruce Matthews and the only daughter of the former lieutenant-governor. Fraser's father was Charles Percival Fell, a stockbroker who had become president of Empire Life Insurance in Kingston in 1934 and of Matthews & Company, the family stockbrokerage, in 1950. Although born in Lawrence Park, Fraser had grown up in the Bridle Path area, perhaps Toronto's most prestigious address. He won acceptance at the demanding University of Toronto Schools (UTS), where he studied with such later notables as John Evans and Fraser Mustard.

As a student Fell would probably have known nothing about it but in April 1951 the partners created a capital fund: what today we refer to as the partners' fixed equity. Traditionally as the money had come into the firm it had been distributed to the partners. Now they were to be required to keep at least some money in the firm: Aitchison $9,000, J.W. Pickup and Calvin $15,000 each, Robinson $4,000, MacKenzie $5,200, Robertson $3,600, J.D. Pickup $4,000, Williston $3,600, and Menzel $3,000.

A revision to the percentage of drawings under the partnership agreement on 13 February the following year showed a further modest shift of income to the junior partners. J.W. Pickup and C.C. Calvin were reduced to 26 percent each, Aitchison was reduced to 12 percent, Robinson was restored to 6 percent, and MacKenzie rose to 8 percent. Robertson went to 5 percent, while J.D. Pickup rose to 6 percent and Williston to 5 percent, the same percentage now given to David Menzel. The remaining 1 percent was unallotted.

<hr />

SHORTLY THEREAFTER, ON 25 February 1952, the David Fasken estate paid another dividend to the firm by way of a motion brought on behalf of its executors. David's will had provided that the bulk of the estate was to accumulate in a capital fund. On his son Robert's death in 1934, two capital accounts had been created, one each for David Jr. and his half-sister, Inez. She died in 1945 at the age of nineteen, however, leaving no issue, and David Jr. became the sole beneficiary of the income from the capital fund, receiving $10,000 a year. During the ten years following Robert's death only $20,000 a year had been distributed, and just $10,000 thereafter. The annual increase in the capital fund at this point would have been in the hundreds of thousands of dollars, and by 1952 the fund was very substantial. The *Accumulations Act* of 1950 prohibited a period of accumulation more than twenty-one years from the death of the testator.[55] This meant that going forward the annual increase in the fund had to be paid out. The question was to whom.

The will had provided a default of Fasken's next of kin. Calvin and Williston made the motion on behalf of the executors for directions on the meaning of *next of kin*. The counsel appearing on the motion were a who's who of Ontario litigators. John Arnup appeared on behalf of Robert's wife, Inez, who sought the money for Robert's estate. Gershom Mason represented David Fasken Jr. Cyril Carson appeared for two of David Sr.'s sisters and thirty-three nieces and nephews, who argued that they were his next of kin. F.T. Watson, the Official Guardian, represented David Jr.'s unborn children.

Justice Barlow, the trial judge, sided with David Jr. He noted that David Fasken "was a barrister and solicitor of this court with a wide knowledge of the law" and found that it was clearly Fasken's intention to leave his estate to his direct descendants.[56] He had chosen the words *next of kin* because they were widely settled to mean direct descendants — and his grandson was the only living direct descendant.

The decision was appealed to the Ontario Court of Appeal. In September, when the appeal was heard, Pickup appeared with Williston. Cyril Carson was very persuasive and a majority of the panel, Justices Henderson and Gibson, found for Fasken's sisters, nieces, and nephews.[57] They held that *next of kin* should be given the meaning found in the *Devolution of Estates Act*, which defined "next of kindred" as "the father and the mother and the brothers and the sisters of the intestate [who] shall be deemed of equal degree but there shall be no representations admitted among collaterals after brothers' and sisters' children."[58] Justice Roach dissented. He would have upheld the trial decision based on the reasoning that paragraph 18 (the default provision) was an attempt by the testator to avoid an intestacy of his estate, and thus *next of kin* should be taken to mean those who would take on an intestacy and should include lineal descendants.

This decision was also appealed. But before it was heard the firm went through a fundamental change that arose from Prime Minister St. Laurent's need to name a new Chief Justice of Ontario.

ROBERTSON HAD ANNOUNCED THAT he intended to retire. Left unannounced was that although the frail eighty-year-old was in failing health, he had told his former co-counsel, St. Laurent, that he would not leave office until he was satisfied with the person who was to succeed him — and Robertson had strong views on Justice McRuer, who was being touted as his likely successor.[59] Some time went by as several other names were put forward and rejected. Only when Robertson's former junior, J.W. Pickup, was suggested did he agree. Pickup knew nothing of this.

He arrived at the firm's offices bright and early on 25 September 1952 only to be told that he had an urgent call from Ottawa. It was the prime minister offering him the job. He was quite surprised at the offer and at the speed with which St. Laurent insisted it be implemented.[60] Of course, St. Laurent knew that much time had already gone by. *Saturday Night* magazine also noted that the process of replacing Robertson had been anything but quick, noting in an editorial that "it was unfortunate that so long a time elapsed between the announcement of Chief Justice Robertson's retirement and the appointment of his successor." It may have been critical of the process, but it had praise for the choice of Pickup, whom it characterized as "a lawyer's lawyer who has acted for both the Federal Liberal Government and the Provincial Conservative Government and has not had time for personal political activity."[61]

On Robertson's retirement the *Globe and Mail* praised him "as one of the finest lawyers Canada has ever produced."[62] The *Toronto Star*, too, was effusive in its praise, referring to him as "a man of supreme gifts, high ideals and sterling character."[63] The *Star* went on to say,

> No member of the legal profession is more respected than he; this not only for his knowledge of the law and his ability to weigh legal arguments, but also for his uprightness and qualities of mind and heart. The capacity for study and interpretation, which had already become evident during his younger years as a practising lawyer in Stratford, had new scope in the wider field which he found in Toronto, where his knowledge of constitutional law became proverbial.

Among the many honours he received was an honorary doctor of laws degree from the University of Toronto. Ironically, this LLD was Robertson's first and only university degree. He had sat on the university's board of governors for many years without a degree of his own, having gone into law as a matriculant.

Pickup's federal appointment came just two weeks after Ontario Attorney-General Dana Porter had retained him to conduct an investigation into the Don Jail escape of the Boyd gang.[64] Pickup had told the newspapers that in the provincial inquiry there was "a great deal of work to be done. We have only scratched the surface."[65] Nevertheless, this work and his many other files had to be turned over to others because his appointment required him to withdraw from practice immediately and cease all appearances before the courts. Pickup was concerned not only that a successor be found to assume the position of special counsel for the Don Jail inquiry but also that the person chosen use his son as his junior, as Pickup himself had intended to do. In order to keep J.D. involved and to ensure the matter was handled properly, J.W. suggested to Dana Porter that his childhood friend George Walsh succeed him as special counsel.[66] Porter took the suggestion and J.D. Pickup was retained as Walsh's junior.

Pickup was not as good at dealing with the transition of his other files. His appointment and St. Laurent's insistence on a quick response meant that he had accepted the position without consulting Calvin. Understandably this greatly upset his long-time colleague and partner. Calvin recalled that in 1937 Robertson had notified Alex Fasken and accepted the offer only after consultation with his partners.[67] Why should this appointment be any different? He was of the view that it was simply not in the spirit of partnership for Pickup to leave the firm without working with those remaining to lessen the impact of his departure. Who, Calvin wondered, was to assume the important and lucrative work that Pickup had been doing? And who was to keep J.D. Pickup busy and productive now that his father would not be providing him with work?

On 1 October 1952 J.W. Pickup became the first partner to claim back his capital from the firm. He had $15,000 to his credit. He received a $7,000 Dominion of Canada 3 percent bearer bond due 1 January 1959, an $8,000 Dominion of Canada 3 percent bearer bond due 1 May 1957, and $470.85 in cash.

• →◦◦←— •

MEANWHILE, THE PARTNERSHIP HAD to be restructured in a way not seen since Alex Fasken's death in 1944. It would now be Calvin to whom the others looked. Although he was only one member of the management committee, he became the senior partner. On 24 September 1952 a new partnership agreement was signed. As had happened when Robertson went to the bench, the name Fasken, Robertson, Aitchison, Pickup & Calvin was retained, but the financial arrangements changed. MacKenzie turned out to be the primary beneficiary of Pickup's departure, replacing him on the management committee and increasing his own share of the profits to 12 percent. Robinson, J.D. Pickup, Williston, and Menzel all went to 9 percent.

One wonders if the lawyers whom J.W. Pickup left behind had any idea that their firm was on the eve of profound changes. Business law, which had long taken second place to litigation in the firm — at least from the perspective of prestige and profile — was about to awake from its decades of slumber.

A NEW BEGINNING,
1953–63

AFTER THREE DECADES OF slow economic growth, "Canada was . . . embarked on the greatest period of development in all her history . . . [and] trade, production, income and real wealth all continued a spectacular, if sometimes jagged, rise."[1] Luckily, the firm's business law practice was in a position to grow alongside the economy, having been freed from the personal limitations of Alex Fasken. Economic expansion meant that business lawyers were much in demand. People were starting new businesses that needed to be incorporated, organized, and financed. Existing businesses were expanding, which often meant mergers and acquisitions. All these activities called for the special skills that business lawyers possessed, especially now that government had grown accustomed to having a large say in the economy.

There was, however, one major hurdle to overcome — the firm had only a few business lawyers. At the time of J.W. Pickup's departure the only lawyers in the firm of eight partners who had any claim to such a designation were Calvin, MacKenzie, and Menzel. Two partners, Aitchison and Robinson, were aging grinders who conducted the firm's real estate practice. J.D. Pickup was a litigator of little value to the firm. J.F. Robertson was not the lawyer his father had been; he had his own practice in estates.[2] It soon became clear to Calvin that he needed more business lawyers.

New, talented people began to be recruited in numbers not seen since the turn of the century. For the first time since then the firm reached fifteen lawyers, and then surpassed that number by the end of the decade with seventeen. Significantly, none of the seventeen was a member of the old guard; Aitchison, Robinson, J.D. Pickup, and J.F. Robertson would all leave during the decade. Calvin died shortly thereafter but not before re-establishing the firm as a strong corporate commercial practice and training the next generation of lawyers to lead it in the last quarter of the twentieth century.

As this period of growth began, Calvin and MacKenzie, two of the three members of the management committee, were the most highly compensated. The only other bright lights on the firm's immediate horizon were Williston and Menzel. In the September 1953 allocation of profits, Calvin was alone at the top with 25 percent; MacKenzie was a distant second at 13 percent, followed by the more senior Aitchison at 12 percent; J.D. Pickup, Williston, and Menzel were all at 10 percent; J.B. Robinson got 9 percent and J.F. Robertson 6 percent. The remaining 5 percent was unallocated and available for bonuses or new hires.

The firm's recent recruiting efforts had not been very fruitful. In 1949 the partners tried Gordon V. Armstrong, who had articled at Mason Foulds.[3] He lasted only one year. Then they brought in John M. Gunn in 1952, but he lasted only until 1954.[4] They were more fortunate with Fraser Fell and Bill Swackhamer, who joined in 1953,[5] and with David Taylor in 1954,[6] Bob Sutherland in 1955,[7] and Harry Macdonell in 1956.[8]

Fell was called to the bar in 1953. In his quiet, soft-spoken, measured way, he would prove to be one of the great business lawyers of his era. He was a tireless worker who commanded instant respect and "never made a dumb statement."[9] He attracted much work to the firm and helped continue Calvin's efforts to rebuild its position as a corporate law firm. He, his uncle, and his brother Tony were later said to have a "blueblood family flair for finance."[10]

James William "Bill" Swackhamer joined the firm as a lawyer the same year as Fell, but he had taken a different road there and was to serve a very different role. He was born in 1922 in Barton, Ontario.[11] His father, Edward Swackhamer, was a house painter. As a young man Bill started at McMaster University but with the war raging in Europe he then enlisted in the Royal Canadian Navy, serving with Canada's naval escort operations in the North Atlantic and attaining the rank of lieutenant-commander. After the war he finished his BA at McMaster, graduating in 1947. He started his articles in Hamilton with Theodore Leslie McCombs. Then off he went to Osgoode Hall Law School, where he first met Walter Williston. In Toronto he completed his articles with John Arnup,[12] then returned to Hamilton to start his legal

Bob Sutherland
Law Society of Upper Canada Archives, Osgoode Hall Law School fonds
"1955 graduating class, Osgoode Hall Law School," P488

career. When Pickup left in 1952 Walter Williston began to look for someone who could help with the firm's extensive litigation practice. Swackhamer — with his terrific voice, physical presence, and intelligence — came to mind.[13] Williston suggested to Swackhamer that he could use his help at the Faskens firm. An interview with Calvin was arranged, and Calvin was won over as soon as he learned that Swackhamer had been a lieutenant in the Canadian Navy, the same rank in the service as he had held himself.

J. David Taylor was born in Toronto in 1938 and raised in Hamilton. He had an honours BA in political economy from McMaster, where he first met Fraser Fell. He followed Fraser to the firm in 1954 on graduating with honours from Osgoode Hall. He was a clever fellow, if somewhat abrupt.[14] He joined the firm as a litigator. Soon, however, Taylor switched to corporate, not only because there was much corporate work to do but also because he had an aptitude for tax, an increasingly important aspect of corporate law.

Robert "Bob" M. Sutherland was born in Grand Mère, Quebec, a pulp and paper town, in 1928. He had received a BA from the University of Toronto in 1950 and had then articled with the firm. He joined as a lawyer on his call to the bar in 1955. Bob was brash and self-confident but quite detail oriented, and one of the few young lawyers who could put up with the temper and extreme demands of J.D. Pickup.

Harry Winsor Macdonell also had an aptitude for tax. Born in Toronto in 1929, he was slightly younger than Fell and Sutherland but considerably older than David Taylor. He had been a medallist on graduating from Carleton University with a BCom in 1952. He had articled with the firm and been called to the bar in 1956.

Georgia Riddell Bentley
Law Society of Upper Canada Archives, Osgoode Hall Law School fonds
"Osgoode Hall Law School, 1954 graduating class," P487

To THIS POINT IN the firm's history, all lawyers had been men, but the next year that changed. It had from time to time brought in a woman law student — J.B. Robinson, for example, recalled that Margery Washington Rowland had been a student in the office when he came to the firm in 1918 — but it had never hired any of them as lawyers.[15] Georgia Bentley was the first female lawyer. She was born Georgia Marianne Riddell in Palmerston, Ontario, in 1929. She had attended the University of Toronto, receiving her BA in 1950, and had been called to the bar in 1954. When she joined the firm four years later, she was married to Rafe Bentley but she initially retained her maiden name. When she became pregnant with her son and began to show, Calvin embarrassed her into adopting her married name by referring to her publicly as Miss Riddell.[16]

From the beginning "Mrs. Bentley" was treated differently. She was on a salary and was assigned to the aging Aitchison and Robinson as a conveyancing lawyer. She also assisted Robertson in wills and estates. It would be many years before a woman in the firm did anything other than these family-related types of legal work. Although she practised with the firm for almost thirty years, developing a deep expertise in real estate, she was never seriously considered for partnership.

Calvin's attitude toward Bentley was reflective of the past. In many, more positive respects, his practice also reminds one of that past, and specifically of W.H. Beatty at his peak. Calvin combined a largely corporate/commercial practice with an active involvement in the business affairs of large, corporate clients. In his level of polish and his social position Calvin was much more like Beatty than either of the Fasken brothers. David had been an aggressive self-starter who rose despite, rather than because of, social or family connections. Alex Fasken had certainly not been the sort to sit on a bank board. But Calvin had the pedigree, the intelligence, and a banker's conservatism.

—————

In 1952 Calvin was elected president of Canada's oldest trust company, Toronto General Trusts Corporation. When that company was formed in 1882 "to act as administrator, executor, guardian, assignee etc, of estates or persons, and to execute trusts under authority of the courts or other corporations," Beatty had been one of the "gentleman of standing and influence" recruited for its board.[17] But Beatty and his firm had not done its legal work. Calvin was the one who brought the trust company into the fold, serving as its president from 1952 to 1961. Again like Beatty, Calvin accumulated many board seats and executive positions. He was on the board of Dome Mines and its affiliate Campbell Red Lake, Yukon Consolidated Gold Corporation Limited, Dominion Magnesium, Moffats Limited, Avco of Canada, Pilot Insurance, Canada Permanent Mortgage Corporation, and Dunham Bush, and he served on the advisory committee of the London and Lancashire Insurance Company and as a governor of McMaster University.[18]

Calvin was a quietly impressive man. In March 1958 the *Globe and Mail* ran a business profile of him under the heading "All Work and No Play — but Not a Dull Boy."[19] It began by characterizing him as "without doubt one of Toronto's (if not Canada's) most modest executives." In his interview Calvin remarked, "The secret of getting ahead is simply to join a firm with brilliant seniors and then, as time goes on, keep it staffed with brilliant juniors. Then all you have to do is just ride along." The *Globe* noted that "the ride has carried him pretty far up the ladder."

From the upper rungs Calvin could see that the growing Canadian economy offered both opportunities and challenges. As legal counsel and president Calvin knew, for example, that Toronto General Trusts needed to grow quickly to keep pace with the economy. He oversaw its purchase of Ottawa Valley Trust Company in 1952 and of Osler and Nanton Trust in Winnipeg in 1953.[20]

The next year Calvin became president and chairman of the board of Toronto Western Hospital, but the bulk of his attention was focused elsewhere. In 1954 the Bank of Toronto entered into exploratory talks with the Dominion Bank about the possibility of a merger. When those talks proved fruitful, serious negotiations began, and for six months the two institutions secretly discussed the terms on which they might merge.

Calvin, as lead legal counsel to the Bank of Toronto, headed its merger committee. His counterpart at the Dominion Bank was also a lawyer, Beverley Matthews of McCarthy's. Calvin and his law firm had acted for the Bank of Toronto for a very long time. Matthews was relatively new to the Dominion Bank, which had to this point been an Osler client. Any link between McCarthy's and the Dominion were in the distant past, when the McCarthy Osler firm had maintained its offices in that bank's building. But in May 1916, when McCarthy and Osler had split, the McCarthy firm had moved out of the building and the Bank had remained with Osler's. Matthews, however, had joined the board of the Dominion Bank in the late 1940s and gradually won its business for McCarthy's. So it was Calvin and Matthews who led the lengthy merger discussions.

Calvin had an advantage in representing the larger of the two institutions, as the final terms evidence. The merged entity was to be known as the Toronto-Dominion Bank. Shareholders of the Dominion Bank received one share in the new bank for each share they held, but shareholders of the Bank of Toronto received one and one-third shares for each of theirs. The president of the Bank of Toronto, B.S. Vanstone, was to be chairman of the board, while the president of the Dominion Bank, Robert Rae, was to be vice-chairman. The president was to be the former general manager at the Dominion Bank, A.C. Ashford, but the vice-president and general manager was to be William Kerr, who had held that office at the Bank of Toronto.[21]

As the discussions proceeded, Calvin and Matthews were also in discussions with the Ministry of Finance in Ottawa because the merger needed ministerial approval. It came on 1 November 1954. Calvin and Matthews then prepared the documentation necessary to win approval of the merger from the shareholders of each bank. The shareholders meetings were held in December and, as expected, the merger was approved on both sides. On 1 February 1955 the branches of the combined bank opened their doors to the public as the Toronto-Dominion Bank.

Calvin and Matthews had become friends and each had a prominent place on the board of the new bank, but Calvin chaired its executive committee. Each law firm retained some of the bank's business. Over time Faskens would do the bulk of the Bank's litigation and secured lending and McCarthy's would do the bulk of its corporate work.

Even after its acquisitions, the Toronto General Trusts continued to face economic pressure to grow. Calvin knew that the Toronto-Dominion Bank was interested in expanding its interest in Canada Permanent Mortgage Corporation, a company that had also been controlled by the Gooderham and Worts families for many years. Canada Permanent Mortgage had a subsidiary, Canada Permanent Trust. Late in the 1950s he and the other members of the Bank's executive committee began to work with Wood Gundy and Company Limited to put together an offer to buy Toronto General Trusts and merge it with Canada Permanent Trust. On 5 January 1961 Wood Gundy, acting as agent for a financial group led by the Toronto-Dominion Bank, made an offer to purchase all the shares of Toronto General Trusts. As chairman of the executive committee of the bank behind the offer and also president of the target company, Calvin was required by law to declare his interest and refrain from voting, but the offer was recommended for acceptance by the shareholders. Again Calvin was off to Ottawa to sell the Ministry of Finance on the deal.

On 21 April, Canada Permanent Trust and Toronto General Trusts applied for permission to merge. After approval was obtained, the materials were prepared to put before the shareholders. They approved the plan on 27 September and the two companies merged on 1 December. Calvin was made chairman of the board of the new Canada Permanent Toronto General Trust Company, which two years later became simply the Canada Permanent Trust Company.[22]

———◆———

CALVIN WAS NOT ONLY the chief administrator of the law firm but also its conscience. He used strong language at times, but he was nonetheless a man of deep religious convictions. He established the rule (unchanged until the 1989 merger with Campbell Godfrey & Lewtas) that no liquor was allowed on the firm's premises. Calvin's views on alcohol are reputed to have cost the firm a client. In the mid-1950s Molson Brewery of Montreal was in a bitter struggle with its arch-rival, E.P. Taylor's Canadian Breweries Limited, which made Carling and O'Keefe beer. Provincial law required that beer sold in a province be brewed in that province.[23] In March 1952 Canadian Breweries expanded into Quebec by gaining control of National Breweries and its Dow plant in Montreal. Molson decided to retaliate by expanding into Ontario.

Bryce MacKenzie, Jim Lewtas, and C.C. Calvin are standing and Minto Pyle and an unknown US lawyer are seated at a closing in 1952. Lewtas and Pyle were with Arnoldi, Parry & Campbell, which later became Campbell Godfrey & Lewtas.

This strategy meant that Molson had to acquire or build a plant in Toronto. Senator Hartland Molson approached Calvin about purchasing land in the city. Was there a way to do so without publicity?

Calvin indicated that he could acquire land on behalf of the company by purchasing as an agent for an undisclosed purchaser. When the 1955 purchase was carried out in this way without the knowledge of Taylor and Canadian Breweries, the senator was very pleased. The plant was built and the Molson Canadian brand was launched. Senator Molson asked Calvin to join the company board but Calvin politely declined, saying that he could not face his sisters if he was on the board of a brewery. So Hal Mockridge of Osler's went on the Molson board instead. In the mid-1960s, when Molson expanded further into Ontario, Purdy Crawford of Osler's got the work.[24]

⁕⎯⬦⎯⁕

ANOTHER COMPANY WAS LOOKING to expand in 1952. Rio Tinto, a UK company with mining operations in South Africa, was considering searching for minerals in Canada. Oscar Weiss, who was principally stationed in South Africa, was given responsibility for Canada.[25] Rio Tinto therefore needed Canadian counsel and turned to Faskens as one of Canada's leading mining law firms. Calvin delegated the work to Bryce MacKenzie. In 1953 Weiss arranged for the incorporation of a federal company cleverly called Ownamin Limited. One of its first projects was a mining option agreement in Quebec. As was typical in such agreements, Rio was entitled to take shares in the new explor-ation company in return for its investment in the property. When Rio Tinto wanted to get credit for the expense of Oscar Weiss in travelling to Canada, the firm was asked to opine on whether such expenses qualified as an in-vestment in the property. MacKenzie prepared the opinion and it gave him the first chance to meet J.N.V. (Val) Duncan, a barrister turned businessman who was Rio's managing director.[26] Duncan's wife was from British Colum-bia and he had developed a strong interest in Canada. He and MacKenzie would come to know each other very well over the next decade

Despite these early moves, Rio Tinto did not become heavily involved in Canada until it joined Joseph Hirshhorn in exploiting Canadian uran-ium deposits. Hirshhorn would later give his name and his art collection to a modern art museum on the Mall in Washington,[27] but what mattered to Rio Tinto was that he and his colleague Franc Joubin had discovered a huge quantity of uranium in Algoma District, directly north of Lake Huron near Blind River.[28] In early 1955 Hirshhorn and his Algom Uranium Mines Limited signed a letter of intent with Duncan and Rio Tinto Company Lim-ited and its Canadian subsidiary, Rio Tinto (Canada) Limited. The deal was hammered out over several days in the Faskens boardroom. Duncan sat with Calvin and MacKenzie opposite Jack Blain of McCarthy's, who represented Algom Uranium, and William Bouck, who was Hirshhorn's primary legal counsel.[29] Various financing companies were also present and represented by Borden & Elliot and Fraser & Beatty. In essence Rio Tinto was to provide the funding and expertise for the uranium development in return for shares, a supply agreement, and five seats on the nine-person board of Algom Uranium Mines.

By 15 October 1955 the Pronto mine and mill was formally opened. MacKenzie took a special train the night before to be in Blind River for the opening. With help from the government, the planned community of Elliot Lake was developed there.

This was only the beginning of many mining deals that the firm would handle for Rio Tinto. By May 1956 Joseph Hirshhorn had merged his inter-ests with Rio Tinto (Canada) Limited, which was renamed Rio Tinto Mining Company of Canada Limited. Through a series of wholly owned or con-trolled companies, it opened a number of other mines in the area. When Robert Winters, the Nova Scotia industrialist turned Liberal minister of public works, went down to defeat in the federal election that brought

John Diefenbaker and the Conservatives to power, he became its president. Winters' colleague and mentor, C.D. Howe, became a director.

By the end of 1957 some 18,000 people were living in Elliot Lake. The company donated money for a hospital and Hirshhorn donated an auditorium. Then its major customer, the US Atomic Energy Commission, decided not to exercise its option to take further uranium after its existing contracts expired in 1962 and 1963. The future of the uranium industry looked bleak. In June 1960 a general meeting of the shareholders of the various Rio Tinto–related companies approved an amalgamation that resulted in Rio Algom Mines Limited. This ensured that the company would survive despite the inevitable closing of some of the mines. To soften the blow to the model community of Elliot Lake, the company bought back the houses of terminated employees and provided separation allowances and help in finding new employment.

The firm continued to act for the Rio Tinto group, assisting it with many projects. It was involved in the company's 1962 acquisition of Atlas Steels Limited. Later Harry Macdonell would play a key role in Rio Tinto's assumption of control of the British Newfoundland Development Corporation (Brinco), which developed the huge Churchill Falls hydroelectric power project.[30]

—◦◦◦—

IN 1960 THE FIRM assisted in a corporate transaction that must have generated a more emotional reaction than others, acting for the shareholders of Excelsior Life Insurance Company in a sale of the business to the large US-based insurer Aetna. Excelsior Life was a company that the firm had not only advised but also guided for decades. But like many financial institutions it needed to expand to survive in the new world. Aetna itself had a long history. The company had begun in 1850 in Hartford, Connecticut, operating an annuity fund to sell life insurance. As Excelsior Life would later do, it chose its general counsel, in this case Judge Eliphalet Adams Bulkeley, for its board of directors and as its president.

In the more than a century since its founding Aetna had grown substantially, but all of its operations had been in the United States. By 1960 it wanted to expand internationally and it looked to Canada. Excelsior's need to grow and Aetna's desire for a Canadian operation fostered a deal. The question was whether this would be the end of the firm's long, special relationship with Excelsior. As it happened, it was not.

Aetna Canada, as Excelsior Life came to be known, continued to look to Faskens for its legal work, but the lawyers at the firm would never again lead that company as they had done so often in the past.

———•◦◆◦•———

On J.W. Pickup's departure Walter Williston, even though relatively junior, assumed the role of lead litigator. One of his first cases was the appeal to the Supreme Court of the Fasken estate motion. Williston and Swackhamer appeared for the executors. A panel of five judges of the Supreme Court of Canada — Justices Kerwin, Rand, Kellock, Locke, and Cartwright — overturned the Court of Appeal and reinstated the trial judgment.[31] David Jr. alone was to get the annual surplus.

Williston was in the midst of developing his reputation as one of Canada's most effective litigators. William Comery recalls that when he joined the firm as a student in the 1950s, Walter Williston, although a relatively junior lawyer, was spending most of his time in the Ontario Court of Appeal or the Supreme Court of Canada.[32] He was not, however, someone who enjoyed the respect and admiration of all. He seldom stood on formality and often said things that shocked and upset people. He was unkempt, looking like he slept in his suit, and he was disorganized. He drank too much too often and collected women as lovers the way a rock star or a top athlete does today. Comery recalls being asked as a student to accompany Williston to the Supreme Court of Canada in late October 1956:

> We left in the afternoon in his Austin Healey convertible, and the wind streaming in through the inevitable crack between the canvas roof and the windscreen almost froze our skulls and our brains. Arriving in Ottawa for dinner we had a long, luxurious, somewhat boozy dinner and then I was ready for bed. Instead, Walter hustled me off to the Supreme Court of Canada library where we proceeded to review the law for the case the next day.

Donald Jack had a similar experience with Williston when he was a student.[33] Again we hear of a drive to Ottawa, in Jack's case with Ron Rolls sleeping in the back seat, a stopover for a boozy dinner, and another late night trip to the library to try, in an inebriated state, to prepare for court the next morning.

Had Williston been nothing more than a partier or a drinker, he would never have become a legend. But he was clearly brilliant and insightful, and a quick study — he needed to be because he did not prepare properly for court, relying heavily on his juniors to prepare the law and brief him on it at the last moment. After a night of drinking and carousing, he would show up at the law library with his junior or a student and review their research. He had an amazing understanding of the law and of civil procedure and would correct their errors and seek out key cases that they had missed, then go off to court and win. Those who worked with him recognized that he depended on them, but rather than resenting the way he exploited them to enjoy his lifestyle, they rose to the occasion time and time again. That says volumes about their resourcefulness and talent and about the respect they had for this maverick. They knew that he was very perceptive and could identify and address a court's concerns, making him a successful, much sought after litigator. They also appreciated that he took on controversial cases and fought for the underdog. As a result, Walter attracted a regular stream of bright, hard-working, resourceful protégés. Williston mentored Dana Porter's son, Julian, as well as Don Jack, John Laskin, John Sopinka, Ron Rolls, Tony Kelly, Bill Graham, Allan Rock, John Campion, and many more.

He taught them what he had learned from J.W. Pickup, who in turn had learned it from R.S. Robertson: "If you want to be effective, be brief. If you want to be brief, shorten your sentences. If you want to shorten your sentences, figure out what it is that you really want to say, and then get to it without a lot of flowery preliminaries. Most important, put your heart into it, because otherwise, it is unlikely to be effective."[34]

Williston continued to teach at the Law Society's school and worked from the inside to foster the change that Wright and his colleagues were still seeking. Finally, in 1957, at a time when the number of law students was making the maintenance of Osgoode Hall Law School an economic burden on the legal profession, the benchers worked out a compromise with the universities. They sanctioned programs at the University of Toronto, University of Ottawa, Queen's, and the University of Western Ontario. All these universities, along with the Osgoode Hall Law School, adopted a three-year LLB program. Where the universities compromised was in the establishment of a one-year articling program and six-month bar admission course to follow the university degree. That way the benchers could ensure that people called to the bar in Ontario had at least some practical experience and that practising lawyers had the opportunity to test the suitability of these candidates through the bar admission examinations. Walter taught civil procedure for many years in the bar admission course and ultimately used the materials for a book that he and Ron Rolls wrote on court forms. Later he ran successfully for bencher, ultimately becoming a life bencher after being elected four times.

∗—➔✧←—∗

As THE FIRM LOOKED more and more to its bright young lawyers, the old guard began to leave. The first to go was R.S. Robertson's son, John Farley. On 15 April 1954 he ceased to be a partner. MacKenzie was the beneficiary, with most of Robertson's 6 percent of the profits going to him. The others stayed largely where they had been. One other person did benefit: J.W. Swackhamer, although not a partner, was paid 2% in addition to his salary "until otherwise directed by any two of Aitchison, Calvin or MacKenzie."[35]

Swackhamer's rising star was confirmed the next year when he became a partner. As of 1 January 1956 the partnership profit allocation was as shown in Table 6.[36] The remaining 4 percent was for the time being unallotted, being available for associate bonuses or new hires.

As of 1 January 1956
the partnership profit
allocation looked like this.*

James Aitchison	11%
C.C. Calvin	24%
J.B. Robinson	9%
B.R.P. MacKenzie	15%
J.D. Pickup	9%
W.B. Williston	11%
D.G.C. Menzel	11%
J.W. Swackhamer	6%

* *Ibid.*

Williston, Menzel, and Swackhamer continued to rise in the partnership over the next few years. Then, in late summer 1958, David Menzel had a fateful chat with his senior partner and mentor. He wanted more than the 12 percent he was receiving and asserted that he would leave if he did not get it. Calvin did not take well to any ultimatum and this was no exception. He bid his promising young partner good prospects and showed him the door. Menzel took $26,000 with him and the promise of an additional $26,000 in five months as his share of work in progress and accounts receivable.[37] With his experience and contacts in mining, he joined Falconbridge and

Ronald Robertson
Law Society of Upper Canada Archives, Osgoode Hall Law School fonds
"1957 graduating class, Osgoode Hall Law School," P490

worked in house in the mining industry for several years before returning to Bay Street practice with Campbell Godfrey & Lewtas. With Menzel's departure MacKenzie would now receive 19 percent and Williston 16 percent. Two up-and-coming associates, Fraser Fell and J. David Taylor, received a 1 percent share of profits.

THE LATE 1950s WAS when the foundations of the modern firm were laid. Fell, Swackhamer, Taylor, Sutherland and Macdonell were joined by Ron Robertson, Ron Rolls, Bob Tuer, Roger Wilson, Robert Shirriff, and Doug Gibson.

Ronald Neil Robertson joined the firm in 1956 as a student. He came with both a distinguished lineage and superb credentials. His father was Colonel John Gordon Robertson, R.S. Robertson's cousin who had been severely injured at Vimy Ridge. His older brother was Gordon Robertson, who was then one of the most experienced and important civil servants in Ottawa.[38] Ron was born in 1930 when Gordon was already thirteen and as a result Ron did not spend much time with his brother growing up. When Ron was five, Gordon had left to go to school in Regina. Then in 1938 Gordon had gone to England on a Rhodes Scholarship. On his return to Canada in 1941 he went to Ottawa, where he worked in the Department of Foreign Affairs for the remainder of the Second World War. For five years thereafter Gordon served as personal secretary to Prime Minister Mackenzie King and then as secretary to the St. Laurent cabinet. When Ron joined the firm his brother was the deputy minister of the Department of Northern Affairs and Natural Resources. The brothers were not particularly close but Gordon was nevertheless an especially good contact for a firm still focused heavily on the North and the mining sector.

Ron was inspired to go into law by his second cousin, R.S. Robertson, whom he met on several occasions when his family came to visit the Chief Justice in Toronto.[39] It seems only right therefore that Ron joined Robertson's former law firm — but that is not where he began. Through the influence of his brother Gordon, Ron commenced his articles at Herridge Tolmie in Ottawa. He soon moved to Toronto and joined Faskens to complete them.

He has to qualify as one of the best-educated people in the firm's history. He left his native Saskatchewan to study at Merchant Taylor's School in England, returning to Canada to pursue a BA at Dalhousie, in Nova Scotia, from whence his father had come. Winning a Rhodes Scholarship as his brother had done, he went back to England and completed a BA (1954) and BCL (1955) at Magdalene College, Oxford. He then received an LLB from Osgoode Hall and was called to the bar in 1957. As if his family connections, superb academic record, and first-class mind were not enough of an advantage, he was also tall and handsome and spoke with a deep, authoritative voice.

Joining the firm shortly after Robertson were five young articling students: Bob Tuer, Roger Wilson, Robert Shirriff, Ron Rolls, and Bill Comery. All but Comery would become lawyers in the firm. The four who joined were a study in contrasts. Bob Tuer, like Bob Sutherland, was from a small town and a rough, uncut diamond. He would become an excellent litigator in the style of a street fighter. Intimidation was an important tool in his arsenal, and he excelled at asking tough questions and insisting on truthful answers. Roger Wilson was ever the gentleman, gregarious, charming, witty, and exceptionally well read. He made a legion of friends and stood out at the many cocktail parties and other social events he organized or attended. He would prove a magnet for legal work and board seats.

Robert Shirriff was also a gentleman with a patrician air, but less gregarious and somewhat more reserved than Roger. He used to wince at the crude jokes shared by Williston and Tuer. Shirriff had given up a promising acting career to go into law. For years he thought of himself as more successful than his fellow Hart House actor and lifelong friend, Donald Sutherland.

Clockwise from top left: Ron Rolls, Robert Shirriff, Roger Wilson, and Bob Tuer
Law Society of Upper Canada Archives, Osgoode Hall Law School fonds
"1958 graduating class, Osgoode Hall Law School," P491

Ron Rolls was even more of the aristocrat than Shirriff. He was exceptionally well organized and spoke with great precision and attention to grammar and enunciation. He hated sloppiness in thinking, expression, or dress and yet he adored Walter Williston, with whom he worked long and often. Walter had a sharp mind but dressed carelessly, spoke with a slur, and was disorganized. They were the odd couple, with Ron as Felix and Walter as Oscar.

Williston and Rolls differed in another way: Rolls was gay and Williston was quite markedly heterosexual. But this did not matter to Walter. Swackhamer was also gay. If anything, recruiting and working with gay lawyers appealed to Walter's iconoclastic nature and sense of social fairness. He wanted bright, articulate, hard-working lawyers irrespective of their sexual orientation.

Others came and went in this period. John F. Varcoe stayed for two years. Norman L. Booth and D.S. Rickerd stayed but a year.[40] For a time in 1960 the firm had nineteen lawyers, including Rickerd and new recruit John Sopinka.[41]

Sopinka was born on 19 March 1933 in Broderick, Saskatchewan, where his Ukrainian-born parents, Metro and Nancy, had settled after emigrating from Wislok, Poland, in 1928. The family moved to Hamilton, Ontario, when John was seven years old. His father worked at International Harvester.[42] John loved playing the violin and at fifteen played with Hamilton's philharmonic orchestra. He attended Saltfleet High School in Stoney Creek and then the University of Toronto, where he earned BA and LLB degrees. John was an amazingly talented and very competitive person. In addition to being a skilled violinist, he was a defensive halfback in the Canadian Football League, playing twenty-nine games with the Toronto Argonauts between 1955 and 1957 and eight with the Montreal Alouettes in 1957. He was called to the bar in 1960 and joined the law firm. (Also joining the firm as a student was another CFL football star, Ron Stewart, who played halfback for the Ottawa Rough Riders.[43] Unlike Sopinka, Stewart put football first and was not asked to join the firm as a lawyer.)

Sopinka worked closely with Williston and would later recall that Walter set "a hard and unrelenting pace in both work and play."[44] To survive, Sopinka developed an approach based on tireless preparation: "The idea was to chase down every possible lead in a case, to go after every avenue of inquiry in search of evidence. The second idea behind the first idea was never to be caught by surprise, but possibly to catch the other side with something unexpected."[45] One of the tasks Sopinka assumed was to run the 1961 campaign to elect Williston as a bencher. Williston's personality and Sopinka's organization and competitive spirit won the day.[46]

As the firm grew bigger and younger, the need for professional management also grew. Despite Calvin's dissent, on 29 October 1961 the firm hired its first full-time office manager.[47] Previously the senior partners had managed the firm with the help of the firm's accountant, but with the increasing demands that the growing firm created and with Calvin busy managing other enterprises, the younger partners all believed it was time to seek professional help.

Sheldon C. Skinner took the position and immediately introduced a number of administrative changes. Central docketing was one of his first innovations. Up to this time lawyers had tracked their own time and prepared accounts for their clients. Skinner thought it was better to have each lawyer keep track of time spent on files and then submit it to accounting, to ensure that accounts were properly billed and make it easier to track how each lawyer was spending his or her time. Skinner also introduced an office manual setting out changes to such matters as the charging of meals and overtime to clients.[48]

In November 1961 J.D. Pickup retired from the partnership for health reasons. He was only forty-four. The firm agreed to pay him $500 a month for the next six years, a total of $36,000 "in respect of profits earned but not collected."[49] On 29 November Pickup became counsel to the firm. His counsel agreement began with a statement,

> The members of our firm are desirous of assisting you in your efforts to recover and maintain your health and our firm agrees that your hours of work and your vacations must be adjusted to meet your requirements and to that end you shall be free to decline for reasons of health any work required of you hereunder without affecting your right to remuneration hereunder.[50]

As counsel he was paid $14,000 per annum, given an office and secretarial assistance, and permitted to accept work from others.

In the firm J.D. Pickup would be remembered as the person who gave impetus to the anti-nepotism policy. He had always been favoured by his father and resented by those who were not. His war injury made him difficult to work with. After he left, the firm quickly adopted a policy to ensure that relatives of partners in the firm could not be hired.[51] The firm that in the 1930s would hire no one but family now refused to hire anyone with family connections.

———◆———

NEW YEAR's DAY 1962 brought much new blood to the partnership. Aitchison, Calvin, MacKenzie, Williston, and Swackhamer, acting as the management committee, decided to admit Fraser Fell, David Taylor, Bob Sutherland, and Harry Macdonell. The percentage drawings under the partnership agreement were varied as shown in Table 7. The firm now had seventeen lawyers. In addition to the ten partners, there were seven associates and a number of students who would soon be lawyers: Georgia Bentley, Ron Robertson, Alex Givens, Doug Gibson, Roger Wilson, Bob Tuer, Ron Rolls, Robert Shirriff, Jay Huckle, John Sopinka, and Terry Brooks.

Aitchison	5%	Swackhamer	12%
Calvin	18%	Fell	6%
Robinson	7%	Taylor	6%
MacKenzie	18%	Sutherland	4%
Williston	17%	Macdonell	6%
R.N. Robertson, not yet a partner			1%

Alex Givens and Franklin Douglas "Doug" Gibson would prove to be the key additions. Givens was the firm's first Roman Catholic and the first tax specialist. He was born in 1927 in Kingston. He had been called to the bar in 1950 and was a well-established tax practitioner working at Philips Electronics when he joined the firm in 1962.[52] Born on 18 November 1929 Doug Gibson, like Fraser Fell, was allied to the Toronto moneyed elite. His father was the Reverend John E. Gibson, a prominent Anglican minister, and his wife was Anne Elizabeth Pollitt, the daughter of Donovan Hoult Pollitt, the president and general manager of Campbell Canada.[53] Gibson attended Ridley College and the University of Toronto, graduating with a BA in 1953. He then articled with Cassels, Brock & Kelley and attended Osgoode Hall, being called to the bar in 1957. On his call he joined Cassels Brock, where he practised for several years. In 1962 he joined Faskens. In a practice that focused on trusts and estate planning for the very well-to-do, he became one of the prime finders for the firm.

Although the firm was collectively getting younger, Jimmy Aitchison was not. He was now seventy-five and quite frail. He resigned from the partnership and became counsel as of 1 January 1963 after fifty-seven years in the firm. The partners decided that in addition to receiving "in respect of profits earned but not collected, . . . $25,000.00," he would be awarded "a special allowance by reason of long years of service of $20,000.00." Of this $45,000, $15,000 was paid immediately and the balance in monthly payments of $500 each.

— —✦— —

THE NEXT MONTH OUGHT to have been a special time for the firm — its 100th anniversary — but 23 February 1963 came and went without fanfare. No one seems to have noticed that on this day in 1863, Beatty and Chadwick had founded the firm. When the lawyers looked back into the firm's past, it was the exploits of David Fasken and the successes in court of R.S. Robertson that brought them pride. Beatty had been alive when Aitchison joined as a student in 1906 but he had ceased to practise by that point. Aitchison and J.B. Robinson both recalled Chadwick, but the man they remembered was an old, largely deaf eccentric who studied genealogy and heraldry. One wonders if Calvin paused on his way to his seat at the head of the TD Bank's board table to glance at Beatty's portrait, which hung there with those of the other presidents, or at the portrait of Beatty that hung in the boardroom of Canada Permanent. If he did, there is no evidence that it motivated him to preserve the memory of the Beatty years.

By this point Calvin was spending much of his time in meetings. His desk diary for 1963 shows board meetings, executive committee meetings, and annual meetings day after day.[54] One day it was a meeting of the Excelsior Life board, another a meeting of the Bank's executive committee. Yet another day would have him in New York for a meeting of the Dome Mines board or back in Toronto for a meeting of Canada Permanent Mortgage or Canada Permanent Trust or the Rio Algom board. Days without meetings he often spent at Toronto Western Hospital dealing with its issues and concerns.

On the morning of 1 August 1963 Calvin attended a meeting of the board of the Toronto-Dominion Bank. That afternoon he was to have chaired a meeting of the executive committee of Canada Permanent Trust Company at its attractive art deco offices at 320 Bay Street, but it was cancelled. He had no appointments for the rest of that day or the next so he worked at the law office, then left to spend the weekend on Garden Island, a place he enjoyed away from the office and the tension of helping to run many companies.[55] He died after dinner on 3 August 1963, at the age of sixty-nine. When people gathered in the office on Monday morning they learned that the "old man" had died. The firm went into mourning, shutting the office and not reopening until Thursday, 8 August.[56]

Calvin's compensation had for some time been a large portion of the firm's profits. Now the firm had to deal with what was owing to his estate and how the profits were to be divided in future. On 30 December 1963 it was decided that the amount to be paid to Calvin's estate in respect of profits earned but not yet collected was $83,505.00, plus eighteen ninety-sevenths of the total actually collected.

MacKenzie, Williston, Fell, and Swackhamer then turned their minds to the compensation of the partners going forward. They now had 18 percent available. Williston was given an additional 1 percent so that he and

MacKenzie were the highest compensated at 18 percent. Fell, Taylor, Macdonell, and Sutherland all received an additional 1 percent, raising them to 7 percent. Robertson, a rising star, was made a partner and given 6 percent. The remaining 11 percent was allocated to the associates. Rolls, Shirriff, Wilson, Tuer, and Gibson received bonuses of 2 percent, and Bentley received 1 percent. This meant that Rolls, Shirriff, Wilson, and Tuer would receive $8,000 as salary, plus 2 percent, with a guaranteed minimum of $1,000 per month by way of salary and drawings. Gibson received $10,000 by way of salary, plus 2 percent, with a guaranteed minimum of $1,250 per month by way of salary and drawings. Bentley received $7,500 by way of salary, plus 1 percent, with a guaranteed minimum of $850 per month by way of salary and drawings.

Following Calvin's death many both inside and outside the firm questioned whether it could survive. He had for years been the principal client finder and client minder. Did the firm have the experience and wisdom to keep existing clients and attract new ones? There was no grey hair left. MacKenzie was now the oldest and he was only fifty-six. Williston was next at forty-four. Most of the lawyers were in their twenties or early thirties. Calvin's friend Beverley Matthews visited Bryce MacKenzie and suggested that a wise course of action for the remaining partners was to merge their practice with McCarthy's. They ought to know that without Calvin to attract the business and manage the firm, they could not make a go of it. MacKenzie conferred with his partners. There was no love lost between the Fasken partners and their long-time rivals. The remaining lawyers rallied around MacKenzie and encouraged him to deliver a definitive *no* to Matthews.

Then the real work began. The weight of carrying on fell on Bryce MacKenzie, Walter Williston, Bill Swackhamer, and Fraser Fell. Meetings were arranged with long-standing clients to assure them that the firm would continue to serve their needs diligently and well. Owing to Calvin's wise management, the clients already knew the partners who had been doing their work and they remained loyal.

Bryce MacKenzie bore the greatest burden, assuming the title of senior partner and taking Calvin's place on the board of Dome Mines, Rio Algom, and other clients. On his death in 1986 the firm acknowledged the "enormous debt of gratitude for the leadership shown by Mr. MacKenzie following Mr. Calvin's death."[57]

IN RETROSPECT, IT IS no surprise that the firm not only survived but prospered. The transition was closer to that following William Gooderham's death than the jarring one necessitated by Worts' early demise. Calvin had done his job well. The executive committee structure meant that others in the firm understood management issues. MacKenzie, in particular, was familiar with and to the firm's major clients and had been supervising the more junior partners and associates for some time. Those lawyers may have been relatively young, but they had been well chosen and well trained. Most went on to very successful careers, many of them with the firm. A new administrator was in place and had started to adopt modern management techniques. The firm had strong ties with its key clients and the newer lawyers, such as Fraser Fell, Roger Wilson, and Doug Gibson, were able to exploit their many contacts (and in Roger's case, his winning personality) to attract new clients.

Rather than facing the dismal future predicted by Matthews, the firm was actually well on its way in a climb back to the sort of prominence in the Toronto legal community that it had enjoyed under Beatty and Blackstock, even if the lawyers in the firm did not recognize those names or the high standard against which history would judge them.

A MULTITUDE OF
CHANGES BUT . . .

UNDER MACKENZIE, THE FIRM's business law practice continued to focus primarily on financial institutions, insolvency, mining, and health law, but he remained the senior partner for only six years. As had happened with Tom Blackstock six decades before, the demands of the office, long hours, and frequent travel to New York and England took a toll on MacKenzie's health. In 1969 he suffered the first of multiple strokes, while on a business trip to New York. His wife, Florence, was immediately flown down to be with him.[1] Although he continued to come into the office for some years after this devastating event, he was never the same. Unable to practise, he turned his mind to the past and prepared the memoirs of both Faskens and Rio Algom referred to in this history.

For the next two decades Williston was the star. He continued to gather about him bright, young litigators, creating a sort of litigation boutique within the law firm. Several of those young lawyers would be appointed to the bench: John Sopinka, who went to the Supreme Court of Canada; John Laskin and Eleanore Cronk, now on the Ontario Court of Appeal; and Sydney Lederman, a judge of the Ontario trial division. Some went on to distinguished teaching careers, including John McCamus, as dean of Osgoode Hall Law School; Bruce Dunlop at the University of Toronto; and John Evans at Osgoode Hall. Still others went into politics, like Bill Graham, who became interim leader of the Liberal Party of Canada, and Allan Rock, who became the federal minister of justice, Canada's ambassador to the United Nations, and now president of the University of Ottawa. Many of those who worked with Williston, however, stayed with the practice of law and became distinguished lawyers: Ron Rolls, Julian Porter, Bob Tuer, John Campion, David Roebuck, Harvey Strosberg (as a student), Tony Kelly, and Don Affleck.

In 1967 the firm settled on the name Fasken & Calvin and moved with thirty lawyers and approximately fifty staff and students from Toronto Street into part of the thirtieth floor of the newly completed Toronto-Dominion Bank Tower, a Mies van der Rohe design. McCarthy & McCarthy, with whom it shared the TD Bank's work, also moved into the building. When I went to that office for my articling interview in the spring of 1979, the firm had grown to sixty-two lawyers, not counting Bryce MacKenzie and John Risk, who were listed as counsel but had ceased to practise. It stayed in that building until the summer of 2010, when it moved into the new Bay Adelaide Centre.

My office on the twentieth floor of the Bay Adelaide Centre looks east. Through the maze of newer buildings I can still make out the Gooderham & Worts complex. It looks nothing like the print on my wall showing that industrial complex as it was in 1890. I tell those who drop in and ask about the print that Gooderham & Worts was the engine that drove the firm in its first half century. I remind today's lawyers that they have links to that complex and the families that ran it, and that the law they practise today has been determined in part by the needs of the Gooderham & Worts business empire. They have trouble accepting this because they focus on how much has changed.

There have indeed been a multitude of changes. Some started with the Fasken brothers, and it is only fitting that as I look east toward the Gooderham & Worts complex, one of the buildings that stands closer to me is the Excelsior Life Building on Toronto Street. David Fasken, who had that building erected, took steps toward the modern firm when he introduced the partnership agreement of 1906. The concepts on which Fasken's draft agreement were built — that all of a partner's time belonged to the firm and that law is a full-time profession — resonate with the modern lawyer.

Nevertheless, David Fasken would not feel entirely at home in the firm of 2013, nor would C.C. Calvin, who followed him and laid its foundations. Their law firm was still made up almost exclusively of white, Protestant men, mostly of British ancestry. As I sat in a recent internal meeting, I looked around the room and realized that not one of the half dozen people in the meeting would have been likely to practise in the firm during its first 100 years — and certainly none of us would have been made a partner. There was a woman, a Jewish person, a Black person, a person of Chinese ancestry, a person of Indian ancestry, and me, a Catholic with Green Irish roots. Faskens can no longer be described as Anglican, Methodist, or Baptist, Conservative or Liberal, establishment or not, and it has certainly ceased to be made up exclusively of men. It comprises a large, diverse group of people of varied background, gender, culture, and religion who conduct a broad, multi-faceted practice. Canada's visible minorities are still underrepresented, but they are present.[2] Then, diversity was largely unknown and unwelcome. Now we glory in what diversity we have achieved and strive for more, celebrating an annual diversity day.

It would be wrong, however, to think of the firm during its first century as an entirely closed shop. While the firm was largely the preserve of white Anglo-Saxon Protestant men, there were Jewish and women students and at least one of each became a lawyer in the firm. Focusing on the firm's earlier WASP character means at times overlooking instances when it demonstrated openness. The president of the Canadian Association of Black Lawyers (CABL), Andrew Alleyne, juniored with me and now, a partner in the firm, sits next to me. He was both pleased and surprised when during the course of my research I learned that the firm had represented Lucie and Thornton Blackburn, two runaway slaves who fled to Upper Canada in 1833 and settled in Toronto.[3] The Blackburns started the first taxi business in Toronto in 1861 and shortly thereafter began to use Beatty & Chadwick for their legal work. Edward Marion Chadwick prepared their wills and the firm administered their estates.[4] How had this come about? As with so much of the early history of the firm, the answer was to be found in links to the Anglican Church and to the Gooderhams. The Blackburns lived near the Gooderham & Worts distillery, attended Anglican services at Little Trinity Church, and came to be loosely considered part of the extended family. Once Andrew learned of this early link to the Black community in Toronto, he, along with the chair of the firm's diversity committee, Doug New, convinced the firm to establish a needs-based scholarship for young minority law students in the name of the firm's first Black clients. It is administered by CABL.

If growing religious, ethnic, and cultural diversity was barely hinted at even in the 1950s, some changes were anticipated, such as the use of a management committee and professional administrators and the adoption of an anti-nepotism policy — no more brothers or sons or cousins. All these trends continue unabated. Collectively they have brought an end to family connections within the firm and have democratized and professionalized its administration.

The law firm of 2013 is managed much more like a corporate business than was the case in its first century. Although technically not shareholders, the partners have shareholder-like rights. It would be impractical to have all partners deal with management issues, yet modern partners would not tolerate a managing partner with anything like the power that the Faskens exercised in the firm. The reaction to the autocratic rule of Alex Fasken was rule by management committee, and that model continues to be used. Today the managing partner and the management committee are elected for fixed terms, but policy matters are dealt with by the committee just as they were in the era of Aitchison, Pickup, and Calvin. Now, however, that committee has a large staff of professional administrators to implement its policies and decisions.

A large administrative staff is necessary because Faskens continued to grow dramatically throughout the 1960s, '70s, and '80s, more than doubling its size every ten years. By the 1970s it had over thirty lawyers, by 1980 over sixty, and by 1990 over 200. That growth was both facilitated and necessitated by the growing size, sophistication, and regulation of corporations and corporate transactions. A firm the size of Faskens in the mid-1950s was able to handle the merger of the Bank of Toronto and the Dominion Bank. By the 1980s a firm of that size could no longer do an adequate job of addressing the many legal aspects of such a merger. A "mega-deal" in the 1980s and '90s involving, for example, the purchase of one publicly traded company by another would require many legal specialists. Each side would have a legal team in each affected jurisdiction consisting of two or three corporate lawyers to draft and negotiate the deal and oversee due diligence, a securities lawyer to ensure compliance with securities regulation, a competition lawyer to ensure that the deal would not be challenged as anti-competitive, a tax lawyer to structure the deal to minimize tax, a labour lawyer to deal with union issues, a pensions lawyer to review the cost and viability of the target's pension obligations, a real estate lawyer to deal with any land transfers or lease obligations, an environmental lawyer to assess any risk of environmental hazards, an intellectual property lawyer to deal with the transfer of trademarks, patents, and copyrighted works, an information technology lawyer to deal with the transfer of IT technology and the transition from the target company's IT system to that of the purchasing company, a government relations lawyer to obtain any necessary approvals or waivers, and numerous students and paralegals to conduct the extensive due diligence. What Calvin would have done with Bryce MacKenzie and a student in the 1950s would keep a team of more than 20 busy for months just three decades later.

The modern era has been notable for increased government regulation and the concomitant move to more and more specialization within the broad practice areas of the firm. The hiring of Alex Givens in 1962 as a tax specialist gave a hint of what was to come. He was soon joined by Allan Schwartz, who would be largely responsible for developing the firm's tax department and in the process earn the distinction of being the first Jewish partner in the firm. Over time other areas of specialization developed. David Corbett, the current national managing partner, was the first labour law specialist in the Toronto office, developing his expertise in the early 1980s under the guidance of Dick Potter, who also mentored me at that time in the development of an information technology law practice. Together Dick and I recruited Colleen Spring Zimmerman to start an intellectual property department. Others have focused on such speciality areas as securities and environmental law. The Faskens of 2013 has more than thirty specialty practice areas.

Even fields such as estates and insolvency, which have had long been practice areas in the firm, have changed. In Beatty and Chadwick's time they were not the intensive areas of exclusive practice that they have become. In 2013 the idea that an estates lawyer like Chadwick would assist with an initial public offering of securities or help a client to buy or sell a company is ludicrous — the height of malpractice. But it was regularly done in the period under study. In 2013 specialist lawyers and their insurers, the Lawyers' Professional Indemnity Company, would protest if someone dabbled in their area. They would note that there are so many laws, regulations, and conventions of practice to master that a non-specialist is bound to falter. Then it was a necessity arising from the smaller firm and it was possible because the law imposed fewer rules and regulations on such commercial activities.

The firm has become a series of overlapping specialty groups using sophisticated technology and serving a wide range of clients in Canada and around the world. Financial institutions, health service providers, and mining companies may still be its principal clients but to them have been added domestic and foreign technology companies, accounting firms, telecom companies, car manufacturers and other industrial enterprises, retailers, consultants, and service firms of every description, and entertainers such as Oscar Peterson and Cirque du Soleil.

The firm has also become highly automated. All lawyers, administrators, paralegals, and staff use smart phones and personal computers in the courtrooms, boardrooms, and everywhere else. Not only does the firm have hundreds of printers, scanners, and copiers but many lawyers have them in their homes and cottages. And, of course, the Internet joins all the lawyers and secretaries in the office with clients and colleagues around the world.

Slowly the firm has become less dominated by men. Georgia Bentley was joined in 1973 by Hilda M. McKinlay, who did estates and trust work. Unlike Georgia, however, Hilda was unwilling to wait endlessly for partnership. She stayed until 1983 and was then appointed to the Ontario Court of Appeal, from which she retired in 1999.[5] The year she left was the year the firm accepted its first woman into the partnership. Eleanore Cronk became a partner 120 years after the firm was founded. She had a distinguished career as a litigator, much of it with Faskens, before she, too, was appointed to the Ontario Court of Appeal. Since then the firm has added many women, a number of whom have become partners and participated in firm management.

The firm of 2013 has over 700 lawyers, but much of that growth has been through mergers with other firms, beginning in 1980 with Risk Cavan Gardner. That merger brought the firm Stephen Risk, Rudy Gardner, and Rand Lomas, among other lawyers. In November 1989 Faskens merged with the equally large firm of Campbell Godfrey & Lewtas to form a 237-person firm, Fasken Campbell Godfrey. When Fraser Fell, who had left the partnership to head Dome Mines, talked to his former partners about the proposed merger, he said that the two firms shared a common culture and history, and indeed they did. Like Faskens, Campbell Godfrey was over 100 years old.[6]

Three years prior to the merger with Campbell Godfrey, Fasken & Calvin had become part of a national firm known as Fasken Martineau Walker, a sort of joint venture between the partners of Faskens and those of the Quebec-based Martineau Walker. The way had been prepared for such interprovincial partnerships by McCarthy & McCarthy, which in 1981 had entered into a partnership with Black & Company in Alberta.[7] When that merger was opposed by the Alberta Law Society, the partnering firms retained Milner Steer and challenged the Law Society in the courts. The law firms lost at trial but in 1986 they prevailed at the Alberta Court of Appeal. That year, Faskens and Martineau Walker entered into their own partnership. Or rather, the two firms created a third firm.

Fasken Martineau Walker was a partnership of the individual partners in each firm but was in addition to, and not in substitution for, the provincial partnerships. It was modified but maintained following the merger with Campbell Godfrey in 1989. This national alliance was entered into in light of the globalization of the business activities of, and the legal services required by, the business community. In Canada it permitted referral of work and cooperation and coordination in training, marketing, and office administration. But from the beginning one of the rationales of Fasken Martineau Walker was expansion abroad. The large number of partners meant that the firm could better afford to open foreign offices. London was opened in 1987 and Brussels shortly thereafter. The first would grow and prosper; the second was a short-lived, unsuccessful attempt to take advantage of the new European Union.

In 1999 Faskens fully merged with Martineau Walker to create a single national firm under the name Fasken Martineau. The next year British Columbia's Russell & DuMoulin joined to create Fasken Martineau DuMoulin LLP. These mergers facilitated further expansion. In May 2003 the firm opened an office in Calgary, Alberta, recruiting a number of lawyers from other established firms. In February 2007 it merged for the first time with non-Canadian lawyers, aligning with London-based Stringer Saul LLP. In doing so it became the world's first full-service law partnership with lawyers practising both English and Canadian law. Later that same year, in April, the now truly international firm strengthened itself in Canada by merging with the Ottawa-based telecom boutique Johnston & Buchan LLP. That Ottawa office was strengthened when, in September 2009, a team of three senior lawyers joined, bringing combined expertise in corporate finance and in the technology, mining, and transportation sectors. That same month, Fasken Martineau opened an office in Paris through a merger with Paris-based Gravel, Leclerc & Partners, including seven lawyers, to which a team of four prominent lawyers from Dewey & LeBoeuf in Paris was added. Then in the fall of 2012, Faskens strengthened its mining practice in Africa by agreeing to merge with seventy-one lawyer Bell Dewar of Johannesburg effective 1 February 2013. The firm, dating back to 1890, had initial success representing gold mining, newspaper, and railway clients.

It is likely that few of the firm's new partners in Canada and elsewhere appreciate how much the practice of the modern Fasken Martineau DuMoulin has been shaped by Faskens' first century. Their due diligence prior to the mergers would have informed them of the numerous financial institutions, mining clients, and hospitals that Faskens represents and revealed that several have been very long-standing clients. They can be forgiven for not being fully conversant with the extensive interactions the Faskens lawyers had with those clients, or how they came to act for them in the first place. Even the Faskens partners themselves have often been unaware of these facts.

But aware or not, they should not doubt the influence of those early years and early interactions — the marriage of Beatty and Blackstock into the Gooderham and Worts families, the Fasken brothers' mining ventures and their transformation of the law firm, Alex Fasken's personality and the reaction of others to his autocratic rule, the courtroom skills of Robertson and Williston, and Calvin's careful preparation of the next generation of lawyers.

A NOTE ON SOURCES

Fasken Martineau DuMoulin LLP Fonds

THE FASKEN MARTINEAU DUMOULIN LLP FONDS is in the Archives of the Law Society of Upper Canada at Osgoode Hall, identified as PF189. The collection contains materials related to both the Fasken & Calvin and Campbell Godfrey & Lewtas branches of the firm, including certain administrative records, some legal opinions, the partnership agreements, some news clippings, and other biographical material, memorabilia, and photographs. Many of the early financial records have been preserved on microfilm. A finding aid is available.

Other Holdings of the Law Society of Upper Canada

THE HOLDINGS OF THE ARCHIVES are described at http://rc.lsuc.on.ca/library/arch_holdings.htm. They include the minutes of Convocation (meetings of the Law Society's board of governors) from 1797 to the present, member files on past lawyers, and records of Standing and Special Committees.

A list of the private fonds and collections housed at the Archives of the Law Society of Upper Canada is also available online. The fonds and collections are listed by name of the creator. Each is assigned a unique Private Fonds, or PF, reference code. Finding aids are available online for several of the private fonds and collections. Some of the private fonds related to the firm are

Chadwick, Edward PF9
Lash, Zebulon PF204
Riddell, William Renwick PF61
Geller, John Arthur PF202

Jack Geller joined Faskens on its merger with Campbell Godfrey.

Gibbs Blackstock Family Papers

THE GIBBS BLACKSTOCK FAMILY PAPERS are in the Thomas Fisher Rare Book Library, University of Toronto, identified as MS Coll 88. This series consists of nine boxes of correspondence exchanged between members of the Gibbs Blackstock family and their acquaintances from 1819 to 1956. Although most of the letters are personal, a number of professional and business letters are included. They are arranged chronologically according to the branches of the family tree. Of most relevance to the firm are letters to or from Thomas Gibbs Blackstock and his brother George.

Miller Family Papers

THE THIRTY-FIVE BOXES OF Miller Family Papers are in the University of Toronto Archives, B76-0007. Box 6 contains a genealogy of the William Miller family written by Professor Lash Miller on the verso of letterhead for the Chemical Laboratory, University of Toronto. There is much material about Nicholas Miller's practice before he joined the Beatty firm, including, in box 3, docket entries for 1861–69 showing a number of cases in the courts of common pleas that he was involved with. Box 9 has a book of accounts for W. Nicholas Miller, Galt, 1864, as well as a ledger for W. Nicholas Miller, Galt, 4 December 1865. The Gore District Mutual Fire Insurance Company was a large regular client and rates sixteen pages in the ledger.

Other Holdings of the University of Toronto Archives

THE HOLDINGS OF THE University of Toronto dealing with University Park in general and William Beatty's home on Queen's Park Crescent in particular are extensive. See University of Toronto Archives, A-73-0008/010(08). They include the agreements for the rental of the land as well as architectural plans for the house to be built on the land. The same archives has pictures of the houses in its picture collection.

Diaries of Edward Marion Chadwick

THE DIARIES OF EDWARD Marion Chadwick, 1855–1921, are in the possession of Dianne Bell of Orillia, a great-granddaughter. These volumes are well written in a clear hand. They are illustrated and a few are indexed by Chadwick himself. More than ten volumes have survived in whole or in part. All are roughly five by seven inches and each about 200 pages. A few (before 1860 and volume 5, for 1863–67) have broken spines and missing pages. Most are in good condition. A microfilm copy is also to be found in Ottawa at the Canadian Heraldic Authority.

Toronto City Directories

THE TORONTO PUBLIC LIBRARY Reference Library has a complete set of the Toronto City Directories, as does the City of Toronto Archives. These directories list the male occupants of each home and their employment or profession. They also have listings for each business in the city.

Library and Archives Canada

LIBRARY AND ARCHIVES CANADA (LAC) has many relevant records, such as correspondence about the firm's incorporation of federal corporations. They can be searched online at www.collectionscanada.gc.ca. Of particular interest are letters between members of the firm and either ministers of justice or prime ministers. The principal collections for ministers of justice are as follows:

1867–73	John A Macdonald fonds (MG 26A)
1875–77	Edward Blake fonds (R4424-0-2-E, MG 27-ID2)
1881–85	Alexander Campbell fonds (R4503-0-8-E, MG 27-IC2)
1885–94	Sir John Thompson fonds (R5240-0-1-E, MG26-D)
1894–96	Charles Hibbert Tupper fonds (R4367-0-8-E, MG27-ID16)

Prime ministerial papers are as follows:

1867–73, 1878–91	Sir John A Macdonald fonds (MG 26A)
1892–94	Sir John Thompson fonds (R5240-0-1-E, MG26-D)
1896	Sir Charles Tupper fonds (R12555-0-4-E, MG 26-F)
1896–1911	Sir Wilfrid Laurier fonds (R10811-0-X-E, MG 26-G)
1911–20	Sir Robert Laird Borden fonds (R6113-8-4-E, MG26-H)

There are also collections for some firm members, such as the George Tate Blackstock fonds (R4562-0-X-E, MG 27-II2) and Charles Robert Webster Biggar fonds (R7560-0-5-E, MG 29-D45) and for the Toronto Board of Trade.

Archives of Ontario (AO)

THE ARCHIVES OF ONTARIO have many relevant records, such as correspondence about the firm's registration of provincial partnerships and corporations, and can be searched online. Other holdings of relevance include the diaries of Chadwick's daughter in the Fanny Marion Chadwick fonds (F 1072) (MS 573), the Riddell Family Papers (F 1078), and the bench books of Riddell, William Renwick, 1852-1945 (RG 22-482), and the Blackstock, Gibbs, and Gooderham (Family) (F 4362).

FIRM CHRONOLOGY
1863–2012

Names by Which
the Firm Has Been Known

Beatty & Chadwick	1863–1866
Robinson, Beatty & Chadwick	1866–1868
Beatty & Chadwick	1868–1870
Beatty, Chadwick & Lash	1870–1876
Beatty, Chadwick & Lash; Beatty, Miller & Lash	1876
Beatty, Chadwick & Biggar; Beatty, Miller & Biggar	1876–1878
Beatty, Chadwick, Biggar & Thomson; Beatty, Miller, Biggar & Blackstock	1879–1882
Beatty, Chadwick, Thomson & Blackstock	1883
Beatty, Chadwick, Blackstock & Galt; Beatty, Chadwick, Blackstock & Neville	1883–1886
Beatty, Chadwick, Blackstock & Galt	1886–1892
Beatty, Blackstock, Nesbitt & Chadwick	1892–1895
Beatty, Blackstock, Nesbitt, Chadwick & Riddell	1895–1898
Beatty, Blackstock, Nesbitt, Chadwick & Riddell; Beatty, Blackstock, Galt & Fasken	1898–1903

Beatty, Blackstock, Nesbitt, Fasken & Riddell;	1903–1904
Beatty, Blackstock, Chadwick & Galt	
Beatty, Blackstock, Fasken, Riddell & Mabee;	1905
Beatty, Blackstock, Fasken, Galt & Gooderham	
Beatty, Blackstock, Riddell & Chadwick;	1905–1906
Beatty, Blackstock, Fasken, Galt & Gooderham	
Beatty, Blackstock, Fasken & Riddell	1906
Beatty, Blackstock, Fasken & Chadwick	1907–1910
Beatty, Blackstock, Fasken, Cowan & Chadwick	1910–1915
Fasken, Cowan, Chadwick & Rose	1915–1917
Fasken, Robertson, Chadwick & Sedgewick	1917–1920
Fasken, Robertson, Chadwick, Sedgewick & Aitchison	1920
Fasken, Robertson, Sedgewick & Aitchison	1920–1922
Fasken, Robertson, Sedgewick, Aitchison & Pickup	1922–1925
Fasken, Robertson, Aitchison, Pickup & Calvin	1925–1961
Fasken, Calvin, MacKenzie, Williston & Swackhamer	1962–1967
Fasken & Calvin	1967–1986
Fasken & Calvin/Fasken Martineau Walker	1986–1989
Fasken Campbell Godfrey/Fasken Martineau Walker	1989–1990
Fasken Campbell Godfrey/Fasken Martineau Davis	1991–1993
Fasken Martineau LLP	1999–2000
Fasken Martineau DuMoulin LLP	2000–

Location of the Firm's Office in Toronto

Location	Name of Firm at Time of Move	Date of Move
Exchange Building	Beatty & Chadwick	1863
Church Street	Robinson, Beatty & Chadwick	1866
56 King Street East	Beatty & Chadwick	1868
Bank of Toronto	Beatty, Chadwick & Lash	1877
Excelsior Life Building	Fasken, Cowan, Chadwick & Rose	1915
Toronto-Dominion Bank Tower	Fasken & Calvin	1967
Bay Adelaide Centre	Fasken Martineau DuMoulin LLP	2010–present

BRIEF HISTORIES OF CAMPBELL GODFREY & LEWTAS, MARTINEAU WALKER, AND RUSSELL & DUMOULIN

Campbell Godfrey & Lewtas

CAMPBELL GODFREY TRACED ITS beginning to 1870, when Frank Arnoldi was called to the Ontario bar.[1] Two years later Oliver Howland joined in partnership with Arnoldi. Although Arnoldi was more senior, they named their firm Howland & Arnoldi, to take advantage of the Howland name. As we have seen, in the Toronto of the last half of the nineteenth century, family was extremely important. Howland and Arnoldi could draw upon the Howland family influence and its many family businesses.

Interestingly, the Howlands lived on William Street, in a house immediately north of the Beatty family home. William Pearce Howland, Oliver's father, was a very prominent grain merchant in Toronto who had offices in the Exchange Building, where Beatty and Chadwick set up their first office. He was also a member of the Legislative Assembly and would become one of the Fathers of Confederation and a lieutenant-governor of Ontario (1868–73), receiving a knighthood. In 1863, when Beatty and Chadwick formed their firm, they could not have realized that the sixteen-year-old boy next door would found a rival firm that would merge with theirs 126 years later.

The Howland family offered the Howland & Arnoldi firm many of the same advantages as the Gooderham and Worts families offered Beatty & Chadwick. Sir William Pearce Howland was at various times president of the Ontario Bank, the Toronto Board of Trade, and Confederation Life

Association. (W.H. Beatty served for years on his board of directors and as his vice-president.) One of William Howland's brothers, Henry Stark Howland, served as vice-president of the Canadian Bank of Commerce from 1867 until he left to help found the Imperial Bank of Canada in 1873. H.S. Howland was the first president of the Imperial Bank of Canada, a post he held until his death. He also headed a wholesale hardware firm known as H.S. Howland, Sons & Company. Sir William's other brother, Peleg Howland, was in the milling industry, a founding director and vice-president of the Dominion Bank, and president of the Farmers' Loan Company.

Oliver's brother, William Holmes Howland, ran the family business when his father's career took him into politics. In 1871 William co-founded the Queen City Fire Insurance Company. In 1874–75 he was elected president of the Board of Trade. An ardent temperance advocate, in 1885 he was elected mayor of Toronto on a temperance, morality, religion, and reform platform.

Like Howland, Frank Arnoldi came from a distinguished family. He was born in Montreal in 1848. His father and grandfather were both doctors — his grandfather had been the first president of the Académie de Médecine in Montreal and the subject of a portrait by Cornelius Krieghoff. Arnoldi's father moved to Belleville, Ontario, after Frank was born and Frank was educated at the Toronto Model School and Upper Canada College. Initially he practised alone but for a period in 1876–77 he went into a partnership known as Fitzgerald & Arnoldi. By the time Arnoldi became Howland's partner he was a well-known and very effective litigator in Toronto.

Both Arnoldi and Howland did some litigation. Frank Arnoldi had a general practice that included a considerable amount of counsel work, appearing before the Privy Council on several occasions. Howland was the solicitor for the London Canada Company and for George T. Jewett, US patentee of the modern process of milling, and as such acted as Jewett's counsel before the Supreme Court of Canada in the case that validated the patent. As we have seen, Howland worked with Beatty and Chadwick on the development of the Annex.

Like Beatty Blackstock, the Howland & Arnoldi firm went through profound changes around the turn of the century. When Strachan Johnston joined in 1894 he became the fifth lawyer in the firm, after Howland, Arnoldi, Edmund Bristol, and William H. Cawthra. Cawthra, who had been a student in the firm, had joined as a lawyer that year. A member of one of the richest and most prominent early families in Toronto, Cawthra married a daughter of W.H. Beatty, providing one more link between the two firms.

For whatever reason, by 1897 Howland, Arnoldi, and Johnston were the only members of the firm, and by 1898 it had dropped to just Arnoldi and Johnston. In 1903 Strachan Johnston also left to become a partner in the firm of Thomson, Johnston & Tilley, which, ironically, had been founded by Daniel Edmund Thomson, a former member of the Beatty & Chadwick firm.

One important contributor to the change was Oliver Howland himself. In 1894 he began the political career that would eventually contribute in 1898 to his leaving the firm. He defeated Sir Charles Moss in the riding of South Toronto and served as a member of the Ontario Legislative Assembly until 1901 when, following in the footsteps of his older brother, William Holmes, he was elected mayor of Toronto.

The 1890s were not without some positive developments for Howland & Arnoldi. Arnoldi served as president of the National Club from 1893 to 1896 and as such carried out a financial reorganization that saved the club. Each day as Alex Fasken arrived to have lunch in that club he passed a bronze portrait of Arnoldi that still hangs in that club's vestibule.

The Campbell of Campbell Godfrey was Gordon Peter Campbell, who joined the Arnoldi Grierson & Parry firm in 1924, specializing in corporate and admiralty law. He was a physically impressive man with close personal and business connections to such men as Gordon C. Leitch, whom he helped to create Upper Lakes Shipping; J.A. "Bud" McDougald of Argus Corporation; and, as we have noted, Bruce Matthews. Campbell had also been active in the federal Liberal Party in Ontario and was appointed to the Senate of Canada in 1943 at the age of forty-four.

Over the years Campbell Godfrey had many distinguished members, including Wilfred Wright Parry, who assisted Thomas Bata in immigrating to Canada from Czechoslovakia and establishing what has become a multinational shoe business; John Morrow Godfrey, who assisted J.W. Pickup with the *Noronic* inquiry and was later made a senator for his contribution to the Liberal Party of Canada; and James Lawrence Lewtas, an outstanding corporate/commercial lawyer who served as a director of the Bank of Canada.

Martineau Walker

MARTINEAU WALKER WAS FORMED in 1907, when two young Montreal lawyers, Henry Noel Chauvin and George Harold Baker, decided to found their own firm.[2] Montreal then had a population of 400,000 and was a political, economic, and cultural centre with one of the busiest ports in North America.

Baker and Chauvin set up offices at 179 St. James Street, then home to Canada's largest banks and financial institutions. Three years later Harold E. Walker joined the firm.

Baker was politically active, serving as a member of Parliament. Although a sitting member he volunteered for active service in the First World War and died in battle in Belgium on 3 June 1916. He became the first member of Parliament to give his life for the preservation of the ideals in which he so strongly believed. A bronze statue was erected in his honour in the Parliament Buildings in Ottawa.

To fill his place Richard Tuson Henecker, KC, joined the firm. His addition was similar to the addition of John Beverley Robinson to Beatty & Chadwick. Almost twenty years older than his partners, Henecker was very well connected. His wife was Alice Abbott, the daughter of Sir John Abbott, one of the string of Conservative prime ministers who had followed the death of Sir John A. Macdonald. Henecker was also very active in the business world and he brought a large number of clients to the firm.

In 1919 Thomas Shearer Stewart and Jean Martineau joined the firm, now located in the Commercial Union Building on St. James Street. Both men were impressive additions. Stewart had been blind since a youthful accident but had obtained a BA at McGill University, winning the Macdonald Award. That permitted him to spend two years studying in France. Martineau, a young Université de Montréal law graduate, would ultimately become the senior counsel to the firm that would bear his name.

Unlike Faskens, the Montreal firm experienced growth in the 1920s, expanding to eight lawyers. The crash of late 1929 and the Depression that followed, however, were difficult times. In 1933 Henry Noel Chauvin was elected Batonnier of the Bar of Montreal and Batonnier Général of the Bar of the Province of Quebec. Robert H.E. Walker, a law graduate from McGill and the son of Harold E. Walker, joined the firm in 1936. Soon after the Second World War began in September 1939, Robert volunteered for active service and went overseas. He became commander of the 15th Canadian Armoured Field Regiment. In 1940 George A. Allison joined the firm but he, too, volunteered for service and spent 1942 to 1946 in Europe.

The end of the war brought the return of Walker and Allison, who were to play a determining role in the direction of the development of the firm. In the late 1940s, under Walker's leadership, the firm began to plan for specialization in tax and commercial law. In 1949 Chauvin, a co-founder of the partnership and its principal inspiration, died at the age of seventy-seven. In the same year Roger L. Beaulieu, a young lawyer and MBA graduate from Harvard, joined the firm. Ironically, the Montreal firm was now located in the Bank of Toronto Building on St. James Street, at the corner of McGill Street.

In 1953 Jean Martineau was elected Batonnier of the Bar of Montreal and Batonnier Général of the Bar of the Province of Quebec. The next year he became a judge of the Quebec Court of Appeal, where he remained for five years. On his return to the firm in 1959, it had ten members. It would grow to twenty-nine in 1969, fifty-three in 1976, and to more than a hundred by the early 1980s.

During the 1950s and '60s, meanwhile, many distinguished lawyers joined the firm. They included the Honourable Gerald LeDain, later appointed a judge of the Federal Court of Appeal and eventually the Supreme Court of Canada; William Tetley, QC, who became minister of revenue and minister of consumers, cooperatives, and financial institutions of Quebec and later a senior professor of law at McGill; Charles A. Phelan, Maurice E. Lagacé, and John H. Gomery, who would become justices of the Superior Court of Quebec; Jérome Choquette, QC, former minister of justice of Quebec; and Jean-Claude Delorme, OC, OQ, who would become president of Teleglobe Canada.

Three events in the 1960s and '70s had a particularly significant influence on the evolution of Martineau Walker: Expo 67, the creation of the Caisse de dépôt et placement du Québec, and the construction of the massive James Bay resource development project. In 1964 the commissioner-general of the Canadian Corporation for the 1967 World Exhibition approached Jean Martineau about taking responsibility for the legal aspects of the world's fair planned for Montreal to mark the centennial of Confederation. The work done for Expo 67 began with the drafting of the general bylaws of the corporation and ended, almost ten years later, with the final settlement of litigation arising from the event.

In 1965 the Quebec government created the Caisse de dépôt et placement du Québec. A few months later its president, Claude Prieur, asked Roger Beaulieu to advise the Caisse on the legal aspects of investments and, generally, on the legal safeguards necessary for the Caisse to play its role as an informed and secured lender and investor. The Caisse became one of the largest public pension funds in the world and vital to the economic life of Quebec.

In 1971 Premier Robert Bourassa of Quebec retained Roger Beaulieu to assist with the James Bay hydro project. Just as Faskens had advised Brinco in the 1960s on the Churchill Falls project, Martineau Walker helped with James Bay. It established the legal framework for the organization of a territory as large as France to be run by a corporation that would have the powers of a municipality. The Tennessee Valley Authority, created by US President Franklin D. Roosevelt in the 1930s, served as the model. Martineau Walker conceived and drafted the legislation that gave birth to the James Bay Development Corporation, the James Bay Energy Corporation, and the other corporations that became part of this large Crown corporate group.

Harold E. Walker died in 1970 at the age of eighty-seven, having worked at the firm until the end. Senator the Honourable Alan A. Macnaughton, PC, OC, QC, former speaker of the House of Commons, became counsel to Martineau Walker in the same year. In 1971 Marcel Cinq-Mars, QC, a former batonnier général, became one of several counsel to the firm.

Martineau Walker started a series of mergers in 1981 intended to add new specialty areas. First it merged with Gagnon, Lafleur & Associés. That firm had been founded in 1965 and specialized in labour and administrative law. Early in 1983 the members of Lazarovitz, Cannon, Lemelin, a Quebec City firm, joined Martineau Walker, as did the firm of Bélanger, Leclerc, transport law specialists. Finally that year Goudreau, Gage, Dubuc, specializing in intellectual property matters, affiliated with Martineau Walker.

Russell & DuMoulin

RUSSELL & DUMOULIN BEGAN in 1888 when Joe Russell, then a twenty-one-year-old lawyer from New Brunswick, started his law practice in Vancouver.[3] It is said that within an hour of his arrival on 11 April 1888 Joe had secured a position as legal adviser to Ross & Keperley, land agents for the Canadian Pacific Railway. Vancouver was then a boom town, and being legal counsel to the agents for the largest land owner kept him very busy. Nevertheless, he left Ross & Keperley in August 1888 to become a member of the Victoria law partnership of Yates & Jay, which was then just opening a Vancouver office. He did not formally become a partner in this firm until 31 July 1889, when he was called to the BC bar.

It was the firm of Yates, Jay & Russell that after a series of name and personnel changes came to be known as Russell & DuMoulin. Curiously, the first firm known as Russell & DuMoulin did not last long. It was formed in 1928 by Alan Russell, the younger of Finley Russell's two sons, and his friend Len DuMoulin. Finley, brother of Joe Russell, the founder of Russell

& DuMoulin, was a member of the family firm. Young Alan, who had been a member of his father and uncle's firm for a time, wanted to strike out on his own. When his father put pressure on him to return to the family firm, he refused the offer unless his new partner, Len DuMoulin, was admitted to the partnership on the same terms as he was.

Leonard DuMoulin was born on 20 May 1902 in Victoria, British Columbia. He later moved with his family, initially to Kelowna and then to Kingston, Ontario. He was educated at Trinity College School in Port Hope. In 1919 he returned to British Columbia, where he articled in Kelowna and then in Vancouver. He was called to the bar 6 October 1924, but given the poor economic conditions in Vancouver at the time he failed to find employment. After a short stint in Montreal as a toy salesman in 1925 he returned once again to Vancouver, where he became close friends with Alan Russell and moved in with the Russell family.

Len DuMoulin had a warm, outgoing disposition. He was quick, witty, friendly, and adept at both boosting morale and encouraging others to achieve their best. His litigation practice was focused principally on insurance matters. He served as a bencher of the Law Society of British Columbia from 1959 to 1967 and its treasurer in 1967. He also became vice-president of the Canadian Bar Association in 1960. He later declined the presidency because his wife, Kitt, did not feel comfortable flying and he did not wish to fulfill the many international obligations of that office alone. He retired from practice in 1972.

NOTES

৩১ Preface ৳৩

1   For a profile of Ronald Joseph Rolls, see Jack Batten, *Learned Friends: A Tribute to 50 Remarkable Advocates, 1950–2000* (Toronto: Advocates' Society, 2005) at 98–99. Rolls died in August 2012 as I was finalizing this book.

2   The letters were subsequently donated by Coyle to the Archives of the Law Society of Upper Canada, where they form the Edward Chadwick Fonds, PF9.

3   Clifford Ian Kyer, *The Papal Legate and the "Solemn" Papal Nuncio: Changing Patterns of Papal Representation 1270–1378* (PhD diss, University of Toronto, 1979) [unpublished].

4   My study of legal education, co-authored with Jerry Bickenbach, would be published as *The Fiercest Debate: Cecil A. Wright, the Benchers and Legal Education in Ontario 1923–1957* (Toronto: Osgoode Society, 1987).

5   C Ian Kyer, "New Light on an Old Firm" (1984) 18 Law Soc'y Gaz 205.

6   C Ian Kyer, "The Transformation of an Establishment Firm: From Beatty Blackstock to Faskens 1902–1915" in Carol Wilton, ed, *Inside the Law: Canadian Law Firms in Historical Perspective* (Toronto: University of Toronto Press for the Osgoode Society for Canadian Legal History, 1996) 161; "Gooderham and Worts: A Case Study in 19th Century Business Organization" in G Blaine Baker & Jim Phillips, eds, *Essays in the History of Canadian Law*, vol 8, *In Honour of R. C. B. Risk* (Toronto: University of Toronto Press for the Osgoode Society for Canadian Legal History, 1999) 335; "The David Fasken Estate: Estate Planning and Social History in Early 20th Century Ontario" in Jim Phillips, Roy McMurtry, & John T Saywell, eds, *Essays in the History of Canadian Law*, vol 10, *A Tribute to Peter Oliver* (Toronto: University of Toronto Press for the Osgoode Society for Canadian Legal History, 2008) 410.

7   See my biographical sketches of William Henry Beatty, Edward Marion Chadwick, Wallace Nesbitt, David Fasken, George Sedgewick, Hiram Augustus Calvin, William George Gooderham, and Albert Edward Gooderham in the *Dictionary of Canadian Biography* (Toronto: University of Toronto Press, 1966–) vols 14, 15, and 16.

8   Richard Potter prepared an "Anatomy of a 1980s Mega-Deal: The Hiram Walker

Take-Over Bid" in 1999. It has been deposited in the Fasken Martineau DuMoulin LLP (FMD) Fonds, PF189, Archives of the Law Society of Upper Canada (LSUC), Toronto.

9 MH Ogilvie, Review of Mitchell and Slinn, *The History of McMaster Meighen* (1991) 70 Can Bar Rev 212–14.

10 *Ibid.*

11 His undated memo to the author (circa 1984) is in the FMD Fonds, PF189, LSUC.

12 CM Blackstock, *All the Journey Through* (Toronto: University of Toronto Press, 1997).

13 Marion, the family historian, was the granddaughter of David Fasken's sister Marion.

14 The photos are now in the FMD Fonds, PF189, 2009006-48P–54P, LSUC, Toronto.

☙ Introduction ❧

1 Every year since the award's inception, Fasken Martineau has been named Law Firm of the Year for Global Mining by *Who's Who Legal*, the strategic research partner for the American Bar Association's Section of International Law.

2 I discuss these mergers in the epilogue and provide a brief history of each of the firm's major merger partners in Appendix 2. I have also listed the firm's many names over its 150-year history in Appendix 1, along with the associated addresses.

3 Franc Joubin makes the same point about Bay Street promoters: they drew their name from the business district but few actually had offices on Bay Street. See Franc Joubin & D McCormack Smyth, *Not for Gold Alone: Memoirs of a Prospector* (Toronto: Deljay Publications, 1986) 136.

4 Gregory P Marchildon, "Corporate Lawyers and the Second Industrial Revolution in Canada" (2001) 64 Sask L Rev 99–112.

5 A genealogical chart showing the relationships between lawyers in the firm and the members of the Gooderham and Worts families is provided at the beginning of Chapter 2.

6 See, by way of comparison, Blaine Baker, "Law, Practice and Statecraft in Mid-Nineteenth Century Montreal: The Torrance-Morris Firm 1828–1868" in Carol Wilton, ed, *Beyond the Law: Lawyers and Business in Canada 1830–1930* (Toronto: University of Toronto Press for the Osgoode Society, 1990) 45-91, a study looking at the Torrance-Morris firm, which served the business interests of the Torrance family in Montreal.

7 See William FE Morley, "Introduction" to Edward Marion Chadwick, *Ontarian Families: Genealogies of United Empire Loyalist and Other Pioneer Families of Upper Canada* 2 vols (Belleville, ON: Mika Silk Screening, 1972).

8 Bruce Patterson, "Edward Marion Chadwick: Pioneer of Canadian Heraldry and Genealogy" (2004) 37 Ontario Branch News (Ontario Genealogical Society) 10–31.

9 Robert Merrill Black, "Shagotyohwisaks: E.M. Chadwick and Canadian Heraldry" (September 1990) 24(3) Heraldry in Canada 2 at 5. See also Conrad Swan, *Canada, Symbols of Sovereignty* (Toronto: University of Toronto Press, 1977) at 163–64 and 203.

10 This was to be a magnificent new Anglican cathedral in the area that came to be known as the Annex. See Jack Batten, *The Annex: The Story of a Toronto Neighbourhood* (Erin, ON: Boston Mills Press, 2004) at 56–60.

11 Marchildon, "Corporate Lawyers" at 99.

12 Peter Waite, *The Man from Halifax: Sir John Thompson, Prime Minister* (Toronto: University of Toronto Press, 1985).

13 On Hart Massey, Timothy Eaton, and Wilmot Matthews, see J Andrew Ross & Andrew D Smith, *Canada's Entrepreneurs: Portraits from the Dictionary of Canadian Biography* (Toronto: University of Toronto Press, 2011) at 250–70, 407–17, and 446–52.

On Flavelle, see Michael Bliss, *A Canadian Millionaire: The Life and Business Times of Sir Joseph Flavelle* (Toronto: University of Toronto Press, 1978).

14   "Fasken Funeral Struggles through Snow-Bound Roads," *Toronto Daily Star* (5 December 1929), at 2, featuring a picture of a "motor car here being pulled out of the snow by a motor truck."

15   "Lawyer Walter Williston Took Controversial Cases" *Toronto Star* (25 August 1980) A5.

16   See Donald Jack, "Recollections of Walter B. Williston, QC" (Autumn 1998) Advocates' J 5; and Jack Batten, *Learned Friends: A Tribute to 50 Remarkable Advocates, 1950–2000* (Toronto: Advocates' Society, 2005) at 56–57.

17   The funeral was announced in the *Globe and Mail* (25 August 1980) 23.

⁓ Chapter 1 ⁓

1   Shirley Ann Brown, *The Windows of St. James* (Toronto: St James Cathedral, 2001) at 15–16.

2   The diaries of Edward Marion Chadwick are described in the Note on Sources.

3   Her birthdate is given on the memorial plaque mounted on the east wall of St James' Cathedral.

4   See Edward Marion Chadwick, *Ontarian Families: Genealogies of United Empire Loyalist and Other Pioneer Families of Upper Canada* (Belleville, ON: Mika Silk Screening, 1972) vol 1 at 160–61.

5   Howland would later play a role in bringing about the confederation of the British North American colonies. See DB Read, *The Lieutenant-Governors of Upper Canada and Ontario 1792–1899* (Toronto: Briggs, 1900) at 207–13; and Harry Feltus Pearce, *Sir William Pearce Howland CB KCMG 1813–1907* (Plymouth, MA: Pilgrim Society, 1976).

6   Graham Parker, "Sir John Hawkins Hagarty" in *Dictionary of Canadian Biography (DCB)* (Toronto: University of Toronto Press, 1966–) vol 12 at 399–400.

7   Toronto had a population of 3,969 in 1831 according to statistics in the appendix to JMS Careless, *Toronto to 1918: An Illustrated History* (Toronto: James Lorimer, 1984) at 200–1.

8   Chadwick diaries, vol 5 (1863–67), 1 July 1864 states that he and Ellen visited Montreal on their honeymoon, to see the monuments in the cemetery for Christ Church Cathedral of Ellen's grandfather, grandmother, aunt Mary, and other relatives.

9   The nature of James Beatty's problem is uncertain. The fact that he was disabled, spending much time in bed, is part of the oral history of the family according to Geoff Beatty, his great-grandson. The *Town of York 1815–34* (Toronto: University of Toronto Press, 1966) at 76, states that Beatty set up his shop on King Street in 1831 but was out of business by 1836. Robert A Harrison in his diaries notes him as as one of the pall bearers for Harrison's father, who was a drunkard. See Peter Oliver, ed, *The Conventional Man: The Diaries of Ontario Chief Justice Robert A. Harrison 1856–1878* (Toronto: University of Toronto Press for the Osgoode Society for Canadian Legal History, 2003) at 233.

10   Chadwick, *Ontarian Families*, vol 1 at 160; *Mitchell's Toronto Directory 1864–5* (Toronto: WC Chewett, 1865) at 10.

11   Three different years were given by Beatty for his birth. On his tombstone in St James Cemetery, it states 1833. When a student at Upper Canada College, he gave 11 December 1833 and 10 December 1834. See AH Young, ed, *The Roll of Pupils of Upper Canada College* (Kingston, ON: Hanson, Crozier, and Edgar, 1917) at 104. His obituary in the *Toronto Public Library Biographical Scrapbooks*, vol 1 at 33, says 1835, as do Charles GD Roberts & Arthur L Tunnell, *A Standard Dictionary of Canadian Biogra-*

phy: The Canadian Who Was Who, 2 vols (Toronto: Trans-Canada Press, 1934–38) vol 1 at 29, and his partner, Chadwick, in *Ontarian Families*, vol 1 at 160.

12 Chadwick diaries, vol 4 (1861–62), 21 May 1862.

13 J Rordan, *The Upper Canada Law List and Solicitors' Agency Book*, 4th ed (Toronto: WC Chewett, 1862) at 9. The term *attorney* ceased to be used in 1881 when the *Ontario Judicature Act, 1881* SO 1881, c 5, provided that thereafter all attorneys and solicitors were to be called solicitors of the Supreme Court of Ontario. On the distinction between barristers, solicitors, and attorneys, see John Honsberger, "Barristers and Solicitors" (1992) 26 Law Soc'y Gaz 177.

14 Chadwick diaries, vol 4 (1861–62) states that on 11 June 1862 he was "calling on the Beattys . . . found the whole of the sheminines on hand save Mrs. Beatty and Miss Jane."

15 If Chadwick knew William Beatty or his sisters before the party the fact goes unmentioned in his diaries.

16 His family had gone to Ireland from England at the time of Oliver Cromwell and formed part of the Irish landed gentry.

17 Chadwick diaries, vol 9 (1902–16) at 110–11, provides a lengthy account of his 1909 return with his wife, Mattie, to the family home known as Cravendale, "only about a mile from Jerseyville on the Brantford branch of the TH&B [Toronto Hamilton & Buffalo Railway]," where he had been born and that he had not visited since he was four. He notes that they came to "rising ground with woods on one side . . . and expected to find on the other side fields sloping down to a creek which the road would cross and sloping up the other side towards the house, and when we got to the top we saw it all as I have remembered it for 65 years" but, "The old white clapboard house was burnt down long ago and there is now a large brick house."

18 He frequently mentions the Peterson firm in his diary for 1858, Chadwick diaries, vol 1 (1858 incomplete). See also Darrel E Kennedy, "An Armorial Mystery: The Origin and History of the Armorial Achievement of the City of Guelph, Ontario, Used by the City Corporation before 1978" (2009) 2 Alta Studia Heraldica 117 at 129 and 133.

19 Chadwick diaries, vol 4 (1861–62), 2 August 1861.

20 In *ibid*, 3 August 1861, he states that it was "Patterson Harrison & Hodgins into whose office I am going." The dominant partner was Robert Harrison (1833–78), a lawyer, author, politician, and judge in Canada West. Harrison would later become Chief Justice of Ontario (1875–78). On Harrison's law practice, see Oliver, *The Conventional Man* at 57–78.

21 *Ibid*, 16 August 1862.

22 Hawkins was probably a nickname for Austin Cooper Chadwick, Marion's younger brother, who was then in Toronto studying law.

23 Leo A Johnson, *History of Guelph 1827–1927* (Guelph, ON: Guelph Historical Society, 1977). There is a picture of Fred at 263.

24 Kennedy, "An Armorial Mystery" at 135.

25 Chadwick diaries, vol 4 (1861–62), 1 November 1862.

26 See the Pew Record for St James, Diocesan Archives, Diocese of Toronto, Anglican Church of Canada. The Beatty family had pew 137 in the west aisle.

27 Rordan, *The Upper Canada Law List*, 4th ed at 9.

28 *Ibid*; Thomas Hutchison, *Toronto Directory, 1862-3* (Toronto: Lovell & Gibson, 1863) at 30. Leys was well known to the Gooderhams. He would later be a commodore of the Royal Canadian Yacht Club, of which they were prominent members, and one of his children would marry a Gooderham. See Chadwick, *Ontarian Families*, vol 1 at 155a. It is interesting to note that many of Toronto's lawyers had their offices within

a short distance of the corner of Church and King, which seems to have been the centre of the legal community. The courthouse was then located on Adelaide near Church.

29 Chadwick diaries, vol 4 (1861–62), 9 June 1862 says that he "spent all day at the office engrossing a deed."

30 RCB Risk, "The Nineteenth-Century Foundations of the Business Corporation" (1973) 23 UTLJ 270 at 272.

31 Chadwick diaries, vol 4 (1861–62), 28 February 1862.

32 Calvin Browne & Edward Marion Chadwick, *Osgoode Hall Examination Questions Given at the Examinations for Call . . . with Concise Answers and the Student Guide* (Toronto: Rollo and Adam, 1862). A review of the book appears in the *Globe* (24 May 1862) at 2 (column 7).

33 J Rordan, *The Upper Canada Law List and Solicitors' Agency Book*, 5th ed (Toronto: WC Chewett, 1866).

34 See Oliver, *The Conventional Man* at 201.

35 Chadwick diaries, vol 5 (1863–67), 29 January 1863, "went up for examinations for call, getting through the paper (which I believe to be the hardest that has yet been given) in 2 hours."

36 See Chadwick diaries, vol 5 (1863–67), 2 February 1863.

37 The lying in state at Osgoode Hall and the funeral at St James is described in Patrick Brode, *Sir John Beverley Robinson: Bone and Sinew of the Compact* (Toronto: Osgoode Society, 1984) at 269.

38 The records in the Archives of the Law Society of Upper Canada show that William Henry Beatty was entered on the Attorney Rolls, Court of Common Pleas Attorney Rolls, and Solicitors Rolls for February 1863. He was not called to the bar until 1880. Edward Marion Chadwick was entered on the Attorney Rolls, Court of Common Pleas Attorney Rolls, and Solicitors Rolls for May 1862. He was called to the bar in February 1863.

39 The lavish opening ceremonies are described in Bruce W Hodgins, "John Sandfield Macdonald" in JMS Careless, ed, *The Pre-Confederation Premiers: Ontario Government Leaders, 1841–1867* (Toronto: University of Toronto Press for Ontario Historical Studies Series, 1980) 246.

40 *Globe* (23 February 1863) 3.

41 The two buildings are pictured and discussed in William Dendy, *Lost Toronto: Images of the City's Past* (Toronto: McClelland and Stewart, 1993) at 70–75.

42 See Eric Arthur, *Toronto: No Mean City*, 3rd ed, rev Stephen A Otto (Toronto: University of Toronto Press, 1986) at 116–18 for a photograph, plans, et cetera. The plans for the building show a door between offices 11 and 12, suggesting that the partners moved into part of a suite of offices occupied by Gooderham & Worts.

43 See Joseph Schull, *100 Years of Banking in Canada: A History of the Toronto-Dominion Bank* (Vancouver: Copp Clark, 1958) at 6.

44 The floor plan is reproduced in Arthur, *Toronto* at 119. The office addresses are found in the *General Directory for the City of Toronto, 1866* (Toronto: Mitchell, 1866) at 169.

45 See Thomas Hutchison, *Toronto Directory, 1856* (Toronto: Lovell & Gibson, 1856). Gooderham and Worts were listed as both distillers and commission merchants.

46 The Fasken firm has long acted for Dun & Bradstreet, a successor firm.

47 EM Chadwick to Violet Baker, 13 March 1913, Edward Chadwick Fonds, PF9, Archives of the Law Society of Upper Canada (LSUC), Toronto (copy in Fasken Martineau DuMoulin LLP [FMD] Fonds, PF189-2-1).

48 See the statistical tables in Careless, *Toronto to 1918* at 200–3.

49 Rordan, *The Upper Canada Law List*, 4th ed at 9.

50 *An Act to Incorporate the Toronto Exchange, 1854* (18 Vict) c 54; and Dendy, *Lost Toronto* at 45.

51 *Proceedings of the Seventh Annual General Meeting*, Bank of Toronto, 15 July 1863, 1, Archives of the Toronto-Dominion Bank (TDB), Toronto.

52 *Proceedings of the Eight Annual General Meeting*, Bank of Toronto, 20 July 1864, 1, *ibid.*

53 *Globe* (18 August 1863) 3.

54 *Ibid* (25 December 1863) 3.

55 Letter to the editor, "City Solicitors" *ibid* (29 April 1864) 2.

56 See, for example, the case of *Beaty v Gooderham* (1867), 13 Grant's Canada Chancery Reports 317 which notes that "Messrs. Gooderham, Worts, Howland and Wilmot" provided mortgages in the 1850s and 1860s.

57 *Ibid.*

58 For a description of this and other small railways of the day, see JM & Edw Trout, *The Railways of Canada for 1870–1* (Toronto: Monetary Times, 1871) at 166.

59 From the family gravestone in St James Cemetery.

60 A very formal printed invitation to her funeral has been preserved and is in the possession of Douglas Worts. It states, "You are requested to attend the funeral of Elizabeth, eldest daughter of James G. Worts, from the residence of Mrs. Bright, Kingston Road (near the Don Bridge), to the place of interment, St James Cemetery, on Sunday afternoon, at 3 o'clock."

61 CM Blackstock, *All the Journey Through* (Toronto: University of Toronto Press, 1997) at 19. See also the Gibbs Blackstock Family Papers, MS Coll 88, Thomas Fisher Rare Book Library, Toronto.

62 Ted Wickson, *Reflections of Toronto Harbour: Two Hundred Years of Waterfront Development* (Toronto: Toronto Port Authority, 2002) at 25, 27–32.

63 Alan L Hayes, *Holding Forth the Word of Life: Little Trinity Church 1843–1992* (Toronto: Corporation of Little Trinity Church, 1991) at 11.

64 Blackstock, *All the Journey Through* at 15–21.

65 See also the Rev Alexander Sanson, *Sermon after the Funeral of William Gooderham, Esq, Churchwarden, Preached in Trinity Church, Toronto* (Toronto: [s.n.], 1881) at 11. A copy is in Gibbs Blackstock Family Papers, MS Coll 88, box 10, folder 40, Thomas Fisher Rare Book Library, Toronto.

66 See the discussion of the founding of the school in Richard B Howard, *Colborne's Legacy: Upper Canada College, 1829–1979* (Toronto: Macmillan, 1979) at 67.

67 Blackstock, *All the Journey Through* at 6–7.

68 *Ibid.*

69 *Proceedings of the Eight Annual General Meeting*, Bank of Toronto, 20 July 1864, 2, and *Proceedings of the Ninth Annual General Meeting*, Bank of Toronto, 19 July 1865, 1, TDB.

70 "Mrs. W.H. Beatty Saw 75 Years of Toronto Life" *Toronto Telegram* (21 May 1928). The Orange Order, originally founded in Ireland in 1795, commemorated the victory of William of Orange over the Irish Catholic uprising on 12 July 1690 in the Battle of the Boyne. The Grand Lodge of British North America had been established in Brockville in 1830. It served as a Protestant fraternal society but had significant political influence in the second half of the nineteenth century. See Gregory S Kealey, *Workers and Canadian History* (Montreal and Kingston: McGill-Queen's University Press, 1995) at 163–208; and the *Canadian Encyclopedia* (Toronto: McClelland and Stewart, 2000) at 1726.

71 J Ross Robertson, *Robertson's Landmarks of Toronto*, 6 vols (Toronto: JR Robertson, 1898–1914) vol 1 at 126.

72   *[Toronto] Leader* (11 February 1865).

73   See *Globe* (28 April 1865) 3. The Gooderham and Worts families were important members of the congregation. Alex Dixon was instrumental in having the church built in 1843. See Hayes, *Holding Forth the Word of Life*.

74   It states, "In memory of Ellen Byrne Chadwick the Beloved Wife of Edward Marion Chadwick Esq. and Daughter of James Beatty Esq. Born 9 November 1843. Married 28 June 1864. Died suddenly 10 February 1865. Him that cometh to me I shall in no wise cast out."

75   Chadwick diaries, vol 6 (1867–71), 1 August 1867.

76   *Ibid*, vol 5 (1863–67), 14 November 1866.

77   See the correspondence between Gooderham & Worts and Lanman & Kemp of New York in the Baldwin Room, Metropolitan Toronto Public Library, manuscript collection. JW Beatty signed the Gooderham & Worts letters starting 15 August 1876. He is termed a clerk in the *Toronto Directory, 1878* (Toronto: Might & Taylor, 1878) at 180 and an accountant in the *Toronto Directory* (Toronto: Might & Taylor, 1880) at 209.

78   *Proceedings of the Ninth Annual General Meeting*, Bank of Toronto, 19 July 1865, 1, TDB.

79   *Globe* (21 September 1865) at 1–2 published the prize list for the Provincial Exhibition. Under "Extra Entries," Chadwick's illuminated manuscript on parchment and title pages and vignette of illuminated manuscript was said to have been awarded a diploma.

80   Chadwick diaries, vol 6 (1867–71), 28 November 1867.

81   On the background to the raids and their political significance, see David A Wilson, *Thomas Darcy McGee*, 2 vols (Montreal and Kingston: McGill-Queen's University Press, 2011) vol 2 at ch 11.

82   Peter Vronsky, *Ridgeway: The American Fenian Invasion and the 1866 Battle That Made Canada* (Toronto: Allen Lane, 2011).

83   Oliver, *The Conventional Man* at 275.

84   Chadwick diaries, vol 5 (1863–67), 2 June 1866

85   They were so labelled by Blackstock. See Gibbs Blackstock Family Papers, MS Coll 88, box 7, folder 4.

86   "Mrs. W.H. Beatty Saw 75 Years of Toronto Life."

87   See Chadwick, *Ontarian Families*, vol 1 at 160.

88   EM Chadwick to Violet Baker, 13 March 1913, Edward Chadwick Fonds, PF9, LSUC, Toronto.

89   Austin Cooper Chadwick would be appointed a junior county court judge for Wellington County on 10 January 1873. See Henry James Morgan, ed, *The Canadian Men and Women of the Time: A Handbook of Canadian Biography* (Toronto: W Briggs, 1898) at 172.

90   Patrick Brode, "John Beverley Robinson" *DCB* vol 12, 906–8.

91   Dendy, *Lost Toronto* at 114–15.

92   Chadwick diaries, vol 5 (1863–67), 16 February 1867. *Globe* (31 July 1868) notes that he was promoted to lieutenant effective 2 June in the volunteer militia 2nd Battalion, Queen's Own Rifles.

93   Chadwick diaries, vol 5 (1863–67), 4 June 1867.

94   It is unlikely that Chadwick and Mattie were aware that the steamer had been rented in September 1866 to the government by the shipping firm of Calvin & Breck of Garden Island, near Kingston. See DD Calvin, *A Saga of the St. Lawrence* (Toronto: Ryerson Press, 1945) at 133–37. They certainly could not have realized that one day Chadwick's law firm would bear the name Calvin prominently. Collamer Chipman Calvin, who would become managing partner of the firm and one of Canada's lead-

ing business lawyers, had not yet been born.

95 See Dendy, *Lost Toronto* at 78–79.

96 Chadwick diaries, vol 6 (1867–71), 30 November 1867.

97 Chadwick's book on his family's genealogy, *The Chadwicks of Guelph and Toronto and Their Cousins, Toronto 1914* (Toronto: Davis and Henderson, 1914) at 57, has the following: "John Craven Chadwick, eldest son of above John Craven Chadwick . . . . Married, firstly, 21st June, 1860, Elinor Tonee, died 9th January, 1868."

98 The premises had previously been occupied by Henry Pellatt, stockbroker, who would later work with Chadwick to raise funds for the building of St Alban's Cathedral. Their office was located between Rice Lewis and Son Hardware Store and Brown's Bank. Brown's Bank was to fail the next year. RT Naylor, *The History of Canadian Business 1867–1914*, 2 vols, Carlton Library Series 207 (1975; repr, Montreal and Kingston: McGill-Queen's University Press, 2006) vol 1 at 167.

99 The Alex Lewis grocery store had been located at 178 King Street, across from the Beatty woollen warehouse at number 177. Rice Lewis and a much younger William Beatty may have come to know each other when their families lived above their respective stores. See George Walton, *City of Toronto and the Home District Commercial Directory, 1837* (Toronto: T Dalton & WN Coats, 1837) at 4 and 27.

100 Trinity Church Marriage Register, Diocesan Archives, Diocese of Toronto, Anglican Church of Canada; Chadwick, *Ontarian Families*, vol 1 at 155.

101 *Globe* (1 March 1869) 2.

102 Rod Clarke, *Narrow Gauge through the Bush: Ontario's Toronto Grey & Bruce and Toronto & Nipissing Railways* (Paris, ON: R Clarke and R Beaumont, 2007).

103 Trout & Trout, *Railways of Canada* at 37.

104 Chadwick, *The Chadwicks of Guelph* at 62.

105 Trout & Trout, *Railways of Canada* at 150–51.

106 See the account of the fire, including a drawing of the building ablaze, in *Robertson's Landmarks of Toronto*, vol 2 at 642–44.

107 See RCB Risk, "The Nineteenth-Century Foundations of the Business Corporation" (1973) 23 UTLJ 270 at 272.

108 *An Act to Provide for the Formation of Incorporated Joint Stock Companies for Manufacturing, Mining, Mechanical or Chemical Purposes, 1850* (13 & 14 Vict) c 28.

109 *An Act to Amend Chapter 63 of the Consolidated Statutes of Canada Respecting Joint Stock Companies, 1861* (23 & 24 Vict) c 19.

110 The firm's financial records indicate that Lash did not become a full partner until 1874. In 1870 it is likely he joined as a junior partner. See Beatty, Chadwick, Thomson, & Blackstock, Private Ledger 8A (1883–1915), 9, Accounting records, FMD Fonds, PF189-5-1, LSUC.

111 Chadwick diaries, vol 6 (1867–71), 21 May 1870. See also the professional card that appeared in the *Globe* (18 May 1870) 3.

112 See the advertisement that he took out in the *Globe* (11 June 1868) 1.

113 *Harty v Gooderham* (1871), 31 UCQB 18. *High-wines* is a term used for alcohol or spirits that have been through a second distillation but have not yet been mixed to produced flavoured whiskey.

114 Theodore Regehr, "Zebulon Aiton Lash" in *DCB*, vol 14 at 605.

115 Rordan, *Upper Canada Law List*, 4th ed.

116 The Miller Family Papers are described in the Note on Sources.

117 W Nicholas Miller to Zebulon Lash, 3 February 1867, Letterbook 1867–68, 401, Miller Family Papers, B76-0007, box 11, U of T Archives.

118 *Register of Ontario Marriages, 1858–69*, vol 66, *Toronto 1858–67*, microfilm reel MS248, reel 15 (LDS reel 1030065), 178, Archives of Ontario, Toronto.

119 (1868) 4 Can LJ 107.
120 Letterbook 1867–68, 972, 977, 981, and 992, Miller Family Papers, B76-0007, box 11.
121 See Kennedy, "An Armorial Mystery" at 132–33.
122 Dianne Newell, "William Gooderham" in *DCB*, vol 11 at 1881–90.
123 The 1871 Petition is in the archives of Confederation Life. See Confederation Life Association, *Confederation Life Insurance Company 1871–1971* (Toronto: Confederation Life Association, 1972) at 3–5; and CR Dent, *Confederation Life Association: The Story of the Founding and Progress of a Great Canadian Institution* (Toronto: Confederation Life, 1939) at 51–55 and 169.
124 James Beaty, QC, was a promoter of Confederation Life. He practised law with the firm of Beaty Snow Smith and Naismyth, which later became Beaty Hamilton and Snow. Beaty and his partner Snow were related by marriage, and one of their descendants, Michael Snow, would later be commissioned to do a sculpture for the Confederation Life building on Bloor Street.
125 Chadwick, *Ontarian Families*, vol 1 at 155a.
126 Southeast quarter of Section 8 in the 8th Concession and the northeast subdivision of Section 8, Township of McTavish in the District of Algoma. See *Beatty v McConnell* (1906), 8 OWR 916 at 917 (Ont CA).
127 The Privy Council would later say that the property was "mining lands" (see *McConnell v Beatty* (1908), 11 OWR 1 at 1), but the property seems to have been sold for settlement. See Morris Zaslow, *The Opening of the Canadian North 1870–1914* (Toronto: McClelland and Stewart, 1971) at 11.
128 On the ending of appeals to the Privy Council and the designation of the Supreme Court of Canada as the court of last resort, see James G Snell & Frederick Vaughn, *The Supreme Court of Canada: History of the Institution* (Toronto: Osgoode Society, 1985) at 178–95.
129 Quoted in *McConnell v Beatty*, [1908] AC 90.
130 Dendy, *Lost Toronto* at 182.
131 See University of Toronto Archives, A-73-0008/010(08). Gearing, who built Deer Park Church in 1870, is described by Eric Arthur as "a successful builder" (*Toronto* at 161). He lived at Yonge and Carlton, and a picture of his Georgian-style home is at 161 of Arthur's book.
132 He had promised the university that the house and stable would be finished by 1877. They seem to have been finished by 1876 (*Toronto Directory*, 1876).
133 Beatty had letterhead printed for personal use with "The Oaks, Queens Park" in the upper right-hand corner. Original in the possession of Geoff Beatty.
134 Dendy, *Lost Toronto*, notes at 183, "The cast-iron fountain stands on the site (now occupied by Hamilton McCarthy's statue of Sir John A. Macdonald) that had been reserved for a statue of Queen Victoria." Arthur, *Toronto* at 194, has a picture that shows the site after the erection of the statue of Sir John A Macdonald. Beatty's home can be seen to the right.
135 Eric Arthur, *From Front Street to Queen's Park: The Story of Ontario's Parliament Buildings* (Toronto: McClelland and Stewart, 1979) at 65. A photograph of two of the Beatty children bundled up in a small horse-drawn sleigh on the road in front of the Oaks can be found in Peter C Newman, *Canada — 1892 Portrait of a Promised Land* (Toronto: Madison Press, 1992) 18. The original is in the Archives of Ontario, S18119.
136 See "Mrs. W.H. Beatty Saw 75 Years of Toronto Life." The family occupied the home until 1930, when the university took over the property and tore the house down to build the Botany Building (now the Tanz Centre for Research in Neurodegenerative Diseases).

❧ Chapter 2 ❧

1   See Bruce W Hodgins, "John Sandfield Macdonald" in JMS Careless, ed, *The Pre-Confederation Premiers: Ontario Government Leaders, 1841–1867* (Toronto: University of Toronto Press for Ontario Historical Studies Series, 1980) at 246; and Joseph Schull, *Ontario since 1867*, Ontario Historical Studies Series (Toronto: McClelland and Stewart, 1978) at 35–44.

2   Chadwick is described in Henry James Morgan, ed, *The Canadian Men and Women of the Time: A Handbook of Canadian Biography* (Toronto: W Briggs, 1898) at 173 as "politically, a Con., but not an active politician." Dianne Newell, "William Gooderham" in *Dictionary of Canadian Biography (DCB)* (Toronto: University of Toronto Press, 1966–) vol 11 at 360 says, "Although his conservative views were well known, Gooderham avoided the public eye."

3   Joseph Beatty to Sir John A Macdonald, 12 March 1891, Macdonald Papers, MG26-A, Letterbooks, 250137–39, Library and Archives Canada (LAC).

4   WH Beatty to Sir John A Macdonald, 13 July 1883, *ibid*, 8665–66.

5   From the obituary for Charlotte Beatty in the *Toronto Telegram* (21 May 1928). Gladstone, of course, had begun his political career as a Tory but had switched parties to become a Liberal and as such served off and on as British prime minister from 1868 to 1894.

6   Newell, "James Gooderham Worts" in *DCB*, vol 11 at 938.

7   Biggar, *Sir Oliver Mowat* at 150.

8   Blake's Ontario government enacted legislation prohibiting anyone from sitting simultaneously in both the federal and provincial legislature, and Blake resigned his provincial seat. See Joseph Schull, *Edward Blake: The Man of the Other Way 1833–1881* (Toronto: Macmillan, 1975) at 99–103; and Schull, *Ontario since 1867* at 49–51.

9   See Pierre Berton, *The National Dream: The Great Railway 1871–1881* (Toronto: McClelland and Stewart, 1970) at 90–144.

10   Beatty, Chadwick, Thomson & Blackstock, Private Ledger 8A (1883–1915), 9, Accounting records, Fasken Martineau DuMoulin (FMD) LLP Fonds, PF189-5-1, Archives of the Law Society of Upper Canada (LSUC), Toronto, indicates that there were two firms known as Beatty, Chadwick & Lash. The old firm was extant from 16 May 1870 to 1 May 1874, and the new firm, in which Beatty, Chadwick, and Lash were equal partners, existed from 1 May 1874 to 13 May 1876.

11   Nicholas Miller was the father of one of Canada's leading chemists, W. Lash Miller, after whom a building is named at the University of Toronto. See Adrian G Brook & WAE McBryde, *Historical Distillates: Chemistry at the University of Toronto since 1843* (Toronto: University of Toronto Press, 2007) at 85–101; and Martin Friedland, *The University of Toronto: A History* (Toronto: University of Toronto Press, 2002) at 157.

12   Theodore Regehr, "Zebulon Aiton Lash" in *DCB*, vol 14 at 605.

13   Each child would go by his middle name so that we now had W. Lash Miller and W. Miller Lash. The former would become one of Canada's leading professors of chemistry. The latter would practise law with his father and become the president of both Brazilian Light and Traction (later known as Brascan) and of the Toronto Club. Each would have a building named after him at the University of Toronto. See Larry Wayne Richards, *University of Toronto: An Architectural Tour* (New York: Princeton Architectural Press, 2009) at 146–47 and 207–8.

14   See W Miller Lash in Robert Brown, "The House That Blakes Built" (unpublished manuscript, 1978) at 128. The author was presented with a copy of this manuscript by the Blakes firm.

15   See Margaret Banks, "The Evolution of the Ontario Courts 1788 to 1981" in David H Flaherty, ed, *Essays in the History of Canadian Law* (Toronto: University of Toronto

Press for the Osgoode Society, 1983) vol 2 at 523–25.

16 Regehr, "Zebulon Aiton Lash" in *DCB*, vol 14 at 605–8. See also Desmond H Brown, *The Genesis of the Criminal Code of 1892* (Toronto: University of Toronto Press for the Osgoode Society, 1989) at 108–9; and Brown, "The House That Blakes Built" at 119.

17 (September 1876) ns 12 CanLJ 241.

18 Chadwick diaries, vol 7 (1871–84), 15 May 1876.

19 CRW Biggar, *Sir Oliver Mowat: A Biographical Sketch*, 2 vols (Toronto: Warwick Brothers and Rutter, 1905) vol 1 at vii.

20 *Ibid* at 147.

21 Biggar, *Sir Oliver Mowat* at 249–50.

22 J Ross Robertson, *Robertson's Landmarks of Toronto*, 6 vols (Toronto: JF Robertson, 1898–1914) vol 1 at 526–27.

23 *Toronto Directory, 1876* (Toronto: Fisher & Taylor, 1876) at 146 shows Mowat living in the fourth house north of Queen on the east side. The other three homes were inhabited by Sir H Parker, baronet, Mrs A Beatty, widow of James, and the Honourable W Howland, Lieutenant-Governor of Ontario. Biggar and his bride moved into a house on the west side of the same street.

24 Biggar, *Sir Oliver Mowat* at 151. At 145 Biggar tells us that his father-in-law had purchased the house shortly after his appointment to the bench "and there, surrounded by his books, he spent many of the happiest hours of his life."

25 Drawing on his own roots and those of his Presbyterian-raised wife, Biggar edited an Anglican version of the Methodist and Presbyterian Sunday School magazines that he and Jane Helen had known. Richard E Ruggle, "The Saints in the Land 1867–1939" in Alan L Hayes, ed, *By Grace Co-workers: Building the Anglican Diocese of Toronto 1780–1989* (Toronto: Anglican Church Centre, 1989) at 199.

26 WH Beatty to his son Charlie, letter headed "The Oaks, Queens Park, Aug. 3, 1892," copy provided by the Beatty family to the author.

27 Toronto Board of Trade, *Souvenir: A History of the Queen City and Her Board of Trade* (Toronto and Montreal: Sabiston Lithographic and Publishing, 1893) at 150. On law firm recruitment based on merit rather than family or other connections, see Jeffrey Haylock, "Cravath by the Sea: Recruitment in the Large Halifax Law Firm, 1900–1955" 31 Dal LJ 401–25.

28 Thomas Gibbs Blackstock described it as a junior partnership in letters to his parents. Chadwick refers to George Sedgewick as a nominal partner. Chadwick diaries, vol 10 (1916–21), 1 January 1917.

29 Chadwick diaries, vol 7 (1871–84), June 1876.

30 JB Robinson Memoirs, Faskens Martineau DuMoulin LLP (FMD) Fonds, PF189-2-1, 2009006-088, Archives of the Law Society of Upper Canada (LSUC), Toronto.

31 Chadwick diaries, vol 7 (1871–84), 6–7 November 1876.

32 Donald Creighton, *John A. Macdonald: The Old Chieftain* (Toronto: Macmillan, 1955) at 218. See also Richards, *University of Toronto* at 63.

33 The Chadwick property is now the site of the Bahen Centre for Computer Science at the University of Toronto. See Richards, *University of Toronto* at 137–39.

34 One wonders whether the need for Beatty to work even longer hours to cover some of Chadwick's work as he toiled to get his house built and to move motivated Beatty and Lottie to take a lengthy vacation in the British Isles in the spring of 1877. In any event, it was the first of many trips they took to England. They were gone a month, leaving Chadwick to cover the workload. Chadwick's diaries, vol 7 (1871–84), 18 May 1877.

35 See various annual reports and lists of shareholders in the Archives of the Toronto-Dominion Bank (TDB), Toronto.

36 Joseph Schull, *100 Years of Banking in Canada: A History of the Toronto-Dominion Bank* (Vancouver: Copp Clark, 1958) at 71.

37 *Ibid* at 211.

38 *Proceedings of the Twentieth Annual General Meeting*, Bank of Toronto, 21 June 1876, 1, TDB.

39 *Proceedings of the Twenty-first Annual General Meeting*, Bank of Toronto, 20 June 1877, 1, *ibid*.

40 William Beatty to Sir John A Macdonald, September 1879, Macdonald Papers, MG 26A, Letterbooks 166547–49, LAC.

41 *Ibid*, where the letterhead of Beatty, Chadwick, Biggar & Thomson/Beatty, Miller, Biggar & Blackstock shows the firm as having "Offices over the Bank of Toronto, Corner Wellington & Church Streets."

42 William Dendy, *Lost Toronto: Images of the City's Past* (Toronto: McClelland and Stewart, 1993) at 54.

43 Tom wrote to his father on 4 September 1876 that he "had the satisfaction of making the highest score in the Q.O.R team, in fact I was the only one in the battalion who took a prize in that match" (Gibbs Blackstock Family Papers, MS Coll 88, box 7, folder 3, Thomas Fisher Rare Book Library, Toronto).

44 Biggar had grown up as a Methodist in Prince Edward County, where Tom's father had influenced him greatly. Decades later Biggar would write to Tom on the occasion of the father's death, saying that he remembered "his appointment in Consecon and how after his first sermon my own father came back and said 'well, at last we have got the right man!' Of his influence there, I cannot speak too highly; and as for myself — it was one of the most helpful in my life. Need I say more?" CRW Biggar to Thomas Gibbs Blackstock, 13 December 1905, *ibid*, folder 15.

45 CM Blackstock, *All the Journey Through* (Toronto: University of Toronto Press, 1997) at 248–49.

46 Two of their brothers, Thomas Nicholson (known as TN) and William Henry, had become large-scale exporters of grain and produce. They had also "built a stately home in the midst of beautiful gardens, embellished by fountains and abundant shrubbery . . . called 'Ellesmere.' On their place in Oshawa as a "dynasty family," see M McIntyre Hood, *Oshawa, the Crossing between the Waters: A History of Canada's Motor City* (Oshawa: McLaughlin Public Library, 1968) chs 15 and 16.

47 Tom hints at his partner's troubles in a letter to his father informing him that "McNabb . . . is a very decent good-hearted fellow . . . whatever faults he has may be traced to his easy going habits." Thomas Gibbs Blackstock to William Schenck Blackstock, 3 September 1877, *ibid*, box 7, folder 3.

48 Blackstock, *All the Journey Through* at xi.

49 Note from Tom to Mary Hodge Blackstock, Gibbs Blackstock Family Papers, MS Coll 88, box 7, folder 4. See also Blackstock, *All the Journey Through* at 169.

50 Tom collected letters of reference from his teachers. His English teacher at UCC said that he was "very industrious and intelligent . . . excelled in English Grammar & in History." James Loudon, his math tutor at University College and a future president of the university, said that he had the "distinction of being ranked in Honors in the Department of Mathematics." E Schluter, his master of French and German, reported that "he greatly distinguished himself while at College both by his gentlemanly conduct and by steady application." Letters of reference for Thomas Gibbs Blackstock, 6–10 December 1870, *ibid*, box 10, folder 30. Gibbs Blackstock Family Papers, MS Coll 88, box 7, folder 3. In the summer of 1873, Tom worked in the Snelling & Wardropoffice that conducted a barristers' practice from No. 1 York Chambers on Toronto Street. When September came, Tom found himself a better job

with Delamere & Brooke, Barristers in Law/Solicitors in Chancery. Gibbs Blackstock Family Papers, MS Coll 88, box 6, folder 9.

51 Gibbs Blackstock Family Papers, MS Coll 88, box 7, folder 3. In the summer of 1873, Tom worked with Snelling & Wardrop in a barristers' practice from No 1 York Chambers on Toronto Street. When September came, Tom found himself a better job with Delamere & Brooke, Barristers in Law/Solicitors in Chancery. Gibbs Blackstock Family Papers, MS Coll 88, box 6, folder 9.

52 Blackstock, *All the Journey Through* at 204.

53 *Ibid* at 206.

54 Tom wrote a brief description of his trip to the Buffalo Land (Gibbs Blackstock Family Papers, MS Coll 88, box 10, folder 29).

55 Blackstock, *All the Journey Through* at 210–11.

56 *Ibid* at 210.

57 Thomas Gibbs Blackstock to Mary Hodge Blackstock, ca 1866–July 1903, Gibbs Blackstock Family Papers, MS Coll 88, box 7, folders 4–12.

58 There is a 28 January 1880 account of a moose hunt in November 1879 in the *ibid*, box 10, folder 31.

59 Mulock would later become a politician, serving as postmaster-general in Laurier's government and as chancellor of the University of Toronto. See WA McKay, ed, *Macmillan Dictionary of Canadian Biography*, 4th rev ed (Toronto: Macmillan, 1978) at 603; and Friedland, *University of Toronto* at 100.

60 See his letterhead as a sole practitioner, T Gibbs Blackstock, 20 July 1877, *ibid*, box 7, folder 7.

61 Thomas Gibbs Blackstock to William Schenck Blackstock, 16 March 1878, *ibid*, box 7, folder 3.

62 William Schenck Blackstock to Thomas Gibbs Blackstock, 1 September 1878, *ibid*, box 6, folder 9.

63 E Wyly Grier, *Autobiography* (unpublished ms, 1953–57), 6, Archives of Ontario, Toronto. Grier, who became one of Canada's great portrait painters, had a relationship with George that, in his own words, "deepened into a friendship of many years."

64 Blackstock, *All the Journey Through* at 249. See his picture facing 83.

65 Thomas Gibbs Blackstock to Mary Hodge Blackstock, 14 April 1879, *ibid*, box 7, folder 12.

66 Thomas Gibbs Blackstock to William Schenck Blackstock, 14 April 1879, *ibid*, box 7, folder 3.

67 *Ibid.*

68 See Beatty, Chadwick, Thomson & Blackstock, Private Ledger 8A (1883–1915), 11.

69 Newell, "William Gooderham" in *DCB*, vol 11 at 360.

70 The pamphlet for the service is in the Gibbs Blackstock Family Papers, MS Coll 88, box 10, folder 5.

71 A set of letters dated December 1879 and January 1880 in the FMD Fonds, PF189-1-1, 2009006-028, LSUC.

72 Blackstock, *All the Journey Through* at 250.

73 A formal invitation to the 28 January 1880 wedding can be found in the Gibbs Blackstock Family Papers, MS Coll 88, box 10, folder 32. It is incorrectly listed in the finding guide as "Wedding invitation from the marriage of George Gooderham and Harriet Dean."

74 Beatty, Chadwick, Thomson & Blackstock, Private Ledger 8A (1883–1915).

75 *Ibid*, 11.

76 *Annual Report of the Bureau of Industries for the Province of Ontario* (Toronto: Warwick and Sons by order of the Legislative Assembly, 1883) at 37.

◆ Chapter 3 ◆

1 *The Ontario Law List and Solicitors' Agency Book,* 9th ed (Toronto: Joshua Rordans, 1882) at 1.

2 See CM Blackstock, *All the Journey Through* (Toronto: University of Toronto Press, 1997); and the biography of William Jr by Leo Johnson, in *Dictionary of Canadian Biography (DCB)* (Toronto: University of Toronto Press, 1966–) vol 9 at 360–61.

3 On the leadership role that Methodists and Baptists played in the early Temperance movement, see Craig Heron, *Booze: A Distilled History* (Toronto: Between the Lines, 2003) at 58.

4 See Dean Beeby, "George Gooderham" in *DCB,* vol 13 at 387–90. The documents for the dissolution of the partnership of William Gooderham and James Gooderham Worts and the formation of the new partnership are in the Series RG 55-17, *York County Copartnership Registry,* doc no 59, Archives of Ontario, Toronto.

5 "Death Removes George Gooderham" *Globe* (2 May 1905) 2.

6 See filings in *York County Copartnership Registry,* 4 February 1882, Series RG 55-17, Archives of Ontario certifying that William Gooderham, James Gooderham Worts, and George Gooderham were the only members of the partnership when it was dissolved on 22 August 1881 on the death of William Gooderham and that thereafter JG Worts and G Gooderham created a new partnership under the same name.

7 *Proceedings of the 26th Annual General Meeting of Shareholders,* Bank of Toronto, 21 June 1882, Archives of the Toronto-Dominion Bank (TDB), Toronto. It is important to note that corporate officers had not yet taken on a significant day-to-day operational role. The Bank of Toronto, for example, was managed by its chief cashier, not its president.

8 See the obituaries in the *Globe* (22 August 1881); *[Toronto] Monetary Times* 15(9) (26 August 1881) 237; *Toronto Daily Star* (22 August 1881).

9 *Globe* (23 August 1881) 3.

10 The Rev Alexander Sanson, *Sermon after the Funeral of William Gooderham, Esq, Churchwarden, Preached in Trinity Church, Toronto* (Toronto: [s.n.], 1881) at 5–6. A copy can be found in the Gibbs Blackstock Family Papers, MS Coll 88, box 10, folder 40, Thomas Fisher Rare Book Library, Toronto.

11 *Robert Summers v Commercial Union Assurance Co.,* [1881] 6 SCR 19.

12 This firm, referred to as Mulock's, was for a time important, but it eventually faded away.

13 The Miller Family Papers, University of Toronto Archives, B76-0007, contain in box 39 a fishing rod and case, ca 1870, "made by John Kay, Galt Ont and given by him to W. N. Miller and given by W. N. M. to Z. A. Lash when W. N. M. moved to England. Given by Z. A. L. to W. Lash Miller December, 1918."

14 Later Biggar would explain that "in 1859 Mr. Mowat asked James Maclennan, then practising in Hamilton, to become his partner. The firm of Mowat & Maclennan was formed in January 1860, and the two senior partners remained together — except while Mr. Mowat was Vice-Chancellor — until Mr. Maclennan became, in 1888, a Judge of the Court of Appeal for Ontario." CRW Biggar, *Sir Oliver Mowat: A Biographical Sketch,* 2 vols (Toronto: Warwick Brothers and Rutter, 1905) vol 1 at 43. See also A Margaret Evans, *Sir Oliver Mowat,* Ontario Historical Studies Series (Toronto: University of Toronto Press, 1992) at 34–35. Mowat's 1860 partnership agreement said that he would dedicate himself to the law practice to the extent "consistent with the due discharge of the duties of a member of the Legislature." He had ceased to be a member of the firm on being appointed to the bench but had rejoined the firm on leaving. Biggar notes, "On January 1, 1873, he resumed the practice of his profession, rejoining his former partner, Mr. James (now Mr. Justice) Maclennan, who was

then the head of the firm of Maclennan, Downey & Ewart. Notwithstanding several subsequent changes in its membership, Mr. Mowat's name continued to appear in the style of the firm as senior partner from that time until his death" (158).

15 G Blaine Baker, "William Albert Reeve" in *DCB*, vol 12 at 887–88. On the roles of local Crown attorney and justice of the peace, see Robert J Sharpe, *The Lazier Murder: Prince Edward County, 1884* (Toronto: University of Toronto Press for the Osgoode Society for Canadian Legal History, 2011) at 47–49.

16 "I heard from Fitch of Brantford asking me to refer him to attorneys previous with whom I served so I expect to get a definite proposition from him soon as soon as he gets a reply from Reeve & Mulock" (Thomas Gibbs Blackstock to William Schenck Blackstock, Toronto, 30 June 1877, Gibbs Blackstock Papers, MS Coll 88, box 7, folder 3, Thomas Fisher Rare Book Library, Toronto).

17 "I consulted Reeve who tho't it would be a good idea for a year at least. He has still ideas of coming to Toronto." Thomas Gibbs Blackstock to William Schenck Blackstock, 3 September 1877, *ibid*, box 7, folder 3.

18 Robert Brown, "The House That Blakes Built" (unpublished ms, 1978) at 120. A copy of this work is in the library of the LSUC Archives. Brown describes the changes that Lash brought: "Hitherto known as a litigation firm, its reputation built upon the achievements of the great counsel work of Edward and Samuel Blake, Walter Cassels, John A. Boyd and others, it now developed under the aegis of Z. A. Lash into a firm noted for its skills in commercial and financial matters as well."

19 Chadwick diaries, vol 7 (22 September 1871–84).

20 William Beatty to Sir John A Macdonald, 13 July 1883, Macdonald Papers, MG26-A, Letterbooks, 8665–6, Library and Archives Canada.

21 *Macdonald et al v Crombie et al* (1883), 2 OR 243; *O'Brien v Clarkson* (1884), 10 OAR 603.

22 See his obituary in the *Globe* (21 June 1882) 1.

23 *Ibid*.

24 "James Gooderham Worts" in *DCB*, vol 11 at 937–39 at 938.

25 A power of attorney respecting the Worts estate in Beatty's favour dated 8 May 1900 is in Fasken Martineau DuMoulin LLP (FMD) Fonds, PF189-1-1, 2009006-028, Archives of the Law Society of Upper Canada (LSUC), Toronto.

26 There were a series of codicils dated 11 January 1878, 27 September 1880, 14 November 1881, 4 May 1882, and 22 May 1882. See *Worts v Worts* (1889), 18 OR 332.

27 *Ibid*.

28 See my article "Gooderham and Worts: A Case Study in 19th Century Business Organization" in G Blaine Baker & Jim Phillips, eds, *Essays in the History of Canadian Law*, vol 8, *In Honour of R. C. B. Risk* (Toronto: University of Toronto Press for the Osgoode Society for Canadian Legal History, 1999) 335–57.

29 RSO 1877, c 150.

30 Corporation Index 1868–1906, MS 480, reel 2, Archives of Ontario, Toronto. On Albert Lee Gooderham and his family, see Edward Marion Chadwick, *Ontarian Families: Genealogies of United Empire Loyalist and Other Pioneer Families of Upper Canada*, 2 vols (Belleville, ON: Mika Silk Screening, 1972) vol 1 at 155.

31 A partial copy of the agreement showing that it was prepared by TG Blackstock is in the Archives of the Toronto-Dominion Bank. A summary of the agreement is in Gooderham and Worts Heritage Plan Report No 4, Inventory of Archival Sources, prepared by Stephen A Otto, March 1994. It is also summarized in *Worts v Worts* (1889), 18 OR 337.

32 See "William George Gooderham" in Charles GD Roberts & Arthur L Tunnell, *A Standard Dictionary of Canadian Biography: The Canadian Who Was Who*, 2 vols (To-

ronto: Trans-Canada Press, 1934–38) vol 2 at 176.

33 See "Albert Edward Gooderham" in *ibid* at 174–75.

34 The profits would have been substantial. *Toronto Illustrated 1893* (Toronto: Ontario Genealogical Society, ON Branch, 1992) states that the distillery business was paying $1,800 a day to the federal government in excise taxes, $650,000 a year, meaning that they had sales in the many millions of dollars.

35 *Worts v Worts* (1889), 18 OR 332 at 337. A footnote to the judgment at 341 indicates that Beatty provided oral evidence.

36 *Ibid* at 343, where Chancellor Boyd states, "I may mention that evidence was tendered as to the wishes of the testator respecting the business of Gooderham and Worts, which I considered not material (even if admissible), having regard to the opinion."

37 *An Act Respecting the Incorporation of Joint Stock Companies by Letters Patent*, RSC 1886, c 119.

38 [1879–80] 4 SCR 215, aff'd (1881–82), 7 AC 96.

39 See Jacob S Ziegel, "Constitutional Aspects of Canadian Companies" in Jacob S Ziegel, ed, *Studies in Canadian Company Law*, 2 vols (Toronto: Butterworths, 1967–73) vol 1 at 150.

40 See RW Wegenest, *The Law of Canadian Companies* (Toronto: Burroughs and Company, 1931) at 30. The company registered in Ontario as an extra-provincial corporation in 1900. (A copy of the extra-provincial charter and a typescript of the original federal letters patent can be found in the Archives of Ontario.)

41 There are copies of the letters patent in RG 55-5 (the dormant corporation files 1868-1977) No TC 1312 (43-28-25-2-12), Archives of Ontario.

42 FMD Fonds, PF189-3, 2009006-120, LSUC.

43 *Toronto Directory, 1885* (Toronto: RL Polk, 1885).

44 This became a very important banking firm, representing the Bank of Nova Scotia. It dissolved in the late 1980s and a number of its partners joined the Faskens firm.

45 See obituary in *Toronto Public Library Biographical Scrapbooks*, vol 5 at 228–29.

46 Toronto Board of Trade, *Souvenir: A History of the Queen City and Her Board of Trade* (Toronto and Montreal: Sabiston Lithographic and Publishing, 1893) at 150.

47 See Henry James Morgan, ed, *The Canadian Men and Woman of the Time: A Handbook of Canadian Biography* (Toronto: W Briggs, 1898) at 150.

48 Curtis Cole, *Osler, Hoskin & Harcourt: Portrait of a Partnership* (Toronto: McGraw-Hill Ryerson, 1995) at 30. See also Christopher Moore, *McCarthy Tétrault: Building Canada's Premier Law Firm 1855–2005* (Vancouver: Douglas and McIntyre, 2005) at 26–27.

49 See the entries in Curtis Cole, *Osler, Hoskin & Harcourt: Portrait of a Partnership* (Toronto: McGraw-Hill Ryerson, 1995) appendix 2 at 295.

50 Beatty was so impressed with the work ethic of "this raw lad from the farm" that in a letter to his son, Charles William, dated 3 August 1892, he compared him to Thomson and suggested that his son emulate the two of them. Beatty added, "You could never give them too much to do — always ready for more" (original in possession of Geoffrey Beatty, copy in possession of the author).

51 "His outstanding traits were a capacity for sustained and concentrated effort, close attention to detail, and absolutely unprejudiced weighing of facts." Charles GD Roberts & Arthur L Tunnell, *A Standard Dictionary of Canadian Biography: The Canadian Who Was Who*, 2 vols (Toronto: Trans-Canada Press, 1934–38) vol 2 at 149.

52 On this 1876 church, see Elysia Delaurentis & Debra Nash-Chambers, *Remembering Pilkington Township Lives, Loves and Labour* (Fergus, ON: self-published, 2006) at 76–78.

53 See "Toronto General Trusts" *Toronto Evening Star* (31 May 1894) 2.

54 Roberts & Tunnell, *Standard Dictionary of Canadian Biography*, vol 1 at 29–30.

55 WH Beatty to his son Charlie, letter headed "The Oaks, Queens Park, Aug. 3, 1892." Copy provided by the Beatty family to the author.

56 Just inside a small room to the left on entering St James Cathedral is a large, attractive plaque in memory of Sir Thomas Galt and his son Thomas Percival Galt.

57 In 1889, when the reconciliation of accounts was being done for the period during which Neville had been a junior partner, amounts that would otherwise have been paid to Neville as a former partner were instead paid to Galt and William Henry Brouse, who were junior partners after Neville, and to Blackstock. The financial records state "R. S. N.'s share for 34 months goes as follows: to T. G. 500, W. H. Brouse 1,200, T. G. Bl. 800 or $66.67 per month for 34 ms = 2,266.78 ÷ 3 = 755.59 to each." Typically a departing partner would have received either a cash payment on leaving the firm with future amounts collected being paid to Beatty or his share of any future collections. That such was not the case with Neville suggests that he was seen as undeserving of his share. Beatty Chadwick Thomson and Blackstock Private Ledger 8A (1883-1915), FMD Fonds, PF189-5-1, LSUC.

58 *Toronto Directory, 1886* (Toronto: RL Polk, 1886) shows the two of them in partnership at 18–20 King Street.

59 The firm's account books show much effort to collect accounts in 1886–87 especially.

60 Beatty Chadwick Thomson and Blackstock Private Ledger 8A (1883-1915), FMD Fonds, PF189-5-1, 2009006-169, 205, LSUC.

61 George Tate Blackstock to Sir John A Macdonald, 2 June 1884, Macdonald Papers, C1764, 190997–191000; and William Beatty to Sir John A Macdonald, 9 September 1885, Macdonald Papers, LB C1773, 203345–6, Library and Archives Canada (LAC).

62 See C Ian Kyer & J Bickenbach, *The Fiercest Debate: Cecil A. Wright, the Benchers, and Legal Education in Ontario 1923–1957* (Toronto: Osgoode Society, 1987) at 30–34.

63 Christopher Moore, *The Law Society of Upper Canada and Ontario's Lawyers, 1797–1997* (Toronto: University of Toronto Press, 1997) at 170.

64 Geoffrey Hunt Stanford, *To Serve the Community: The Story of the Toronto Board of Trade* (Toronto: University of Toronto Press for the Board of Trade of Metropolitan Toronto, 1974) at 31.

65 *Ibid* at 18.

66 Marilyn M Litvak, *Edward James Lennox, "Builder of Toronto"* (Toronto: Dundurn Press, 1995) at 7.

67 Letter to WH Beatty from Sir John A Macdonald, 1 October 1886, Macdonald Papers, MG26-A, Letterbook 24, LAC.

68 See *Toronto Illustrated 1893* (1893; repr, Toronto: Ontario Genealogical Soceity, Toronto Branch, 1992) at 25–26 for a description of the board and of Beatty's position as its solicitor.

69 Photograph e002505606, Toronto Board of Trade, 1850-1977 Fonds MG28-III56, R3087-0-7-E., LAC reproduced in Stanford, *To Serve the Community.*

70 Toronto Board of Trade, 1850–1977 Fonds, MG28-III56, R3087-0-7-E, microfilm reels C-9827, 9850, and 9853, LAC.

71 Chadwick, *Ontarian Families*, vol 1 at 157 and 179.

72 *An Act to Incorporate the Royal Canadian Insurance Company, SO 1868* (31 Vict) c 53.

73 Craig Heron, *Booze: A Distilled History* (Toronto: Between the Lines, 2003) at 87.

74 "Guarantee Company The Dominion of Canada an Enterprising and Successful Institution" *Toronto Daily Star* (15 March 1901) 2.

75 On the distinction, see DC Masters, "The Anglican Evangelicals in Toronto, 1870–1900" (September–December 1978) J Can Church Historical Soc'y 51.

76 EM Chadwick to Violet Baker, 23 September 1921, Edward Chadwick Fonds PF9, LSUC.

77 Chadwick diaries, vol 7 (22 September 1871–84), 1 January 1873: "Celebrated this festive occasion by making my first attempt at oil painting." In later entries he notes that what he is painting are heraldic crests and the like. See, for example, his entry for New Year's Day 1909, where he says, "spent most of the rest of the day painting (heraldic as usual)."

78 HG Hart, *The New Annual Army List for 1882* (London: John Murray, 1882) at 1015g. It notes that he had been made an honorary major, 28 January 1876.

79 These firms would merge in 1989 to form Fasken Campbell Godfrey. The deed transferring title from William Howland to the syndicate was prepared by the Howland Arnoldi firm, but all other legal work for the syndicate seems to have been prepared by Beatty's firm.

80 A detailed history of the cathedral project can be found in the Heritage Impact Statement prepared by Goldsmith Borgal & Company Limited for Royal St George's College in June 2006, available in the archives of the college. A shorter but more readily accessible account can be found in Mark Osbaldeston, *Unbuilt Toronto: A History of the City That Might Have Been* (Toronto: Dundurn Press, 2008) at 70–77.

81 EM Chadwick, *Monograph of the Cathedral of St. Alban the Martyr Toronto* (Toronto: Self-published, 1920–21) at 9.

82 Pews were bought and sold. The Archives of St James Cathedral have copies of the conveyances. In 1911, for example, Charlotte Louisa Beatty and her siblings sold their father's pew, 190 in the west aisle, to the churchwardens for $250. The conveyance was prepared by Beatty Blackstock Fasken Cowan & Chadwick.

83 46 Vic c 63. See Chadwick, *Monograph of the Cathedral* at 14.

84 Chadwick, *Monograph of the Cathedral* at 15–16 states, "The purchase was therefore made, in December 1884. Being at the time outside the city limits, application was made to the Legislature for an Act to enable the Cathedral to be located outside the city limits, which was duly passed. (48 Vic., Ca 93–1st February, 1885.)"

85 *The Canadian Churchman* was the Anglican High Church weekly newspaper. It began in 1875 as the *Dominion Churchman* and in 1890 changed its name to the *Canadian Churchman*. See Alan L Hayes, ed, *By Grace Co-workers: Building the Anglican Diocese of Toronto 1780–1989* (Toronto: Anglican Book Centre, 1989) at 52.

86 Pasted into the Chadwick diaries, vol 9 (1902–21 September 1916), 5 September 1912. Chadwick added the note, "After working for the Church for nearly 40 years, this is, I think, the first time that anything that I have done has received a public recognition."

87 Records of St Alban the Martyr, collection 1601, Archives of the Ecclesiastical Province of Ontario, Toronto.

88 There are extensive materials (compiled by Chadwick) in St Alban's Cathedral, Diocesan Archives, Diocese of Toronto, Anglican Church of Canada.

89 See DC Masters, *Henry John Cody: An Outstanding Life* (Toronto: Dundurn Press, 1995) at 88–96. George Horace Gooderham was on the Finance Committee for the new St Paul's and Mrs Thomas Gibbs Blackstock donated the organ to the new church. Her daughter, Barbara Blackstock, married Canon Cody after his first wife died. *Ibid* at 188–89.

90 A bill of costs for Moss Falconbridge & Barwick, consisting of $20 to examine title and the documentation as well as $5.10 disbursements, can be found in St Alban's Cathedral, Diocesan Archives, Diocese of Toronto, Anglican Church of Canada. The minutes of the final negotiations, also in the archives, mention that they were held in Chadwick's office at the firm but he is not mentioned as speaking for either party.

91 Chadwick, *Monograph of the Cathedral of St. Alban the Martyr Toronto* at 7.
92 Cynthia Monaco, "The Difficult Birth of the Typewriter" (Spring–Summer 1988) American Heritage of Invention and Technology 9 at 15.
93 See 1881–85, Alexander Campbell Fonds, R4503-0-8-E, MG 27-IC2, and 1885–94, Sir John Thompson Fonds, R5240-0-1-E, MG26-D, both in LAC.
94 William Beatty to Sir John A Macdonald, 22 July 1887, Macdonald Papers, MG26-A, LB C1495, 8924, LAC.
95 William Beatty to Sir John A Macdonald, 9 January 1888, Macdonald Papers, MG26-A, 224982-4, LAC.
96 William Beatty to Sir John A Macdonald, 14 April 1888, Macdonald Papers, MG26-A, 58801-8, LAC.
97 Thomas Blackstock to Sir John Thompson, 14 April 1888, Sir John Thompson Fonds, R5240-0-1-E, MG26-D, vol 70/C9242, 7708, LAC.
98 Thomas Gibbs Blackstock to William Schenck Blackstock, 23 February 1888, Gibbs Blackstock Family Papers, MS Coll 88, box 7, folder 3, Thomas Fisher Rare Book Library, Toronto.
99 Dr James Frederick William Ross was then thirty-one years old and had become an MD the year before. See Henry James Morgan, ed, *The Canadian Men and Women of the Time: A Handbook of Canadian Biography of Living Characters*, 2d ed (Toronto: W Briggs, 1812) at 973. Ross would become a key figure at the Toronto General Hospital. See JTH Connor, *Doing Good: The Life of Toronto's General Hospital* (Toronto: University of Toronto Press, 2000) at 171, 176–77.
100 Beatty, Chadwick, Thomson & Blackstock, Private Ledger 8A (1883–1915), Accounting records, FMD Fonds, PF189-5-1, 2009006-169, LSUC.

⇜ Chapter 4 ⇝

1 James Plomer with Alan R Capon, *Desperate Venture: Central Ontario Railway* (Belleville, ON: Mika Publishing, 1979) at 107.
2 Ron Brown, *Ghost Railways of Ontario* (Peterborough, ON: Broadview Press, 1994) at 136–43.
3 Plomer, *Desperate Venture* at 44 and 69. See also Arnold Hoffman, *Free Gold: The Story of Canadian Mining* (New York: Associated Book Service, 1947) at 53. On Ritchie as a supporter of Canada's commercial union with the United States, see Christopher Pennington, *The Destiny of Canada: Macdonald, Laurier and the Election of 1891* (Toronto: Allan Lane Canada, 2011) at 54–55.
4 See, for example, *Toronto General Trusts Corporation v Central Ontario RW Co* (1904), 10 OLR 347.
5 *Confederation Life Insurance Company 1871–1971* (Toronto: Confederation Life Association, 1972) at 10–11. See also CR Dent, *Confederation Life Association: The Story of the Founding and Progress of a Great Canadian Institution* (Toronto: Confederation Life, 1939) at 114.
6 There is a discussion of the announcement and the competition for the design of the building in Mark Osbaldeston, *Unbuilt Toronto 2* (Toronto: Dundurn Press, 2011) at 93–100.
7 *Montreal Herald* (30 December 1890). Tellingly, the Toronto press did not run the story.
8 Robert Merrill Black, "Shagotyohgwisaks: E.M. Chadwick and Canadian Heraldry" (September 1990) 24(3) Heraldry in Canada 2 at 5.
9 See the photo of the pyramid visit in CM Blackstock, *All the Journey Through* (Toronto: University of Toronto Press, 1997) at 198–99.

10 George's palatial home is still at Bloor and St George, where it now serves as the York Club. Tom and Hattie's home was torn down to make way for the St George subway station, although part of their fence survives. The Royal Canadian Yacht Club later built its mainland clubhouse on the site. A picture of the Blackstock house can be seen in the entrance hall to the club. Pictures of the house and its interior can also be found in William Dendy, *Lost Toronto: Images of the City's Past* (Toronto: McClelland and Stewart, 1993) at 218–19.

11 Blackstock, *All the Journey Through* at 22–25.

12 On the donation and its impact on Canadian parks, see SE (Ted) Hart, *J.B. Harkin, Father of Canada's National Parks* (Edmonton: University of Alberta Press, 2010) at 16.

13 See Christopher Moore, *The Law Society of Upper Canada and Ontario's Lawyers, 1797–1997* (Toronto: University of Toronto Press, 1997) at 181–84; John Hagan & Fiona Kay, "Hierarchy in Practice: The Significance of Gender in Ontario Law Firms" in Carol Wilton, ed, *Inside the Law: Canadian Law Firms in Historical Perspective* (Toronto: University of Toronto Press for the Osgoode Society for Canadian Legal History, 1996) 530–72 at 535.

14 Hagan & Kay, "Hierarchy in Practice" at 535.

15 The same held true in the other large firms. The first woman lawyer in McCarthy's was Edith Sheppard in 1921. See Christopher Moore, *McCarthy Tétrault: Building Canada's Premier Law Firm, 1855–2005* (Vancouver: Douglas and McIntyre, 2005) at 57. The first woman in Osler's was Bertha Wilson in 1959. See Curtis Cole, *Osler, Hoskin & Harcourt: Portrait of a Partnership* (Toronto: McGraw-Hill Ryerson, 1995) at 143.

16 In 1899 Brouse left the firm to become secretary and treasurer of the Toronto Stock Exchange, where he would become president in 1910–11.

17 We know very little about Harper Armstrong. The records of the Law Society of Upper Canada indicate that he was admitted as a student-at-law in the Easter term of 1885 and was called to bar in the Easter term of 1890.

18 *Toronto Directory, 1887* (Toronto: RL Polk, 1887) vol 2 at 281, lists Harper Armstrong as a student with Beatty, Chadwick, Blackstock & Galt boarding at 86 Bond Street. He continued to be so listed in 1888, 1889, and 1890 although he changed boarding houses, moving to Seaton Street. *Toronto Directory, 1890* (Toronto: RL Polk, 1890) vol 2 at 940, lists McKay as a student with Beatty, Chadwick, Blackstock & Galt boarding at 292 Queen Street East. He continued to be so listed in 1890 and 1891.

19 See *Gooderham et al v The Corporation of the City of Toronto* (1890), 21 OR 120. Nesbitt and young McKay would take an appeal to the Supreme Court of Canada in 1894. See [1894] 25 SCR 246.

20 Charles Moss was the brother of the Honourable Thomas Moss (1836–81) and the brother-in-law of Glenholme Falconbridge. All three would serve as Chief Justice of Ontario. See Christopher Moore, *The Law Society of Upper Canada and Ontario's Lawyers, 1797–1997* (Toronto: University of Toronto Press, 1997) at 191.

21 *The Utterson Lumber Company (Limited) v Simpson Rennie*, [1892] 21 SCR 218.

22 S Craig Wilson, "George Tate Blackstock" in *DCB*, vol 15 at 117.

23 *Ibid.*

24 WHC Boyd, "The Last Chancellor" (1981) 15 Law Soc'y Gaz 356 at 363–64.

25 See Curtis Cole, "McCarthy, Osler, Hoskin, and Creelman, 1882–1902: Establishing a Reputation, Building a Practice" in Carol Wilton, ed, *Beyond the Law: Lawyers and Business in Canada 1830–1930* (Toronto: Osgoode Society, 1990) at 162 on the role of Britton Bath Osler as prosecutor in the case.

26 Wyly Grier, "Autobiography" (unpublished manuscript, 1943) at 47, MU 8225, Archives of Ontario, Toronto.

27 *Ibid.*
28 Blackstock, *All the Journey Through* at 272.
29 George Tate Blackstock to Hon CH Tupper, 17 December 1891, 17694 vol 143/C-9255, Library and Archives Canada (LAC).
30 David Cruise & Alison Griffiths, *The Lords of the Line: The Men Who Built the CPR*, rev ed (Toronto: Penguin Books, 1996) at 182–89.
31 Charles GD Roberts & Arthur L Tunnell, *A Standard Dictionary of Canadian Biography: The Canadian Who Was Who*, 2 vols (Toronto: Trans-Canada Press, 1934–38) vol 1.
32 Stephen Leacock, *Canada, the Foundations of Its Future* (Montreal: Privately printed, 1941) at 193.
33 See the letters from TG Blackstock to Thompson in the Sir John Thompson Fonds, R5240-0-1-E, MG26-D, LAC, especially 15 April 1894, vol 206/C-10537, 25883; and 3 August 1894, vol 217/C-10539,27273. *Lady Aberdeen Diaries*, 13 December 1894, LAC.
34 *Lady Aberdeen Diaries*, 13 December 1894, LAC.
35 Dr Ross was also George Gooderham's personal physician. See Henry James Morgan, ed, *The Canadian Men and Women of the Time: A Handbook of Canadian Biography of Living Characters*, 2d ed (Toronto: W Briggs, 1812) at 973.
36 PB Waite, *The Man from Halifax: Sir John Thompson, Prime Minister* (Toronto: University of Toronto Press, 1985) at 415.
37 *Lady Aberdeen Diaries*, 13 December 1894, LAC.
38 *DuMoulin v Burfoot*, [1893] 22 SCR 120. The opposing counsel was Frank Arnoldi, whose firm would become Campbell Godfrey & Lewtas and merge with Faskens in 1989.
39 "Thenceforth his success was both speedy and sustained. He showed a firm grasp of principle and a fine faculty of discrimination, and while in great demand as a trial lawyer in both civil and criminal cases, was on occasion employed in cases of enquiry into public affairs" (Roberts & Tunnell, *A Standard Dictionary of Canadian Biography*, vol 1 at 379).
40 See, for example, *Charlebois v Delap*, [1895] 26 SCR 221; *Jermyn v Tew*, [1898] 28 SCR 497; *London Assurance Corporation v Great Northern Transit Company*, [1899] 29 SCR 577.
41 *Henry Headford v The McClary Manufacturing Company*, [1894] 24 SCR 291.
42 See his obituary in the *Globe and Mail* (24 March 1954).
43 Reginald Stewart & A Munro Grier, "Gilbert and Sullivan: Two Addresses," 17 March 1932, 121, online: Empire Club http://speeches.empireclub.org/61166/data?n=1.
44 Augustus Bridle, *The Story of the Club* (Toronto: Arts & Letters Club, 1945) at 52–53. When Grier died in 1954 at ninety-three, his obituary in the *Globe* said "Lawyer, Speaker, Actor A. Munro Grier Dies."
45 Hilary Bates Neary, "William Renwick Riddell: Judge, Ontario Publicist and Man of Letters" (1977) 11 Law Soc'y Gaz 144.
46 Allan Levine, *King: William Lyon Mackenzie King, a Life Guided by the Hands of Destiny* (Vancouver: Douglas and McIntyre, 2011) at 40.
47 ML Friedland, *The University of Toronto: A History* (Toronto: University of Toronto Press, 2002) at 167–68.
48 *Ibid* at 164–66.
49 See, for example, the petition that Nesbitt, Chadwick and Riddell prepared on behalf of the Toronto Board of Trade for an act to amend its act of incorporation in 1896 and the petition by Nesbitt for an act to incorporate the Manufacturers Life Assurance Company of North America in 1901. Both are in RG6-A-1, LAC.
50 Kenneth Jarvis, "Chief Justice Hugh Rose" (1968) 11 Law Soc'y Gaz 17 at 19.

51 Robert J Sharpe, *The Last Day, The Last Hour: The Currie Libel Trial* (Toronto: Osgoode Society, 1988) at 98.

52 FMD Fonds, PF189, 2009006-028, LSUC, Toronto.

53 Richard B Howard, *Colborne's Legacy: Upper Canada College 1829–1979* (Toronto: Macmillan, 1979) at 124.

54 *Ibid*, 125.

55 WH Beatty & Wallace Nesbitt, *The Boards of Trade General Arbitrations Act* (Toronto: Board of Trade, 1894); and *Rules of the Toronto Chamber of Arbitration with Notes and Suggestions as to the Conduct of a Reference* (Toronto: Board of Trade, 1894). See also Geoffrey Hunt Stanford, *To Serve the Community: The Story of the Toronto Board of Trade* (Toronto: University of Toronto Press for the Board of Trade of Metropolitan Toronto, 1974) at 62–63.

56 Stanford, *To Serve the Community* at 62.

57 Albert Tucker, *Steam into Wilderness: Ontario Northland Railway 1902–1962* (Toronto: Fitzhenry and Whiteside, 1978) at 1–4.

58 HV Nelles, *The Politics of Development: Forest, Mines and Hydro-electric Power in Ontario 1849–1941*, 2d ed (Montreal and Kingston: McGill-Queen's University Press, 2005) at 120.

59 On Cox, see J Andrew Ross & Andrew D Smith, eds, *Canada's Entrepreneurs: From the Fur Trade to the 1929 Stock Market Crash* (Toronto: University of Toronto Press, 2011) at 418–24.

60 The following is drawn from letters in the Sir Wilfrid Laurier Fonds, R10811-0-X-E, MG 26-G, LAC (hereafter Laurier Letters). The quotation is from letter of TG Blackstock to AG Blair, Minister of Railways, 14 December 1897, Laurier Letters, 18265–66. A copy of the letter was sent to Laurier on 7 January 1898, Laurier Letters, 19637–40.

61 Thomas Blackstock to Sir Richard Cartwright, 26 November 1897, Laurier Letters, 18256.

62 Copy of letter to Sir Richard Cartwright, 10 December 1897, Laurier Letters, 18261–62.

63 Thomas Gibbs Blackstock to TG Shaughnessy, 14 December 1897, Laurier Letters, 18263–64, LAC. On Shaughnessy and his role at the CPR, see Cruise & Griffiths, *Lords of the Line* at 259–92, especially 282–87.

64 Thomas Gibbs Blackstock to AG Blair, Minister of Railways, 14 December 1897, copy, Laurier Letters, 18265–66.

65 Thomas Gibbs Blackstock to Sir Wilfrid Laurier, 7 January 1898, Laurier Letters, 19637–40.

66 Sir Wilfrid Laurier to Thomas Gibbs Blackstock, 23 June 1899, Laurier Letters, 34793.

67 Thomas Gibbs Blackstock to Sir Wilfrid Laurier, 12 July 1901, Laurier Letters, 57530.

68 See Jeremy Mouat, *Roaring Days: Rossland's Mines and the History of British Columbia* (Vancouver: UBC Press, 1995) at 104–5. Blackstock, George Gooderham, and others are pictured, *ibid* at 142. The strike was an important chapter in labour history. See Gregory S Kealey, *Workers and Canadian History* (Montreal and Kingston: McGill-Queen's University Press, 1995) ch 11 and especially 429–31.

69 See Levine, *King* at 50–54.

70 WLM King, *Diary*, 19 November 1901 (available online through LAC); Kealey, *Workers*, discusses the diary entry at 429–31.

71 WLM King, *Diary*, 10 January 1902.

72 Mouat, *Roaring Days* at 104–5.

73 J Castell Hopkins, ed, *Canadian Annual Review of Public Affairs 1901* (Toronto: Annual Review Publishing, 1901) at 55.

74 Quoted in Blackstock, *All the Journey Through* at 273.

75 Chadwick, *Ontarian Families*, vol 1 at 157a.

76 Beatty's other daughter, Alice Maud Beatty, married William Hubert Cawthra, a member of the wealthy and influential Cawthra family, when he was a partner in the Howland Arnoldi firm. In 1936 Maud and William donated the St George's Chapel to St James Cathedral. See William Cooke, ed, *The Parish and Cathedral Church of St. James', Toronto 1797–1997: A Collaborative History* (Toronto: Printed for the Cathedral by University of Toronto Press, 1998) at 114 and 210.

77 *An Encyclopaedia of Canadian Biography*, 3 vols (Montreal and Toronto: Canadian Press Syndicate, 1904–7) vol 2 at 24.

78 See Eric Arthur, *Toronto: No Mean City*, 3rd ed, rev Stephen A Otto (Toronto: University of Toronto Press, 1986) at 196.

79 See the letters in the Laurier Letters, R10811-0-X-E, MG 26-G, Library and Archives Canada.

80 On the tunnel, see Lucy Booth Martyn, *The Face of Early Toronto: An Archival Record 1797–1936* (Sutton West, ON: Paget Press, 1972) at 16.

81 See *An Act to Incorporate the Toronto Hotel Company*, SO 1899, c 110; and Marilyn M Litvak, *Edward James Lennox, "Builder of Toronto"* (Toronto: Dundurn Press, 1995) at 52–54. That Lennox was a client is confirmed by *Sylvester Neelon v City of Toronto and E.J. Lennox*, [1895] 25 SCR 579. Nesbitt and Grier appeared on behalf of Lennox.

82 Norman R Ball, *The Canadian Niagara Power Company Story* (Erin, ON: Boston Mills Press in association with FortisOntario, 2005) at 31–37.

83 *Ibid* at 11 and 279.

84 Grier would lead a very interesting life after his departure from the firm. In 1913 he joined the five-year-old Arts & Letters Club. His brother, Wyly Grier, had been a charter member in 1908 and its second president in 1909–10. Both in the club and outside, Munro became a noted amateur actor. Then in 1924–26 he followed his brother into the presidency of the club. See Augustus Bridle, *The Story of the Club* (Toronto: Arts & Letters Club, 1945) at 52–53. Munro Grier would later become counsel to Osler Hoskin & Harcourt. See *Canada Law List 1940*.

85 Reginald Stewart & A Munro Grier, "Gilbert and Sullivan: Two Addresses," 17 March 1932, 121, online: Empire Club http://speeches.empireclub.org/61166/data?n=1.

86 "Mrs. W.H. Beatty Saw 75 Years of Toronto's Life" *Toronto Telegram* (21 May 1928).

87 Roberts & Tunnell, *A Standard Dictionary of Canadian Biography*, vol 2 at 149.

88 The details of Fasken's shareholdings and acquisition of control are set out in his evidence in Canada, Royal Commission on Life Insurance, *Report*, 4 vols (Ottawa: The Commission, 1907) vol 2 at 1278–96. Undated 1980s memo to the author from Morgan S Crockford, which is in the FMD Fonds.

89 Undated 1980s memo to the author from Morgan S. Crockford, which is in the FMD Fonds. Crockford was with Excelsior Life from 1926 to 1970, rising to Corporate Secretary.

90 For a description and picture of the Fasken home, see Litvak, *Edward James Lennox* at 54 and 67.

91 There is a picture of the stately home in the *[Toronto] Mail and Empire* (2 August 1930), together with a discussion of David's purchase and renovations.

92 Marion MacKenzie, "Hardscrabblers of Hardscrabblers: Kenneth and Margaret Jane MacDonald MacKenzie and FAMILY: Dr. Donald (M.D.); Alexander James, Ph. M.B. (Druggist); Kenneth Robertson (Undertaker and Embalmer); and Marion Fasken (School teacher) and Their Clans: 1. MacDonald–Ross; 2. Fasken–Mitchell; 3. MacKenzie–Robertson" (unpublished manuscript, 1959). She stresses that as rich as David Fasken became he was always very careful with his money. He "learned the

hard way the value of EVERY COPPER." She quotes him as saying "I walked when others rode" and remarks, "At home he had learned how to do without and live on a minimum; while an apprentice he had continued learning it even more so, and as a Graduate Lawyer, even after he became a very wealthy one, the same practice was followed." She illustrates her point by telling a story. Fasken, the multimillionaire, wanted a cup of coffee while travelling by train from New York to Toronto. He went to the dining car and asked what a coffee would cost. When he learned it would cost 35 cents, he tried to bargain with the waiter, arguing that no coffee was worth that sum. The waiter explained that that was the price that he was required to charge and Fasken left without the coffee (ch 20, Fasken–Mitchell).

93 *Ibid*, ch 19, Fasken–Mitchell.
94 Marion Mackenzie and her mother visited Fasken at his law office "and as soon as his Dad introduced him to Mother and me, I knew that Bob would be of no help to his Dad at any time as a lawyer or as a Business Man" (*ibid*, ch 21, Fasken–Mitchell).
95 *Register of the Graduates of University of Toronto* (Toronto: University of Toronto Press, 1920).
96 On Reeve's important place in Ontario legal education, see C Ian Kyer & Jerome Bickenbach, *The Fiercest Debate: Cecil A. Wright, the Benchers, and Legal Education in Ontario 1923–1957* (Toronto: Osgoode Society, 1987) at 30–34.
97 Some of the papers from Alex's days as a sole practitioner are in the Fasken Martineau DuMoulin LLP (FMD) Fonds, PF189, 2009006-016, Archives of the Law Society of Upper Canada (LSUC), Toronto.
98 CM Blackstock, *All the Journey Through* (Toronto: University of Toronto Press, 1997) at 274.
99 (1903) 3 Can Rev of Annual Affairs at 126.
100 See Robert Bothwell, *A Short History of Ontario* (Edmonton: Hurtig Publishers, 1986) at 101–2; and (1903) 3 Can Rev of Annual Affairs at 126–48. For the Liberal perspective, see Margaret Prang, *N.W. Rowell, Ontario Nationalist* (Toronto: University of Toronto Press, 1975) at 53–55.
101 Charles P Girdwood, Lawrence F Jones, & George Lonn, *The Big Dome: Over Seventy Years of Gold Mining in Canada* (Toronto: Cybergraphics, 1983) at 119.
102 MacKenzie, "Hardscrabblers," ch 21, Fasken–Mitchell.
103 See the memoranda in [1903] 33 SCR. On Justice Mills, see *The Supreme Court of Canada and Its Justices 1875–2000* (Ottawa: Dundurn Group and the Supreme Court of Canada in cooperation with Public Works and Government Services Canada, 2000) at 92.
104 James G Snell & Frederick Vaughn, *The Supreme Court of Canada: History of the Institution* (Toronto: Osgoode Society, 1985) at 86, say, "Though lacking judicial experience, Nesbitt had an outstanding reputation as counsel, and his nomination to the Supreme Court was widely acclaimed." John Sopinka, another member of the firm, would later be appointed to the Court, but more than ten years after he had left the firm.
105 (1903) Can Law J 338.
106 Quoted in Philip Girard, "Politics, Promotion, and Professionalism: Sir Wilfrid Laurier's Judicial Appointments" in Jim Phillips, R Roy McMurtry, & John T Saywell, eds, *A Tribute to Peter N. Oliver* (Toronto: University of Toronto Press for Osgoode Society for Canadian Legal History, 2008) 169–99 at 184.
107 *Chandler & Massey v Kny-Scheerer Co*, [1905] 36 SCR 130 at 134–35.
108 Jamie Benidickson, "James Pitt Mabee" in *Dictionary of Canadian Biography* (Toronto: University of Toronto Press, 1966–) vol 14 at 670–72.
109 *The Canadian Almanac and Repository of Useful Knowledge for the Year 1894* (Toronto:

Copp Clark, [1893?]) at 259.

110 Obituary, *Toronto Daily Star* (6 May 1912) 1.

111 Davis is listed as a student at Beatty Blackstock in Might's *Toronto Directory*, 1905, 1906, 1907, 1908, and 1909. He first appears in the 1905 directory at 432. In the 1910 directory at 541 he is listed as a barrister with Beatty Blackstock.

112 See his obituary in *Toronto Public Library Biographical Scrapbooks*, vol 8 at 566; and also Christopher Moore, *The Law Society of Upper Canada and Ontario's Lawyers, 1797–1997* (Toronto: University of Toronto Press, 1997) at 179.

113 See Sigmund Samuel, *In Return: The Autobiography of Sigmund Samuel* (Toronto: University of Toronto Press, 1963) at 10.

114 Thomas Gibbs Blackstock to Mary Hodge Blackstock, 25 July 1903, Gibbs Blackstock Family Papers, MS Coll 88, box 7, folder 12, Thomas Fisher Rare Book Library, Toronto.

115 "Millions for His Children" *Toronto Star* (23 August 1905) 7 notes that Joe Beatty and David Fasken were the witnesses to his will. Annual report of the Bank of Toronto, 1907, TD Bank Archives.

116 Annual report of the Bank of Toronto, 1907, TD Bank Archives.

117 He resigned on 4 October 1905. See the memoranda in [1905] 36 SCR and Snell & Vaughn, *Supreme Court of Canada* at 88 and 260.

118 Christopher Moore, *McCarthy Tétrault: Building Canada's Premier Law Firm, 1855–2005* (Vancouver: Douglas and McIntyre, 2005) at 40.

119 His resignation spurred an editorial in (1905) Canadian Law Times 562. They distinguished his case from that of more long-standing judges who retired with an allowance and then sought to return to practice. Nesbitt, like Oliver Mowat, Samuel Blake, and John Thompson before him, had retired without an allowance. "There is certainly nothing to prevent such a person from doing as he pleases, nor would any sane man propose to fetter him by legislation."

120 Moore, *McCarthy Tétrault* at 41–42.

121 Moore, *Law Society* at 346. Nesbitt is buried with his father-in-law Beatty in the family plot in St James Cemetery in Toronto. A single headstone has a memorial to Beatty on one side and to Nesbitt on the other.

122 Jack Batten, *The Annex: The Story of a Toronto Neighbourhood* (Erin, ON: Boston Mills Press, 2004) at 141–43.

123 His diary notes on 9 February 1905 that he "dined at the Beattys' for annual Smart Est[ate] meeting." Beatty's sister-in-law Emelie-Ardelia Worts had married David Smart. See Edward Marion Chadwick, *Ontarian Families: Genealogies of United Empire Loyalist and Other Pioneer Families of Upper Canada*, 2 vols (Belleville, ON: Mika Silk Screening, 1972) vol 1 at 159. It was a troubled marriage leading to a much-publicized divorce. David died not long after. It was his estate that Beatty and Chadwick managed.

124 Macdonell continued to be underappreciated until finally, in the 1970s, singer/songwriter Stan Rogers composed a song to his memory, "Macdonell on the Heights."

125 In 1911 he funded the Bathurst Street building (and convinced his friend, architect Edward James Lennox, to do the design without charge). A few years later, he financed the building of a nurses' home known as the Edith Cavell Memorial Nurses' Home. The hospital trained many of the Fasken women. See *The Toronto Western Hospital*, pamphlet, no 978.208, Archives of Toronto Western Hospital.

126 *Beatty v McConnell* (1905), 6 OWR 882. The trial judge calls him Sterling but the Court of Appeal and the Judicial Committee of the Privy Council talk of a Mr Gregory.

127 *Assessment Act*, RSO 1887, c 23, s 31, quoted by Street J in *Beatty v McConnell* (1906), 7

OWR 11 at 11.

128 Beatty had to be able to convince a judge that his brother knew nothing of this dispute and Beatty's title defect and that he would have agreed to purchase the property at the same value as the option that had been granted for its sale, meaning that he would not profit from the purchase.

129 *Beatty v McConnell* (1906), 7 OWR 11.

ᴑᴥ Chapter 5 ᴥᴑ

1 Quoted in GB Stevens, *The Canada Permanent Story, 1855–1955* (Toronto: Canada Permanent Mortgage Corporation, 1955) at 38.

2 Melville Ross Gooderham, known as Ross, was the third son of George Gooderham.

3 *City of Hamilton v Hamilton Distillery Company*, [1906] 38 SCR 239 (with Hugh Rose); *Lockhart v Wilson*, [1907] 39 SCR 541; *Canadian Casualty & Boiler Ins Co v Boulter Davies & Co*, [1907] 39 SCR 558 (with Hugh Rose); *Hamilton Street Railway v City of Hamilton*, [1907] 39 SCR 673 (with Hugh Rose).

4 One suspects that his director's fees and salary as an officer of numerous companies brought Beatty considerable income. We know that at Confederation Life he received $1,904 in 1902, $2,935.87 in 1903, and $2,916.20 in 1904. See the evidence given in Canada, Royal Commission on Life Insurance, *Minutes of Evidence*, 4 vols (Ottawa: The Commission, 1907) vol 2 at 836.

5 *Dominion of Canada & Newfoundland Gazetteer and Classified Business Directory* (Toronto: Canadian Gazetteer, 1915) at 824 shows him as a sole practitioner at 59 Victoria Street. The *Canadian Who's Who 1936–7* (Toronto: University of Toronto Press, 1936–37) says, "formerly a member of his father's firm; sometime President of B. Kerr & Verner, wholesale dry goods." He was also a founder of the York Club, which was established in 1910 in his late father-in-law's mansion at the corner of Bloor and St George, just a short distance from his own home at 121 St George.

6 Hilary Bates Neary, "William Renwick Riddell: Judge, Ontario Publicist and Man of Letters" (1977) 11 Law Soc'y Gaz 144 at 148.

7 On the creation and role of the bar associations, see C Ian Kyer & Jerome Bickenbach, *The Fiercest Debate: Cecil A. Wright, the Benchers, and Legal Education in Ontario 1923–1957* (Toronto: Osgoode Society, 1987) ch 2.

8 "The Lawyer: An Address to the Ontario Bar Association by the Hon. Justice W.R. Riddell" (December 1907) Can LT, reprinted in *Law Society Gazette 2002: Professionalism: A Century of Perspectives* at 11–12.

9 Donald Jones, "Canada's Early History Brought to Life by Judge" *Toronto Star* (12 February 1983) G18, says, "In the official history of Ontario he is remembered as one of the province's great jurists; but it was his work as a writer and historian . . . that once made the name of William Renwick Riddell familiar across the entire country."

10 See W Wesley Pue, "Becoming 'Ethical': Lawyers' Professional Ethics in Early Twentieth Century Canada" (1991) 20 Man LJ 227; and WR Riddell, "A Code of Legal Ethics" (1919) 4 Reports of the Can Bar Assn 136.

11 Excerpt from the agreement between William Henry Beatty, Edward Marion Chadwick, David Fasken, Mahlon K Cowan, Harper Armstrong, Alexander Fasken, and Hugh E Rose, Partnership agreement, 1 May 1910, FMD Fonds, PF189-1-3, LSUC.

12 The commission was established because of fears of mismanagement and irregularities in the insurance industry arising out of a New York State investigation. On the circumstances of the commission proceedings, hearings, and findings, see Castell Hopkins, ed, *Canadian Annual Review of Public Affairs* 1906 (Toronto: Annual Review Publishing, 1906) at 215.

13   Wallace Nesbitt acted for Canada Life and began the inquiry by addressing the commissioners' focus on his client and its dealings. See Royal Commission on Life Insurance, *Report*, vol 1 at 1.
14   The inquiry also looked into what the various parties earned in salary. Edwin Marshall, the general manager of Excelsior Life, testified that he was paid a salary of $2,500, while David Fasken as president was paid $2,000 and Dr John Ferguson as medical referee was paid $1,200. See *Toronto Star* (21 June 1906) 1.
15   Royal Commission on Life Insurance, *Report*, vol 2 at 1287. As evidence of the changed relationship, David Fasken testified that up to his death, George Gooderham had purchased mortgages placed by Excelsior Life on properties in Manitoba, Saskatchewan, and Alberta to provide Fasken's insurance company with cash flow. This practice stopped when Ross Gooderham became executor. See *ibid* at 1293.
16   *Toronto Star* (27 November 1951).
17   Wallace Nesbitt, for example, served on the board, and the firm gave a legal opinion in connection with the public offering by AE Ames of shares in the Gold Ring Consolidated Mining Company. See the advertisement for the shares in the *Toronto Star* (17 October 1896) 3.
18   Michael Barnes, *Fortunes in the Ground: Cobalt, Porcupine and Kirkland Lake* (Toronto: Stoddard Publishing, 1993) at 13–17. See also Albert Tucker, *Steam into Wilderness: Ontario Northland Railway, 1902–1962* (Toronto: Fitzhenry and Whiteside, 1978) at 11–17.
19   *Toronto Star* (17 May 1906) 1. See also John Patrick Murphy, *Yankee Takeover at Cobalt* (Cobalt: Highway Book Shop, 1977) at 1–3.
20   The Excelsior Life Banner 18(1) (January 1930) 9.
21   "Cobalt the World's Richest Silver Camp," *Cobalt Daily Nugget* (September 1910) 10.
22   Quoted in SA Pain, *Three Miles of Gold: The Story of Kirkland Lake* (Toronto: Ryerson Press, 1960) at 3.
23   Quoted in HV Nelles, *The Politics of Development: Forest, Mines and Hydro-electric Power in Ontario 1849–1941*, 2d ed (Montreal and Kingston: McGill-Queen's University Press, 2005) at 148.
24   Obituary for David Fasken, *Toronto Star* (4 December 1929) 1.
25   *[Toronto] Monetary Times* (15 September 1905) 331.
26   *[Toronto] Monetary Times* (22 September 1905) 363.
27   WA Parks, "Cobalt Mineral Conditions," address with stereopticon views before the Empire Club of Canada, Toronto, 15 November 1906.
28   Census Division, *Chronological Record of Canadian Mining Events from 1604 to 1943 and Historical Tables of the Mineral Production of Canada* (Ottawa: Dominion Bureau of Statistics, 1945) at 8.
29   Morris Zaslow, *The Opening of the Canadian North, 1870–1914* (Toronto: McClelland and Stewart, 1971) at 184.
30   Douglas Owen Baldwin, "Cobalt: Canada's Mining and Milling Laboratory, 1903–1918" (1984) 8 HSTC Bulletin: J Hist Can Science, Tech & Medicine 95 at 99–100.
31   Quoted in Robert Bothwell, *A Short History of Ontario* (Edmonton: Hurtig, 1986) at 109.
32   Joseph Schull, *100 Years of Banking in Canada: A History of the Toronto-Dominion Bank* (Vancouver: Copp Clark, 1958) at 91–92.
33   *Ibid* at 64–65.
34   Richard Tatley, *Northern: Steamboats Timiskaming, Nipissing and Abitibi* (Toronto: Stoddard Boston Mills Press, 1996) at 180–87. See also Michael Barnes, *Temagami* (Toronto: Stoddard Boston Mills Press, 1992), which has pictures of the hotels at 67 and of *Belle* and the other steamboats at 11, 53, and 59–60.

35   Isabel Fasken is an interesting person in her own right. She had had a crush on Ly-
      man Duff. In fact she had assumed that they would be married, but he rejected her
      in favour of another local girl and then moved to British Columbia. Although she
      continued for a time to write to him, she eventually got the message and subse-
      quently accepted an offer of marriage from Alex Fasken. See David Williams, *Duff, A
      Life in the Law* (Toronto: Osgoode Society, 1984).

36   See Lovat Dickson, *Wilderness Man: The Amazing Story of Grey Owl* (London: Macmil-
      lan, 1997) at 51. See also Barnes, *Temagami* at 43–48.

37   See Bruce Hodgins & James Benidickson, *The Temagami Experience* (Toronto: Univer-
      sity of Toronto Press, 1989) at 119 and 186.

38   "Cobalt Has Made Twenty-Five Millionaires," *Montreal Star* (14 April 1909) 12. An-
      other of the Canadians made rich by Cobalt was Reuben Wells Leonard. See Bruce
      Ziff, *Unforeseen Legacies: Reuben Wells Leonard and the Leonard Foundation* (Toronto:
      University of Toronto Press for the Osgoode Society for Canadian Legal History,
      2000) at 20.

39   Zaslow, *Opening of the Canadian North* at 185.

40   Baldwin, "Cobalt" at 109.

41   Charles P Girdwood, Lawrence F Jones, & George Lonn, *The Big Dome: Over Seventy
      Years of Gold Mining in Canada* (Toronto: Cybergraphics, 1983) at 30–36, 70, 119.

42   Robert J Surtees, *The Northern Connection: Ontario Northland since 1902* (North York:
      Captus Press, 1992) at 75–76. See also Albert Tucker, *Steam into Wilderness: Ontario
      Northland Railway 1902–1962* (Toronto: Fitzhenry and Whiteside, 1978) at 46–48.

43   *Canadian Annual Review of Public Affairs 1912* (Toronto: Annual Review Publishing,
      1912) at 644.

44   A review of the history of the Flin Flon mine and David Fasken's role appeared in
      "Sulphide in Assay Led to Development of Flin Flon," *[Toronto] Mail and Empire* (10
      December 1927) 17, complete with pictures of Fasken with his Indian guides, canoe-
      ing to the site and riding a large ox. See also Arnold Hoffman, *Free Gold: The Story of
      Canadian Mining* (New York: Associated Book Service, 1947) at 230–52.

45   Marion MacKenzie, "Hardscrabblers of Hardscrabblers: Kenneth and Margaret Jane
      MacDonald MacKenzie and FAMILY: Dr. Donald (M.D.); Alexander James, Ph. M.B.
      (Druggist); Kenneth Robertson (Undertaker and Embalmer); and Marion Fasken
      (School teacher) and Their Clans: 1. MacDonald–Ross; 2. Fasken–Mitchell; 3. MacK-
      enzie–Robertson" (unpublished manuscript, 1959), ch 21, Fasken–Mitchell. The
      history includes an unidentified news clipping hand-dated 1906 and headed "Young
      Wife Seeks to Annul the Marriage." Given the ongoing interest of the *Toronto Daily
      Star* in the story it may well be from that paper.

46   SO 1907, c 23, s 8.

47   "Parr–Faskin Marriage Has Been Annulled" *Toronto Daily Star* (9 August 1907).

48   Hugh Rose to Charles Murphy, 17 September 1909, Sir Wilfrid Laurier Fonds,
      R10811-0-X-E, MG 26-G, C-880, 589, Library and Archives Canada. (A copy is also
      found at *ibid*, 159872–75.)

49   *55th Annual Report and List of Shareholders*, Bank of Toronto, November 1910, 4, Ar-
      chives of the Toronto-Dominion Bank (TDB). See also Minutes of the Board, Bank of
      Toronto, 11 January 1911, *ibid*.

50   On the battle for public power, see Joseph Schull, *Ontario since 1867*, Ontario Histori-
      cal Studies Series (Toronto: McClelland and Stewart, 1978) ch 8. On the role of Nes-
      bitt, see Norman R Ball, *The Canadian Niagara Power Company Story* (Erin, ON: Boston
      Mills Press in association with FortisOntario, 2005) at 102–3.

51   *Minutes of the Bank of Toronto Board of Directors*, 27 November 1912, TDB. Henry
      James Morgan, ed, *The Canadian Men and Women of the Time: A Handbook of Canadian*

Biography of Living Characters, 2d ed (Toronto: W Briggs, 1812) at 76; Beatty obituary, *Globe* (21 November 1912) 9.

52 Charles GD Roberts & Arthur L Tunnell, *A Standard Dictionary of Canadian Biography: The Canadian Who Was Who*, 2 vols (Toronto: Trans-Canada Press, 1934–38) vol 1 at 126–27.

53 Letter to Laurier, 2 March, 1912 in the FMD Fonds, PF189, LSUC Archives.

54 He later became "the dean of police court lawyers." Obituary, *Globe and Mail* (23 April 1963).

55 MacKenzie, "Hardscrabblers," Fasken–Mitchell–Robert, ch 19.

56 *Ibid.*

57 The choice and the reaction it created are discussed in Mark Osbaldeston, *Unbuilt Toronto 2* (Toronto: Dundurn, 2011) at 109–15. See also William Dendy, *Lost Toronto: Images of the City's Past* (Toronto: McClelland and Stewart, 1993) at 124–25.

58 *A Historical Look at King and Bay*, TD Bank pamphlet, c 1990, TDB.

59 Dendy, *Lost Toronto* at 125.

60 "Lawyer Suing for $600,000 for Sale of La Rose Mines" *Toronto Daily Star* (23 September 1912) 5.

61 For a discussion of the development of codes of ethical conduct, see W Wesley Pue, "Becoming 'Ethical': Lawyers' Professional Ethics in Early Twentieth Century Canada" (1991) 20 Man LJ 227.

62 Hoffman, *Free Gold* at 238–47.

63 "Shake-Up in La Rose," *New York Times*, 21 October 1909.

64 "La Rose Profits Increased" *New York Times* (21 April 1911).

65 "Still on Stand in Big La Rose Case" *Toronto Daily Star* (24 September 1912) 17.

66 *Ibid.*

67 EM Chadwick to Violet Baker, 13 March 1913, Edward Chadwick Fonds, PF9, LSUC.

68 Wyly Grier was then one of Canada's best portrait painters and the brother of Munro Grier, a former partner.

69 Sworn answers to interrogatories given by William Harvey, 1 September 1925, in connection with the legal action brought by WJ Moran against Midland Farms Company et al in the District Court of Midland County, Texas, copy, Fasken Oil and Ranch Properties Limited files (FORP files), Nina Stewart Haley Memorial Library, Midland, Texas.

70 OW Kerr to Attorney Caldwell, 24 September 1913, in connection with the threatened legal action by WJ Moran against Midland Farms Company et al in the District Court of Midland County, Texas, copy, FORP files.

71 David Fasken testified as to Harvey's role. Canada, Royal Commission on Life Insurance, *Minutes of Evidence*, 4 vols (Ottawa: The Commission, 1907) vol 2 at 1293–94.

72 Sworn answers to interrogatories given by William Harvey, 1 September 1925.

73 OW Kerr to Attorney Caldwell, 24 September 1913.

74 *Ibid.*

75 Sworn answers to interrogatories given by William Harvey, 1 September 1925.

76 Historical plaque on the ranch house.

77 Sworn answers to interrogatories given by William Harvey, 1 September 1925.

78 See W Harvey to David Fasken, 21 July 1913, copy, FORP files; sworn affidavit of William Harvey, 8 October 1913, in connection with the legal action brought by WJ Moran against Midland Farms Company et al in the District Court of Midland County, Texas, copy,

79 See David Fasken to W Harvey, 15 May 1913, copy, FORP files.

80 See David Fasken to W Harvey, 4 October 1914, copy, FORP files.

81 See David Fasken to W Harvey, 15 May 1913, copy, FORP files. He would later write

to Harvey that "nobody else outside of yourself could have sold it to me" (David Fasken to W Harvey, 25 November 1913, copy, FORP files).

82   Tupper Tupper McTavish & Co of Winnipeg to Harvey, 17 June 1913, FORP files. See also *Fasken v Minister of National Revenue*, [1949] 1 DLR 810 at 812–14.

83   Kenneth J Lipartito & Joseph A Pratt, *Baker & Botts in the Development of Modern Houston* (Austin: University of Texas Press, 1991).

84   In a letter dated 30 October 1913 on his law firm stationery, David wrote to GW Kerr, the agent trying to sell the property that David had had "no report of a good well on the property . . . . I feared that we merely had a ranching proposition on our hands." The purchase agreement and related correspondence are in the FORP files.

85   David Fasken to GW Kerr, 30 October 1913, FORP files.

86   *Ibid*. On the same day he wrote Harvey, "I feel we went into this proposition without having the ends properly tied . . . but we will have to . . . work out that proposition as best we can."

87   During my visit the local historical museum had a display about the floods of 1912.

88   John Leffer, "Midland County" and William R Hunt, "Andrews County," in Wallace Prescott Webb, *The Handbook of Texas* (Austin: Texas State Historical Association, 1952–76).

89   *Ibid*.

90   David Fasken to W Harvey, 6 October 1913, FORP files.

91   Andrew Fasken testified as to this sequence of events in an examination for discovery conducted on 25 August 1926 in Midland in connection with the action by the *State of Texas v David Fasken et al* (transcript copy, FORP files).

92   See "Fasken, Texas" in Webb, *Handbook of Texas* (1976) vol 3 at 293. There are several Texas historical plaques on the C Ranch, one of which, erected in 1967, describes the Midland & Northwestern Railroad as a "standard gauge 66-mile line built by David Fasken Sr." It operated from 1916 to 1920, when it was washed out and abandoned. See also the *Midland Reporter-Telegram* (15 March 1959) 6 and (14 October 1968) 4B; and *San Antonio Standard-Times* (19 January 1966) B.

93   "Fasken, Texas" in Webb, *Handbook of Texas* (1976) vol 3 at 293.

94   From Fasken, Robertson, Chadwick & Sedgewick, Private Ledger 2, Fasken Martineau DuMoulin LLP (FMD) Fonds, Accounting records, PF189-5-1, Archives of the Law Society of Upper Canada (LSUC), Toronto.

95   By 1929 the firm was known as Galt, Gooderham & Towers. It prepared a conveyance of pew 56 from William George Gooderham to Aileen Smith, 14 October 1929. A copy can be found in the St James Cathedral Archives.

96   *Toronto Directory, 1913* at 645.

97   This was to be Lennox's last major building. One wonders if it was because David Fasken was soon to move to Texas and Beatty and Blackstock, who had sent their work to him, were dead.

98   *Toronto Directory, 1916* at 1286.

99   Marilyn M Litvak, *Edward James Lennox, "Builder of Toronto"* (Toronto: Dundurn Press, 1995) at 89. The building was designated a property of architectural value under the *Ontario Heritage Act* on 14 February 1984. The notice stated, "This building is an important part of the significant group of historic buildings flanking Toronto Street."

100 EM Chadwick to Violet Baker, 20 September 1915, Edward Chadwick Fonds, PF9.

101 Memoirs of Bryce MacKenzie, FMD Fonds, PF189-2-1, 2009006-082, LSUC.

102 Memoirs of JB Robinson, FMD Fonds, PF189-2-1, 2009006-088 and 2009006-094, LSUC.

103 See the note on his withdrawal in FMD Fonds, PF189-2-1, 2009006-072, LSUC.

104 Memoirs of JB Robinson, FMD Fonds, PF189-2-1, 2009006-088, LSUC.

105 *Canadian Who's* at 888. See also Anne Bigelow, "Descendants of Richard Balkwill and Joan Contyn," online: www.annebigelowfamily.ca.

106 See "Chief Justice Native Son of Millbrook," *Peterborough Examiner*, FMD Fonds, PF189-2-1, 2009006-091, LSUC, on Pickup's appointment as Chief Justice of Ontario in 1952.

107 "Pickup Family Envy of Town" *Peterborough Examiner* (11 October 1952) 14.

108 Robert R Hall QC, "George Theopholius Walsh, QC" (1976) 10(2) Law Soc'y Gaz 99–102 at 100.

109 Ontario Bar Biographical Research Project database, Archives of the Law Society of Upper Canada.

110 Might's *Toronto Directory*, 1911 at 1011; 1912 at 1127; and 1913 at 1185.

111 *Ibid*, 1914 at 1278.

112 John Honsberger, QC, "Lewis Duncan, QC" (1977) 11(1) Law Soc'y Gaz 25 at 27.

113 "Wife of New Chief Justice Hopes Life Won't Change," unidentified news clipping, FMD Fonds, PF189-2-1, 2009006-091, LSUC.

114 See *Who's Who in Canada 1940–41* (Toronto: International Press, 1941) at 1344.

115 Both his grandfather and father are in the *Dictionary of Canadian Biography*. Much of what follows is drawn from either Donald Swainson's biography of DD Calvin in vol 11 or from my biography of HA Calvin in vol 16. See also Brian Osborne & Donald Swainson, *Kingston Building on the Past* (Westport, ON: Butternut Press, 1988) at 150–51 and 195–96.

116 "All Work No Play but Not a Dull Boy" *Globe and Mail* (15 March 1958) 28.

117 Might's *Toronto Directory*, 1915 at 610. He is shown as a student at Beatty Blackstock, residing at 40 College Street.

118 Quoted by DD Calvin in *A Saga of the St. Lawrence* (Kingston: Queen's University Press, 1945) at 30.

119 Partnership agreement, 1 May 1915, FMD Fonds, PF189-1-3, 2009006-072, LSUC.

120 *Canada Law List 1916* at 79 and 82. In Might's *Toronto Directory*, 1916 at 802, the ad under the new name added, "Formerly Beatty, Blackstock, Fasken, Cowan & Chadwick."

121 Partnership agreement, 1 May 1915, FMD Fonds, PF 189-1-3, 2009006-072, LSUC.

122 *Toronto Star* (11 November 1916) 1.

123 Joseph Schull, *Ontario since 1867*, Ontario Historical Studies Series (Toronto: McClelland and Stewart, 1978) at 216–17.

124 See, for example, their work together in 1915–16 on *Singer v Singer*, [1916] 52 SCR 447.

125 Charles GD Roberts & Arthur L Tunnell, *A Standard Dictionary of Canadian Biography: The Canadian Who Was Who* 2 vols (Toronto: Trans-Canada Press, 1934–38) vol 1 at 126–27.

126 "His fine, natural courtesy made him popular with lawyers who appeared before him and he was held in great affection by his fellow judges. In essence, he is remembered as a thorough, impartial and exceedingly capable judge." See "Chief Justice Hugh Rose" (1968) 2(1) Law Soc'y Gaz 17 at 17.

127 A few months earlier Chadwick had noted in his diary, vol 10 (22 September 1916–21) that on 16 October 1916, "Dick and Josephine persuaded me to go with them to the 'movies' to see moving pictures of scenes of the war . . . exhibited with official approval. (For a long time I have had no taste for the movies which have appeared to me to be vulgar and sometimes worse and I have refused to go to them.)"

128 Memoirs of Bryce MacKenzie, FMD Fonds, PF189-2-1, 2009006-082, LSUC.

129 Much of this account is taken from WE Elliott, "Scots Pioneers in Huron 'Slept under

a Huge Elm Tree,'" *Goderich Signal-Star* (20 April 1978) 1a, 2a, and 14a.

130 See *Who Was Who 1951–60* (Toronto: International Press, 1960) at 936.

131 See *The Supreme Court of Canada and Its Justices 1875–2000* (Toronto: Dundurn Group and the Supreme Court of Canada in cooperation with Public Works and Government Services Canada, 2000) at 100.

132 "Robertson Retires, McRuer Reported New Chief Justice," *Globe and Mail* (4 September 1952) 1. A copy is in FMD Fonds PF189-2-1, 2009006-100, LSUC.

133 Craig Heron, *Booze: A Distilled History* (Toronto: Between the Lines, 2003) at 174–77.

134 *Re Stratford Fuel, Ice, Cartage and Construction Co.*, [1914] 50 SCR 100.

135 Gordon Robertson, *Memoirs of a Very Civil Servant: Mackenzie King to Pierre Trudeau* (Toronto: University of Toronto Press, 2000) at 3–5. Robert Gordon describes his father's role at Vimy Ridge as a lieutenant in 195th Battalion of Canadian Corps, leading the charge. The elder son was born a month after the battle at a time when his father was fighting for his life in France. His father spent two years in hospitals in France and England, where he had four operations on a shattered leg. He initially came back to Nova Scotia as a soldier-settlement commissioner, responsible for helping veterans to find a place in Nova Scotia. In 1919 he returned to Saskatchewan as livestock commissioner. See also John Hawkes, *The Story of Saskatchewan and Its People*, 3 vols (Chicago and Regina: SJ Clarke, 1924) vol 3.

136 "All Work No Play but Not a Dull Boy" *Globe and Mail* (15 March 1958) 28.

137 A copy of the issue of the journal with Calvin's article is in FMD Fonds, PF189-2-1, 2009006-095, LSUC.

138 "Miners of Cobalt Voted to Strike," *Toronto Star* (26 June 1917) 12.

139 Gregory S Kealey, *Workers and Canadian History* (Montreal and Kingston: McGill-Queen's University Press, 1995) at 300.

140 Charles P Girdwood, Lawrence F Jones, & George Lonn, *The Big Dome: Over Seventy Years of Gold Mining in Canada* (Toronto: Cybergraphics, 1983) at 150.

141 Gregory S Kealey, "Strikes in Canada 1891–1950" in *Workers and Canadian History* at 368.

142 "Liberals Appeal for Union Government" *Toronto Star* (15 December 1917) 13.

143 Réal Bélanger, "Sir Wilfrid Laurier" in *Dictionary of Canadian Biography* (Toronto: University of Toronto Press, 1966–) vol 14, 610–28, reprinted in Ramsay Cook & Réal Bélanger, eds, *Canada's Prime Ministers: Macdonald to Trudeau, Portraits from the Dictionary of Canadian Biography* (Toronto: University of Toronto Press, 2007) at 189–90.

144 On the leadership convention and Mackenzie King's leadership of the Liberal Party, see Allan Levine, *King: William Lyon Mackenzie King, a Life Guided by the Hands of Destiny* (Toronto: Douglas and McIntyre, 2011) at 108–10.

ᴄ⅋ Chapter 6 ⅌ᴄ

1 From the minute book of St Mary's Cement Limited, now in St Mary's Museum.

2 Arnold Hoffman, *Free Gold: The Story of Canadian Mining* (New York: Associated Book Service, 1947) at 237.

3 *Ibid*, 233, 235.

4 *Ibid*, 237.

5 Harvey in his sworn examination for discovery in the Moran lawsuit tells us that he first met David Fasken when Harvey was an articled clerk in the Beatty firm. He had gone west to Manitoba and had been David's agent in land deals in Manitoba and Alberta. When Harvey learned the C ranch in Texas was for sale, he came to Toronto to convince David to buy it. Relying on Harvey and insisting that there must be

water on the property, he agreed to do so. *WJ Moran v Midland Farms Company, et al*, District Court of Midland County No 1724, Nina Stewart Haley Memorial Library, Midland, Texas.

6 Unidentified newsclippings hand dated 2 and 9 November 1921 headed "Robert Fasken Seeks Divorce: Wife Wins in Texas Court" and "Robt. Fasken Awarded Divorce: Wife Will Enter an Appeal," included with Marion MacKenzie, "Hardscrabblers of Hardscrabblers: Kenneth and Margaret Jane MacDonald MacKenzie and FAMILY: Dr. Donald (M.D.); Alexander James, Ph. M.B. (Druggist); Kenneth Robertson (Undertaker and Embalmer); and Marion Fasken (School teacher) and Their Clans: 1. MacDonald–Ross; 2. Fasken–Mitchell; 3. MacKenzie–Robertson" (unpublished manuscript, 1959).

7 *May Fasken v Robert Fasken* (1924), 260 SW 701 at 702.

8 *Ibid.*

9 "He tried to give her a life full of thrills and excitement which she had always loved, and great parties were held for her benefit to which the most eligible young men were invited but she would have naught to do with any of them . . . . She would trust herself to no one but her Uncle Dave." MacKenzie, "Hardscrabblers," ch 21, Fasken–Mitchell.

10 *Ibid.*

11 *Ibid.*

12 *Ibid.*

13 *Ibid.*

14 Memoirs of JB Robinson, Fasken Martineau DuMoulin (FMD) Fonds, PF189-2-1, 2009006-088, Archives of the Law Society of Upper Canada (LSUC), Toronto.

15 *Ibid.*

16 *Ibid.*

17 Memoirs of Bryce MacKenzie, FMD Fonds, PF189-2-1, 2009006-082, LSUC.

18 Memoirs of JB Robinson, FMD Fonds, PF189-2-1, 2009006-088, LSUC.

19 *Ibid.*

20 In an interview with Don Affleck, 7 February 1974, FMD Fonds, PF189-2-1, 2009006-083, LSUC, Bryce MacKenzie would later say, "David Fasken could attract business with his little finger, Alex could lose it the same way." I agree that David was excellent at attracting business, but I disagree that Alex lost clients. He drove lawyers out of the firm but he seemed quite good at keeping clients happy.

21 Robert Shirriff, interview with author, 19 December 2011.

22 For two different perspectives on the split of McCarthy Osler into McCarthy & McCarthy and Osler Hoskin & Harcourt, see Christopher Moore, *McCarthy Tétrault: Building Canada's Premier Law Firm, 1855–2005* (Vancouver: Douglas and McIntyre, 2005) ch 2; and Curtis Cole, *Osler, Hoskin & Harcourt: Portrait of a Partnership* (Toronto: McGraw-Hill Ryerson, 1995) ch 3.

23 The following is based on the memoirs of JB Robinson.

24 Memoirs of Bryce MacKenzie.

25 *Shilson v Northern Ontario Light and Power Co*, [1919] 59 SCR 443.

26 [1920] 60 SCR 375.

27 Memoirs of Bryce MacKenzie.

28 Shirriff interview; Richard B Potter, interview with author.

29 *Income War Tax Act, 1917*, SC 1917 c 28.

30 *Succession Duty Act*, RSO 1927, c 26. Ontario had enacted legislation in 1892 to collect succession duties.

31 Gifts and trusts are categorized as *inter vivos* and testamentary. An *inter vivos* trust is created and comes into effect during the life of the person settling the trust. A

testamentary trust is created during the life of the person settling the trust in his or her will and comes into effect on that person's death.

32   A discretionary trust involves some element of discretion or judgment on the part of the trustee. The discretion is often when, how, if, or to whom the trust property is distributed.

33   MacKenzie, "Hardscrabblers," ch 21, Fasken–Mitchell.

34   Preamble to *Succession Duty Act* (55 Vict) c 6.

35   A history of the statute and its many amendments can be found in LR Mactavish, ed, *Ontario Statute Annotations, R.S.O. 1970 edition* (Aurora, ON: Canada Law Book, 1974) at 719. It was passed as 55 Vict c 6 and then re-enacted in 1907 as 7 Edwd VII c 10 and again in 1909 as 9 Edwd VII c 12. Provincial succession duty legislation in Canada was repealed in the 1970s, with Ontario the last to make the change, in 1979. This was done in part because Alberta refused to implement such legislation, making it a "death tax haven," and in part because of the federal taxation of estates and the desire to avoid double taxation. See Wolfe D Goodman, "Death Taxes in Canada, in the Past and in the Possible Future" (1995) 43 Can Tax J 1360.

36   *Succession Duty Act*, RSO 1927, c 26, s 19.

37   See the discussion of the difference between succession duty and estate tax in Ralph R Loffmark, *Estate Taxes* (Toronto: Carswell, 1960) at 1–2.

38   *Succession Duty Act* (55 Vict) c 6, s 4, later in RSO 1927, c 26, s 3.

39   MacKenzie, "Hardscrabblers," ch 20, Fasken–Mitchell, says that "he didn't salt away his money in vaults, but used it to better the lives of his nearest relatives, especially the older members of the Fasken Clan who had not been able to acquire too many of this world's comforts. To each of them was paid a monthly instalment, sufficient to ensure them comfortable lives as long as they lived, and arrangements were made legally to ensure that no matter what happened to him nor when, that money would be forthcoming . . . as long as they should live." She continues, "He also had a Trust Fund set up whereby such of his relatives who should ever really need any financial aid that they were unable to provide for themselves, should get as much help as his Trustees decided was necessary." In 1959, she notes, the "Trust Fund is still active. But, any relative who can earn or who has enough to manage on comfortably without such help gets nothing from the Trust Fund."

40   The plaque was put up years later at the suggestion of Sam Bowman, a local Mennonite farmer turned township reeve. See preface.

41   *Canada Trust Co v Fasken* (1990), 69 DLR (4th) 575.

42   On similar conditions attached to the Leonard Foundation scholarships, see Bruce Ziff, *Unforeseen Legacies: Reuben Wells Leonard and the Leonard Foundation* (Toronto: University of Toronto Press for the Osgoode Society for Canadian Legal History, 2000) at 78–83 and 176. Ironically 1990, the year of the Fasken estate litigation, was also the year that the Ontario Court of Appeal ruled the Leonard scholarship conditions unenforceable as contrary to public policy.

43   *Canada Trust Co v Fasken* (1990), 69 DLR (4th) 575 at 578.

44   It is described very briefly in *ibid* at 577.

45   MacKenzie, "Hardscrabblers," ch 20, Fasken–Mitchell.

46   *The Toronto Western Hospital*, pamphlet, no 978.208, Archives of Toronto Western Hospital. A copy is also in FMD Fonds, PF189-2-1, 2009006-080, LSUC.

47   *Toronto Daily Star* (3 December 1929) 1.

48   Ziff, *Unforeseen Legacies* at 13.

49   MacKenzie, "Hardscrabblers," includes an unidentified news clipping, hand-dated 5 December, that summarizes the oration. From its text it seems to be from a local Elora paper.

50   Marion MacKenzie, noting that Staff Captain McCoy of the Salvation Army had attended Fasken's funeral, tells us, "Dave had been a special friend of the Salvation Army helping them in their work with the needy, with his money, of which no one knew anything about except the Officers of the Army" ("Hardscrabblers," ch 22, Fasken–Mitchell).
51   *Ibid*, ch 8, Fasken–Mitchell.
52   Cited in *Fasken v Minister of National Revenue*, [1948] Ex CR 580 at 583; *Texas v Fasken*, US Supreme Court, (1927) 274 US 724, 47 S Ct 762, 71 L Ed 1329.
53   *Texas v Fasken*.
54   Memoirs of JB Robinson.
55   *[Toronto] Mail and Empire* (16 December 1921).
56   See William FE Morley, "Introduction" to Edward Marion Chadwick, *Ontarian Families: Genealogies of United Empire Loyalist and Other Pioneer Families of Upper Canada* (Belleville, ON: Mika Silk Screening, 1972), vol 1.
57   Robert Merrill Black, "Shagotyohwisaks; E.M. Chadwick and Canadian Heraldry" (September 1990) 24 Heraldry in Canada 5.
58   Her diaries are in the Chadwick Papers, MSS MS573, Archives of Ontario, Toronto. Portions have been published in Frances Hoffman & Ryan Taylor, *Much to Be Done: Private Life in Ontario from Victorian Diaries* (Toronto: Natural Heritage/Natural History, 1996). See also Jack Batten, *The Annex: The Story of a Toronto Neighbourhood* (Erin, ON: Boston Mills Press, 2004) at 141–43.
59   See Eric Arthur, *Toronto: No Mean City*, 3rd rev ed (Toronto: University of Toronto Press, 1986) at 243. See also the discussion of his work at Osgoode Hall in John Honsberger, *Osgoode Hall: An Illustrated History* (Toronto: Osgoode Society for Canadian Legal History, 2004) at 224–26. His work on the Albany Club is discussed online: www.albanyclub.ca/abt_003.php.
60   Dick Chadwick was the founder and president of the Foundation Company of Canada, which was responsible for many bridges and dams across Canada as well as for the Festival Theatre in Stratford. Dick was awarded the Julian C Smith medal by the Engineering Institute of Canada in 1953 and was inducted into the Alumni Hall of Distinction of the University of Toronto Faculty of Applied Science and Engineering in 1984. See online: MyAlumni.utoronto.ca http://alumni.utoronto.ca/s/731/index. aspx?sid=731&gid=36&pgid=2071.
61   Brian's carvings of heraldic symbols like the gryphon are a feature of the Barristers' Lounge at Osgoode Hall. See Honsberger, *Osgoode Hall* at 224–26.
62   *Ontario Metal Products Co v Mutual Life Ins Co* (1923), 54 OLR 299.
63   *Ontario Metal Products Co v Mutual Life Ins Co*, [1924] SCR 35.
64   On Tilley, see David Ricardo Williams, *Just Lawyers: Seven Portraits* (Toronto: Osgoode Society for Canadian Legal History, 1995) ch 2.
65   On Rowell, see Margaret Prang, *N.W. Rowell, Ontario Nationalist* (Toronto: University of Toronto Press, 1975).
66   Newton Rowell articled with Hellmuth, whom Margaret Prang in her biography of Rowell terms "one of the most distinguished lawyers in the province" (*ibid* at 17).
67   Shaver would become a bencher of the Law Society. On his role in the fight over legal education, see C Ian Kyer & Jerome Bickenbach, *The Fiercest Debate: Cecil A. Wright, the Benchers, and Legal Education in Ontario 1923–1957* (Toronto: Osgoode Society, 1987) at 220 and 231.
68   On the background behind the banking difficulties, see Michael Bliss, *Northern Enterprise: Five Centuries of Canadian Business* (Toronto: McClelland and Stewart, 1987) ch 14.
69   For a summary of these and a discussion of the difficulties facing the banks, see

Joseph Schull, *100 Years of Banking in Canada: A History of the Toronto-Dominion Bank* (Vancouver: Copp Clark, 1958) at 125–36.

70 *[Toronto] Monetary Times* (10 February 1882), quoted in Basil Skodyn, ed, *The Permanent Story 1855–1980: An Historical Review of the 125-Year Growth of the Canada Permanent Mortgage Corporation, Its Subsidiaries, and Amalgamated Companies* (Toronto: Canada Permanent Mortgage Corporation, 1980) at 37.

71 Patrick Boyer, *A Passion for Justice: The Legacy of James Chalmers McRuer* (Toronto: Osgoode Society for Canadian Legal History, 1994) at 68–69.

72 *R v Gough et al*, [1925] 57 OLR 426, 28 OWN 391 and 394.

73 Boyer, *A Passion for Justice* at 53.

74 Memoirs of JB Robinson.

75 *Toronto Public Library Biographical Scrapbooks*, vol 7 at 675–80.

76 Memoirs of JB Robinson.

77 *[Toronto] Mail and Empire* (17 December 1930). See also *Toronto Public Library Biographical Scrapbooks*, vol 7 at 675–80.

78 *Canadian Who's Who* (Toronto: University of Toronto Press, 1936–37).

79 Obituaries, *Toronto Star* (14 March 1939); and Obituaries, *Globe* (15 March 1939).

80 See notice in [1930–31] 66 OLR.

81 His resignation 2 March 1933 is in [1933] OR. For the Court of Appeal's analysis of one of his judgments, see *Re Sawtell ex parte Bank of Montreal*, [1933] OR 295.

82 On the commission, see John D Arnup, *Middleton: The Beloved Judge* (Toronto: Osgoode Society, 1988) at 101–2. For the political context, see Neil McKenty, *Mitch Hepburn* (Toronto: McClelland and Stewart, 1967) at 42–45.

83 See John Boyko, *Bennett: The Rebel Who Challenged and Changed a Nation* (Toronto: Key Porter Books, 2010) at 225.

84 *Tariff Board Act*, SC 1931 (21–22 George V), c 55, as amended by SC 1933 (23–24 George V), c 51.

85 On this case see AB McKillop, *The Spinster and the Prophet: Florence Deeks, H.G. Wells, and the Mystery of the Purloined Past* (Toronto: Macfarlane, Walter and Ross for the Osgoode Society for Canadian Legal History, 2000).

86 *Ibid* at 261.

87 *Ibid* at 349.

88 "David Fasken, KC, Dies at Home after Long Illness" *Globe* (3 December 1929) 1; "David Fasken, Wealthy Mining Magnate Dies" *Toronto Daily Star* (3 December 1929) 1.

89 "Many Attend Funeral of the Late David Fasken" *Toronto Daily Star* (4 December 1929) 1; and *Globe* (5 December 1929) 1. "Fasken Funeral Struggles through Snow-Bound Roads" *Toronto Daily Star* (5 December 1929) featured a picture of a "motor car here being pulled out of the snow by a motor truck."

90 The Surrogate Court inventory of his assets dated 13 December 1929 is in the Archives of Ontario.

91 Bruce Ziff makes a similar comment on the value for succession duty purposes of the Reuben Wells Leonard estate in *Unforeseen Legacies* at 47.

92 On his role and that of his wife, Barbara, in the Laredo, Texas, community, see (5 May 2003) LMT Bus J 3.

93 Michael Bliss, *Northern Enterprise: Five Centuries of Canadian Business* (Toronto: McClelland and Stewart, 1987) at 411.

94 Charles P Girdwood, Lawrence F Jones, & George Lonn, *The Big Dome: Over Seventy Years of Gold Mining in Canada* (Toronto: Cybergraphics, 1983) at 119.

95 *Ibid.*

96 See, for example, Robertson to Messrs German, Lennox & Deacon, Barristers,

October 1927, and Robertson to Messrs Hughes & Agar, Barristers, 29 January 1929, Fasken Martineau DuMoulin LLP (FMD), PF189-2-1, 2009006-065(1), Archives of the Law Society of Upper Canada (LSUC), Toronto.

97 Memoirs of Bryce MacKenzie, FMD Fonds, PF189-2-1, 2009006-082, LSUC.

98 On this long and bitter battle, see C Ian Kyer & Jerome Bickenbach, *The Fiercest Debate: Cecil A. Wright, the Benchers, and Legal Education in Ontario 1923–1957* (Toronto: Osgoode Society, 1987).

99 Quoted in Christopher Moore, *The Law Society of Upper Canada and Ontario's Lawyers, 1797–1997* (Toronto: University of Toronto Press, 1997) at 217.

100 "The property at Cobalt was not operated during the year, but a clean-up at the various plants resulted in a shipment of 39 tons of ore, containing 39,959 gross ounces of silver. Shipments of base bullion contained 39,781 fine ounces of silver, valued at $17,940. In addition, approximately 875,000 ounces of bullion, having a value of $375,000, was sold from New York stocks." Bulletin No 94, *Mines and Metallurgical Works of Ontario in 1933* (Toronto: Ontario King's Printer, 1934) at 50.

101 Marion MacKenzie, "Hardscrabblers of Hardscrabblers: Kenneth and Margaret Jane MacDonald MacKenzie and FAMILY: Dr. Donald (M.D.); Alexander James, Ph. M.B. (Druggist); Kenneth Robertson (Undertaker and Embalmer); and Marion Fasken (School teacher) and Their Clans: 1. MacDonald–Ross; 2. Fasken–Mitchell; 3. MacKenzie–Robertson" (unpublished manuscript, 1959), ch 22.

102 *Ibid.*

103 *Ibid.*

104 Hoffman, *Free Gold* at 61 and 290–91.

105 Obituary notice prepared by Excelsior Life for its employees, September 1944.

106 See *The Toronto Western Hospital*, pamphlet, No 978.208, Archives of Toronto Western Hospital.

107 *Ibid.*

108 This account is drawn from the minutes of the meetings held between 1931 and 1937, Fasken Oil and Ranch Properties Limited files, Nina Stewart Haley Memorial Library, Midland, Texas.

109 Bliss, *Northern Enterprise* at 406.

110 Memoirs of Bryce MacKenzie, FMD Fonds, PF189-2-1, 2009006-082, LSUC.

111 *Attorney-General for Ontario v Fasken et al*, [1935] OR 115.

112 *Toronto Telegram* (13 November 1933).

113 *Toronto Daily Star* (17 October 1935).

114 *Succession Duty Act*, RSO 1927, c 26, s 1(g).

115 *Attorney-General for Ontario v Fasken et al*, [1935] OR 288. See also *Toronto Telegram* (9 May 1935).

116 John D Arnup, *Middleton: The Beloved Judge* (Toronto: Osgoode Society, 1988).

117 Memoirs of Bryce Mackenzie. See also MacKenzie, "Hardscrabblers."

118 Brad Francis, *The Life and Times of Bryce R. MacKenzie, Q.C., 1907–1986* (MA thesis, University of Calgary, 2004) [unpublished]. A copy was provided to the author by Francis, a grandson of MacKenzie.

119 An clipping from the *Moose Jaw Times Herald*, June 1932, provided to the author by Ann MacKenzie in March 2004.

120 Memoirs of Bryce MacKenzie. The Ontario Bar Biographical Research Project database, Archives of the Law Society of Upper Canada, lists him as Deputy Public Trustee, 1946–58, and Ontario Public Trustee, 1958–68.

121 Bryce Mackenzie, Memo to Don Affleck, 13 June 1973, FMD Fonds, PF189-2-1, 2009006-046, LSUC.

122 *Ibid.*

123 *Ibid.*

124 He appeared in at least one later appeal to the Privy Council. In 1937 he represented the Yukon Consolidated Gold Corporation Limited in an appeal from the Ontario Court of Appeal by Leslie Colbatch Clark, trustee of the estate of Vernon Wright Worsdale, a bankrupt. Robertson's appeal book is in FMD Fonds, PF189-2-1, 2009006–128, LSUC.

125 H Blair Neatby, "William Lyon Mackenzie King" in Ramsay Cook & Réal Bélanger, eds, *Canada's Prime Ministers: Macdonald to Trudeau, Portraits from the Dictionary of Canadian Biography* (Toronto: University of Toronto Press, 2007) at 279.

126 John T Saywell, *The Lawmakers: Judicial Power and the Shaping of Canadian Federalism* (Toronto: University of Toronto Press for the Osgoode Society for Canadian Legal History, 2002) ch 9.

127 Margaret Prang, *N.W. Rowell, Ontario Nationalist* (Toronto: University of Toronto Press, 1975) at 485–86.

128 Memoirs of Bryce MacKenzie.

129 The correspondence is in FMD Fonds, PF189-2-1, 2009006–116, LSUC.

130 William Rodney, *Joe Boyle: King of the Klondike* (Toronto: McGraw-Hill Ryerson, 1974).

131 There is correspondence of August 1945 in which Pickup and Calvin discuss a handwritten letter that the firm had received from Justice Greene on an aspect of the *Patton v Yukon* case. FMD Fonds, PF189-2-1, 2009006–117, LSUC.

132 *Patton v Yukon Consolidated Gold Corporation*, [1934] 3 DLR 400.

133 *Patton v Yukon Consolidated Gold Corporation*, [1936] OR 308.

134 *Patton v Yukon Consolidated Gold Corporation*, [1942] OR 92.

135 Allan Levine, *King: William Lyon Mackenzie King, a Life Guided by the Hands of Destiny* (Toronto: Douglas and McIntyre, 2011) at 278–87.

136 Prang, *N.W. Rowell* at 496.

137 Memoirs of Bryce MacKenzie.

138 *Ibid.*

139 *Ibid.*

140 *Ibid.*

⚓ Chapter 7 ⚓

1 See the letters from CC Calvin to JW Pickup, February 1942, Fasken Martineau DuMoulin (FMD) Fonds, PF189-3, 2009006–123, Archives of the Law Society of Upper Canada (LSUC).

2 Partnership agreement, 1 January 1939, FMD Fonds, PF189-1-3, LSUC.

3 Marion MacKenzie, "Hardscrabblers of Hardscrabblers: Kenneth and Margaret Jane MacDonald MacKenzie and FAMILY: Dr. Donald (M.D.); Alexander James, Ph. M.B. (Druggist); Kenneth Robertson (Undertaker and Embalmer); and Marion Fasken (School teacher) and Their Clans: 1. MacDonald–Ross; 2. Fasken–Mitchell; 3. MacKenzie–Robertson" (unpublished manuscript, 1959), ch 19, Fasken–Mitchell. A copy can be found in FMD Fonds, PF189-2-2, 2009006–108.

4 On his death he left a $100 life annuity to Willows. An undated and unidentified newspaper clipping was given to me by Ann MacKenzie headed "$100 Annuity Left to One-Eyed Caddy."

5 The pleadings and sworn statements in evidence are in FMD Fonds, PF189-3, 2009006–126, LSUC.

6 The judgment signed by the judge and annotated as to costs is also in *ibid*. There is also an unidentified news clipping about the case, "Suit against City Lawyer Is

Dismissed," 26 May 1942, FMD Fonds, PF189-2-1, 2009006-080, LSUC.

7   *Patton v Yukon Consolidated Gold Corporation*, [1942] OR 92.

8   *Patton v Yukon Consolidated Gold Corporation*, [1945] 4 DLR 801.

9   *Ibid.*

10 See "Name J.W. Pickup Special Counsel," *Toronto Telegram* (14 January 1943).

11 On the Department of Justice under Varcoe and especially on the role of WR Jackett, see Richard W Pound, *Chief Justice W.R. Jackett: By the Law of the Land* (Montreal and Kingston: McGill-Queen's University Press and the Osgoode Society for Canadian Legal History, 1999).

12 *Ibid* at 124.

13 *Re Gardner et al*, [1948] 1 DLR 611.

14 Christopher Armstrong, *Moose Pastures and Mergers: The Ontario Securities Commission and the Regulation of Share Markets in Canada 1940–1980* (Toronto: University of Toronto Press, 2001) at 54–63.

15 Chief Justice Robertson wrote the judgment, "The appeals . . . raise important questions as to the powers of the Commission, the nature of the proceedings before it, and the powers of this court on an appeal from a review by the commission." *Re Gardner et al*, [1948] 1 DLR 611 at 612.

16 *Ibid* at 617.

17 *Who's Who in Canada 1940–41* (Toronto: International Press, 1941) at 1341.

18 *Re Dairy Corporation of Canada Limited*, [1934] OR 436 at 439. In this motion with respect to a plan of arrangement between a corporation and its shareholders, Pickup was counsel for the Bank of Toronto and Calvin deposed to the facts.

19 Memoirs of Bryce MacKenzie, FMD Fonds, PF189-2, 2009006-082 and 2009006-082, LSUC.

20 See opinion letters, FMD Fonds, PF189-1-2, 2009006-065 to 069, LSUC.

21 Memoirs of Bryce MacKenzie.

22 Christopher Moore, *The Law Society of Upper Canada and Ontario's Lawyers, 1797–1997* (Toronto: University of Toronto Press, 1997) at 179.

23 David Menzel, interview with author, September 2005.

24 MacKenzie, "Hardscrabblers," ch 22, Fasken–Mitchell.

25 Letter sent on behalf of Mrs Fasken to Mr Hilary G Bedford, manager of the Midland Farms, 29 September 1944, FMD Fonds, PF189-2-1, 2009006-080, LSUC.

26 Unidentified news clipping, FMD Fonds, PF189-2-1, 2009006-080, LSUC.

27 Bryce MacKenzie, interview with Don Affleck, 7 February 1974, FMD Fonds, PF189-2-1, 2009006-083, LSUC.

28 Obituary notice prepared by Excelsior Life, FMD Fonds, PF189-2-1, 2009006-080 LSUC.

29 On the appointment of Matthews to the post of lieutenant-governor, see Neil McKenty, *Mitch Hepburn* (Toronto: McClelland and Stewart, 1957) at 143–44.

30 "Gen. A. Matthews Led Army Division" *Toronto Star* (21 September 1991) at 14.

31 *Ibid.*

32 "$100 Annuity Left to One-Eyed Caddy" an unidentified newsclipping in FMD Fonds, PF 189-2-1, 2009006-081, LSUC.

33 MacKenzie, "Hardscrabblers," ch 22, Fasken–Mitchell.

34 N Jane Pepino, CM, QC, Call to the Bar Speech, Roy Thomson Hall, Toronto, 22 July 2005.

35 John M Godfrey "Personal Reminisences and a History of the Law Firm of Campbell, Godfrey & Lewtas 1870–1975" (unpublished MS, 1983), FMD Fonds PF 189-2-1, 2009006-098, LSUC.

36 *Toronto Telegram* (3 July 1945) 2, FMD Fonds, PF189-2-1, 2009006-089, LSUC.

37 *Globe and Mail* (20 December 1945) 7, FMD Fonds, PF189-2-1, 2009006-089, LSUC.
38 Peter C Newman, *The Establishment Man: A Portrait of Power* (Toronto: McClelland and Stewart, 1982) at 102–3. See also the undated memo to the author from Morgan S Crockford in the FMD Fonds, PF 189, LSUC. Matthews would become president of Massey-Ferguson and one of the principals with Bud MacDougal of Argus Corporation, figuring prominently in Peter C Newman's *Debrett's Illustrated Guide to the Canadian Establishment* (Toronto: Methuen Publications, 1981).
39 Menzel interview.
40 The 22 December 1948 revision to the percentage of drawings for the firm states, "These percentages do not make any provision for W. B. Williston, but leave 1% which for the time being will be paid to D. G. C. Menzel as per instructions which have been issued to the Accountant . . . Menzel gets 1% but not as a partner."
41 C Ian Kyer & Jerome Bickenbach, *The Fiercest Debate: Cecil A. Wright, the Benchers, and Legal Education in Ontario 1923–1957* (Toronto: Osgoode Society, 1987) at 210.
42 Christopher Moore, *The Law Society of Upper Canada and Ontario's Lawyers, 1797–1997* (Toronto: University of Toronto Press, 1997) at 252.
43 *Fasken v Minister of National Revenue*, [1949] 1 DLR 810, [1948] Ex CR 580.
44 *Income War Tax Act 1917*, SC 1927, c 10, s 12.
45 Donald Jack, "Recollections of Walter B. Williston, QC" (Autumn 1998) Advocates' J 5 at 5–6.
46 Laskin's role in his case is discussed by Philip Girard in *Bora Laskin: Bringing Law to Life* (Toronto: University of Toronto Press for the Osgoode Society for Canadian Legal History, 2005) at 252–58. The case is also discussed in William Kaplan, *Canadian Maverick: The Life and Times of Ivan C. Rand* (Toronto: University of Toronto Press for the Osgoode Society for Canadian Legal History, 2009) at 139–40.
47 Canada *Report of Court of Investigation into the Circumstances Attending the Loss of the S.S. Noronic in Toronto Harbour, Ontario, on 17 September 1949* (Ottawa: Department of Transport, 1949).
48 John Craig, *The Noronic Is Burning* (Don Mills, ON: General Publishing, 1976) at 3.
49 Monday 19 September. *Ibid*, 104.
50 *Ibid*, 105.
51 *Ibid*, 106.
52 *Ibid*, 2.
53 Partnership agreement, 1 August 1950, FMD Fonds, PF189-1-3, LSUC.
54 Fraser Fell, interview with author, 20 December 2011.
55 *Accumulations Act*, RSO 1950, c 9.
56 [1952] OR 802 at 806.
57 [1952] OR 807.
58 RSO 1950, c 4.
59 Memoirs of Bryce MacKenzie.
60 "Name Pickup Chief Justice" *Toronto Star* (25 September 1952) 1.
61 "The New Chief Justice" *Saturday Night* (11 October 1952) 6.
62 "Robertson Retires, McRuer Reported New Chief Justice" *Globe and Mail* (5 September 1952); "Chief Justice Retires" *Toronto Daily Star* (4 September 1952) 1.
63 "Chief Justice Retires" *Toronto Daily Star* (4 September 1952) 1.
64 *Toronto Daily Star* (10 September 1952) 2.
65 "J.W. Pickup Appointed Ontario Chief Justice" *Globe and Mail* (26 September 1952) 4.
66 "G.T. Walsh Named to Succeed Pickup in Don Jail Probe" *Globe and Mail* (1 October 1952) 23.
67 Memoirs of Bryce MacKenzie.

❧ Chapter 8 ❧

1   Joseph Schull, *100 Years of Banking in Canada: A History of the Toronto-Dominion Bank* (Vancouver: Copp Clark, 1958) at 189.

2   Fraser Fell, interview with author, 20 December 2011.

3   *Toronto Directory 1949* (Toronto: Might's Directory Company, 1949) at 495, and *Toronto Directory 1948* (Toronto: Might's Directory Company, 1948) at 43.

4   *Toronto Directory 1952* (Toronto: Might's Directory Company, 1952) at 502.

5   The society section of the *Globe and Mail* of 26 June 1953 featured a picture of Fraser Fell at the graduation with his wife-to-be, Margot Crossgrove of Guelph. They were married the day after his call to the bar. *Toronto Directory 1954* (Toronto: Might's Directory Company, 1954) at 411.

6   *Toronto Directory, 1955* (Toronto: Might's Directory Company, 1955) at 414; *Canadian Who's Who* (Toronto: University of Toronto Press, 1979) at 973.

7   *Toronto Directory, 1956* (Toronto: Might's Directory Company, 1956) at 444.

8   *Canadian Who's Who* (1979) at 614.

9   Henry (Hal) Jackman quoted in Diane Francis, "Building a Corporate Dynasty" *Toronto Star* (10 July 1983) H1.

10 *Ibid.*

11 Obituary, *Toronto Star* (8 August 1973).

12 Ontario Bar Biographical Research Project database, Archives of the Law Society of Upper Canada (LSUC), Toronto.

13 Robert Shirriff, interview with author, 18 December 2011.

14 Fell interview.

15 Memoirs of JB Robinson, Fasken Martineau DuMoulin LLP (FMD) Fonds, PF189-2-1, 2009006-094, LSUC.

16 Robert Shirriff, interview with author, 19 December 2011.

17 *[Toronto] Monetary Times* (10 February 1882), quoted in Basil Skodyn, ed, *The Permanent Story 1855–1980: An Historical Review of the 125-Year Growth of the Canada Permanent Mortgage Corporation, Its Subsidiaries, and Amalgamated Companies* (Toronto: Canada Permanent Mortgage Corporation, 1980) at 37.

18 Obituary, *Toronto Star* (6 August 1963) 31. A copy can be found in FMD Fonds, PF189-2-1, 2009006-095, LSUC.

19 *Globe and Mail* (15 March 1958) 28.

20 His annual report for Toronto General Trusts reporting on the acquisitions is in Biographical subject files, FMD Fonds, PF189-2-1, 2009006-095, LSUC.

21 Schull, *100 Years of Banking* at 189–97.

22 Skodyn, *The Permanent Story* at 45.

23 Craig Heron, *Booze: A Distilled History* (Toronto: Between the Lines, 2003) at 303.

24 On the Molson battle with Canadian Breweries, see Douglas Hunter, *Molson the Birth of a Business Empire* (Toronto: Viking, 2001) at 430–32; and Heron, *Booze* at 302–7. On Osler's winning the Molson business, see Curtis Cole, *Osler, Hoskin & Harcourt: Portrait of a Partnership* (Toronto McGraw-Hill Ryerson, 1995) at 130–31.

25 The following account is based upon notes prepared by Bryce MacKenzie in February 1974, FMD Fonds, PF189-2-1, 2009006–127, LSUC.

26 Philip Smith, *Brinco: The Story of Churchill Falls* (Toronto: McClelland and Stewart, 1975) at 20.

27 Franc Joubin & D McCormack Smyth, *Not for Gold Alone: Memoirs of a Prospector* (Toronto: Deljay Publications, 1986) at 251–63.

28 *Ibid,* 199–221.

29 *Ibid,* 189.

30 See Smith, *Brinco* at 300-80.

31 [1953] 3 DLR 431

32 William F Comery, "Walter Williston — Another Side" (1980) 14(4) Law Soc'y Gaz 345–49 at 345–46.

33 Donald H Jack, "Recollections of Walter B. Williston, QC" (Autumn 1998) Advocates' J 5.

34 *Ibid* at 9.

35 Cited in the recitals to the agreement of 1 January 1962 in Partnership agreements, FMD Fonds, PF189-1-3, LSUC.

36 *Ibid.*

37 *Ibid.*

38 Gordon Robertson, *Memoirs of a Very Civil Servant: Mackenzie King to Pierre Trudeau* (Toronto: University of Toronto Press, 2000) at 208: there are pictures of Ron Robertson as a boy with his brother and sister in Montreal in the summer 1942 and also at his brother's wedding in London 14 August 1943. His father was then the wartime Canadian Agricultural Commissioner in London.

39 Ronald Neil Robertson, interview with author, 2010.

40 See the Might's *Toronto Directory* for the years 1957–60.

41 *Ibid*, 1961 at 405.

42 Jack Batten, *Learned Friends: A Tribute to 50 Remarkable Advocates, 1950–2000* (Toronto: Advocates' Society, 2005) at 102.

43 Bob Tuer, interview with author, 1988.

44 Quoted in Batten, *Learned Friends* at 103.

45 *Ibid.* John Campion, email to author, 18 June 2012.

46 Campion, email to author, 18 June 2012.

47 Shirriff interview.

48 See Office manual, FMD Fonds, PF189-1-1, 2009006-049, LSUC.

49 Document determining the partnership of John Douglas Pickup, 29 November 1961, Partnership agreements, FMD Fonds, PF189-1-3, LSUC.

50 *Ibid.*

51 Bob Sutherland, interview with author.

52 *Toronto City Directory*, 1961 at 480.

53 *Canadian Who's Who* (Toronto: University of Toronto Press, 1985) at 446; *Who's Who in Canada, 1958–59* (Toronto: International Press, 1959) at 178.

54 CC Calvin, day planner for 1963, FMD Fonds, PF189-1-1, 2009006-015, LSUC.

55 *Toronto Daily Star* (6 August 1963) 31.

56 Memo to staff, 6 August 1963, FMD Fonds, PF189-1-1, 2009006-048, LSUC.

57 *Ibid.*

✑ Epilogue ✑

1 Brad Francis, *The Life and Times of Bryce R. MacKenzie, Q.C., 1907–1986* (MA thesis, University of Calgary, 2004) [unpublished].

2 An informal survey in 2007 showed that of the firm's Toronto office's 234 lawyers, 51 were women, 13 were of Asian descent, and 4 were Black.

3 See Karolyn Smardz Frost, *I've Got a Home in Glory Land: A Lost Tale of the Underground Railway* (Thomas Allen: Toronto, 2007) at 331–32.

4 *Ibid* at 348. One of the terms of the will concerned the family of Robert Smith. There is a letter in Library and Archives Canada in which Joe Beatty wrote to Sir John A Macdonald about Bob Smith, a Black porter at Gooderham & Worts who was a strong supporter of Sir John A because he stood up to the United States. JW Beatty et al to John A Macdonald, photo enclosed, 2 March 1891, John A Macdonald Papers,

MG26-A, 250137–39, Library and Archives Canada.

5   Based on her citation as a distinguished alumna of Osgoode Hall Law School, awarded in February 2003.

6   A brief history of Campbell Godfrey & Lewtas is provided in an appendix.

7   Christopher Moore, *McCarthy Tétrault: Building Canada's Premier Law Firm 1855–2005* (Vancouver: Douglas and McIntyre, 2005) at 139–58.

৩১ Appendix 2 ৯৬

1   The following is drawn from John M Godfrey, "Personal Reminiscences and a History of the Law Firm of Campbell, Godfrey & Lewtas 1870–1975," Fasken Martineau DuMoulin LLP (FMD) Fonds, PF189-2-1, 2009006-098, Archives of the Law Society of Upper Canada (LSUC), Toronto.

2   The following is drawn from a short history entitled *Martineau Walker* (Montreal: Self-published, 1984).

3   The following is drawn from Christine Harvey & Arthur E Mullins, *Russell & DuMoulin: The First Century 1889–1989* (Vancouver: Russell and DuMoulin, 1989).

Index

PUBLICATIONS OF THE OSGOODE SOCIETY FOR CANADIAN LEGAL HISTORY

2013   R. Roy McMurtry, *Memoirs*
Charlotte Gray, *Carrie's Case: The Maid who Shot a Massey and Shocked the Nation*
C. Ian Kyer, *Lawyers, Families, and Businesses: The Shaping of a Bay Street Law Firm*
G. Blaine Baker and Donald Fyson, eds., *Essays in the History of Canadian Law: Volume XI — The Canadas*

2012   R. Blake Brown, *Arming & Disarming: A History of Gun Control in Canada*
Eric Tucker, James Muir & Bruce Ziff, eds., *Property on Trial: Canadian Cases in Context*
Shelley Gavigan, *Hunger, Horses & Government Men: Criminal Law on the Aboriginal Plains, 1870–1905*
Barrington Walker, ed., *The African-Canadian Legal Odyssey: Historical Essays*

2011   Robert J. Sharpe, *The Lazier Murder: Prince Edward County, 1884*
Philip Girard, *Lawyers and Legal Culture in British North America: Beamish Murdoch of Halifax*
John McLaren, *Dewigged, Bothered and Bewildered: British Colonial Judges on Trial*
Lesley Erickson, *Westward Bound: Sex, Violence, the Law and the Making of a Settler Society*

2010   Judy Fudge and Eric Tucker, eds., *Work on Trial: Canadian Labour Law Struggles*
Christopher Moore, *The British Columbia Court of Appeal: The First Hundred Years*
Frederick Vaughan, *Viscount Haldane: The Wicked Step-father of the Canadian Constitution*
Barrington Walker, *Race on Trial: Black Defendants in Ontario's Criminal Courts, 1850–1950*

2009   William Kaplan, *Canadian Maverick: The Life and Times of Ivan C. Rand*
R. Blake Brown, *A Trying Question: The Jury in Nineteenth-Century Canada*
Barry Wright and Susan Binnie, eds., *Canadian State Trials, Volume III: Political Trials and Security Measures, 1840–1914*
Robert J. Sharpe, *The Last Day, the Last Hour: The Currie Libel Trial*

2008   Constance Backhouse, *Carnal Crimes: Sexual Assault Law in Canada, 1900–1975*
Jim Phillips, R. Roy McMurtry & John Saywell, Eds., *Essays in the History of Canadian Law, Vol. X: A Tribute to Peter N. Oliver*
Gregory Taylor, *The Law of the Land: Canada's Receptions of the Torrens System*
Hamar Foster, Benjamin Berger & A.R. Buck, Eds., *The Grand Experiment: Law and Legal Culture in British Settler Societies*

2007   Robert Sharpe & Patricia McMahon, *The Persons Case: The Origins and Legacy of the Fight for Legal Personhood*
Lori Chambers, *Misconceptions: Unmarried Motherhood and the Ontario Children of Unmarried Parents Act, 1921–1969*
Jonathan Swainger, Ed., *The Alberta Supreme Court at 100: History & Authority*
Martin Friedland, *My Life in Crime and Other Academic Adventures*

2006   Donald Fyson, *Magistrates, Police and People: Everyday Criminal Justice in Quebec and Lower Canada, 1764–1837*
Dale Brawn, *The Court of Queen's Bench of Manitoba 1870–1950: A Biographical*

History
R.C.B. Risk, *A History of Canadian Legal Thought: Collected Essays*, edited and introduced by G. Blaine Baker & Jim Phillips

2005   Philip Girard, *Bora Laskin: Bringing Law to Life*
Christopher English, Ed., *Essays in the History of Canadian Law, Vol. IX: Two Islands, Newfoundland and Prince Edward Island*
Fred Kaufman, *Searching for Justice: An Autobiography*

2004   John D. Honsberger, *Osgoode Hall: An Illustrated History*
Frederick Vaughan, *Aggressive in Pursuit: The Life of Justice Emmett Hall*
Constance Backhouse & Nancy Backhouse, *The Heiress versus the Establishment: Mrs. Campbell's Campaign for Legal Justice*
Philip Girard, Jim Phillips & Barry Cahill, Eds., *The Supreme Court of Nova Scotia, 1754–2004: From Imperial Bastion to Provincial Oracle*

2003   Robert Sharpe & Kent Roach, *Brian Dickson: A Judge's Journey*
George Finlayson, *John J. Robinette: Peerless Mentor*
Peter Oliver, *The Conventional Man: The Diaries of Ontario Chief Justice Robert A. Harrison, 1856–1878*
Jerry Bannister, *The Rule of the Admirals: Law, Custom and Naval Government in Newfoundland, 1699–1832*

2002   John T. Saywell, *The Law Makers: Judicial Power and the Shaping of Canadian Federalism*
David Murray, *Colonial Justice: Justice, Morality and Crime in the Niagara District, 1791–1849*
F. Murray Greenwood & Barry Wright, Eds., *Canadian State Trials, Volume Two: Rebellion and Invasion in the Canadas, 1837–8*
Patrick Brode, *Courted and Abandoned: Seduction in Canadian Law*

2001   Ellen Anderson, *Judging Bertha Wilson: Law as Large as Life*
Judy Fudge & Eric Tucker, *Labour Before the Law: Collective Action in Canada, 1900–1948*
Laurel Sefton MacDowell, *Renegade Lawyer: The Life of J.L. Cohen*

2000   Barry Cahill, *'The Thousandth Man': A Biography of James McGregor Stewart*
A.B. McKillop, *The Spinster and the Prophet: Florence Deeks, H.G. Wells, and the Mystery of the Purloined Past*
Beverley Boissery & F. Murray Greenwood, *Uncertain Justice: Canadian Women and Capital Punishment*
Bruce Ziff, *Unforeseen Legacies: Reuben Wells Leonard and the Leonard Foundation Trust*

1999   Constance Backhouse, *Colour-Coded: A Legal History of Racism in Canada, 1900–1950*
G. Blaine Baker & Jim Phillips, Eds., *Essays in the History of Canadian Law, Vol. VIII: In Honour of R.C.B. Risk*
Richard W. Pound, *Chief Justice W.R. Jackett: By the Law of the Land*
David Vanek, *Fulfilment: Memoirs of a Criminal Court Judge*

1998   Sidney Harring, *White Man's Law: Native People in Nineteenth-Century Canadian Jurisprudence*
Peter Oliver, *Terror to Evil-Doers': Prisons and Punishments in Nineteenth-Century Ontario*

1997   James W. St. G. Walker, *'Race', Rights and the Law in the Supreme Court of Canada: Historical Case Studies*
Lori Chambers, *Married Women and Property Law in Victorian Ontario*
Patrick Brode, *Casual Slaughters and Accidental Judgments: Canadian War Crimes*

and Prosecutions, 1944–1948
Ian Bushnell, *The Federal Court of Canada: A History, 1875 – 1992*

1996   Carol Wilton, Ed., *Essays in the History of Canadian Law, Vol. VII: Inside the Law — Canadian Law Firms in Historical Perspective*
William Kaplan, *Bad Judgment: The Case of Mr. Justice Leo A. Landreville*
Murray Greenwood & Barry Wright, Eds., *Canadian State Trials, Volume I: Law, Politics and Security Measures, 1608–1837*

1995   David Williams, *Just Lawyers: Seven Portraits*
Hamar Foster & John McLaren, Eds., *Essays in the History of Canadian Law, Vol. VI: British Columbia and the Yukon*
W.H. Morrow, Ed., *Northern Justice: The Memoirs of Mr. Justice William G. Morrow*
Beverley Boissery, *A Deep Sense of Wrong: The Treason,Trials and Transportation to New South Wales of Lower Canadian Rebels after the 1838 Rebellion*

1994   Patrick Boyer, *A Passion for Justice: The Legacy of James Chalmers McRuer*
Charles Pullen, *The Life and Times of Arthur Maloney: The Last of the Tribunes*
Jim Phillips, Tina Loo, & Susan Lewthwaite, Eds., *Essays in the History of Canadian Law, Vol. V: Crime and Criminal Justice*
Brian Young, *The Politics of Codification: The Lower Canadian Civil Code of 1866*

1993   Greg Marquis, *Policing Canada's Century: A History of the Canadian Association of Chiefs of Police*
Murray Greenwood, *Legacies of Fear: Law and Politics in Quebec in the Era of the French Revolution*

1992   Brendan O'Brien, *Speedy Justice: The Tragic Last Voyage of His Majesty's Vessel Speedy*
Robert Fraser, ed., *Provincial Justice: Upper Canadian Legal Portraits from the Dictionary of Canadian Biography*

1991   Constance Backhouse, *Petticoats and Prejudice: Women and Law in Nineteenth-Century Canada*

1990   Philip Girard & Jim Phillips, Eds., *Essays in the History of Canadian Law, Vol. III: Nova Scotia*
Carol Wilton, Ed., *Essays in the History of Canadian Law,Vol. IV: Beyond the Law — Lawyers and Business in Canada 1830–1930*

1989   Desmond Brown, *The Genesis of the Canadian Criminal Code of 1892*
Patrick Brode, *The Odyssey of John Anderson*

1988   Robert Sharpe, *The Last Day, the Last Hour: The Currie Libel Trial*
John D. Arnup, *Middleton: The Beloved Judge*

1987   C. Ian Kyer & Jerome Bickenbach, *The Fiercest Debate: Cecil A. Wright, the Benchers and Legal Education in Ontario, 1923–1957*

1986   Paul Romney, *Mr. Attorney: The Attorney General for Ontario in Court, Cabinet and Legislature,1791–1899*
Martin Friedland, *The Case of Valentine Shortis: A True Story of Crime and Politics in Canada*

1985   James Snell and Frederick Vaughan, *The Supreme Court of Canada: History of the Institution*

1984   Patrick Brode, *Sir John Beverley Robinson: Bone and Sinew of the Compact*
David Williams, *Duff: A Life in the Law*

1983   David H. Flaherty, Ed., *Essays in the History of Canadian Law, Vol. II*

1982   Marion MacRae and Anthony Adamson, *Cornerstones of Order: Courthouses and Town Halls of Ontario, 1784–1914*

1981   David H. Flaherty, Ed., *Essays in the History of Canadian Law, Vol. I*
G. Blaine Baker and Donald Fyson, eds., *Essays in the History of Canadian Law: Volume XI — The Canadas*